THE NEW SCIENCE
OF
GIAMBATTISTA VICO

THE NEW SCIENCE OF GIAMBATTISTA VICO

Revised Translation of the Third Edition (1744)

THOMAS GODDARD BERGIN

AND MAX HAROLD FISCH

Cornell University Press

ITHACA, NEW YORK

❀❀❀

To the Memory of

FAUSTO NICOLINI

1879–1965

B
3581
.P73E43
1968

First published 1968

Library of Congress Catalog Card Number: 68–16393

PRINTED IN THE UNITED STATES OF AMERICA BY KINGSPORT PRESS, INC.

PREFACE

This translation of Giambattista Vico's *Scienza nuova* is based on the text of the third edition (Naples, 1744) as edited by Fausto Nicolini in Volume 112 and in the first 166 pages of Volume 113 of the *Scrittori d'Italia* (Bari, Laterza, 1928). Nicolini used Vico's manuscript to correct the text, broke up long paragraphs and sentences, put curved brackets around parenthetical remarks, modernized the punctuation in other ways, numbered the sections and chapters, supplied titles for sections that lacked them, and numbered the paragraphs for convenience of reference. (In later printings and in his commentary and bibliography, Nicolini used the phrase "the second *New Science*" for the third edition *plus* those passages in the second and in numerous manuscript revisions of it that were "suppressed or substantially altered" in the third. Such passages occupy pages 169–309 of Volume 113 in the printing of 1928; other additions were made by Nicolini in subsequent printings.)

Our translation, begun in 1939 at Naples and on Capri in consultation with Nicolini and Croce, was interrupted by World War II, completed after the war, and first published by Cornell University Press in 1948. In 1961, we revised and abridged it for an Anchor Books edition. The entire translation has now undergone a further revision; the changes of course are more frequent and extensive in the parts that had not been included in the abridgment.

Vico's edition of 1744 had neither index nor footnotes. The text itself had therefore to be heavily larded with references of three kinds: (1) forward and backward references to other parts of the text; (2) citations of primary sources of evidence; and (3) references to the learned literature of the sixteenth, seventeenth, and early eighteenth centuries.

There are numerous defects in all three kinds of references. Vico quotes inexactly from memory; his references are vague; his memory is often not of the original source but of a quotation from it in some secondary work; he ascribes to one author what is said by another, or to one work what is said in another by the same author; he makes historical assertions for which his evidence has so far not been found; his promises of subsequent discussion are sometimes unfulfilled; and his backward references are sometimes to nonexistent passages. The New Science, we are sometimes tempted to say, is a great vision; the backward and forward references connect the parts of the vision, and only secondarily and imperfectly the parts of the book; and the vision, though loosely tied here and there to historical facts, floats free of them elsewhere, if it does not fly in their face, and yet is true to them in its fashion.

Nicolini's genial, erudite, and indispensable *Commento storico* exposes Vico's "philological" [paragraph 139] errors and deficiencies with chastening love, corrects and supplies most of them, and leaves it to lesser scholars to discover supporting evidence where he found none, or stronger evidence where what he found was weak, and thus to show that Vico's scholarship was not quite so erratic, at this point or at that, as Nicolini sadly concluded it was. But alas, there are errors even in *il gran comento*, both typographical and substantive, that are detectable only by pursuing the references; these errors have already been many times repeated from it by editors, translators, and commentators who shirked the pursuit; and it may take a generation or two to slough them off.

An English commentary, making full use of Nicolini's but accepting nothing on its authority, and bringing to bear the resources of the social sciences and of modern historical scholarship, is certainly a desideratum, and the time is nearly ripe for it, but it is beyond our competence. In the present edition, however, we have gone much farther than in that of 1948 toward completing and correcting Vico's references, and a word is in order as to our treatment of each of the three kinds mentioned above.

(1) The numbering of the paragraphs has permitted us to substitute paragraph numbers in square brackets for phrases like "as we have laid down in the Axioms," "as we have already demonstrated," "which we have several times quoted," "as we shall shortly see," "as will later be shown in full detail." (Sometimes we keep the phrase and add the number.) By the same device, we have added hundreds of other cross references. In cases involving proper names, the index will enable the reader to supply still others.

(2) Vico often refers to his primary sources by the name of the author only, and almost never adds more than the name of the particular work. In most cases we have supplied more exact references in square brackets. For Greek and Latin works included in the Loeb Classical Library, we use the English titles and the numbered divisions of those editions: books, chapters, sections, pages, columns, lines, as the case may be. See "Abbreviations and Signs" below (page xvii).

(3) Since the learned literature to which Vico refers has largely been forgotten, since ample references are supplied in Nicolini's commentary, and since any library that has the literature will have the commentary, we have in most cases contented ourselves with giving the author's name in the language he spoke, and the title of his work in the language in which it was written, or in English. English readers who do not have a research library at hand, or who lack the leisure to use it for the purpose, but who nevertheless wish help in placing Vico in relation to what was for him the recent and contemporary scholarly literature of his subjects, will find such help in two recent works by Frank E. Manuel: *The Eighteenth Century Confronts the Gods* and *Isaac Newton Historian* (Harvard University Press, 1959 and 1963). As Manuel remarks (on page 43 of the latter book), Vico sent Newton a copy of the first edition of the *New Science*, but "if Newton ever received it he would not have remotely comprehended its meaning."

Vico refers also to two previous works of his own: his *Universal Law* (1720–22) and the first edition of the *New Science* (1725). The paragraphs in which such references occur are listed in the index under Vico's name.

With slight changes, the introduction to our abridged edition is reprinted here. A long historical introduction, which serves as a more general guide, was published in 1944 with our translation of Vico's *Autobiography*. The present Introduction is expository and interpretive, not critical. It aims only to explain, as far as possible from within the work itself, the nature, scope, and claims of that historico-systematic science of human society that Vico called his "new science concerning the common nature of nations." It is cast in the form of an explanation of the full title as it appeared in the third edition. By using letters for the sections of the Introduction and numbers for the paragraphs, we have been able to include it in our scheme of square-bracketed references and thus to permit it to fill a small part of the place of the commentary that we have not attempted.

The dozen footnotes we have allowed ourselves are but samples of a kind of annotation that would be needed throughout to constitute the most meager sort of commentary. Since we do not undertake even that, but only to correct and sharpen Vico's own references, as with leisure and clerical help he might have done, we have done it by square-bracketed insertions in the text, where he would have put them, and have spared ourselves the temptation to expand that nearly every footnote would have presented (those to paragraphs 359 and 1084 for example).

The problems and policies of the translation itself are illustrated at length in the Introduction, but a few further remarks are appended here. We have carried the breaking up of sentences much farther than Nicolini did. Otherwise, though we translate quite freely some difficult passages which would be opaque in a literal rendering, and though we now and then recast an entire paragraph, we have tried on the whole to keep as close to Vico's style and idiom as English will permit. At the expense of occasional awkwardness, we have also tried to respect his technical and quasi-technical terms. *Certo* and its cognates, for example, are with rare exceptions translated "certain" and the like, even when it is not certain that Vico is using them in the technical sense explained in paragraph 321. *Umano* and its cognates, which we were often tempted to render "humane" or "civilized," are usually allowed to stand as "human" and the like, in order to preserve a possible reference either (*a*) to the age of men as distinguished from the age of gods and the age of heroes, or (*b*) to the ages of heroes and men together as distinguished from the age of gods, as in paragraph 629 [C7, J5]. *Tempi* are nearly always "times," not ages (*età*) or periods or epochs, to preserve a possible allusion to Vico's chronology or "doctrine of times." And—may the reader forgive us—"*tre sètte di tempi*" [975] are "three sects of times" or time-sects to preserve the ambiguity of "sect" as division and as following. A time-sect is a cut of time such that there are sectarian differences between one time-sect and another. Each time-sect is characterized by a following of usages, customs, and institutions peculiar to itself, and by a *Zeitgeist* or time-mind—the cut and fashion of a time [979] rather than of a place, a class, or a party. In this ambiguous sense of "sect," Vico's ideal eternal history [393] is a tri-sect history.

A few terms for which there are no exact English equivalents are represented by the half-naturalized Latin forms of the same words: *connubio* by connubium [110, 598], *famoli* by famuli [555ff], *conato* and *conati* by conatus [340, 388, 504, 689, 696, 1098], for examples. *Repubblica*, on the other hand, is uniformly rendered "commonwealth" to avoid the misleading associations of "republic" in English. *Dominio* (Latin *dominium*) we have usually translated "ownership," but sometimes "dominion" or (particularly in the phrase *dominio eminente*) "domain" [25, 266]. And lastly, *principio* we have sometimes rendered "principle" and sometimes "beginning" [736]. As a quasi-technical term with Vico, it means both at once, and it may fairly be said that the ambivalence of this term is one of the keys to Vico's thought [A3, I·1–14].

Yale University   T. G. B.
University of Illinois   M. H. F.
September 1967

CONTENTS

BOOK FOUR: THE COURSE THE NATIONS RUN

BOOK FIVE: THE RECOURSE OF HUMAN INSTITUTIONS
WHICH THE NATIONS TAKE WHEN THEY RISE
AGAIN

CONCLUSION OF THE WORK

BIBLIOGRAPHICAL NOTE

The standard edition of Vico's works is by Fausto Nicolini (8 vols. in 11; Bari, 1911–41). For a bibliography, see Benedetto Croce, *Bibliografia vichiana*, as rewritten by Nicolini (2 vols.; Naples, 1947). For full commentary on the *New Science*, see Nicolini, *Commento storico alla seconda Scienza nuova* (2 vols.; Rome, 1949–50). A shorter commentary may be found in Nicolini's one-volume edition of Vico's *Opere* in *La letteratura italiana* (Milan and Naples, 1953). Ariel Doubine's translation of the *New Science* (*La science nouvelle*, Paris, 1953) is accompanied by a French version of this shorter commentary, as well as of an introductory essay by Nicolini. The English translation of Vico's *Autobiography* by M. H. Fisch and T. G. Bergin (Ithaca, N.Y., 1944; London, 1945; revised, Great Seal Books, 1963) is preceded by a 107-page essay which supplies a historical introduction to the *New Science* as well as to the *Autobiography*. For further exposition and criticism, see Croce, *La filosofia di Giambattista Vico* (Bari, 1911; revised edition, 1947; English translation by R. G. Collingwood, *The Philosophy of Giambattista Vico*, London, 1913). See also Robert Flint, *Vico* (London, 1884); C. E. Vaughan, *Studies in the History of Political Philosophy, Before and After Rousseau* (Manchester and New York, 1925), I, 207–53; H. P. Adams, *The Life and Writings of Giambattista Vico* (London, 1935); A. Robert Caponigri, *Time and Idea: The Theory of History in Giambattista Vico* (Chicago and London, 1953; critically reviewed by M. H. Fisch in *Journal of Philosophy*, LIV, 648–52, 1957). On Neapolitan intellectual life in Vico's time, see M. H. Fisch, "The Academy of the Investigators," in *Science, Medicine and History: Essays . . . in Honour of Charles Singer*, edited by E. A. Underwood (London and Toronto, 1953), I, 521–63. For the independent value of Vico's chief earlier work, the *Universal Law* (*Il diritto universale*), see M. H. Fisch, "Vico on Roman Law," in *Essays in Political Theory presented to George H. Sabine*, edited by M. R. Konvitz and A. E. Murphy (Ithaca, N.Y., and London, 1948), pp. 62–88. Vico's *On the Study Methods of Our*

Time has been translated by Elio Gianturco (Indianapolis, 1965); and a translation of his *On the Ancient Wisdom of the Italians* is being prepared by Lucia Marchetti Palmer. The tercentenary of Vico's birth (1968) will be honored by an international volume of essays on his thought and influence, edited by Giorgio Tagliacozzo and Hayden V. White and published by The Johns Hopkins Press. See also page vii above.

The University of Chicago Library has supplied a photograph of the plate facing page 3 from its copy of Giambattista Vico's *Scienza nuova* (Naples, 1744).

ABBREVIATIONS AND SIGNS

(References are to divisions or lines as numbered in Loeb Classical Library editions where such editions exist; otherwise to Teubner or other standard editions of the original texts.)

A.	*Aeneid* of Vergil
	Annals of Tacitus
A.A.	*Against Apion* of Josephus
A.P.	*Art of Poetry* (*Ad Pisones*) of Horace
C.	*Code* of Justinian
C.G.	*City of God* of St. Augustine
D.	*Digest* of Justinian
E.	*Nicomachean Ethics* of Aristotle
G.	*Germany* of Tacitus
G.W.	*Gallic War* of Caesar
H.	*History* of Tacitus
I.	*Iliad* of Homer
J.	*Institutes* of Justinian
L.	*Law of War and Peace* of Grotius
	Laws of Cicero
	Laws of Plato
O.	*Odyssey* of Homer
Op.	*Opere* of Vico (referred to by pages in vol. 2, by paragraphs in vol. 3)
P.	*Politics* of Aristotle
R.	*Republic* of Plato
S.	*On the Sublime* of Dionysius Longinus
[ ]	inserted by the translators (or, in a few cases, by Vico's editor, Nicolini)

! Vico misremembers, misquotes, distorts, or misrepresents the sources to which he refers or on which he is presumably relying. (This sign might have been used with great frequency, but we have forborne. We content ourselves with a general caveat in this place and a reference to Nicolini's *Commento storico* for full particulars.)

Square-bracketed numbers 1–1112 refer to paragraphs of the translation; A1–M10 to paragraphs of the Introduction; v–viii to pages of the Preface.

INTRODUCTION

PRINCIPI DI SCIENZA NUOVA DI GIAMBATTISTA VICO D'INTORNO ALLA COMUNE NATURA DELLE NAZIONI . . . .

A1 *Principles of New Science of Giambattista Vico concerning the Common Nature of the Nations. . . .* So reads the title page of the third edition, which appeared in July 1744, six months after Vico's death. It is this edition that is here translated. The title of the first edition (1725) had contained an additional clause that was dropped in the second (1730) and third editions. That longer title ran: *Principles of a New Science concerning the Nature of the Nations, by which are found the Principles of Another System of the Natural Law of the Gentes.* A lost draft preceding that from which the first edition was printed seems to have borne the title *New Science concerning the Principles of Humanity*; and, in a letter accompanying a presentation copy of the first edition itself, Vico referred to it as his work on the *principles of humanity.*

A2 We propose to introduce both our translation and the science by explaining the title of the third edition. More exactly, we seek to make the title mean to the reader in advance what it might otherwise mean to him only after a careful study of the entire book. We shall begin with a general remark that applies particularly to three of the terms of the title. After that, we shall consider the terms of the title one by one, in reverse order, beginning with the last and ending with the first. At convenient points, however, we shall digress to explain the phrase "Natural Law of the Gentes" in the title of the first edition [E1–8], and the phrase "principles of humanity" in the title of the lost draft [J1–5]. And at the end we shall try to explain why, though Vico's new science is in fact a science of institutions, the term *istituzione* does not appear in the title, and occurs only once in the text [M1–10].

A3 Our general remark is that Vico was professor of Latin Eloquence at the University of Naples, and that in the years 1709–22 he had published four works in Latin before turning to Italian for the *New Science*. We should expect, therefore, that he would use Italian words of Latin origin with a lively sense of their etymological overtones. It only gradually becomes apparent to us, however, that, when he uses such words with emphasis, as when they are the key terms of a sentence or clause, it is usually the etymological meaning that is emphasized. This remark applies in particular to three terms in the title: principles [I·1–14], nature [C1–7], and nations [B1–9]. The etymological meaning of the first is "beginning"; of the second and third, "birth." Thus, besides (or, as it often seems, instead of) their usual relatively abstract philosophical or scientific meanings, all three have a relatively concrete genetic meaning. It is the genetic meaning that is emphatic, and the technical meaning is either explicitly redefined genetically or, without redefinition, undergoes a displacement in that direction.

A4 The controlling methodological postulate of Vico's new science is that doctrines or theories must begin where the matters they treat begin [314]. This is to assume that genesis, or becoming, is of the essence of that which the new science treats: that, at least for the new science, nascence and nature are the same. If we are not ready to grant this as a postulate for all science, we may perhaps grant it provisionally within the scope of Vico's new science. Once we grant it, we are prepared to expect that "the common nature of nations" will turn out to be or to involve an ontogenetic pattern exhibited by each nation in its origin, development, maturity, decline, and fall [349, 393].

We proceed now to consider the terms of the title one by one, beginning with the last.

NATIONS

B1 A "nation" is etymologically a "birth," or a "being born," and hence a race, a kin or kind having a common origin or, more loosely, a common language and other institutions. (There is no reference to the modern national state as such, and no exclusive reference to political institutions.) In Vico's usage, however, there are three differences of emphasis. In the first place, in his ideal or typical case, the important thing is not race or lineage but a system of institutions. In the second place, in his ideal or typical case, a nation is assumed to be isolated from other nations, not to insure purity of racial stock, but to insure that its system of institutions shall develop independently of every other, and that correspondences between one system and another shall not be ascribed to cultural diffusion. In the third place, a nation is identified not merely in cross section by a set of institutions shared by a group of people at a given time, but genetically by a system of institutions continually changing, whose changes are due not to external influences but to internal stresses, to a sort of internal logic in which, for example, the class struggle plays a principal role. There is not only an original and individual birth for each system but a continual birth of new institutions within it, a continual transformation of old institutions, and even a rebirth of the nation after death.

B2 Vico uses the term "nation" not only in this broad sense, for that which exhibits the entire ontogenetic pattern, but also in a narrower sense, for what is there only at maturity. In the latter case, he needs other terms for the earlier stages of social evolution. The most important of these is the Latin term *gens* (plural nominative *gentes*, plural genitive *gentium*), for which the Italian is *gente* (plural *genti*). In the technical sense, this term occurs only in the plural, and for Vico's *genti* we use the Latin plural *gentes*. This term also is used in a broader and in a narrower sense. In paragraph 982, for example, it occurs in the narrower sense: "On these boundaries were to be fixed the confines first of families, then of gentes or houses, later of peoples, and finally of nations." In other passages, such as 631, Vico adopts and adapts the Latin distinction between major and minor gentes (*gentes maiores, gentes minores*) and identifies the former with the families and the latter with the peoples of 982.

B3 The etymology of *gens* is the same as that of *natio*; that is, generation or begetting, genesis or birth. It has the same genetic emphasis [555f]. The importance of this term will appear when we come to "the natural law of the gentes" [E1].

B4 The adjective for the noun *gens* is "gentile." This adjective has two chief uses. One is a technical use in Roman law, where it denotes a degree of relationship for purposes of inheritance, as in Vico's recurring phrase "direct heirs, agnates, and gentiles" [110, 592, 598, 985, 987, 988, 1023]. The other and much more frequent use is to emphasize the fact that the nations with whose nature the new science is concerned are the "gentile" nations. Such a nation as he contemplates is isolated in the first place from the Hebrew people, and only in the second place from other gentile nations [B1]. Vico, of course, never uses the redundant phrase "gentile gentes"; the term "gentes" has the emphatic meaning without the adjective. But we are to understand throughout that the families, gentes, peoples, and nations in question are gentile. All statements about the Hebrews are to be understood as asides or obiter dicta; they are no part of the science.

B5 The nations of which Vico speaks constitute a world, which he calls "the world of nations," *il mondo delle nazioni;* and the nature of the nations will be, or will be continuous with, the nature of this world. "World," *mondo,* has here the cosmetic sense of the Greek *kosmos* and the Latin *mundus,* a beautiful order that has been created out of an ugly chaos [725]. The chaos in question was that of the confusion of human seeds by promiscuous intercourse [688] among the beasts into which the non-Hebraic descendants of Noah had degenerated; and the cosmos was, in the first place, that of the primitive institutions of religion, marriage, and burial, and especially that of marriage; and in the second place, the whole complex of social institutions that developed out of these primitive ones.

B6 The world of nations is a world constituted by all the gentile nations taken together, even at a time when they are as yet completely isolated from one another; a world not first created when these nations enter into relations of commerce, diplomacy, alliance, federation, and war and peace-by-treaty with one another, but a world then recognized as already there, though as undergoing further development in and through these relations [146].

B7 Over against the world of nations Vico sets the world of nature [331, 722] (and sometimes also "the world of minds and of God" [42] or "the world of the sciences" [498, 779]). The importance of this contrast will appear under the head of "Science" below [F3].

B8 Vico has other names for the world of nations. When he wants a phrase to balance "the natural world," as "world of nations" balances "world of nature," he uses most often the phrase "the civil world" [331]. That is, he uses the adjective corresponding to the noun "city" (as Aristotle uses "political" to correspond to *polis,* or city-state) rather than that corresponding to "nation." Still another name for the word of nations is "the world of men" [689, 690]. "Polity," "civility," and "humanity" are synonyms in Vico's language [J2, 783, 899].

B9 In a last name for the world of nations, Vico uses the term "city" in another way, for which Augustine's *City of God* is his precedent. He speaks of "this great city of the human race" [342] and even of "the great city of the nations, founded and governed by God" [1107]. It must be emphasized, however, that this is Augustine's earthly city, or city of men, not his heavenly city, or city of God. The new science is a science of the former. It has nothing to do with the latter.

NATURE

C1 The genetic sense of "nature" is made quite explicit in paragraphs 147–148. We may apply what is there said to the particular case of nations somewhat as follows. The nature (*natura*) of nations is nothing but their birth (*nascimento*) in certain times and in certain guises (*guise*, modes or modifications). Whenever the time and guise are thus and so, it is a nation and not something else that is born. The inseparable properties of nations must be due to the modification or guise with which nations are born. Of whatever has these properties, and is therefore a nation, we may be sure that the nature or birth (*natura o nascimento*) was thus and not otherwise.

C2   To illustrate, we may take what Vico supposes to be the very first step in the birth of a nation; namely, the birth of a religion, which coincides with the birth of Zeus or Jupiter or Jove, the first god of the gentile nations. In this case, the "certain time" was when the sky first thundered—a hundred years after the flood in Mesopotamia, two hundred elsewhere [192ff]. The certain guise was as follows. The descendants of Ham and Japheth and the non-Hebraic descendants of Shem, having wandered through the great forest of the earth for a century or two, had lost all human speech and institutions and had been reduced to bestiality, copulating at sight and inclination. These dumb beasts naturally took the thundering sky to be a great animated body, whose flashes and claps were commands, telling them what they had to do [377, 379]. The thunder surprised some of them in the act of copulation and frightened copulating pairs into nearby caves [387ff]. This was the beginning of matrimony and of settled life [504ff, 1098]. What might otherwise have been a random act, preceded by other such acts with other mates and succeeded by others with others, became a permanent lifelong companionship sanctified by the god of the thundering sky who had frightened them into the cave. The two institutions, religion and matrimony, have thus a common birth. Every other institution will have its nature, its time and guise of birth; and it is by the birth of all in due course that a nation is born and lives [J3].

C3   It will be instructive to compare this genetic conception of the nature of nations with Aristotle's teleological conception of the nature of city-states, to which at first glance it seems diametrically opposed. "When several villages are united in a single complete community, large enough to be nearly or quite self-sufficing, the *polis*, or city-state, comes into existence, originating in the bare needs of life, and continuing in existence for the sake of a good life. And therefore, if the earlier forms of society are natural, so is the *polis*, for it is the end of them, and *the nature of a thing is its end. For what each thing is when fully developed, we call its nature*, whether we are speaking of a man, a horse, or a family. Besides, the final cause and end of a thing is the best, and to be self-sufficing is the end and the best. Hence it is self-evident that the *polis* is a natural institution, and that man is by nature a political or city-state animal." (Aristotle: *Politics* 1.2, Oxford translation slightly modified.)

C4 Vico seems at first to be saying that the nature of a thing is its beginning, and Aristotle that its nature is its end. On a closer look, however, the difference seems less radical. Both are genetic or developmental conceptions of nature. When Aristotle says that man is by nature a political animal, he means that he is an animal that becomes a man only in the *polis*. The question of the nature of man is a question of becoming; there is nothing more natural than becoming; and the becoming of the *polis* is as natural as that of man, because these are not two becomings but one.

C5 There was a standing distinction between nature on the one hand and *nomos* (law, contract, convention, arbitrary institution) on the other. The Sophists had exaggerated the distinction, and they had put man on the side of nature and the *polis* on the side of arbitrary institution. Aristotle meant to reduce the distinction, or at least to put man and *polis* on the same side of it rather than on opposite sides.

C6 Now Vico here agrees with Aristotle. When he calls the world of nations the world of men, he means that what were beasts in the world of nature become men in the world of nations, and it is by the becoming of the world of nations that they become men. Or, as he puts it otherwise, in a sense they make the world of nations, and in the same sense they make themselves by making it [367, 520, 692].

C7 Vico distinguishes three successive ages in the nature or development of nations—that of gods, that of heroes, and that of men; and he distinguishes three corresponding natures—divine, heroic, and human [916ff]. It is true that this is only one of three senses in which he uses the term "human." In one sense, all three natures are human; in a second sense, the second and third in contrast with the first [629]; in a third sense, the third in contrast with the first and second [viii]. But this third sense is the strict or proper sense of the term. That is, Vico identifies the nature of man more particularly with what men become in the third of the three ages. For example, in paragraph 973 he speaks of the "rational humanity" of the age of men as "the true and proper nature of man." In 927 this is called "the intelligent nature, which is the proper nature of man," and in 326 and 924 it is called "human reason fully developed." It may be concluded, therefore, that Vico does not really disagree with Aristotle's identification of a thing's nature with what it is when fully developed [J5].

COMMON

D1 It is obvious that in the phrase "common nature of nations," "common" is used in a sense different from that in which things and women are "common" in the *comunione infame*, the infamous commonness, or promiscuity, of the bestial vagrants in the forest [16f]. In that sense, common is the opposite of certain [321] and the effect of an institution of matrimony is that men become "certain fathers of certain children by certain women" [1098].

D2 (In the first edition of our translation, for the *comunione* or commonness of this primeval chaos we put "communism." This was perhaps misleading, by suggesting a system of some sort, whereas Vico's *comunione* denotes a complete absence of system, prior to all institutions. In the present revision, we have rendered it "promiscuity." This also may mislead, by suggesting a defect of individual character in the midst of a society in which that defect is not common. Alas, the revision of translations is at best a matter in large part of substituting ways of misleading the reader less for ways of misleading him more.)

D3 But again, in the phrase here in question, "common" does not, at least in the first instance, mean public, at large, joint, reciprocal, mutually agreed upon. It does not presuppose consideration, deliberation, communication, mutual influence, transaction, convention, or agreement.

D4 What it does mean is "independently exemplified by many, or by all." Here are some examples of the term in this sense in phrases other than "the common nature of nations." "Common sense is judgment *without reflection*, shared by an entire class, an entire people, an entire nation, or the entire human race" [142]. (Obviously Vico means to exclude the possibility of common sense having become common by communication.) "Uniform ideas originating among entire peoples *unknown to each other* must have a common ground of truth" [144].

D5 Consider now two subsequent passages in which the last-quoted "axiom" is cited. Vico says there were as many Joves, with as many names, as there were nations; and, "since in their beginnings these nations were forest-bred and *shut off from any knowledge of each other*," the Jove fable in each nation contained a civil truth which was the common ground of truth that uniform ideas under such circumstances must have [198]. Again: "Since this world of nations has been made by men, let us see in what institutions all men agree and always have agreed. For these institutions will be able to give us the universal and eternal principles . . . on which all nations were founded and still preserve themselves. We observe that all nations, barbarous as well as civilized, *though separately founded because remote from each other in time and space,* keep these three human customs: all have some religion, all contract solemn marriages, all bury their dead. And in no nation, however savage and crude, are any human actions performed with more elaborate ceremonies and more sacred solemnity than the rites of religion, marriage, and burial. For, by the axiom that 'uniform ideas, born among peoples unknown to each other, must have a common ground of truth,' it must have been dictated to all nations that from these three institutions humanity began among them all, and therefore they must be most devoutly guarded by them all, so that the world should not again become a bestial wilderness. For this reason we have taken these three eternal and universal customs as three first principles of this Science" [332f].

D6 Another example: "There must in the nature of human institutions be a mental language common to all nations, which uniformly grasps the substance of things feasible in human social life, and expresses it with as many diverse modifications as these same things may have diverse aspects. A proof of this is afforded by proverbs or maxims of vulgar wisdom, in which substantially the same meanings find as many diverse expressions as there are nations ancient and modern. This common mental language is proper to our Science, by whose light linguistic scholars will be enabled to construct a mental vocabulary common to all the various articulate languages living and dead" [161f]. This is the sense in which two entirely different words belonging to two languages that have developed in complete independence of each other may nevertheless have a common meaning.

D7 Our illustrations have so far been drawn from passages having to do with the common nature of nations though the phrase itself does not occur in them. But it is in a more restricted context that Vico comes nearest to using a technical expression for the relevant sense of commonness. "Now, because laws certainly come first and philosophies later, it must have been from observing that the enactment of laws by Athenian citizens involved their coming to agreement in an idea of an equal utility *common to all of them severally—partitamente comune a tutti—*that Socrates began to adumbrate intelligible genera or abstract universals by induction; that is, by collecting uniform particulars which go to make up a genus of that in respect of which the particulars are uniform among themselves" [1040]. That is, the commonness to which Vico refers is of the sort usually assumed by scientific induction. The importance of this will appear under the head of "Science" below [F1, F5].

NATURAL LAW OF THE GENTES

E1   So far we have remained within the title of the third edition of the *New Science*. It will be convenient at this point to digress and consider the last phrase of the title of the first edition [A1]. In that edition the title was: Principles of a New Science concerning the Nature of Nations, by which are found the Principles of Another System of *the Natural Law of the Gentes*. By "another system," Vico meant a new system, different from those of the seventeenth-century natural-law theorists, Grotius, Selden, and Pufendorf [394]. The sense of the title is that it is the principles of the common nature of nations which disclose the principles of the new system of the natural law of the gentes.

E2   Though Vico dropped this clause from the titles of his second and third editions, it was not because this topic had been omitted in those editions but only because it had become less prominent. His new "system of the natural law of the gentes" is still one of the "principal aspects" of the new science in the third edition [G3, 394]. Indeed, we meet this aspect in the introductory "Idea of the Work" in a sentence which would fit the first edition perfectly: "This New Science studies the common nature of nations in the light of divine providence, discovers the origins of institutions, divine and human, among the gentile nations, and thereby establishes a system of the natural law of the gentes, which proceeds with the greatest equality and constancy through the three ages which the Egyptians handed down to us as the three periods through which the world had passed up to their time" [31]. In a series of chapters in the first edition, Vico had distinguished a first, a second, and a third "natural law of the gentes," proper, respectively, to the three ages he proceeds to distinguish, divine, heroic, human.

E3   From distinctions that were familiar in late if not already in classical Roman law, we may reach Vico's "natural law of the gentes" by the following route. The most general distinction was that between public law and private law. Under private law, a further distinction was made between civil law and *ius gentium*. Though *ius gentium* is literally translated by Vico as *il diritto delle genti*, and though we translate his phrase literally as "the law of the gentes," it is probable that *ius gentium* was an idiomatic phrase like *ubi gentium*, "where in the world," and meant "law everywhere prevailing," or "universal law." In any case, it was not international public law in the sense of law governing relations between nations; nor was it even international private law in the sense of law applied by international tribunals to relations between citizens or corporations of different nations. It was simply that part of the private law of Rome, or of any state, which was also a part of the private law of every other; whereas the civil law of each state was that part of its law which was peculiar to itself. But, further, the *ius gentium,* by virtue of being common to all peoples with whom the Romans had dealings, seemed to be a natural and necessary expression or condition of human society. It obtained everywhere because it was dictated by a natural reason shared by all men and perhaps by other animals. It was *ius gentium* just because it was *ius naturale,* or natural law. It need not follow that *ius gentium* and natural law were identical or even coextensive. One might, however, use the phrase *ius gentium naturale* for so much of the *ius gentium* as was also *ius naturale;* or the phrase *ius naturale gentium* for so much of the *ius naturale* as was also *ius gentium.* Either or both of these phrases might be used without prejudice to the further question whether there was *ius gentium* that was not natural law, or natural law that was not *ius gentium.* In this way we reach Vico's phrase, *ius naturale gentium,* or *il diritto naturale delle genti,* which we render "the natural law of the gentes." It remains to explain what he meant by it, and why we so translate it.

E4 We must begin by reminding the reader of a constant source of confusion and misunderstanding in English translations from the legal literature of continental Europe. English uses the one word "law" in two very different senses for which European languages have distinct and contrasting terms: Latin *ius* and *lex,* Italian *diritto* and *legge,* French *droit* and *loi,* Spanish *derecho* and *ley,* German *Recht* and *Gesetz.* The second term of each pair properly denotes enacted law, law which has been *made* law by the authority of some lawmaking body, at some time and place; law, therefore, by will. The first term of each pair denotes the legal order, structure, or system, conceived as, ideally at least, a rational whole; law, therefore, by reason. The distinction is between what is law because it has been so decided, and what is law because it is in itself straight, right, or reasonable. Thus, only the first term, not the second, could be used in translating such English expressions as "principles of law" or "philosophy of law." Now there are three equally unsatisfactory ways in which we might have sought to prevent misunderstanding of Vico in this connection. We might have kept the terms *diritto* and *legge* without translation. We might have put them in parentheses after the ambiguous translation "law": law (*diritto*), law (*legge*). Or we might have used subscripts: law$_1$

for *legge,* law$_d$ for *diritto.* We shall illustrate by using all three devices in the following paragraph.

E5 Vico deliberately sharpens the distinction between *diritto* and *legge* by starting with the distinction between custom (*consuetudine*) and law (*legge*) and then putting "the natural law$_d$ of the gentes" under the former rather than under the latter. He lays down as an axiom Dio's dictum that "custom is like a king and law$_l$ like a tyrant; which we must understand as referring to reasonable custom and to law$_l$ not animated by natural reason." He says this axiom decides the dispute "whether law$_d$ resides in nature or in the opinion of men," or, what comes to the same thing, "whether man is naturally sociable." "In the first place, the natural law (*diritto*) of the gentes was instituted by custom (which Dio says commands us by pleasure like a king) and not by law (*legge*) (which Dio says commands us by force like a tyrant). For it began in human customs springing from the common nature of nations (which is the adequate subject of our Science) and it preserves human society. Moreover, there is nothing more natural (for there is nothing more pleasant) than observing natural customs (*naturali costumi*). For all these reasons, human nature, in which such customs have had their origin, is sociable" [308f].

E6 The reader will have perceived that this passage sheds some further light on the meaning of "nature" and "natural." Besides the genetic meaning, there is the closely related meaning of spontaneity, of absence of reflection or deliberation. By contrast with the *ius gentium* as natural, the civil law will be that part of the law of a nation which, being peculiar to it, must have been deliberately adopted. There is an interesting passage in which Vico, rejecting the diffusion theory of culture and asserting the multiple-independent-origin theory [F5], argues that if "the natural law of the gentes" had spread by diffusion, it would in all places but that of its origin have had the character of imposed or of deliberately adopted law, and therefore of civil, not natural, law; which is contradictory. ". . . the *natural* law of the gentes . . . has been thought to have come out of one first nation and to have been received from it by the others. . . . If that had been the case, it would have been a *civil* law communicated to other peoples by *human* provision, and not a law which *divine* providence instituted naturally in all nations along with human customs themselves. On the contrary, as it will be one of our constant labors throughout this book to demonstrate, the natural law of the gentes had *separate origins* among the several peoples, *each in ignorance of the others,* and it was only subsequently, as a result of wars, embassies, alliances and commerce, that it came to be recognized as common to the entire human race" [146].

E7 Vico does not stop with the paradox that, on the diffusion theory, the natural law of the gentes would have existed by human foresight, provision, or providence. In rejecting that theory, he sets up over against it the theory of divine providence [F5–6]. But this is put forward not merely as an alternative theory adopted by Vico but as an idea associated from the beginning with the very idea of law. In Latin etymology, it was not uncommon in Vico's time to connect the term *ius* with the name *Ious* or *Jovis*, Jove or Jupiter. Since a theory must begin where what it treats began [314], Vico's theory of "the natural law of the gentes" begins where law began, and that began not only in an act of divine providence but in a rudimentary form of the *belief* in divine providence [398].

E8 It remains to explain our not continuing, as we did in the first edition of our translation, to use the familiar phrase "law of nations" for *ius gentium* and *il diritto delle genti*. One reason is that Vico himself twice uses the phrase *diritto delle nazioni* and we wished to reserve "law of nations" for rendering those two passages [998, 1023]. A more important reason is that the phrase "law of nations" has become associated with international law, and we wished to avoid that confusion.* Lastly, in the complete phrase "natural law of nations," there would be greater risk of the term "natural law" arousing associations with the ideally just, the perfectly rational law which Vico calls "the natural law of the philosophers" [313, 1084].

SCIENCE

F1 The initial distinction here is that between *coscienza*, consciousness or conscience, and *scienza*, knowledge or science. *Coscienza* has for its object *il certo*, the certain; that is, particular facts, events, customs, laws, institutions, as careful observation and the sifting of evidence determine them to be; and *scienza* has for its object *il vero*, the true; that is, universal and eternal principles [137]. (Otherwise put, *scienza* is of the common [321].) The pursuit of *coscienza* of the certain is philology or history; the pursuit of *scienza* of the true or the common is philosophy. Thus far, *scienza* in the narrow sense. But it is in a wider sense that the term *scienza* is used in the title of Vico's work, and in that wider sense it embraces both philology and philosophy. "Philosophy contemplates reason, whence comes knowledge of the true; philology observes that of which human choice is author, whence comes consciousness of the certain. This axiom by its

---

* There is one passage, however, in which Vico extends the phrase "natural law of the gentes" to include international law [632]. And in the first edition of the *New Science* [Op. 3.56] he envisaged a "united nations of the world."

second part includes among the philologians all the grammarians, historians, critics, who have occupied themselves with the study of the languages and deeds of peoples: deeds at home, as in their customs and laws, and deeds abroad, as in their wars, peaces, alliances, travels, and commerce. This same axiom shows how the philosophers failed by half in not giving certainty to their reasonings by appeal to the authority of the philologians, and likewise how the latter failed by half in not taking care to give their authority the sanction of truth by appeal to the reasoning of the philosophers. If they had done this they would have been more useful to their commonwealths *and they would have anticipated us in conceiving this Science*" [138–140].

F2 So far we have satisfied the requirement that science should be knowledge of the universal and eternal [163]. But there was a requirement of equally long standing that science should be knowledge by causes, and the new science is even more emphatic in its claim to meet this requirement [345, 358, 630]. Not only so, but, along this line, Vico had developed a theory of knowledge according to which we can know, or have *scienza* of, only what we ourselves make or do. Thus, we can have *scienza* in mathematics, because we are there deducing the consequences of our own definitions, axioms, and postulates; and we can have *scienza* in physics to the extent of our capacity for experiment. But mathematics and physics fall short of perfect *scienza*. Mathematics falls short because its objects are fictions. Physics falls short because the scope of our experiments can never encompass nature as a whole.

F3 *Scienza* of the world of nature, in the strict sense, is therefore reserved for God, who made it. But *scienza* of the world of nations, the civil world, the world of human institutions, is possible for men, because men have made it, and its principles or causes "are therefore to be found within the modifications of our own human mind" [331]. Moreover, such *scienza* would have the advantage over physics of being complete, and the advantage over mathematics of being real. For, "as geometry, when it constructs the world of quantity out of its elements, or contemplates that world, is creating it for itself, just so does our Science [create for itself the world of nations], but with a *reality* greater by just so much as the institutions having to do with human affairs are *more real* than points, lines, surfaces, and figures are" [349].

F4 There are, however, two obvious objections to be met. (1) According to the Hebrew-Christian view of history, the basic institutions, both sacred and secular, were established by God or Christ. (2) The meaning of history, in that same view, is to be found in a single series of unique acts. In what sense, then, is *scienza* of the world of nations (1) knowledge of what men themselves have made, and in what sense is it (2) knowledge of universals?

F5 These objections are met (a) by excluding the Hebrew-Christian tradition and its institutions from the range within which the new science claims full competence, (b) by conceiving the world of the gentile nations as having indefinitely numerous independent origins [E6], such that in each nation the same "ideal eternal history" is exemplified, and (c) by distinguishing two kinds of providence: (1) the direct and transcendent providence of unique and special acts, which was a privilege of the chosen people, and (2) the immanent providence operating according to uniform laws and using means as natural and easy as human customs themselves, which was all the gentiles had [313]. Of these two kinds of providence, the former is incompatible with full human agency in the making of institutions, and so also is any combination of the former with the latter, but the latter by itself is not.

F6 It is not quite sufficient, however, to say that Vico held, in the case of gentile nations, a theory of providence that enabled him to answer the question how a science of the common nature of these nations is possible. The theory of providence is not merely a presupposition of the science but an integral part or "principal aspect" of it. As a presupposition, divine providence is an article of faith, under which the aforesaid distinction is required in order that Vico may be free to take the first steps toward constructing his science. As a part or aspect of that science, his "rational civil theology of divine providence" [385] may best be understood as a hypothesis to account for what Wundt later called "the heterogony of ends"; that is, for the uniform ways in which, while consciously pursuing their particular ends, men have unconsciously served wider ends [342, 344, 1108]. (This may be compared also with Mandeville's earlier "private vices, public benefits," with Adam Smith's "invisible hand," and with Hegel's "cunning of reason." Vico may have had Mandeville in mind when he said that the "public virtue" of the heroic Romans was nothing but a good use which providence made of their "grievous, ugly and cruel private vices" [38].)

F7 Though the Hebrew-Christian tradition is formally excluded from the range within which Vico's science claims full competence, and though Vico notes many decisive differences between the Hebrews and the gentiles [126, 165ff, 301, 313, 329, 350, 369ff, 396, 401, 481, 948], he nevertheless draws many parallels between Hebrew and gentile history and institutions [165, 423, 433, 527, 530, 533, 557, 658, 715]. Moreover, the distinction loses importance, if it does not quite disappear, in the second cycle of ages in Christian Europe.

F8 This will perhaps suffice to indicate in what sense Vico's work claimed to be science, and how, on his premises, a science of its scope and nature was possible.

NEW

G1 Though Vico wrote and published in the eighteenth century, he was a child of the seventeenth, "the century of genius." He was born in 1668 and he attained in 1699 the professorship of rhetoric which he held until his retirement. Now the seventeenth century is marked, above all others, by the frequency with which, in the titles of scientific and pseudo-scientific works, such words as "new" and "unheard of" appear. It was more honorable to create a new science singlehanded than to continue or extend or even to revolutionize an old one. Vico lived in Naples, which was then near the fringe or frontier of the learned world in which this fever and pride of novelty was epidemic. Naples had, however, in the Academy of the Investigators, an active cell in which the new sciences and the new philosophies of the century were cultivated, and in which some contributions to them were made. It was almost certainly by this Academy that the ambition to found a new science was aroused and sustained in Vico. But the novelties of the seventeenth century had been chiefly in mathematics, in the physical and biological sciences, and in medicine. Vico's ambition was to create a science of human society, a science that should do for "the world of nations" what men like Galileo and Newton had done for "the world of nature" [B5–7, F2–3]. Now Vico does not claim that his is the first attempt at such a science; he claims only that it is the first successful attempt. The only predecessors to whom he refers are the natural-law theorists [394] and Hobbes.

G2 Hobbes had indeed made a claim similar to Vico's when he boasted that "civil philosophy" was no older than his own *De cive* (1642). In Vico's eyes, Hobbes had attempted something much closer to his own new science than in fact Hobbes had intended; namely, the study of "man in the whole society of the human race"—"*L'uomo in tutta la società del gener umano*" [179]. But Hobbes failed, and the reason for his failure was that he thought it possible to derive human society from human deliberation, counsel, and provision, and did not see that gentile society could have arisen only by divine providence.

G3 Vico had himself begun by attempting only "a new system of the natural law of the gentes" to take the place of that of the natural-law theorists. He first conceived the new science in connection with this attempt. Only gradually did the new science itself come to seem important in its own right, and not merely as a foundation on which to build the new system. The new system then dropped into place as merely one of the "principal aspects" of the new science [E2]. Thus, Vico does not ascribe to the natural-law theorists an intent as close to his own as he thinks Hobbes's was. But the natural-law theorists failed, he says, in what they did attempt; and they failed "by beginning in the middle; that is, with the latest times of the civilized nations (and thus of men enlightened by fully developed natural reason) from which the philosophers emerged and rose to meditation of a perfect idea of justice" [394]. That is, what they give us is "the natural law of the philosophers," the ideally just law, and not "the natural law of the gentes," which was a law of force [1084].

G4 If Vico errs, it is in ascribing to his predecessors intentions nearer his own than they in fact were. And if we look further, within or beyond the range of the authors he cites, we shall find not even a remote approach to what he has done. In the end, therefore, if we concede that what he has done is science, we must also concede that it is new science.

GIAMBATTISTA VICO'S

H1 The science concerning the common nature of nations not only is new but is Vico's. It is not a work of collaboration, not a synthesis of results previously attained by others and waiting only to be brought together, organized, and given the form of a science. It is a science in which not even the first steps could be taken until a certain discovery was made. Vico had himself made that discovery, and it was only when he was in possession of it that he was able to proceed to construct the science. "To discover the way in which this first human thinking arose in the gentile world, we encountered exasperating difficulties which have cost us the research of a good twenty years. [We had] to descend from these human and refined natures of ours to those quite wild and savage natures, which we cannot at all imagine and can comprehend only with great effort" [338]. "We find that the principle of these origins both of languages and of letters lies in the fact that the first gentile peoples, by a demonstrated necessity of nature, were poets who spoke in poetic characters. This discovery, which is the master key of this Science, has cost us the persistent research of almost all our literary life, because with our civilized natures we [moderns] cannot at all imagine and can understand only by great toil the poetic nature of these first men" [34].

H2 It was because the natural-law theorists and Hobbes had not made this discovery and were not in possession of this key that they could not so much as make a beginning of the new science, whatever intimations of it may be found in their works.

I·1 We have already noted the systematic ambiguity and the genetic emphasis which the term "principles" shares with the terms "nature" and "nations" [A3]. We must now notice that the term "principles" occurs not only in the title of the work as a whole but also in the title of Book One, *Dello stabilimento de' principi*, "Of the Establishment of the Principles," and in that of Section III of Book One, *De' principi*, "Of the Principles."

I·2 Let us begin with the innermost box of the nest and work outward. The principles of Section III of Book One are the primary institutions of religion, marriage, and burial [330–337]. These are principles in the sense that they are the necessary and sufficient generative conditions of the *gens*, the minimal society that can outlive its members and thus make possible an evolution of culture. "Now since this world of nations has been made by men, let us see in what institutions all men have perpetually agreed and still agree. For these institutions will be able to give us the universal and eternal principles (such as every science must have) on which all nations were founded *and on which they still preserve themselves*" [332]. Farther on, in Section IV: "In reasoning of the origins of institutions, divine and human, in the gentile world, we reach those first beginnings beyond which it is vain curiosity to demand others earlier; and this is the defining character of *principles*. We explain the particular guises of their birth, that is to say their nature, the explanation of which is the distinguishing mark of science. And finally these origins are confirmed by the eternal properties the institutions preserve, which could not be what they are if the institutions had not come into being just as they did, in those particular times, places, and guises, which is to say with those particular natures" [346].

I·3 What Vico has done is to trace the origin of gentile society and thereby of gentile humanity to the origins of these three institutions, and to show how the rest of culture is involved in or derives from them. For a summary statement of the way in which everything grows out of religion, for example, the reader is referred to paragraph 629. But Vico gives little attention to the transformations of these institutions in the later stages of social evolution.

I·4 In the title of Book One itself, "Of the Establishment of the Principles," it may appear that the same term, if it applies to all four sections, must mean the principles of the science itself. These would then be: (1) the chronological table and the annotations upon it, in which the essential philological materials are put in order; (2) the elements in the Euclidian sense, that is to say the axioms, definitions, and postulates; (3) the principles in the narrow sense above indicated; (4) the method. That is, out of these materials, by means of these elements, starting from these principles, and using this method, Vico proposes in the subsequent books to construct (a) the world of nations and (b) the science of that world.

I·5   But it may be that even here the principles are at least primarily those of Section III. This would appear from the last paragraph of Section IV, where Vico says: "From all that has been set forth in general concerning the establishment of the principles of this Science, we conclude that, since its principles are (1) divine providence, (2) marriage and therewith moderation of the passions, and (3) burial and therewith immortality of human souls . . ." [360].

I·6   It is worth noting, perhaps, that two of these institutions, religion and marriage, along with two others not here included, asylums and the first agrarian law, are later referred to as causes and "as it were, four elements of this civil world" [630].

I·7   In the title of the work as a whole, we might expect that the term "principles" should mean not merely the principles as such but the science and the world of nations as constructed from those principles; much in the way that by Euclid's Elements we understand not merely the elements in the strict sense—that is, the definitions, axioms, and postulates—but the system of geometry constructed from those elements.

I·8   But just as Euclid's Elements as a system is susceptible of indefinite further development without addition to or change in the definitions, axioms, or postulates, so Vico's new science is susceptible of indefinite further development without change in its principles, whether in the narrower or in the wider sense. By beginning his title "Principles of New Science," that is, Vico disclaims any pretension to completeness. Of the seven principal aspects of the science [385–399], none is completed within Vico's work. This is particularly evident in the case of the third, "a history of human ideas," or intellectual history. Of one passage coming under this head [1040ff], Vico says that it may serve as "a particle of the history of philosophy narrated philosophically" [1043].

I·9   Vico speaks several times of a Mental Dictionary of which he had given a specimen in the first edition of the *New Science*, of which he gives another example in this edition [473–482], and of which he says he makes continual use. But the Dictionary itself remains a project barely begun.

I·10 Vico prophesies that scholars of the German language will make marvelous discoveries if they apply themselves to seeking its origins in the light of his principles [153, 471].

I·11 Though the new science is thus confessedly incomplete in execution, it does claim to be perfect in idea or conception. In making this claim (which he does only indirectly), Vico quotes from a famous passage in Seneca's *Natural Questions*, near the end of his chapter on comets. In ancient times there were various theories about the "planets," or "wanderers," that reduced their movements to law, but no such law had been discovered for comets. Seneca takes the view that their movements are lawful like those of the planets, but that we so far lack sufficient observations for determining their orbits. When a future age shall have accumulated sufficient data, we may expect that their orbits too will be plotted. Speaking of the world of nature at large, Seneca adds: "Many discoveries are reserved for the ages still to be, when our memory shall have perished. The world is a poor affair if it do not contain matter for investigation for the whole world in every age" [1096].

I·12 We are tempted to say that whereas Seneca was obviously speaking of the world of nature, Vico means by "this world" the world of nations, and means merely that this world, as well as the world of nature, will yield fresh discoveries to the researchers of all future ages. But Vico's memory has given a twist to Seneca's second sentence, changing *nisi in illo quod quaerat* to *nisi id, quod quaerit*, so that the meaning is not "unless it holds something for all the world to seek," but "unless it holds what all the world seeks." It appears, therefore, that "this world" is the new science itself; or, if not that, the world of nations as constructed in and by the new science; or the model world of the "ideal history of the eternal laws which are instanced by the deeds of all nations . . ." [1096]. And what Vico means is that the model world of his science is a poor affair unless whatever future ages discover in the actual history of nations and then look for in his model is found to be covered by "the ideal history" of the model; that is, is seen to be an instance of one or more of the "eternal laws." It is this capacity of a science to accommodate future observations and the results of future experiments that is the mark of a science that is "perfect in its idea."

I·13 This raises the question what degree of conformity with empirical fact Vico considered necessary to confirm the principles of his science. The answer to this question is clear from the third chapter of Book Five [1088ff], the chapter which concludes with the misquotation from Seneca. Vico admits that the nations which do not quite conform to his ideal eternal history are more numerous than those that do. In the ancient world of nations, only Rome approximates it at all closely; in the modern, only certain European nations. The deviations and deformations require special explanations. For example, in the new world across the Atlantic, "the American Indians would now be following this course of human institutions *if they had not been discovered by the Europeans*" [1095]. But the general explanation provided by the model suffices for the typical or exemplary nations.

I·14 But even in the title of the work as a whole, the term "principles" retains the genetic meaning, at least as an overtone; both in the sense that Vico's work presents only the beginnings of the new science and in the sense that the part it presents is focused on the beginnings of the world of nations. Vico has dealt in some detail with the most difficult part of the science, the origins of the institutions which constitute that world; he has dealt only briefly with the beginnings of the second cycle in Europe; beyond that there are only scattered indications. So there is plenty for further workers to do, even within the first two cycles. There is matter for the researchers of all ages to come, in Seneca's sense. But whatever those ages find, the new science will be found to have contained *in principle*.

PRINCIPLES OF HUMANITY

J1 Preceding the draft from which the first edition of the *New Science* was printed in 1725, there was a quite different draft, since lost, which seems to have borne the title *New Science concerning the Principles of Humanity*. In a letter accompanying a presentation copy of the first edition itself, Vico referred to it as his work on the "principles of humanity." And within the work itself in its third edition, the phrase "principles of humanity" occurs now and then [118, 123, 163, 338].

J2 We may safely take it that the phrase "principles of humanity" is at least roughly equivalent to the phrase "common nature of nations." But this means that the term "humanity" is at least roughly equivalent to the terms "civility" and "polity" [B8]. And it means further that the term "humanity," like the terms "nature," "nation," and "principle," has a genetic sense. The principles of humanity are the principles by which creatures who are not men *become* men [C6]. The principles by which the kosmos or world of nations is generated out of the chaos of the infamous bestial commonness or promiscuity of things and women are the same principles by which the men-beasts of the bestial wandering in the great forest of the earth settle down and humanize themselves [B5].

J3 It is not any and every sort of bestiality out of which humanity can

be generated, and in order to obtain as his raw material beasts that have it
in them to become men, Vico, as a good Catholic, starts from the universal
flood [369ff] and allows two centuries for the descendants of Ham and
Japheth and the non-Hebraic descendants of Shem to lapse into a bestiality
suitable for his purpose [C2].

J4   Vico shares with the Marxists and existentialists the negative view
that there is no human essence to be found in individuals as such, and with
the Marxists the positive view that the essence of humanity is the ensemble
of social relations, or the developing system of institutions.

J5   We have already remarked [C7], in connection with the three
ages—gods, heroes, men—that there is a weak sense in which all three are
human by contrast with the antecedent bestial chaos; a stronger sense in
which the second and third are human in contrast with the first [629]; and
a strongest sense in which only the third is human as over against the first
and second. Vico's way of putting this is to speak of the humanity of the
third as *tutta spiegata*, completely unfolded, fully developed.

POETIC WISDOM

K1   We believe we have now made clear the meaning of the terms of
the title of Vico's work, and thereby the meaning of the title as a whole
and the nature and scope of the new science. In connection with the term
"principles," we have had occasion to touch also upon the title of Book
One and even upon the titles of its four sections [I·1, I·4]. Some further
clarification could be achieved by considering the titles of the other four
"books," of some of their subsections, and of the introduction and conclusion. We shall content ourselves, however, with examining only the title of
Book Two, "Poetic Wisdom," and the term "recourse" in the title of Book
Five.

K2   There was a tradition, old enough to be attacked in Plato's
Republic, that the founders of civilization, who were poets like Homer,
were at the same time wise men; that Homer and the tragedians were
masters of all technical knowledge and also moral and religious guides to
the conduct of life. It was supposed that each city-state had been founded
by some great legislative hero, some wise lawgiver, as Sparta, for example,
had been by Lycurgus. There were traditions, much exaggerated by Vico,
to the effect that these lawgivers also were poets [469].

K3   These are forms of the conceit of scholars, who will have it that
whatever they know is as old as the world [127]. A modern form of this
same conceit was the natural-law theories of the seventeenth century,

which, whatever the barbarities and inconveniences they ascribed to the state of nature, imputed to men in that state an ability to recognize the dictates of natural reason and to be guided by them [394].

K4 Now Vico does not doubt that the founders of humanity were poets and sages of a sort. The problem is to determine the sort. Since they founded humanity by creating institutions, they were poets in the Greek sense of makers or creators. To be good at making anything is doubtless in some sense to know how to make it, and the "know-how" is doubtless a sort of knowledge or wisdom. But what sense, and what sort? It was the discovery of the nature of this poetic or creative wisdom, the wisdom of the poets or makers of human institutions, that was the master key of the new science; a discovery which had cost Vico the research of a good twenty years [338]. "In such fashion the first men of the gentile nations, children of nascent mankind, created things according to their own ideas. But this creation was infinitely different from that of God. For God, in his purest intelligence, knows things, and, by knowing them, creates them; but they, in their robust ignorance, did it by virtue of a wholly corporeal imagination. And because it was quite corporeal, they did it with marvelous sublimity; a sublimity such and so great that it excessively perturbed the very persons who by imagining did the creating, for which they were called 'poets,' which is Greek for 'creators' " [376].

K5 Vico went so far as to discern in this poetic wisdom the crude beginnings of the arts and sciences: a poetic or creative metaphysics, out of which there developed in one direction logic,* morals, economics, and politics, all poetic; and in another direction physics, cosmography, astronomy, chronology, geography, all likewise poetic. This provides the outline or framework for Book Two. "We shall show . . . how the founders of gentile humanity by means of their natural theology (or metaphysics) imagined the gods; how by means of their logic they invented languages; by

---

* To illustrate, the branch of logic called topics, as developed by Aristotle and later authors, was the theory of the art of employing common "places" (topoi) for the purpose of inventing probable arguments concerning matters of fact, and eventually of discovering the most probable; for instance, the most probable explanation of a given fact or class of facts, such as thunder. What Vico does in this case is to trace the art back to what he calls the "sensory topics" [495] of primitive men. It was by a topos, or common "place" (startling sounds are likely in the first "place" to be utterances of some being or other), that primitive men passed from the thundering sky to Jupiter Tonans, Jove the Thunderer; but this was a "sensory" topos in that the passage had the immediacy of feeling rather than the discursiveness of deliberate inference. To be hearing thunder was to be listening to Jove. Only by a much later criticism could observed fact and invented explanation be distinguished, and only then could the topos itself be identified and formulated, and rules for its use drawn up.

morals, created heroes; by economics, founded families, and by politics, cities; by their physics, established the beginnings of things as all divine; *by the particular physics of man, in a certain sense created themselves*; by their cosmography, fashioned for themselves a universe entirely of gods; by astronomy, carried the planets and constellations from earth to heaven; by chronology, gave a beginning to [measured] times; and how by geography the Greeks, for example, described the [whole] world within their own Greece" [367].

K6 The sciences in their fully developed, deliberate, systematic, methodologically self-conscious forms, are of course achievements of the age of men. Bacon was the great prophet of the sciences in the second age of men. His projected but unfinished *Great Instauration* (two of whose six parts are represented by the *Advancement of Learning* and the *Novum Organum*) loomed in Vico's view as the monument of seventeenth-century thought with which he would like his *New Science* to be compared. In the second edition (1730) paragraph 37 had had a continuation which somehow dropped out in the third: "Hence in Book Two, which makes almost the entire body of this work, a discovery is made which is just the opposite of that of Bacon in his *Novus orbis scientiarum,* or New World of Sciences, where he considers how the sciences as they now stand may be carried on toward perfection. This work of ours discovers the ancient world of the sciences, how rough they had to be at birth, and how gradually refined, until they reached the form in which we have received them." Vico means not merely that Book Two forms half the bulk of the work, but that it contains nearly all its substance. If the reader will forgive a Vichian pun, it contains nearly everything that is original. All the rest is accessory. Book One prepares the way for Book Two; Books Three and Four expand certain of its insights, or repeat its content in different forms; and Book Five does for the second cycle of ages what Book Two has done for the first cycle.

K7 Presumably the new science, a creation of the eighteenth century, itself belongs to that "New World of the Sciences" which Bacon envisaged. But it is a science which faces in the opposite direction. Though created in the second-cycle age of men, its creation has been made possible by a return to the poetic wisdom by which the world of nations was first created. In devoting half the book to poetic wisdom, Vico exhibits scientific and philosophic wisdom seeking to know itself by recovering its own origins in vulgar or poetic or creative wisdom. In doing this, it becomes itself creative, or recreative. Doubtless all science is in some sense constructive, but the new science is so in a special way. For in *this* science, philosophic or scientific wisdom comprehends, though with the greatest difficulty [338], that vulgar or creative wisdom which is the origin and presupposition of all science and all philosophy. The new science, like all science, must begin where its subject matter begins. But its subject matter is institution-building wisdom, and that began with the first beginnings of institutions (when men first "began to think humanly" [338]). Geometry need not begin where surveying began, nor mechanics where machine-building began, nor chemistry where cooking, smelting, and dyeing began. Perhaps botany must begin where plants began, but it need not inquire when, where, and how botanizing began. But the new science must inquire when, where, and how it itself began. It is Vico's in one sense [H1–2], and in another sense it is simply the coming to self-consciousness of the institution-building wisdom which is as old as the building of institutions. The sciences are themselves institutions, and the same vulgar wisdom that created families, commonwealths, and laws, created also a poetic metaphysics, logic, morals, economics, politics, physics, etc., so that the new science re-creates itself by re-creating the first science, that of augury or divination, out of which all the others grew [365, 391, 661, 734]. Thus wisdom comes full circle in the new science.

RECOURSE

L1 The primary meaning of this term will be apparent if we compare the titles of Books Four and Five: *Del corso che fanno le nazioni*, "Of the Course that the Nations Run"; and *Del ricorso delle cose umane nel risurgere che fanno le nazioni*, "Of the Recourse of Human Institutions that the Nations Take in Rising Again" (or "Of the Recourse of Human Institutions in the Resurrection of Nations"). That Vico means the two titles to be taken together and to interpret each other appears from paragraph 393: "Wherever, emerging from savage, fierce, and bestial times, men begin to domesticate themselves by religion, they begin, proceed, and end by those stages which are investigated here in Book Two, to be encountered again in Book Four, where we shall treat of the course the nations run, and in Book Five, where we shall treat of the recourse of human institutions."

L2 Course and recourse, as in the flow and ebb of the tides, may mean traversing the same stages in opposite directions; or recourse may mean simple recurrence, a coming back or around of some particular event or state of affairs; but the strongest and most literal meaning is a retraversing of the same stages in the same order [41]. This is the meaning of the term in the title of Book Five and in the titles of its first two chapters.

L3 But the term "recourse" has a further meaning. A *ricorso* does not, like the recurrence of a cosmic cycle, merely repeat the *corso*. It is a historical, not a purely natural, process, and it has the legal sense of a retrial or appeal. Since the historical *corso* has not received justice, it must, as it were, appeal to a higher court for a rehearing of its case. The highest court of justice, however, is providential history as a whole; and it requires an age of disintegration and oversophistication, of "the barbarism of reflection" [1106], in order to return to the creative barbarism of sense—*la barbarie ricorsa*, the recourse of barbarism [67, 571, 574]—and thus begin anew. As in the famous verse which Hegel later adapted from Schiller's poem *Resignation*, "the history of the world is the Last Judgment"—"*die Weltgeschichte ist das Weltgericht.*"

INSTITUTION

M1 We conclude our introduction with some remarks concerning a term which occurs in the title of Book Five as here translated, "The Recourse of Human Institutions Which the Nations Take When They Rise Again," and which occurs with considerable frequency throughout our translation, but which, in this sense, does not occur at all in Vico's Italian. Vico uses the Italian word *istituzione* only once, and then in the technical legal sense (derived from the Latin *institutio haeredis* for the appointment of the heir in a will), in the phrase *istituzione de' postumi*, institution of posthumous children as heirs [993].

M2 In Latin and in the Romance languages, the verb "to institute," its past participle used as a noun for what has been instituted, and the noun "institution" itself, all imply deliberate contrivance, artifice, choice, will, intent. One of their chief senses is formal education—planned systematic instruction—as distinguished from uncontrolled learning.

M3 But in Italian this group of cognate words was little used in Vico's time. In place of *istituire*, the verb, the Italians used *ordinare*; in place of *istituto*, the participial noun, they used *ordinamento*; in place of *istituzione*, the noun, they used *ordine*. Vico uses all three: *ordinare*, *ordinamento*, *ordine*. We often translate "institute" for the verb and "institution" for the participle and noun; but sometimes "ordain," "ordinance," and "order," respectively [965f].

M4 Vico's usual word for institution, however, is the common word for thing, *cosa*. In this he is following a rare Latin usage in which *res* was used in the sense of institution, as in the title of Varro's work *Antiquitates rerum humanarum et divinarum*, "Antiquities of Human and Divine Institutions" [6, 52, 284, 364, 990]. For Varro's *res humanae*, Vico uses *cose* *umane;* for his *res divinae, cose divine.* Vico's usage differs from Varro's, however, in that by *cose divine* he often means the institutions of the age of the gods, and by *cose umane* the institutions of the ages of heroes and of men, or even exclusively of the latter.

M5 Among the other terms which we have occasionally rendered "institution" are *ragione,* reason; *diritto,* law; *pianta,* plant or plan, basis, "basic institution" [618ff].

M6 Why did Vico avoid the term "institution" (and its cognate verb and participle), and why did he prefer for the most part the term *cosa?* Because the term "institution" was theoretically loaded; loaded, moreover, with the very theory he was most concerned to discredit; and because the term *cosa* was theoretically neutral, or innocent. Why have we, nevertheless, rendered his *cosa* "institution"? Because in the course of the later eighteenth and the nineteenth century, and in part as a consequence of Vico's own work, the term "institution" was gradually unloaded; because it no longer carries, built in as it were, the rationalistic theory of the origin and nature of institutions, which in Vico's day was still the accepted theory.

M7 The rationalistic theory assumed that the institutions of society were made by "men," in the sense of human beings who were already fully human, in whom the humanity of Vico's "age of men" was already fully developed. What Vico wanted to assert was that the first steps in the building of "the world of nations" were taken by creatures who were still (or who had degenerated into) beasts, and that humanity itself was created by the very same processes by which the institutions were created. Humanity is not a presupposition, but a consequence, an effect, a product of institution building [C6, J2]. Vico indeed carries this so far as to assert that it was not only in respect of mind or spirit, but in respect of body, or "corporature," also, that these creatures-not-yet-human made themselves human [520, 692].

M8 The kind of making involved in the making of the world of nations by men was therefore not that of deliberate contrivance, but that conveyed by the term "poet," which in Greek means maker; conveyed at least when once with Vico we have abandoned the rationalistic theory of poetry itself and adopted a theory according to which the essence of poetry is imagination, passion, sense, rather than intellect [K4].

M9 It is not human but divine providence that uses the passions as means to bring about an end, that of preserving the human race upon the earth [E7, F5–6, 344, 1108]. The rational intelligence that employs means toward ends is therefore involved in the making of the world of nations, but its seat is not in the minds of the men who made it, but in divine providence. Men have themselves made this world of nations, but it was not only without drafting, it was even without seeing the plan that they did just what the plan called for. They builded better than they knew. Yet it was, after all, by a kind of wisdom that men made the world of nations: poetic or creative, common or vulgar wisdom, wisdom common to whole peoples. And it is possible now for philosophic or recondite wisdom to discern how, by that poetic wisdom, they did it.

M10 Since now, by benefit of Vico's work, we can use the familiar term "institution" without violence to his intent, we have freely used it in revising our translation.

M. H. F.

PRINCIPLES

OF

NEW SCIENCE

OF

GIAMBATTISTA VICO

CONCERNING

THE COMMON NATURE

OF THE NATIONS

IDEA OF
THE WORK

Dom. Ant. Vaccaro I.   Sesone Sculp.

EXPLANATION OF THE PICTURE

PLACED AS FRONTISPIECE

TO SERVE AS INTRODUCTION TO THE WORK

1   As Cebes the Theban made a table of moral institutions, we offer here one of civil institutions. We hope it may serve to give the reader some conception of this work before he reads it, and, with such aid as imagination may afford, to call it back to mind after he has read it.

2   The lady with the winged temples who surmounts the celestial globe or world of nature is metaphysic, for the name means as much. The luminous triangle with the seeing eye is God with the aspect of His providence. Through this aspect metaphysic in the attitude of ecstasy contemplates Him above the order of natural institutions through which hitherto the philosophers have contemplated Him. For in the present work, ascending higher, she contemplates in God the world of human minds, which is the metaphysical world, in order to show His providence in the world of human spirits, which is the civil world or world of nations. The latter has as the elements of which it is formed all the institutions represented by the hieroglyphs displayed in the lower half of the picture. The globe, or the physical, natural world, is supported by the altar in one part only, for, until now, the philosophers, contemplating divine providence only through the natural order, have shown only a part of it. Accordingly men offer worship, sacrifices and other divine honors to God as to the Mind which is the free and absolute sovereign of nature, because by His eternal counsel He has given us existence through nature, and through nature preserves it to us. But the philosophers have not yet contemplated His providence in respect of that part of it which is most proper to men, whose nature has this principal property: that of being social. In providing for this property God has so ordained and disposed human institutions that men, having fallen from complete justice by original sin, and while intend-

ing almost always to do something quite different and often quite the contrary—so that for private utility they would live alone like wild beasts—have been led by this same utility and along the aforesaid different and contrary paths to live like men in justice and to keep themselves in society and thus to observe their social nature. It will be shown in the present work that this is the true civil nature of man, and thus that law exists in nature. The conduct of divine providence in this matter is one of the things whose rationale is a chief business of our Science, which becomes in this aspect a rational civil theology of divine providence [342].

3   In the belt of the zodiac which girds the celestial globe the two signs of Leo and Virgo, more than the others, appear in majesty, or, as is said, in perspective. The former signifies that our Science in its beginnings contemplates first the Hercules that every ancient gentile nation boasts as its founder, and that it contemplates him in his greatest labor. This was the slaying of the lion which, vomiting flame, set fire to the Nemean forest, and adorned with whose skin Hercules was raised to the stars. The lion is here found to have been the great ancient forest of the earth, burned down and brought under cultivation by Hercules, whom we find to have been the type of the political heroes who had to precede the military heroes. This sign also represents the beginning of time[-reckoning]s, which among the Greeks (to whom we owe all our knowledge of gentile antiquity) began with the Olympiads, based on the games of which we are told that Hercules was the founder. They must have begun with the Nemean games to celebrate his victory over the lion he slew. Thus the time[-reckoning]s of the Greeks began when cultivation of the fields began among them.

The second sign, that of the Virgin, whom the astronomers found described by the poets as crowned with ears of grain, signifies that Greek history began with the golden age. The poets expressly relate that this was the first age of their world, when through the long course of centuries the years were counted by the grain harvests, which we find to have been the first gold of the world. This golden age of the Greeks has its Latin counterpart in the age of Saturn, who gets his name from *sati*, sown [fields]. In this age of gold, the poets assure us faithfully, the gods consorted on earth with the heroes. For we shall show later that the first men among the gentiles, simple and crude, and under the powerful spell of most vigorous imaginations encumbered with frightful superstitions, actually believed that they saw the gods on earth [713]. We shall see further that by uniformity of ideas the orientals, Egyptians, Greeks and Latins, each in ignorance of the others, afterwards raised the gods to the planets and the heroes to the fixed stars [727ff]. Thus from Saturn (whose Greek name

Chronos means time) new principles are derived for chronology or the theory of times.

4 You must not think it improper that the altar is under and supports the globe. For it will be found that the world's first altars were raised by the gentiles in the first heaven of the poets, who in their fables faithfully passed on to us the story that Heaven had reigned on earth over men and had left great blessings to mankind. These first men, children as it were of the growing human race, believed that the sky was no higher than the summits of the mountains, as even now children believe it to be little higher than the roofs of their houses. Then as the Greek intelligence developed heaven was raised to the summits of the highest mountains, such as Olympus, where Homer relates that the gods of his day had their dwelling. Finally it was raised above the spheres, as we are now taught by astronomy, and Olympus was raised above the heaven of the fixed stars. Thither likewise was transported the altar, which is now a celestial sign, and the fire upon it passed into the neighboring house (as you see here) of the Lion. (This was the Nemean forest [3], to which Hercules set fire to bring it under cultivation.) For the lion's skin was raised to the stars in token of the triumph of Hercules.

5 The ray of the divine providence illuminating a convex jewel which adorns the breast of metaphysic denotes the clean and pure heart which metaphysic must have, not dirty or befouled with pride of spirit or vileness of bodily pleasures, by the first of which Zeno was led to put fate, and by the second Epicurus to put chance, in the place of divine providence. Furthermore it indicates that the knowledge of God does not have its end in metaphysic taking private illumination from intellectual institutions and thence regulating merely her own moral institutions, as hitherto the philosophers have done. For this would have been signified by a flat jewel, whereas the jewel is convex, thus reflecting and scattering the ray abroad, to show that metaphysic should know God's providence in public moral institutions or civil customs, by which the nations have come into being and maintain themselves in the world.

6 The same ray is reflected from the breast of metaphysic onto the statue of Homer, the first gentile author who has come down to us. For metaphysic, which has been formed from the beginning according to a history of human ideas from the commencing of truly human thinking among the gentiles, has enabled us finally to descend into the crude minds of the first founders of the gentile nations, all robust sense and vast imagination. They had only the bare potentiality, and that torpid and stupid, of using the human mind and reason. From that very cause the

beginnings of poetry, not only different from but contrary to those which have been hitherto imagined, are found to lie in the beginnings of poetic wisdom, which have from that same cause been hitherto hidden from us. This poetic wisdom, the knowledge of the theological poets, was unquestionably the first wisdom of the world for the gentiles. The statue of Homer on a cracked base signifies the discovery of the true Homer. (In the first edition of the *New Science* [Op. 3.295ff] we sensed it but did not understand it. In the present edition it is fully set forth after due consideration [780–914].) Unknown until now, he has held hidden from us the true institutions of the fabulous time among the nations, and much more so those of the dark time which all had despaired of knowing, and consequently the first true origins of the institutions of the historic time. These are the three times of the world which Marcus Terentius Varro, the most learned writer on Roman antiquities, recorded for us in his great work entitled [*The Antiquities*] *of Divine and Human Institutions* [M4], which has been lost [40, 52].

7   Moreover, it may here be pointed out that in the present work, with a new critical art that has hitherto been lacking [348], entering on the research of the truth concerning the authors of these same [gentile] nations (among which more than a thousand years had to pass in order to bring forth the writers with whom criticism has hitherto been concerned), philosophy undertakes to examine philology (that is, the doctrine of all the institutions that depend on human choice; for example, all histories of the languages, customs, and deeds of peoples in war and peace), of which, because of the deplorable obscurity of causes and almost infinite variety of effects, philosophy has had almost a horror of treating; and reduces it to the form of a science by discovering in it the design of an ideal eternal history traversed in time by the histories of all nations [349]; so that, on account of this its second principal aspect, our Science may be considered a philosophy of authority [350]. For by virtue of new principles of mythology herein disclosed as consequences of the new principles of poetry found herein, it is shown that the fables were true and trustworthy histories of the customs of the most ancient peoples of Greece. In the first place, the fables of the gods were stories of the times in which men of the crudest gentile humanity thought that all institutions necessary or useful to the human race were deities. The authors of this poetry were the first peoples, whom we find to have been all theological poets, who without doubt, as we are told, founded the gentile nations with fables of the gods. And here, by the principles of this new critical art, we consider at what determinate times and on what particular occasions of human necessity or utility felt by the

first men of the gentile world, they, with frightful religions which they themselves feigned and believed in, imagined first such and such gods and then such and such others. The natural theogony or generation of the gods, formed naturally in the minds of these first men, may give us a rational chronology of the poetic history of the gods. [In the second place,] the heroic fables were true stories of the heroes and their heroic customs, which are found to have flourished in the barbarous period of all nations; so that the two poems of Homer are found to be two great treasure houses of discoveries of the natural law of the gentes among the still barbarous Greeks. In the present work this period of barbarism is determined to have lasted among the Greeks until the time of Herodotus, called the father of Greek history, whose books are for the most part full of fables and whose style retains very much of the Homeric. This is a characteristic retained by all the historians who came after him, as they used a phraseology half way between the poetic and the vulgar. But Thucydides, the first scrupulous and serious historian of Greece, at the beginning of his account, declares that down to his father's time (and thus to that of Herodotus, who was an old man when Thucydides was a child) the Greeks were quite ignorant of their own antiquities, to say nothing of those of other peoples (which, apart from the Roman, have all come down to us through the Greeks) [101]. These antiquities are the deep shadows which the picture shows in the background, against which there stand forth, in the light of the ray of divine providence reflected by metaphysic upon Homer, all the hieroglyphs which represent the principles, known until now only by the effects, of this world of nations.

8 Among these [hieroglyphs] the most prominent is an altar, because among all peoples the civil world began with religion, as we have briefly noted a while back [2] and as we shall shortly observe more fully [9].

9 Upon the altar, at the left, the first object we see is a lituus, the staff with which the augurs took auguries and observed the auspices. This signifies divination, from which, among the gentiles, the first divine institutions took their origin. The Hebrews thought God to be an infinite Mind beholding all times in one point of eternity, whence God, either Himself or through the angels that are minds or through the prophets to whose minds God spoke, gave notice of what was in store for His people. The gentiles fancied bodies to be gods, that by sensible signs they might give notice of what was in store for the peoples. On account of the attribute of His providence, as true among the Hebrews as it was imagined among the gentiles, all humankind gave to the nature of God the name divinity by one common idea, which the Latins expressed in *divinari*, to foretell the

future [342]; but with the aforesaid fundamental difference from which derive all the other essential differences shown by our Science between the natural law of the Hebrews and the natural law of the gentes. The Roman jurisconsults defined the latter as having been ordained by divine providence along with human customs themselves. Thus the aforesaid lituus represents also the beginning of gentile universal history, which is shown by physical and philological evidence to have begun with the universal flood [369]. After an interval of two centuries (as fabulous history relates), Heaven reigned on earth and bestowed many and great blessings on mankind, and, by uniformity of ideas among orientals, Egyptians, Greeks, Latins and other gentile nations, there arose equally the religions of as many Joves. For at the end of this period of time after the flood, heaven must have thundered and lightened, and from the thunder and lightning of its Jove each nation began to take auspices. This multiplicity of Joves, which led the Egyptians to call their Jove Ammon the oldest of them all, has hitherto been a marvel to the philologians [47]. The same twofold evidence proves the religion of the Hebrews more ancient than those by which the gentes were founded, and hence the truth of the Christian religion.

10   On the altar near the lituus may be seen the water and fire, the former contained in a jar. For with a view to divination sacrifices arose among the gentiles from that common custom of theirs which the Latins called *procurare auspicia*, i.e., to sacrifice in order to understand the auguries well so that the divine warnings or commands of Jove might be duly obeyed. These are the divine institutions among the gentiles, from which came later all their human institutions [332ff].

11   The first of these [human institutions] was marriage, symbolized by the torch lit from the fire on the altar and leaning against the jar. For marriage, as all statesmen agree, is the seed-plot of the family, as the family is the seed-plot of the commonwealth. To denote this, the torch, although it is the hieroglyph of a human institution, is placed on the altar along with the water and the fire, which are hieroglyphs of divine ceremonies; just as the ancient Romans celebrated nuptials *aqua et igni*, because it was understood that by divine counsel these two common things (and, before fire even, perennial water as a thing more necessary to life) had led men to live in society.

12   The second human institution is burial. (Indeed *humanitas* in Latin comes first and properly from *humando*, burying.) This institution is symbolized by a cinerary urn, placed to one side within the forest, indicating that burial goes back to a time when men ate fruit in summer and

acorns in winter. The urn is inscribed *D. M.*, which means "to the good souls of the dead." This motto represents the common consent of all mankind in the opinion later proved true by Plato, that human souls do not die with their bodies but are immortal.

13 The urn indicates also the origin among the gentiles of the division of the fields, to which is to be traced the distinction of cities and peoples and finally of nations. For it will be found that the races, first of Ham, then of Japheth, and finally of Shem, without the religion of their father Noah, which they had repudiated (and which alone, in what was then the state of nature, could have held them by marriages in a society of families), were lost from one another by roving wild in the great forest of the earth, pursuing shy and indocile women, and fleeing from the wild animals with which the great ancient forest must have abounded. They were scattered further in search of pasture and water, and as the result of it all were reduced, at the end of a long period, to the condition of beasts. Then, on certain occasions ordained by divine providence (occasions which our Science studies and discovers), shaken and aroused by a terrible fear, each of the particular Uranus and Jove he had feigned and believed in, some of them finally left off wandering and went into hiding in certain places. There, settled with certain women, through fear of the apprehended divinity, in religious and chaste carnal unions they solemnized marriages under cover and begat certain children and so founded families. By long residence and burial of their dead they came to found and divide the first dominions of the earth, whose lords were called giants, a Greek word meaning "sons of earth," i.e., descendants of those who have been buried. Hence they considered themselves noble, justly ascribing their nobility in that first state of human institutions to their having been humanly engendered in the fear of the divinity. From this manner of human engendering and not from anything else, what is called human generation took its name. The houses which had branched out into several families thus formed were called the first gentes because of such generation. As the subject matter of the natural law of the gentes begins at so early a time, so in this work the doctrine begins there too [314ff]. This is a third principal aspect under which our Science should be viewed. Now there are both physical and moral reasons, apart from the authority of history, to show that the giants must have been of disproportionate strength and stature. Since these reasons did not obtain in the case of believers in the true God, creator of the world and of Adam the prince of all humankind, the Hebrews from the very beginning of the world were of proper stature. So, after the first principle of divine providence and the second of solemn

matrimony, the universal belief in the immortality of the soul, which had its beginnings in the institution of burial, is the third of the three principles on which this Science bases its discussions of the origins of all the innumerable various and diverse institutions of which it treats [332ff].

14 From the forests where the urn is placed a plough stands forth, signifying that the fathers of the first gentes were the first strong men of history. Hence the founders of the first gentile nations above mentioned were the Herculeses (of whom [according to Servius's note on Vergil A. 8.564] Varro counted a good forty and the Egyptians claimed theirs to be the most ancient), for these Herculeses subdued the first lands of the world and brought them under cultivation. Thus the first fathers of the gentile nations—who were (1) just in virtue of the supposed piety of observing the auspices which they believed divine commands of Jove (from whose Latin name *Ious* came the old word *ious* for law, later contracted to *ius*; so that justice among all peoples is naturally taught along with piety); (2) prudent in sacrificing to obtain or clearly to understand the auspices, and thus to take good counsel of what, by the commands of Jove, they should undertake in life; and (3) temperate in the institution of matrimony—were also, as is here indicated, (4) strong men [516]. Hence new principles are given to moral philosophy, in order that the esoteric wisdom of the philosophers may conspire with the vulgar wisdom of lawmakers. By these principles all the virtues have their roots in piety and religion, by which alone the virtues are made effective in action, and by reason of which men propose to themselves as good whatever God wills [502ff]. New principles are given also to economic doctrine, by which sons, so long as they are in the power of their fathers, must be considered to be in the family state, and consequently are in no other way to be formed and confirmed in all their studies than in piety and religion [520ff]. Since they are not yet capable of understanding commonwealth and laws, they are to reverence and fear their fathers as living images of God, so as to be naturally disposed to follow the religion of their fathers and to defend their fatherland, which preserves their families for them, and so to obey the laws ordained for the preservation of their religion and fatherland. (For divine providence ordered human institutions with this eternal counsel: that families should first be founded by means of religions, and that upon the families commonwealths should then arise by means of laws [25].)

15 The plough rests its handle against the altar with a certain majesty, to give us to understand that ploughed lands were the first altars of the gentiles, and to denote also the natural superiority which the heroes believed they had over their *socii*. (The latter, as we shall see shortly, are

symbolized by the rudder which is seen bowing near the base of the altar.) On this superiority of nature, it will be shown, the heroes grounded the law, the science, and hence the administration of divine institutions (i.e., the auspices), which were in their keeping.

16 The plough shows only the point of the share and hides the moldboard. Before the use of iron was known, the share had to be made of a curved piece of very hard wood, capable of breaking and turning the earth. The Latins called the moldboard *urbs*, whence the ancient *urbum*, curved. The moldboard is hidden to signify that the first cities, which were all founded on cultivated fields, arose as a result of families being for a long time quite withdrawn and hidden among the sacred terrors of the religious forests. These [cultivated fields] are found among all the ancient gentile nations and, by an idea common to all, were called by the Latin peoples *luci*, meaning burnt lands within the enclosure of the woods [564]. (The woods themselves were condemned by Moses to be burned wherever the people of God extended their conquests [481].) This was by counsel of divine providence to the end that those who had already arrived at humanity should not again become confounded with the wanderers who still remained in the nefarious promiscuity of things and women [D1–2].

17 There may be seen at the left side of the altar a rudder, symbolizing the origin of the migration of peoples by means of navigation. And by its seeming to bow at the foot of the altar, it symbolizes the ancestors of those who later were the authors of these migrations. These [ancestors] were at first impious men, who recognized no divinity; they were nefarious, since relations among them were not distinguished by marriages, and sons often lay with mothers and fathers with daughters; and finally because, not understanding society in the midst of this infamous promiscuity of things, they were all alone like wild beasts, and hence weak and lastly miserable and unhappy because they were in want of all the goods that are needed to keep life safe. Fleeing the several ills they suffered in the dissensions which this wild promiscuity produced, and seeking escape and safety, they betook themselves to the cultivated lands of the pious, chaste, strong, and even powerful, that is, of those who were already united in family society. From these lands, it will be found, cities were called *arae*, altars, throughout the ancient world of the gentiles [775]. For they must have been the first altars of the gentile nations, and the first fire lighted on them was that which served to clear the forests of trees and bring them under cultivation, and the first water was that of the perennial springs, which were necessary in order that those destined to found humanity should no longer wander in bestial vagrancy in search of water, but settle for a long time in one place

and give up vagabondage. And since these altars were evidently the first asylums of the world (which Livy [1.8.5] defines generally as *vetus urbes condentium consilium,* an old counsel of founders of cities, as we are told that within the asylum opened in the Lucus [or clearing, 16] Romulus founded Rome), hence the first cities were almost all called altars. To this minor discovery let us add a major one: that among the Greeks (from whom we have learned all that we know of gentile antiquity [3]) the first Thrace or Scythia (i.e., the first North), the first Asia and the first India (i.e., the first East), the first Mauretania or Libya (i.e., the first South), and the first Europe or first Hesperia (i.e., the first West), and along with all these the first Ocean, were born within Greece itself; and then the Greeks, going abroad in the world, extended these names by analogy to its four parts and to the ocean that surrounds it. These discoveries, we assert, give new principles to geography, which, like the new principles already promised for chronology [3], are necessary if we are to read the ideal eternal history [7]. For chronology and geography are the two eyes of history [732–769].

18   To these altars then, the impious-nomadic-weak, fleeing for their lives from the stronger, came seeking refuge, and the pious-strong killed the violent among them and took the weak under their protection. Since the latter brought with them nothing but their lives, they were accepted as *famuli* and given the means of sustaining life. The family took its name principally from these *famuli,* whose status roughly approximated that of the slaves who came later with the taking of prisoners in war. Hence like several branches from one trunk spring the origins (1) of the asylums [17]; (2) of families, from which cities later arose [25]; (3) of the founding of cities, that men might live secure from the unjust and the violent; (4) of jurisdictions to be exercised within prescribed territories; (5) of the extension of empires, which comes by the practice of justice, strength and magnanimity, which are the most luminous virtues of princes and states; (6) of family coats-of-arms, whose first fields-of-arms are found to have stood for the first seed-fields [484ff]; (7) of fame, from which the *famuli* derived their name, and of glory, which is eternally inherent in serving the human race; (8) of true nobility, which arises naturally from the practice of the moral virtues; (9) of true heroism, which is to put down the proud and give aid to those in danger (in which heroism the Roman people surpassed all other peoples of the earth and so became master of the world) [553]; and lastly, (10) of war and peace, the former taking its start in the world from self-defense, in which the true virtue of strength consists. In all these origins one can trace the eternal plan of commonwealths, on

which states, though acquired by violence and fraud, must take their stand in order to survive, as on the other hand those acquired by way of these virtuous origins afterwards fall to ruin through fraud and violence. This plan of commonwealths is founded on the two eternal principles of this world of nations, namely the mind and the body of the men who compose it. For men consist of these two parts, one of which is noble and should therefore command, and the other of which is base and should serve. But because of the corruption of human nature, the generic character of men cannot without the help of philosophy (which can aid but few) bring it about that every individual's mind should command and not serve his body. Therefore divine providence ordered human institutions with this eternal order: that, in commonwealths, those who use their minds should command and those who use their bodies should obey [630].

19   The rudder bows at the foot of the altar because these *famuli*, as men without gods, had no share in divine institutions and consequently no community even of human institutions with the nobles. Above all, they lacked the right to celebrate solemn nuptials, which the Latins called *connubium*. The most solemn part of the ceremony was the taking of the auspices, by reason of which the nobles thought themselves to be of divine origin and held the *famuli* to be of bestial origin, as generated by nefarious couplings. Bound up with this distinction of a nobler nature we find, equally among the Egyptians, Greeks and Latins, a presumed natural heroism, as is more than sufficiently made plain to us in ancient Roman history [917].

20   Finally the rudder is at some distance from the plough, which is in front of the altar and displays to the rudder a hostile aspect, menacing it with its point. For the *famuli*, having no share, as we have seen, in the ownership of lands, which were all in the hands of the nobles, grew weary of being obliged always to serve their lords. At last, after a long period, they laid claim to the lands and rose in mutiny to enforce the claim, and revolted against the heroes in agrarian contests which, we shall learn, were much more ancient than and very different from those that we read of in later Roman history [583]. Many leaders of bands of *famuli* which had rebelled and been conquered by the heroes (as the serfs of Egypt often were by their priests, according to the observation of Peter van der Kuhn, *De republica hebraeorum*), in order to avoid oppression and to find escape and safety along with the members of their factions, committed themselves to the hazards of the sea and went in search of unoccupied lands along the shores of the Mediterranean, toward the West where the coasts were not then inhabited. This is the origin of the migration of peoples already

humanized by religion, starting from the East (Phoenicia above all) and from Egypt, as happened later, for the same reasons, in the case of the Greeks. In such wise not inundations of peoples, which cannot take place by sea; nor the jealous desire of keeping remote acquisitions by means of recognized colonies, since we do not read of any empire of the East or of Egypt or Greece being extended into the West; nor reasons of trade, for the western coasts were not yet inhabited; but rather heroic law made it necessary for such bands of men in these nations to abandon their own lands, a thing which naturally happens only under some extreme necessity. By means of such colonies, which will accordingly be called "heroic overseas colonies," the human race was spread abroad in the rest of our world by sea, just as by means of the savage wanderings a long time before it had been spread abroad by land [299f, 560, 736].

21   Standing a little further out, in front of the plough, there is a tablet inscribed with an ancient Latin alphabet (which, as Tacitus [A. 11.14] relates, was similar to the ancient Greek) and, underneath, the latest alphabet that has come down to us. This tablet symbolizes the origin of the languages and letters that are called vulgar. These are found to have come into being a long time after the founding of the nations, and letters much later than languages [428ff, 928–36]. To signify this, the tablet rests on a fragment of a column of the Corinthian order, which came quite late among the architectural orders.

22   The tablet lies near the plough and far from the rudder, to signify the origin of native languages, which were first formed each in its own land, where the founders of the nations, scattered and dispersed through the great forest of the earth [13], finally came together by chance and ceased their bestial wandering. With these native languages the Eastern or Egyptian or Greek tongues long afterwards mingled, on the occasion of the above-mentioned migration of peoples to the shores of the Mediterranean and the Ocean [20]. Here we get new principles of etymology, abundantly illustrated throughout this work, by which the origins of native words may be distinguished from those that are unquestionably of foreign origin. The important difference is that native etymologies are histories of institutions signified by the words in the natural order of ideas. First the woods, then cultivated fields and huts, next little houses and villages, thence cities, finally academies and philosophers: this is the order of all progress from the first origins. Foreign etymologies, on the other hand, are mere stories of words taken by one language from another [239f, 304].

23   The tablet shows only the first letters of the alphabets and lies facing the statue of Homer. For the letters, as Greek tradition tells us of

Greek letters, were not all invented at one time; at least they cannot all have been invented by Homer's time, for we know that he left none of his poems in writing [66]. But of the origin of native languages more particular information will be given further on [428ff].

24 Lastly, in the plane most illuminated of all, because the hieroglyphs there displayed represent the most familiar human institutions, the ingenious artist exhibits in capricious arrangement the Roman fasces, a sword and a purse leaning against the fasces, a balance and the caduceus of Mercury [435ff].

25 The first of these symbols is the fasces because the first civil empires arose on the union of the paternal powers of the fathers. Among the gentiles these fathers were sages in auspicial divinity, priests who sacrificed to take the auspices or make sure of their meaning, and certainly monarchs who commanded what they believed to be the will of the gods as shown in the auspices, and consequently were subject to no one but God. So the fasces are a bundle of *litui* or rods of divination, which we find to be the first scepters of the world [617]. These fathers, in the agrarian disturbances we have mentioned above [20], in order to resist the bands of *famuli* aroused against them, were naturally led to unite and enclose themselves in the first orders of reigning senates (or senates made up of so many kings of families) under certain heads-of-orders [584]. These are found to have been the first kings of the heroic cities. Ancient history tells us, though too obscurely, that in the first world of the peoples kings were created by nature; our studies discover the manner. Now these reigning senates, to content the revolting bands of *famuli* and reduce them to obedience, granted them an agrarian law, which is found to have been the first civil law born in the world; and naturally the first plebs of the cities were composed of these *famuli*, subdued by this law. What the nobles granted the plebeians was natural ownership of the fields, civil ownership remaining with the nobles, who were the only citizens of the heroic cities. Thence arose the eminent ownership [or domain] of the orders which were the first civil or sovereign powers of the peoples [viii, 266]. All three kinds of ownership were formed and distinguished one from another at the birth of the commonwealths, which among all the nations, by one idea variously expressed, are found to have been called Herculean commonwealths or commonwealths of Curetes, armed men in public assembly [592f]. This clears up the origins of the famous *ius Quiritium*, which the interpreters of Roman law have thought to be peculiar to the citizens of Rome, as in later times it was; but in the ancient Roman times it was evidently a natural law of all the heroic gentes [595]. And thence, as various streams from a

common source, numerous origins spring forth. (1) The origin of cities, which arose from the families not of sons only but of *famuli* also. Thus they will be seen to be founded by nature on two communities, one of the nobles, to command, the other of the plebs, to obey. Of these two parts is composed the entire polity or law of civil governments. For it is shown that the first cities, of this or indeed any other kind, could not arise from families of sons only [553ff]. (2) The origins of public empires, which were born from the union of private father-sovereign empires in the family state [585]. (3) The origins of war and peace, whereby all commonwealths were brought into being by force of arms and then composed by laws. From the nature of these [two] human institutions derives their eternal property: that wars are waged so that peoples may live secure in peace. (4) The origin of fiefs, for by one sort of rustic fiefs the plebeians became subject to the nobles, and by another sort of noble or military fiefs the nobles, who were sovereign in their own families, became subject to the greater sovereignty of their heroic orders [599ff]. We find that the kingdoms of barbarian times have always had a feudal basis. This sheds light on the history of the modern kingdoms of Europe [1057ff], which arose in those latest barbarian times that are more obscure to us than the first barbarian times of which Varro wrote [6]. For these first fields were given by the nobles to the plebs under burden of a payment [variously] called tithe of Hercules (among the Greeks) [541] or census (which we find to be what Servius Tullius instituted for the Romans) or tribute. The plebs were further obliged to serve the nobles in war at their own expense, as is plain to be seen in ancient Roman history. Here appears (5) the origin of the census which remained the basic institution of the popular commonwealths. Of all our researches into Roman institutions, the most difficult has been that of tracing the process by which this [popular census] developed from that of Servius Tullius, which will be found to have been the basic institution of the ancient aristocratic commonwealths. The relation between the two has made everyone fall into the error of assuming that Servius Tullius ordained the census [as the basic institution] of popular liberty [107, 111, 619ff].

26   From the same beginning come also: (6) The origin of commerce, which, in the form we have indicated, began in real estate with the beginnings of the cities themselves [606]. The term "commerce" is derived from that first *merces* or payment in the world, the fields which the heroes gave the *famuli* under the aforesaid law obliging the latter to serve them. (7) The origin of public treasuries [603], the rudiments of which were there from the birth of the commonwealths but which assumed the recognizable form properly called *aeraria* (from *aes aeris* in the sense of "money")

when the public had to supply money to the plebs in war time. (8) The origin of colonies, which are found to have been bands first of peasants who served the heroes for the sustenance of their lives, then of vassals who cultivated the fields for themselves under the aforesaid real and personal obligations. These we shall call heroic inland colonies to differentiate them from the overseas colonies mentioned above [20]. And finally (9) the origins of the commonwealths, which had at their birth a most severe aristocratic form, in which the plebeians had no share in the civil law. In this connection the Roman commonwealth is found to have been an aristocratic kingdom which fell under the tyranny of Tarquinius Superbus, who sadly misgoverned the nobles and almost destroyed the senate. When Lucretia stabbed herself, Junius Brutus seized the occasion to arouse the plebs against the Tarquins, and, having freed Rome from their tyranny, reëstablished the senate and reorganized the commonwealth on its first principles. For by substituting two annual consuls for one king for life, he did not introduce popular liberty but rather reaffirmed the liberty of the nobles [664]. This is found to have lasted till the Publilian Law, which won for the dictator Publilius Philo the epithet "popular" by declaring that the Roman commonwealth had become popular in constitution. Indeed it expired only with the Petelian Law, which completely freed the plebs from the feudal rustic right of private imprisonment which the nobles had over their plebeian debtors. These two laws, which contain the two major points in Roman history, have been pondered neither by statesmen nor by jurists nor by the learned interpreters of Roman law [104–15]. For they have been misled by the fable that the Law of the Twelve Tables came from free Athens to set up popular liberty in Rome, whereas these two laws declare it to have been set up at home by the natural customs of the Romans themselves. (This fable was exposed in the *Principles of Universal Law,* printed many years ago [Op. 2.564–80].) Therefore, since the laws of a commonwealth must be interpreted according to its constitution, these principles of Roman government involve new principles for Roman jurisprudence.

27 The sword leaning on the fasces indicates that heroic law was a law of force but subject to religion, which alone can keep force and arms in their place where judiciary laws do not yet exist or are no longer recognized. This law is precisely that of Achilles, the hero sung by Homer to the Greeks as an example of heroic virtue, who made arms the arbiter of right [923]. Here is revealed the origin of duels [959ff]; which, as they were certainly celebrated in the last barbarian times, so they are found to have been practiced in the first barbarian times when the mighty were not yet so

tamed as to avenge offenses and injuries by appeal to judiciary laws. The duels they practiced were appeals to certain divine judgments [955ff]. They called on God as witness and made God judge of the offense, and accepted with such reverence the decision that was given by the fortune of the combat that even if the outraged party fell vanquished he was considered guilty. This was a lofty counsel of divine providence, to the end that, in fierce and barbarous times in which law was not understood, it might be measured by God's favor or disfavor, so that such private wars might not sow the seeds of [greater] wars which would have ended in the extinction of the human race. This natural barbarian sense can only be grounded in the innate concept which men have of that divine providence in which they must acquiesce when they see the good oppressed and the wicked prospering. For all these reasons the duel was thought to be a kind of divine purgation, and in barbarian times the belief in its necessity was quite as firm as the prohibition of it in the humanity of our day with its civil and criminal courts instituted by law. In such duels or private wars is found the origin of public wars which are waged by civil powers subject to no one but God, in order that God may settle them by the fortune of victory; so that the human race may rest on the certainty of civil states. This is the principle of the external justice, as it is called, of wars [350, 964].

28   The purse resting against the fasces shows that commerce carried on by means of money began late, after the civil empires were founded, so that we read of no coined money in either of the two poems of Homer. This same hieroglyph indicates the origin of such coined money, which is found to have been the same as that of family coats-of-arms. The latter (as we have intimated above [18] in connection with the first fields-of-arms) are discovered to have signified rights and titles of nobility belonging to one family rather than to another. Thence came the origin of public emblems, or ensigns of the people, which were then raised as military ensigns used as a mute language by military discipline; and finally among all peoples they gave their imprint to coins [487]. Here are given new principles to numismatics, and thereby also to the science of blazonry as it is called; which is one of the three topics on which we find ourselves satisfied with the first edition of the New Science [Op. 3.329; 33, 35].

29   The balance next to the purse is meant to indicate that, after the aristocratic governments, which were heroic governments, there came human governments, at first popular in character. The people had finally come to understand that the rational nature (which is the true human nature) is equal in all men. From this natural equality (by occasions

conceived in the ideal eternal history and encountered exactly in Roman history) they gradually brought the heroes to civil equality in popular commonwealths. This civil equality is symbolized by the balance, because, as the Greeks said, in the popular commonwealths everything goes by lot or by balance. But finally, as the free peoples could not by means of laws maintain themselves in civil equality because of the factions of the powerful, but were being driven to ruin by civil wars, it came about naturally that, obeying a natural royal law or rather natural custom of human peoples, they sought protection under monarchies, which constitute the other type of human government [927, 994ff, 1007f]. (This natural royal law is common to all peoples in all times in popular states which have grown corrupt, but the civil royal law, which is said to have been commanded by the Roman people to legitimize the Roman monarchy in the person of Augustus, is shown in our *Principles of Universal Law* to have been a fable. Our demonstration of this, and of the legendary nature of the story that the Law of the Twelve Tables came from Athens, are two passages [Op. 2.169f,564–80] which permit us to believe that we did not write that work in vain.) In the humanity of our day, there are alternations of these last two forms of government, both human, but neither of the two passes by nature into an aristocratic state where only the nobles command and all the others obey. Hence the commonwealths of nobles now left in the world are few and far between: Nuremberg in Germany; Ragusa in Dalmatia; Venice, Genoa, and Lucca in Italy [1018,1094]. These, then, are the three types of states that divine providence, through the natural customs of the nations, has caused to come into the world, and they succeed one another in this natural order. Since other types, arising by human providence as mixtures of these three, are not supported by the nature of nations, they were characterized by Tacitus (who saw only the effects of the causes we here point out and later treat more fully) as "more laudable than susceptible of attainment, and if by chance any do occur they are not at all lasting" [A. 4.33; 1004]. By this discovery new principles are given to political theory, not merely different from but contrary to those which have been imagined hitherto.

30 The caduceus [604] is the last of the hieroglyphs, to tell us that the first peoples, in their heroic times when the natural law of force reigned supreme, looked upon each other as perpetual enemies, and pillage and piracy were continual because, as war was eternal between them, there was no need of declarations [636–41]. (Indeed, as in the first barbarian times the heroes considered it a title of honor to be called robbers, so in the returned barbarian times the powerful rejoiced to be called pirates [1053].)

But when human governments had been established, whether popular or monarchical, by the law of human gentes heralds were introduced to give warning of wars, and periods of hostility began to be terminated by treaties of peace. And this by a high counsel of divine providence, to the end that nations in their period of barbarism, when they were new in the world and needed to take root, should remain circumscribed within their confines and not, fierce and untamed as they were, cross them to exterminate each other in wars; but after they had grown up and at the same time become familiar with each other and hence tolerant of each other's customs, it should then be easy for conquering peoples to spare the lives of the conquered by the just laws of victory.

31 This New Science or metaphysic, studying the common nature of nations in the light of divine providence, discovers the origins of divine and human institutions among the gentile nations, and thereby establishes a system of the natural law of the gentes, which proceeds with the greatest equality and constancy through the three ages which the Egyptians handed down to us as the three periods through which the world had passed up to their time [E2; 52]. These are: (1) The age of the gods, in which the gentiles believed they lived under divine governments, and everything was commanded them by auspices and oracles, which are the oldest institutions in profane history. (2) The age of the heroes, in which they reigned everywhere in aristocratic commonwealths, on account of a certain superiority of nature which they held themselves to have over the plebs. (3) The age of men, in which all men recognized themselves as equal in human nature, and therefore there were established first the popular commonwealths and then the monarchies, both of which are forms of human government [29, 916ff, 925ff].

32 In harmony with these three kinds of nature and government, three kinds of language were spoken [928ff] which compose the vocabulary of this Science: (1) That of the time of the families when gentile men were newly received into humanity. This, we shall find, was a mute language of signs and physical objects having natural relations to the ideas they wished to express [401, 431, 437]. (2) That spoken by means of heroic emblems, or similitudes, comparisons, images, metaphors, and natural descriptions, which make up the great body of the heroic language which was spoken at the time the heroes reigned [438, 456ff]. (3) Human language using words agreed upon by the people, a language of which they are absolute lords, and which is proper to the popular commonwealths and monarchical states; a language whereby the people may fix the meaning of the laws by which the nobles as well as the plebs are bound [439ff]. Hence,

among all nations, once the laws had been put into the vulgar tongue, the science of laws passed from the control of the nobles [953]. Hitherto, among all nations, the nobles, being also priests, had kept the laws in a secret language as a sacred thing. That is the natural reason for the secrecy of the laws among the Roman patricians until popular liberty arose [999ff].

Now these are the same three languages that the Egyptians claimed had been spoken before in their world, corresponding exactly both in number and in sequence to the three ages that had run their course before them [437ff]. (1) The hieroglyphic or sacred or secret language, by means of mute acts. This is suited to the uses of religion, for which observance is more important than discussion. (2) The symbolic, by means of similitudes, such as we have just seen the heroic language to have been. (3) The epistolary or vulgar, which served the common uses of life. These three types of language are found among the Chaldeans, Scythians, Egyptians, Germans, and all the other ancient gentile nations; although hieroglyphic writing survived longest among the Egyptians, because for a longer time than the others they were closed to all foreign nations (as for the same reason it still survives among the Chinese [50]), and hence we have a proof of the vanity of their imagined remote antiquity.

33   We here bring to light the beginnings not only of languages but also of letters [428–472], which philology has hitherto despaired of finding. We shall give a specimen [430] of the extravagant and monstrous opinions that have been held up to now. We shall observe that the unhappy cause of this effect is that philologists have believed that among the nations languages first came into being and then letters; whereas (to give here a brief indication of what will be fully proved in this volume) letters and languages were born twins and proceeded apace through all their three stages. These beginnings are precisely exhibited in the causes of the Latin language, as set forth in the first edition of the New Science (which is the second of the three passages on whose account we do not regret that book) [Op. 3.368–73; 28, 35, 63]. By the reasoning out of these causes many discoveries have been made in ancient Roman history, government, and law, as you will observe a thousand times, O reader, in this volume. From this example, scholars of oriental languages, of Greek, and, among the modern languages, particularly of German, which is a mother language, will be enabled to make discoveries of antiquities far beyond their expectations and ours [153].

34   We find that the principle of these origins both of languages and of letters lies in the fact that the first gentile peoples, by a demonstrated necessity of nature, were poets [216] who spoke in poetic characters. This

discovery, which is the master key of this Science, has cost us the persistent research of almost all our literary life, because with our civilized natures we [moderns] cannot at all imagine and can understand only by great toil the poetic nature of these first men [H1]. The [poetic] characters of which we speak were certain imaginative genera (images for the most part of animate substances, of gods or heroes, formed by their imagination) to which they reduced all the species or all the particulars appertaining to each genus [412–427]; exactly as the fables of human times, such as those of late comedy, are intelligible genera reasoned out by moral philosophy, from which the comic poets form imaginative genera (for the best ideas of the various human types are nothing but that) which are the persons of the comedies [808]. These divine or heroic characters were true fables or myths [401], and their allegories are found to contain meanings not analogical but univocal, not philosophical but historical, of the peoples of Greece of those times [210, 403].

Since these genera (for that is what the fables in essence are) were formed by most vigorous imaginations, as in men of the feeblest reasoning powers, we discover in them true poetic sentences [219, 825], which must be sentiments clothed in the greatest passions and therefore full of sublimity and arousing wonder. Now the sources of all poetic locution are two: poverty of language and need to explain and be understood. Heroic speech followed immediately on the mute language of acts and objects that had natural relations to the ideas they were meant to signify, which was used in the divine times. Lastly, in the necessary natural course of human institutions, language among the Assyrians, Syrians, Phoenicians, Egyptians, Greeks, and Latins began with heroic verses, passed thence to iambics, and finally settled into prose [232f, 463]. This gives certainty to the history of the ancient poets [464ff] and explains why in the German language, particularly in Silesia, a province of peasants, there are many natural versifiers [471], and in the Spanish, French and Italian languages the first authors wrote in verse [438].

35   From these three languages is formed the mental dictionary [145] by which to interpret properly all the various articulated languages, and we make use of it here wherever it is needed. In the first edition of the *New Science* [Op. 3.387f] we gave a detailed illustration of it, in which this idea of it was presented: that from the eternal properties of the fathers, which we in virtue of this Science considered them to have had in the state of the families and of the first heroic cities in the time when the languages were formed, we find proper meanings [of terms] in fifteen different languages,

both dead and living, by which they were diversely called, sometimes from one property and sometimes from another. (This is the third passage in which we take satisfaction in that edition of our book [28, 33].) Such a lexicon is necessary for learning the language spoken by the ideal eternal history traversed in time by the histories of all nations [7, 349, 393], and for scientifically adducing authorities to confirm what is discussed in the natural law of the gentes and hence in every particular jurisprudence.

36 Along with these three languages—proper to the three ages in which three forms of government prevailed, conforming to three types of civil natures, which succeed one another as the nations run their course—we find there went also in the same order a jurisprudence suited to each in its time [915–941].

37 Of these [three types of jurisprudence] the first was a mystic theology, which prevailed in the period when the gentiles were commanded by the gods [938]. Its wise men were the theological poets (who are said to have founded gentile humanity) who interpreted the mysteries of the oracles, which among all nations gave their responses in verse [464]. Thus we find that the mysteries of this vulgar wisdom were hidden in the fables. In this connection we inquire into the reasons why the philosophers later had such a desire to recover the wisdom of the ancients, as well as into the occasions the fables provided them for bestirring themselves to meditate lofty things in philosophy, and into the opportunities they had for reading their own hidden wisdom into the fables [K6, 515, 779].

38 The second was the heroic jurisprudence [939], all verbal scrupulosity (in which Ulysses was manifestly expert). This jurisprudence looked to what the Roman jurisconsults called civil equity and we call reason of state [320, 949]. With their limited ideas, the heroes thought they had a natural right to precisely what, how much and of what sort had been set forth in words; as even now we may observe in peasants and other crude men, who in conflicts between words and meanings obstinately say that their right stands for them in the words. And this by counsel of divine providence to the end that the gentiles, not yet being capable of universals, which good laws must be, might be led by this very particularity of their words to observe the laws universally. And if, as a consequence of this [civil] equity, the laws turned out in a given case to be not only harsh but actually cruel, they naturally bore it because they thought their law was naturally such. Furthermore they were led to observe their laws by a sovereign private interest, which the heroes identified with that of their fatherlands, of which they were the only citizens [584]. Hence they did not

hesitate, for the safety of their various fatherlands, to consecrate themselves and their families to the will of the laws, which by maintaining the
common security of the fatherland kept secure for each of them a certain
private monarchical reign over his family. Moreover it was this great
private interest, in conjunction with the supreme arrogance characteristic
of barbarous times, which formed their heroic nature, whence came so
many heroic actions in defense of their fatherlands. To these heroic deeds
we must add the intolerable pride, profound avarice and pitiless cruelty
with which the ancient Roman patricians treated the unhappy plebeians,
as is clearly seen in Roman history precisely during that period which Livy
himself describes as having been the age of Roman virtue and of the most
flourishing popular liberty yet dreamed of in Rome [668]. It will then be
evident that this public virtue was nothing but a good use which providence made of such grievous, ugly and cruel private vices, in order that the
cities might be preserved during a period when the minds of men, intent
on particulars, could not naturally understand a common good [F6].
Thence are derived new principles by which to demonstrate the argument
of St. Augustine's discussion of the virtue of the Romans [C.G. 5.12]; and
the opinion hitherto held by the learned concerning the heroism of primitive peoples is put to rout [666]. Civil equity of this sort we find naturally
observed by the heroic nations in peace as well as in war (shining examples
are adduced from the history of the first barbarian times as well as from
that of the last); and it was practiced privately by the Romans as long as
theirs was an aristocratic commonwealth, that is to say down to the times
of the Publilian and Petelian laws [104ff], until which time everything was
based on the Law of the Twelve Tables [985].

39   The last type of jurisprudence [940] was that of natural equity
[324ff, 951], which reigns naturally in the free commonwealths, in which
the people, each for his own particular good (without understanding that
it is the same for all), are led to command universal laws. They naturally
desire these laws to bend benignly to the least details of matters calling for
equal utility. This is the *aequum bonum*, subject of the latest Roman
jurisprudence, which from the times of Cicero had begun to be transformed by the edict of the Roman praetor. This type is also and perhaps
even more connatural with the monarchies, in which the monarchs have
accustomed their subjects to attend to their own private interests, while
they themselves have taken charge of all public affairs, and desire all
nations subject to them to be made equal by the laws, in order that all may
be equally interested in the state. Wherefore the emperor Hadrian re-

formed the entire heroic natural law of Rome with the aid of the human natural law of the provinces, and commanded that jurisprudence should be based on the Perpetual Edict which Salvius Julianus composed almost entirely from the provincial edicts [1023].

40 We may now recapitulate all the prime elements of this world of nations by reference to the hieroglyphs which stand for them. The lituus, water and fire on the altar, the cinerary urn within the forest, the plough leaning against the altar, and the rudder prostrate at the foot of the altar signify divination, sacrifices, the first families including sons only, the practice of burial, the cultivation of the fields and their division, the asylums, the later families including *famuli*, the first agrarian conflicts and hence the first heroic inland colonies and, when these failed, the overseas colonies and with these the first migrations of peoples. All these came within the Egyptian age of the gods, which Varro through ignorance or negligence called the dark time [6, 52]. The fasces signify the first heroic commonwealths, the distinction of the three ownerships (natural, civil, and eminent), the first civil empires, the first unequal alliances accorded under the first agrarian law by which these first cities were founded on rustic fiefs of the plebeians, which in turn were subfiefs of the noble fiefs of the heroes, who, though themselves sovereigns, became subjects of the higher sovereignty of the reigning heroic orders. The sword leaning on the fasces signifies the public wars that were waged by these cities, beginning with pillage and piracy. (Duels, or private wars, must have started much earlier within the state of the families [959ff].) The purse signifies devices of nobility or family coats-of-arms carried over onto medals, the first ensigns of the peoples, which later became military ensigns and finally coins, which here stand for the extension of trade to movable goods by means of money. (Trade in real estate, with natural prices in produce or work, had begun before in divine times with the first agrarian law, on the basis of which the commonwealths were born.) The balance signifies the laws of equality, which are laws properly speaking. Finally the caduceus signifies formally declared public wars, terminated by treaties of peace. All the hieroglyphs of this second group are far from the altar because they all stand for civil institutions of the times in which the false religions were slowly disappearing, beginning with the heroic agrarian conflicts, which gave the name to the Egyptian age of heroes, called by Varro the fabulous time. The tablet with the alphabets is put between the divine and human symbols because with letters, from which philosophies had their beginning, the false religions began to disappear; in contrast with the true, which is

our Christian religion, which indeed is humanly confirmed to us by the most sublime philosophies, the Platonic and the Peripatetic (insofar as it conforms to the Platonic).

41 The whole idea of this work may be summed up as follows. The darkness in the background of the picture is the material of this Science, uncertain, unformed, obscure, which is set forth in the Chronological Table and in the Notes upon it. The ray with which divine providence lights up the breast of metaphysic represents the Axioms, Definitions, and Postulates that this Science takes as Elements from which to deduce the Principles on which it is based and the Method by which it proceeds. All these things are contained in the first book. The ray that is reflected from the breast of metaphysic onto the statue of Homer is the proper light which is given to poetic wisdom in the second book and by which the true Homer is elucidated in the third book. By "The Discovery of the True Homer" all the institutions that make up this world of nations are clarified, proceeding from their origins according to the order in which the hieroglyphs come forth into the light of the true Homer. This is the Course of Nations considered in the fourth book. And having arrived finally at the foot of the statue of Homer, they begin a Recourse in the same order [L2, 393]. Of this we treat in the fifth and last book.

42 Last of all, to state the idea of the work in the briefest summary, the entire engraving represents the three worlds in the order in which the human minds of the gentiles have been raised from earth to heaven. All the hieroglyphs visible on the ground denote the world of nations to which men applied themselves before anything else. The globe in the middle represents the world of nature which the physicists later observed. The hieroglyphs above signify the world of minds and of God which the metaphysicians finally contemplated [B7].

BOOK ONE

ESTABLISHMENT OF PRINCIPLES [I·1; I·4–6]

[SECTION I]

NOTES ON THE CHRONOLOGICAL TABLE,

IN WHICH THE MATERIALS ARE SET IN ORDER

I

[Chronological table, based on the three epochs of the times of the Egyptians, who said all the world before them had passed through three ages: that of the gods, that of the heroes, and that of men] [52].

43 This Chronological Table sets forth in outline the world of the ancient nations, starting from the universal flood and passing from the Hebrews through the Chaldeans, Scythians, Phoenicians, Egyptians, Greeks, and Romans down to the Second Carthaginian War. On it there appear men and deeds of the greatest renown, assigned to certain times and places by the community of scholars. These men and deeds either did not have their being at the times or in the places to which they have been commonly assigned, or never existed at all. On the other hand, from the long dark shadows where they have lain buried, notable men and most pertinent deeds emerge, through whom and by which the decisive changes in human institutions have come about. All this is set forth in these Notes, to show how uncertain, unseemly, defective, or vain are the beginnings of the humanity of the nations.

44 Moreover this Table takes a position quite opposed to that of the Chronological Canon [Canon chronicon, aegyptiacus, hebraicus, graecus] of John Marsham, in which he tries to prove that the Egyptians preceded all the nations of the world in government and religion, and that their sacred rites and civil ordinances, transported to other peoples, were received with some emendation by the Hebrews. In this opinion he was followed by [John] Spencer in his dissertation De Urim et Tummim, in which he expresses the opinion that the Israelites had taken from the Egyptians all their knowledge of divine institutions by means of the sacred Cabala. Finally Marsham was acclaimed by van Heurn in his Antiquitates philosophiae barbaricae, in which, in the part entitled Chaldaicus, he

writes that Moses, instructed in the knowledge of them by the Egyptians, had brought divine institutions to the Hebrews in his laws. Against this line of argument arose Hermann Wits in his *Aegyptiaca*. He thinks that the first gentile author to give certain information about the Egyptians was Dio Cassius, who flourished under the philosopher Marcus Aurelius. But on this point he may be confuted by the *Annals* of Tacitus [2.60], in which we are told that Germanicus, having gone into the East, proceeded thence to Egypt to see the famous antiquities of Thebes, and had one of the priests there interpret to him the hieroglyphs inscribed on some of the monuments. The priest, talking foolishly, told him that those characters preserved the memory of the boundless power that their king Ramses [II] had held in Africa, in the East and even in Asia Minor, equal to the power of the Romans in their own time, which was very great. But this passage, perhaps because it was contrary to his position, Wits said nothing about.

45 But certainly such boundless antiquity did not yield much recondite wisdom to the inland Egyptians. For in the time of Clement of Alexandria, as he recounts in his Miscellanies [*Stromata* 6.4], their so-called priestly books were in circulation to the number of forty-two, and they contained the greatest errors in philosophy and astronomy, for which Chaeremon, teacher of St. Dionysius the Areopagite, is often scoffed at by Strabo [17.1.29]. Their ideas about medicine are found by Galen in his discussion of Hermetic medicine [*On Simples* 6.pr.] to be obvious nonsense and mere quackery. Their morality was dissolute, for it not only tolerated or permitted harlots but made them respectable. Their theology was full of superstition, magic and witchcraft. And the magnificence of their pyramids and other monuments might well have sprung from barbarism, which accords well with hugeness [816]. Egyptian sculpture and casting are regarded even today as extremely crude. For delicacy is the fruit of philosophy, wherefore Greece alone, which was the nation of philosophers, shone with all the fine arts that human genius has ever discovered: painting, sculpture, casting, and the arts of engraving, which are most delicate because they are compelled to abstract the surfaces of the bodies they represent [794].

46 This ancient wisdom of the Egyptians was raised to the stars by Alexandria, founded on the sea by Alexander the Great. Uniting African acuteness with Greek delicacy, it produced distinguished philosophers in divinity, through whom the city gained such renown for high divine wisdom that the Alexandrian Museum was later as much celebrated as the Academy, the Lyceum, the Stoa, and the Cynosarges all together had been in Athens. Alexandria was called on this account "the mother of the

sciences." Such was its excellence that the Greeks called it simply *Polis*, The City, as Athens was called *Astu* and Rome *Urbs*. Thence came Manetho, the Egyptian high priest, who turned all Egyptian history into a sublime natural theology [222], just as the Greek philosophers had previously done with their fables, which will here be found to have been their most ancient histories. Thus the same thing happened to the Greek fables as to the Egyptian hieroglyphs.

47 With such a show of high wisdom, the nation, arrogant by nature (and hence mockingly called "animals of glory"), in a city which was a great emporium of the Mediterranean and, through the Red Sea, of the Ocean and the Indies (a city among whose abominable customs was that related by Tacitus in a golden passage [A. 2.60], that it was "avid of new religions"), believed that the false gods which were scattered abroad in the world (as they learned from the nations which met there for maritime trade) must all have originated in their Egypt, and that their Jove Ammon was the oldest of all Joves (of which every gentile nation had one), and that the Herculeses of all the other nations (Varro enumerated as many as forty [14]) must have taken their names from their Egyptian Hercules. These [pretensions], both reported to us by Tacitus, were due in part to the prejudiced opinion of their exceptional antiquity, which they vainly boasted over all other nations of the world, adding that in ancient times they had lorded it over a great part of the world. They were due in part also to their not knowing the way in which uniform ideas of gods and heroes were born among the gentile peoples without their having any knowledge of each other, as we shall fully demonstrate later on [145f]. Now for all the too flattering judgments with which Diodorus Siculus (who lived in the times of Augustus) adorns the Egyptians, he does not accord them more than two thousand years of antiquity [1.23!], and his judgments are overthrown by Jacques Cappel in his *Historia sacra et exotica*, who puts them in the same class with those which Xenophon had ascribed to Cyrus (and we may add those which Plato often feigns of the Persians [as in his *Alcibiades I* 120E]). Finally all this concerning the vanity of the high ancient wisdom of the Egyptians is confirmed by the hoax of the *Poimander*, palmed off as Hermetic doctrine. Saumaise considered this fragment a disordered and badly composed collection of things, and Casaubon found that it contained no doctrine more ancient than that which the Platonists set forth in the same phraseology.

48 This false opinion of their great antiquity was caused among the Egyptians by a property of the human mind—that of being indefinite [120f]—by which it is often led to believe that the things it does not know

are vastly greater than in fact they are. The Egyptians were in this respect like the Chinese, who grew to so great a nation shut off from all foreign nations, for the Egyptians were similarly shut off until Psammeticus, and the Scythians until Idanthyrsus. The Scythians [or Russians] indeed, according to a vulgar tradition, surpassed the Egyptians in antiquity. This vulgar tradition must have taken its start from [the legendary episode] with which profane universal history begins. It sets up, in Justin's version [1.1, 3], as two pre-beginnings antedating the monarchy of the Assyrians, two powerful kings, Tanaus the Scythian and Sesostris the Egyptian, who have until now made the world seem older than it really is. [The story goes] that Tanaus had moved first through the [near] East with a great army to subdue Egypt, which is by nature very difficult to penetrate with an army, and that then Sesostris with an equally great host had moved to subdue Scythia. Yet Scythia lived unknown to the Persians themselves (who had extended their monarchy over that of the Medes, their neighbors) down to the time of Darius called the Great, who declared war on Idanthyrsus, king of the Scythians; and this king was so barbarous even in the days of a most civilized Persia that he answered him with five real words in the form of five objects, since he did not even know how to write with hieroglyphs [99, 435]. And we are to believe that these two great and mighty kings crossed Asia with two great hosts without making it a province either of Scythia or Egypt, but leaving it in such liberty that there later grew up there the first of the four most famous monarchies in the world, that of Assyria!

49 For the same reason, perhaps, the Chaldeans did not fail to enter the lists in this contest of antiquity. They too were an inland people and, as we shall show, more ancient than the other two, who vainly boasted that they had preserved the astronomical observations of a good twenty-eight thousand years. This was perhaps the reason that Flavius Josephus the Jew [in his *Jewish Antiquities* 1.70] erroneously regarded as antediluvian the observations described on the two columns, one of marble and one of brick, raised against the two floods, and thought that he himself had seen the marble one in Syria. So important was it to the ancient nations to preserve astronomical records, whereas this sense was quite dead among the nations that followed them! Wherefore this column finds its proper place in the museum of credulity.

50 But the Chinese are found writing in hieroglyphs [83] just as the ancient Egyptians did [435] (to say nothing of the Scythians, who did not even know how to put their hieroglyphs in writing [48]). For many thousands of years they had no commerce with other nations by whom they

might have been informed concerning the real antiquity of the world. Just as a man confined while asleep in a very small dark room, in horror of darkness [on waking] believes it certainly much larger than groping with his hands will show it to be, so, in the darkness of their chronology, the Chinese and the Egyptians have done, and the Chaldeans likewise. It is true that Father Michele Ruggieri, a Jesuit, declares that he has himself read books printed before the coming of Jesus Christ. It is true further that Father Martini, another Jesuit, in his *Sinica historia* ascribes a great antiquity to Confucius, which has led many into atheism, as we are informed by Martin Schoock in his *Diluvium Noachi universale*, in which he says that Isaac de la Peyrère, author of the *Preadamitae*, perhaps for that reason abandoned the Catholic faith and then wrote that the flood spread over the lands of the Hebrews only. Nevertheless Nicolas Trigault, better informed than Ruggieri or Martini, writes in his *De christiana expeditione apud Sinas* that printing was in use in China not more than two centuries earlier than in Europe, and that Confucius flourished not more than five hundred years before Christ. And the Confucian philosophy, like the priestly books of the Egyptians, in its few references to physical nature is rude and clumsy, and it is almost wholly devoted to a vulgar morality, the morality commanded to the people by their laws.

51 Premising such reflections on the vain opinion of their own antiquity held by these gentile nations and above all by the Egyptians, we should begin our study of gentile learning [*tutto lo scibile gentilesco*] by scientifically ascertaining this important starting-point—where and when that learning had its first beginnings in the world—and by adducing human reasons thereby in support of Christian faith [*tutto il credibile cristiano*], which takes its start from the fact that the first people of the world were the Hebrews, whose prince was Adam, created by the true God at the time of the creation of the world. It follows that the first science to be learned should be mythology or the interpretation of fables; for, as we shall see, all the histories of the gentiles have their beginnings in fables, which were the first histories of the gentile nations [202]. By such a method the beginnings of the sciences as well as of the nations are to be discovered, for they sprang from the nations and from no other source. It will be shown throughout this work that they had their beginnings in the public needs or utilities of the peoples and that they were later perfected as acute individuals applied their reflection to them [498]. This is the proper starting-point for universal history, which all scholars say is defective in its beginnings [399].

52   In this undertaking we shall be greatly helped by the antiquity of the Egyptians, for they have preserved for us two great fragments not less marvelous than their pyramids, namely these two great philological verities. The first is narrated by Herodotus [2.36; cf. Diodorus Siculus 1.44]: that the Egyptians reduced all the preceding time of the world to three ages, the first that of the gods, the second that of the heroes, the third that of men. The other (as related in Scheffer's *De natura et constitutione philosophiae italicae seu pythagoricae*) is that, with corresponding number and sequence, through all that period three languages had been spoken: the first hieroglyphic, with sacred characters; the second symbolic, with heroic characters; the third epistolary, with characters agreed on by the peoples [173, 432ff]. This division of times was not followed by Marcus Terentius Varro; we must not say because he did not know of it, for, with his boundless erudition, he deserved the honor bestowed on him in the title "most learned of the Romans" in their most enlightened period, the age of Cicero; but rather because he did not choose to; perhaps because he applied [only] to Roman history what by our principles will be found true of all the ancient nations, namely that all Roman institutions, divine and human, were native to Latium. He therefore studied to give them all Latin origins in his great work [*The Antiquities*] *of Divine and Human Institutions* [M4], of which the injustice of time has deprived us. (So far was Varro from believing in the legendary bringing of the law of the Twelve Tables from Athens to Rome!). [According to Censorinus, *Natal Day* 21,] he divided the times of the world into three: a dark time, corresponding to the Egyptian age of the gods; a fabulous time, corresponding to their age of the heroes; and a historic time, corresponding to their age of men [364, 990].

53   Furthermore the antiquity of the Egyptians will help us with two pretentious memories, examples of that conceit of nations by which, as Diodorus Siculus observed [1.9.3], every nation barbarian or civilized has considered itself to be the oldest and to have preserved its records from the beginning of the world [125]; a privilege, as we shall see, of the Hebrews alone [54]. These two pretentious memories we have observed to be, first, the legend that their Jove Ammon was the oldest of all the Joves in the world, and second, that the Herculeses of all the other nations had taken their name from the Egyptian Hercules [47]. That is, that all nations had passed first through the age of gods, the king of whom was by all these nations held to be Jove; and then through the age of heroes, who considered themselves sons of the gods, and of whom Hercules was believed to be the greatest.

II

[The Hebrews]

54 The first column is dedicated to the Hebrews, who, on the most reliable authority of Flavius Josephus the Jew and Lactantius Firmianus [94], lived unknown to all the gentile nations. And yet they reckoned rightly the account of the times passed through by the world, now accepted as true by the severest critics, according to the calculation of Philo the Jew. If his estimate varies from that of Eusebius, the difference is one of a mere fifteen hundred years, which is a very short period of time compared with the variations among the chronologies made up by the Chaldeans, Scythians, Egyptians, and in our own day by the Chinese. And this should be an invincible proof that the Hebrews were the first people in our world and that in the sacred history they have truthfully preserved their memories from the beginning of the world [165f].

III

[The Chaldeans]

55 The second column is devoted to the Chaldeans, both because in geography it is clear that the most inland monarchy of all the habitable world must have been in Assyria, and because in this work it is shown that the inland nations were populated first, and then the maritime nations [736]. And certainly the Chaldeans were the first gentile sages, and the common opinion of philologians regards Zoroaster the Chaldean as their prince. And without question universal history takes its beginning from the monarchy of the Assyrians, which must have begun to take shape among the Chaldean people; from whom, when it had grown to great size, it must have passed to the nation of the Assyrians under Ninus, who must have founded that monarchy not with people brought in from outside but with those born within Chaldea itself, whereupon he did away with the Chaldean name and brought forward the Assyrian in its stead. It must have been the plebeians of that nation through whose support Ninus made himself king. It will be shown in this work that such was the political custom in almost all nations, as we know certainly it was of the Roman. Now the same [universal] history tells us that Zoroaster was slain by Ninus. We shall see that this was said, in heroic language, in the sense that the kingdom of the Chaldeans which had been aristocratic (and of which Zoroaster had been the heroic character) was overthrown by means of the popular liberty of the plebeians of that people. We shall see that in heroic times these plebeians were a different nation from the nobles, and that with the aid of this nation Ninus established himself as monarch. Otherwise, if things are not as we have stated them, this monster of chronology would emerge in Assyrian history: that within the lifetime of one man, Zoroaster, Chaldea had grown from [a land of] lawless vagabonds to such greatness of empire that Ninus was able to found on it a mighty monarchy. For lack of these principles, Ninus, taken as the initiator of universal history, has hitherto made the monarchy of Assyria seem to have been born all at once, as a frog is born in a summer shower [738].

IV
[The Scythians]

56 The third column is set up for the Scythians, who surpassed the Egyptians in antiquity, as we learned not far back [48] from a vulgar tradition.

V
[The Phoenicians]

57 The fourth column is assigned to the Phoenicians rather than to the Egyptians, to whom the Phoenicians brought from the Chaldeans the use of the quadrant and the knowledge of the elevation of the polestar [727]. Of so much there is a vulgar tradition. We shall show later that they brought also vulgar [alphabetic] characters [440].

VI
[The Egyptians]

58 For all the reasons discussed above, the Egyptians, to whom Marsham in his *Canon* accords the distinction of being the most ancient of all the nations, merit the fifth place in our Chronological Table.

VII
[Zoroaster, or the kingdom of the Chaldeans. Year of the world 1756.]

59 Zoroaster is shown in this work to have been a poetic character of founders of peoples in the East. There are as many of these founders scattered through that great part of the world as there are Herculeses scattered through the opposite part, the West. And perhaps the Herculeses whom Varro [14] observed to exist in the likeness of the western ones even in Asia, such as the Tyrian or Phoenician, were considered by the Easterners as so many Zoroasters. But the conceit of scholars, who will have it that whatever they know is as old as the world, has made of them one individual man brimming with the highest esoteric wisdom, and has attached to him the oracles of philosophy, which do nothing but palm off as old a very

new doctrine, namely that of the Pythagoreans and the Platonists. But this conceit of the scholars did not stop here, for it swelled even further by deriving from him the scholastic succession among the nations. According to them, Zoroaster taught Berosus for Chaldea; Berosus, Thrice-great Hermes for Egypt; Thrice-great Hermes, Atlas for Ethiopia; Atlas, Orpheus for Thrace; and finally Orpheus founded his school in Greece. But we shall see shortly how [far from] easy these long journeys were for the ancient nations, who, because of their recent savage origin, lived everywhere unknown even to their nearest neighbors, and came to know each other only by occasion of war or by reason of trade [93].

60   But concerning the Chaldeans the philologians themselves, confused by the various vulgar traditions which they have themselves collected, do not know whether they were individual men or entire families or a whole people or nation. All these doubts will be resolved by the following principles. They were first individuals, then entire families, later a whole people, and finally a great nation on which the monarchy of Assyria was founded. Their wisdom was at first in vulgar divinity, by means of which they divined the future from the path of falling stars at night, and then in judicial astrology. Thus among the Latins a judicial astrologer was still called a Chaldean.

VIII
[Iapetus, from whom spring the giants. Year of the world 1856.]

61   Giants, as we shall show by physical histories found in the Greek fables and by proofs both physical and moral drawn from civil histories, existed in nature among all the first gentile nations [369–373].

IX
[Nimrod, or the confusion of tongues. Year of the world 1856.]

62   The confusion of tongues came about in a miraculous way so that on the instant many different languages were formed. The Fathers will have it that through this confusion of tongues the purity of the sacred antediluvian language was gradually lost. This should be understood as referring to the languages of the Eastern peoples among whom Shem propagated the human race. It must have been otherwise in the case of the nations of all the rest of the world; for the races of Ham and Japheth were destined to be scattered through the great forest of this earth in a savage migration of two hundred years. Wandering and alone, they were to bring forth their children, with a savage education, destitute of any human custom and deprived of any human speech, and so in a state of wild animals. It was necessary that just so much time should pass before the

earth, having at last dried off from the wetness of the universal flood, could send off dry exhalations of the sort wherein lightning could be generated, which stunned and terrified men into abandoning themselves to the false religions of so many Joves that Varro was able to count forty of them, and the Egyptians claimed their Jove Ammon to be the oldest of all [14! Tertullian *Apology* 14.8 says three hundred]. They turned to a kind of divination which consisted in divining the future from the thunder and lightning and from the flights of eagles which they held to be birds of Jove. But among the Easterners there was born a more refined divination from the observation of the movements of the planets and the aspects of the stars. Thus Zoroaster is honored as the first wise man among the gentiles. Bochart gives him the title "contemplator of the stars." Just as the first vulgar wisdom was born among the Easterners, so also among them arose the first monarchy, that of Assyria.

63   This chain of reasoning disposes of all those recent etymologists who attempt to trace all the languages of the world back to the origins of the eastern tongues. The fact is that all the nations sprung from Ham and Japheth first developed their native languages inland, and [only] then, having descended to the sea, began to deal with the Phoenicians, who were famous for navigation and colonies along the shores of the Mediterranean and of the Ocean. We have shown in the first edition of our New Science [Op. 3.368ff] that this is true of the origins of the Latin language and that, by analogy with the Latin, it must hold for all the others as well.

X

[One of these giants, Prometheus, steals fire from the sun. Year of the world 1856.]

64   From this fable we perceive that Heaven reigned on earth, when it was believed to be no higher than the mountain tops, according to the vulgar tradition that also tells that it left great and numerous benefits to the human race.

XI

[Deucalion]

65   In his time Themis, or divine justice, had a temple on Mount Parnassus, and she judged on earth the disputes of mortals.

XII

[Thrice-great Hermes the elder, or the Egyptian age of the gods.]

66   This is the Hermes who, on the authority of Cicero, *On the Nature of the Gods* [3.22.56], was called by the Egyptians [Thoth or]

Theuth (from which the Greeks are said to have derived *theos*), and who brought the Egyptians letters and laws. They in turn (according to Marsham) taught them to the other nations of the world. But the Greeks did not write their laws with hieroglyphs but with vulgar letters, which up to now Cadmus has commonly been thought to have brought to them from Phoenicia, though, as we shall see, they made no use of them for seven hundred years and more thereafter [679]. For within this period there came Homer, who in none of his poems so much as mentions *nomos* (as Feith observed in his *Antiquitates homericae*), and who left his poems to the memory of his rhapsodes because in his time vulgar letters had not yet been discovered, as Flavius Josephus the Jew resolutely maintains against Apion, the Greek grammarian [A.A. 1.2.11f]. Moreover, after Homer, Greek letters turned out so different from Phoenician!

67 But these are minor difficulties by comparison with the following: how can there be nations already founded and yet without laws? and how within Egypt itself, before this Hermes, had the dynasties been founded? As if letters were essential to laws, and as if the laws of Sparta were thus not laws, where a law of Lycurgus himself forbade the knowledge of letters! As if it were an institution impossible in civil nature to devise laws orally and orally to publish them! As if we did not in fact find in Homer two sorts of assembly: one, called the *boulê*, secret, where the heroes met to consult by word of mouth about the laws; and another called the *agora*, public, in which, also by word of mouth, the laws were published! [624]. And as if, finally, providence had not made provision for this human necessity: so that, lacking letters, all nations in their barbarous period were first founded on customs, and [only] later, having become civilized, were governed by [statutory] laws! Just as in the recourse of barbarism [L1–3] the first laws of the new nations of Europe were born in customs, of which the feudal are the oldest. This should be remembered because of what we shall have to say later: that fiefs were the first origins of all the laws that grew up later among all nations both ancient and modern, and hence the natural law of the gentes was established not with [statutory] laws but with these same human customs [599ff].

68 Now as to what touches on that great theme of the Christian religion—that Moses did not learn from the Egyptians the sublime theology of the Hebrews—there seems to be one great obstacle, chronology, which places Moses after Thrice-great Hermes. But this difficulty, besides being met by the reasons set forth above [44], is completely overcome by means of the principles expressed in a really golden passage of Iamblichus, *On the Mysteries of the Egyptians* [1], where he says that the Egyptians

ascribed to this same Hermes all they discovered that was necessary or useful to human civil life. He must therefore have been, not an individual man rich in esoteric wisdom who was subsequently made a god, but a poetic character of the first men of Egypt who were wise in vulgar wisdom and who founded there first the families and then the peoples that finally composed that great nation. From this same passage just cited from Iamblichus it follows that, if the Egyptian division stands of the three ages of gods, heroes and men, and this Thrice-great was their god, then the life of this Hermes must embrace the entire Egyptian age of the gods.

XIII

[The golden age, or the Greek age of the gods.]

69 Fabulous history acquaints us with one of the peculiarities of this age, namely that the gods consorted with men on earth. To give certainty to the principles of chronology, we shall consider in this work a natural theogony or generation of the gods [317], formed naturally in the imaginations of the Greeks on certain occasions of human need or utility, in which they felt they had received help or comfort in the early childhood of the world, when it was overwhelmed by most frightful religions. For whatever men saw or imagined, or even did themselves, they took to be divinity [183]. Now by making twelve short epochs of the twelve gods of the so-called greater gentes [B2], that is the gods consecrated by men in the time of the families, a rational chronology of poetic history leads us to assign to the age of the gods a duration of nine hundred years [734]. This gives us the beginnings of universal profane history.

XIV

[Hellen—son of Deucalion, grandson of Prometheus, great grandson of Iapetus—through his three sons, spreads three dialects in Greece. Year of the world 2082.]

70 From this Hellen the native Greeks were called Hellenes; but the Greeks of Italy were called Graii and their land Graikia, whence they were called Graeci by the Latins. So well did the Greeks of Italy know the name of the mother country beyond the sea, whence they had come as colonists into Italy! For no such word as Graikia is found in any Greek writer, as Jacques Le Paulmier observes in his *Graeciae antiquae descriptio*.

XV

[Cecrops the Egyptian brings twelve colonies into Attica, of which Theseus later makes up Athens.]

71 When Strabo [9.1.8] judges on the contrary that Attica, because of its rocky soil, could not attract foreigners to come and live there, he does

so in order to support the further assertion that the Attic dialect is one of the first among the native dialects of Greece.

XVI

[Cadmus the Phoenician founds Thebes in Boeotia and introduces vulgar letters into Greece. Year of the world 2448.]

72 Since he introduced the Phoenician alphabet there, Boeotia should have been from its literate beginnings the most ingenious of all the nations of Greece; but it produced men of such doltish minds that "Boeotian" became a proverbial term for a man of slow wit.

XVII

[Saturn, or the Latin age of the gods. Year of the world 2491.]

73 This is the age of the gods beginning among the nations of Latium and corresponding in character to the golden age of the Greeks, among whom our mythology will show [544ff] that the first gold was grain, by the harvests of which for many centuries the first nations counted their years [407]. Saturn was so called by the Latins from *sati*, sown [fields], and is called Chronos by the Greeks, among whom *chronos* means time, whence comes the word chronology.

XVIII

[Thrice-great Hermes the younger, or the Egyptian age of the heroes. Year of the world 2553.]

74 This Hermes the younger must be a poetic character of the age of the heroes in Egypt. This age in Greece comes only after an age of the gods lasting nine hundred years; but among the Egyptians the age of the gods lasts only through the time of a father, son, and grandson. Corresponding to this anachronism in Egyptian history we have already noticed a similar one in Assyrian history, the case of Zoroaster [55, 59].

XIX

[Danaus the Egyptian drives the Inachids out of the kingdom of Argos. Year of the world 2553.]

75 These royal successions are great canons of chronology: thus Danaus occupies the kingdom of Argos, which had previously been ruled by nine kings of the house of Inachus, during whose time there must have passed three hundred years (according to the rule of the chronologers), as there must have passed nearly five hundred years during the time of the fourteen Latin kings who reigned in Alba.

76 But Thucydides [1.5] says that in heroic times the kings drove one

another off the throne almost daily; as Amulius drives Numitor from the kingdom of Alba and Romulus then dethrones Amulius and restores Numitor. This came about through the savagery of those times, and also because the heroic cities were without walls, nor were fortresses then in use. We shall see later that this was true also of the returned barbarian times [645, 1014].

XX

[The Heraclids, spread abroad through Greece, bring in the age of the heroes there. Curetes in Crete, in Saturnia or Italy, and in Asia, bring in the kingdoms of priests. Year of the world 2682.]

77   These two great fragments of antiquity, as Denis Petau observes, fall in Greek history before the heroic time of the Greeks. The Heraclids or sons of Hercules are scattered abroad through Greece more than a hundred years before the coming of Hercules their father, whereas, in order to propagate so many descendants, he would have had to be born many centuries earlier.

XXI

[Dido of Tyre goes to found Carthage.]

78   We place her at the end of the heroic time of the Phoenicians, and thus [conceive her to have been] driven out of Tyre because she had been conquered in a heroic contest, as she professes to have left the city on account of the hatred of her brother-in-law. This multitude of Tyrian men was called in heroic diction a woman because it was made up of the weak and vanquished [989].

XXII

[Orpheus, and with him the age of the theological poets.]

79   This Orpheus, who reduces the wild beasts of Greece to humanity, is evidently a vast den of a thousand monsters. He comes from Thrace, a country of fierce warriors, Marses, not of humane philosophers, for the Thracians were through all later time so barbarous that Androtion the philosopher removed Orpheus from the number of sages simply because he had been born in Thrace. [Aelian, *Various History* 8.6.] And [yet] in her beginnings he came forth so skilled in the Greek language that he composed in it verses of marvelous poetry, with which he tamed the barbarians through their ears; for though already organized in nations they were not restrained by their eyes from setting fire to cities full of marvels. And he finds the Greeks still wild beasts [though] Deucalion a thousand years before had taught them piety by his reverence and fear of divine justice.

On Mount Parnassus, in front of the temple raised to divine justice (which was later the dwelling of the Muses and Apollo, the god and the arts of humanity), Deucalion with Pyrrha his wife, both with veiled heads (that is, with the modesty of human cohabitation, meaning marriage), seize the stones that lie before their feet (that is, the stupid brutes of the former savage times) and make them into men by throwing them over their shoulders (that is, by the discipline of household economy in the state of the families) [523]. Hellen too, seven hundred years before, had brought [the Greeks] together by means of language and had sown the three dialects among them by means of his three sons. And the house of Inachus could show that it had founded its kingdoms three centuries before and had continued the royal successions through that period. Finally comes Orpheus to teach the Greeks humanity; and, from the savage condition in which he finds it, he brings Greece into such splendor as a nation that he is a companion of Jason on the naval enterprise of the Golden Fleece (naval enterprises and navigation being the last discoveries of peoples), and he is accompanied on this expedition by Castor and Pollux, the brothers of Helen, for whose sake the famous Trojan War was fought. So, in the life of one man, so many civil institutions are formed, for which the extent of a thousand years would hardly suffice! Such a monstrosity of Greek chronology in the person of Orpheus [735] is like the other two we have observed above: one in Assyrian history in the person of Zoroaster [55, 59], and another in Egyptian history in the two Hermeses [66ff, 74]. It was perhaps because of all this that Cicero in his *On the Nature of the Gods* [1.38.107] suspected that such a person as Orpheus never existed in the world.

80   To these great chronological difficulties may be added others no less serious of a moral and political nature. For Orpheus then founds the humanity of Greece on the examples of an adulterous Jove, a Juno who is the mortal enemy of the virtues of the Herculeses, a chaste Diana who solicits the sleeping Endymions at night, an Apollo who gives oracular responses and pursues to the point of death modest maiden Daphnes, a Mars who, as if it were not enough for the gods to commit adultery on earth, carries it even into the sea with Venus. Nor is this unrestrained licentiousness of the gods satisfied by forbidden intercourse with women: Jove burns with wicked love for Ganymede; indeed this lust reaches the point of bestiality and Jove, transformed into a swan, lies with Leda. This licentiousness, practiced on men and beasts, was precisely the infamous evil of the outlaw world. Many of the gods and goddesses in heaven do not contract matrimony at all. One marriage there is, that of Jove and Juno, and it is sterile; and not only sterile but full of atrocious wrangling. Jove

indeed fixes in the air his chaste and jealous wife and he himself gives birth to Minerva, who springs from his head. And finally Saturn, if he begets children, devours them. Such examples, powerful divine examples as they are (though such fables may contain all the recondite wisdom desired by Plato and in our time by Bacon of Verulam in his *Wisdom of the Ancients*), if taken at face value would corrupt the most civilized peoples and would incite them to become as bestial as the very beasts of Orpheus; so apt and efficacious they are to transform men from the state of beasts to that of humanity! In view of these things it is a very slight reproof that Saint Augustine makes of the gods of the gentiles in his *City of God* [2.7], apropos of the scene in Terence's *Eunuch* [580–606] in which Chaerea, tempted by a painting of Jove lying with Danae in a shower of gold, summons up the hardihood, which he had lacked, to violate the slave girl with whom he was so madly and violently in love.

81   But these treacherous reefs of mythology will be avoided by the principles of this Science, which will show that such fables in their beginnings were all true and severe and worthy of the founders of nations, and only later (when the long passage of years had obscured their meanings, and customs had changed from austere to disolute, and because men to console their consciences wanted to sin with the authority of the gods) came to have the obscene meanings with which they have come down to us. As for the rough chronological tempests, they will be cleared up for us by the discovery of poetic characters, one of whom was Orpheus, considered as a theological poet, who through the fables, in their first meaning, first founded and then confirmed the humanity of Greece. This character stood out more clearly than ever in the heroic contests with the plebeians of the Greek cities. That was the age in which the theological poets distinguished themselves, as for example Orpheus himself, Linus, Musaeus, and Amphion. The last of these, with self-moving stones (i.e., the doltish plebeians) erected the walls of Thebes, which Cadmus had founded three hundred years before; just as Appius, grandson of the decemvir, about as long after the foundation of Rome, fortifies the heroic state for the Romans by singing to the plebs the strength of the gods in the auspices, the knowledge of which was held by the patricians. From such heroic contests the heroic age got its name [661, 734].

XXIII

[Hercules, with whom the heroic time of Greece reaches its climax.]

82   The same difficulties recur for Hercules if we take him for a real man, the companion of Jason in the expedition to Colchis, and not, as we

shall find him to be in respect of his labors, a heroic character of the founder of peoples [514].

XXIV

[Sancuniates writes histories in vulgar letters. Year of the world 2800.]

83   Called also Sanchuniathon and entitled "the historian of truth" (on the authority of Clement of Alexandria in his *Miscellanies* [i.e., by Porphyry *Against the Christians* as quoted by Eusebius *Preparation for the Gospel* 1.9 and 10.9]). He wrote the history of Phoenicia in vulgar characters, while the Egyptians and the Scythians, as we have seen, wrote in hieroglyphs, as the Chinese have been found to do down to our own days. The latter, like the Scythians and the Egyptians, boast a monstrous antiquity because in the darkness of their isolation, having no dealings with other nations, they had no true idea of time. And Sancuniates wrote in vulgar Phoenician characters at a time when vulgar letters had not yet come into use among the Greeks, as we have said above [66].

XXV

[Trojan war. Year of the world 2820.]

84   This war, as it is recounted by Homer, is thought by circumspect critics never to have taken place; and authors like Dictys of Crete and Dares of Phrygia, who as historians of their time gave prose accounts of it, are by these same critics relegated to the library of imposture.

XXVI

[Sesostris reigns in Thebes. Year of the world 2949.]

85   This king brought under his empire the three other dynasties of Egypt, and is evidently the king Ramses of whom the Egyptian priest tells Germanicus in Tacitus [44].

XXVII

[Greek colonies in Asia, in Sicily, in Italy. Year of the world 2949.]

86   This is one of the very few things in which we do not follow the authority of chronology. Constrained by an overpowering reason, we put the colonies brought by the Greeks into Italy and Sicily about a hundred years after the Trojan War, and thus three hundred years before the time at which the chronologists place them; that is, about the time where the chronologists place the wanderings of the heroes such as Menelaus, Aeneas, Antenor, Diomed, and Ulysses. Nor should this cause surprise when they [the chronologists] themselves vary as much as four hundred and sixty years

in dating Homer, the author nearest to these affairs of the Greeks [803]. [Our reason is that] in magnificence and delicacy Syracuse at the time of the Punic wars had nothing to envy Athens itself, and luxury and splendor of customs reach the islands later than the continents. The Croton of Livy's time calls forth his compassion [23.30.6] because of its small number of inhabitants, when it had once had a population of several million.

XXVIII
[Olympic games, first founded by Hercules, then suspended, and restored by Isiphilus. Year of the world 3223.]

87   Since it is found that the years were numbered by Hercules from harvest to harvest [3, 73], but from Isiphilus [i.e., Iphitus] on by the course of the sun through the signs of the zodiac, the certain [or historic] time of the Greeks [52] begins with Isiphilus.

XXIX
[Founding of Rome. Year of Rome 1.]

88   But just as the clouds are dispersed by the sun, so all the magnificent opinions that have been held up to now concerning the beginnings of Rome and of all the other cities that have been capitals of famous nations, are dispersed by this golden passage of Varro (quoted by St. Augustine in his *City of God* [3.15]): that Rome under the kings, who reigned there for two hundred and fifty years, subdued more than twenty peoples and did not extend her empire more than twenty miles.

XXX
[Homer, who came at a time when vulgar letters had not yet been invented, and who never saw Egypt. Year of the world 3290, of Rome 35.]

89   Regarding this first light of Greece we have been left in the dark by Greek history in both its chief aspects, geography and chronology, for nothing certain has come down to us regarding either his fatherland or the age in which he lived. In our third book we shall find him quite different from what he has been thought up to now. But, whoever he was, he certainly never saw Egypt; for he says in the *Odyssey* [4.354] that the island on which there now stands the pharos of Alexandria was as far from the mainland as an unloaded boat with a north wind in the poop could sail in an entire day. Nor did he see Phoenicia; for he says [O. 5.43ff] that the island of Calypso, Ogygia, was so far away that Hermes, a god—and a winged god—could get there only with great difficulty, as if it were as far from Greece (where the gods reside on Mt. Olympus, as he himself sings in

the *Iliad*) as America is from our world. So, if the Greeks in the times of Homer had had dealings with Egypt and Phoenicia, he would have lost credit in both his poems.

XXXI

[Psammeticus opens Egypt, but only to the Ionian and Carian Greeks. Year of the world 3334.]

90 It is from the time of Psammeticus that Herodotus [2.151ff] begins to relate better ascertained facts about the Egyptians. This confirms our opinion that Homer did not see Egypt; and the many items of information that he narrates about Egypt and other countries of the world are either institutions and deeds within Greece itself, as we shall show in the Poetic Geography [741ff], or they are traditions, altered by the passage of a long time, of the Phoenicians, Egyptians, and Phrygians who had colonized among the Greeks; or they are tales of Phoenician travelers who traded on Greek shores long before the time of Homer.

XXXII

[Aesop, vulgar moral philosopher. Year of the world 3334.]

91 In the Poetic Logic [424] it will be found that Aesop was not an individual man in nature, but an imaginary type or poetic character of the *socii* or *famuli* of the heroes, who certainly came before the Seven Sages of Greece.

XXXIII

[Seven Sages of Greece: of whom one, Solon, institutes popular liberty in Athens; another, Thales the Milesian, gives a beginning to philosophy with physics. Year of the world 3406.]

92 Thales began with too simple a principle: water; perhaps because he had seen gourds grow on water.

XXXIV

[Pythagoras, of whom, according to Livy, not so much as the name can have been known at Rome during his lifetime. Year of the world 3468, of Rome 225.]

93 Livy [1.18.2] puts him in the time of Servius Tullius (so far was he from believing that Pythagoras had been the teacher of Numa in divinity!); and in these very times of Servius Tullius, almost two hundred years after Numa, he says that it was impossible, because of the barbarous character of inland Italy in that era, not merely for Pythagoras himself but even for his name to reach Rome from Croton, passing through so many peoples of varying languages and customs. It may thence be inferred how

quick and easy were the really long journeys of Pythagoras to visit the disciples of Orpheus in Thrace, the mages in Persia, the Chaldeans in Babylonia, the gymnosophists in India; then, on his return, the priests of Egypt and, after crossing Africa at its widest, the disciples of Atlas in Mauretania; then, crossing the sea, the Druids in Gaul! Thence he is supposed to have returned to his fatherland, rich in what van Heurn calls barbarian wisdom from those barbarous nations to which, long years before, Hercules the Theban, slaying monsters and tyrants, had gone on his civilizing mission about the world; nations to whom the Greeks bragged, a long time after, that they had taught culture, but not to such profit that they did not remain barbarous. So sound and weighty is the succession of the schools of barbarian philosophy related by the aforesaid van Heurn, which the conceit of scholars has so much applauded! [59].

94 Need we go so far as to appeal here to the authority of Lactantius [*Divine Institutions* 4.2], who firmly denies that Pythagoras was the disciple of Isaiah? This authority is strongly supported by a passage in the *Jewish Antiquities* [12.14] of Josephus the Jew, which proves that the Hebrews in the times of Homer and Pythagoras lived unknown to their nearest inland neighbors, to say nothing of remote nations overseas. For when Ptolemy Philadelphus expressed surprise that no poet or historian had ever made any mention of the Mosaic laws, Demetrius the Jew answered that some who had attempted to tell the gentiles about them had been miraculously punished by God; Theopompus for example had lost his mind and Theodectes his sight. Josephus himself [A.A. 1.12.60] freely admits their obscurity and gives these reasons for it: "We do not live," he says, "on the seashore, nor do we delight in trading or in having dealings with foreigners for the sake of trade." Lactantius reflects that this custom was a counsel of divine providence, so that the religion of the true God might not be profaned by trafficking with gentiles. In this opinion Lactantius is followed by Peter van der Kuhn in his *De republica hebraeorum*. It is all confirmed by public confession of the Hebrews themselves, who, in expiation of the Septuagint, held a solemn fast each year on the eighth day of Tebet, which is our December; because when it was finished there were three days of darkness over all the world, according to the rabbinical books referred to by Casaubon (*Exercitationes in Baronium*), Buxtorf (*Synagoga iudaica*) and Hottinger (*Thesaurus philologicus*). And because the Grecizing Jews called Hellenists, among them Aristeas, who is said to have been in charge of it, claimed divine authority for this translation, the Jews of Jerusalem mortally hated them.

95 But by the nature of these civil institutions [it is to be considered impossible] that over confines [such as those] whose trespass was forbidden even by the highly civilized Egyptians (who were so inhospitable to the Greeks that even a long time after they had opened Egypt to them it was forbidden to use a Greek pot, spit, or knife, or even [to eat] meat cut by a Greek knife), over harsh and forbidding paths, without any language in common, and among the Hebrews of whom it was proverbially said by the gentiles that they would not so much as point the way to a fountain for a thirsty foreigner, the prophets should have profaned their sacred doctrine by making it accessible to foreigners, new men unknown to them; for in all nations of the world the priests kept such doctrine secret even from their own plebs [999f], whence indeed it was everywhere called sacred doctrine, for sacred is as much as to say secret. And from this there emerges a most luminous proof of the truth of the Christian religion: that Pythagoras and Plato, by virtue of a most sublime human science, had exalted themselves to some extent to the knowledge of the divine truths which the Hebrews had been taught by the true God; and on the other hand there arises a weighty confutation of the errors of recent mythologists, who believe that the fables are sacred stories corrupted by the gentile nations and especially by the Greeks. And although the Egyptians had dealings with the Hebrews in their captivity, yet, by a custom common to primitive peoples, namely that of holding the conquered to be men without gods [958], they rather mocked than heeded the Hebrew religion and history. Often, as the sacred book of Genesis narrates [!], they scornfully asked the Hebrews why the God they adored did not come to liberate them from their hands.

XXXV
[Servius Tullius king. Year of the world 3468, of Rome 225.]

96 By a common error it has hitherto been believed that this king instituted the census in Rome as a basis of popular liberty, whereas we shall see [619ff] that the census was a basis of lordly liberty. And this error is in accord with that other one according to which it has been believed up to now that, in those times in which the sick debtor had to appear on an ass or in a cart before the praetor, Tarquinius Priscus instituted the insignia, togas, devices, and chairs of ivory (made of the tusks of elephants, which, because the Romans had first seen them in Lucania in the war with Pyrrhus, they called Lucanian oxen) and finally the triumphal golden chariot, in which splendid equipage the Roman majesty shone brightest in the times of the popular commonwealth.

XXXVI
[Hesiod. Year of the world 3500.]

97 By the proofs we shall advance concerning the time when vulgar writing was introduced among the Greeks [440?], we put Hesiod about the time of Herodotus or a little before. The chronologists with too much boldness put him thirty years before Homer, on whose period the authorities vary by as much as 460 years. Besides, Porphyry (according to Suidas [in the article on Hesiod]) and Velleius Paterculus [1.7.1] state that Homer preceded Hesiod by a great length of time. As for the tripod that Hesiod consecrated to Apollo on Helicon, with the inscription that he had surpassed Homer in song, although Varro accepts it (according to Aulus Gellius [3.11.3]), it is to be kept in the museum of imposture, for it is a hoax similar to those perpetrated in our day by the falsifiers of medals who seek by such deceit to reap a rich profit.

XXXVII
[Herodotus, Hippocrates. Year of the world 3500.]

98 Hippocrates is placed by the chronologists in the time of the Seven Sages of Greece. But, partly because his life is too much tinged with fable (he is said to be the son of Aesculapius and grandson of Apollo), and partly because he is known to be the author of works written in prose with vulgar characters, he is here placed near the time of Herodotus, who likewise wrote prose with vulgar characters and wove his history almost entirely out of fables [101].

XXXVIII
[Idanthyrsus king of Scythia. Year of the world 3530.]

99 This king answered Darius the Great, who had threatened to make war on him, with five real words (which, as we shall later show, the first peoples must have used before they came to vocal words and finally to written ones). These real words were a frog, a mouse, a bird, a plough-share, and a bow for shooting arrows. Further on we shall show the natural and proper meaning of these objects [435]. It would be tedious to report what St. Cyril [i.e., Clement] of Alexandria relates of the council that Darius held to discuss the meaning of this reply, for the interpretations his counselors put upon it are obviously ridiculous. And this Idanthyrsus was the king of those Scythians who surpassed the Egyptians in point of antiquity, and yet at that late epoch did not even know how to write with

hieroglyphs! Idanthyrsus must have been like one of the Chinese kings who, up to a few centuries ago shut off from the rest of the world, vainly boast an antiquity greater than that of the world, and, after so long a time, are still found writing with hieroglyphs, and, although on account of the great mildness of the climate they have most refined talents and make so many marvelously delicate things, do not yet know how to make shadows in painting, against which highlights can stand out; whence, since it has neither relief nor depth, their painting is most crude. And as for the statuettes of porcelain which come from there, they show the Chinese to be just as unskilled as the Egyptians were in casting; whence it may be inferred that the Egyptians were as unskilled in painting as the Chinese are now.

100 To these Scythians belongs Anacharsis [i.e., Abaris], author of the Scythian oracles, as Zoroaster was of the Chaldean. They must first have been oracles of soothsayers, which later, by the conceit of scholars [127], were turned into oracles of philosophers. From the Hyperboreans of Scythia (either this one or another born anciently within Greece itself) there came to Greece the two most famous oracles of the gentiles, the Delphic and the Dodonian; so Herodotus believed [4.33], and after him Pindar [*Olympian* 3.28f; *Pythian* 10.30] and Pherenicus [as quoted in a scholium on the first Pindar passage], who are followed by Cicero in his *On the Nature of the Gods* [3.23.57]. This may explain why Anacharsis was proclaimed a famous author of oracles and numbered among the most ancient soothsaying gods, as we shall see in the Poetic Geography [745]. Meanwhile, to show how learned Scythia was in esoteric wisdom, let it suffice that the Scythians would stick a knife in the ground and adore it as a god, in order to justify the killings they were about to perform. From this wild religion emerged all the civil and moral virtues narrated by Diodorus Siculus, Justin, Pliny, and lauded to the skies by Horace. Thence Abaris [i.e., Anacharsis], wishing to order Scythia by the laws of Greece, was killed by Caduidas his brother. Such was his profit from the 'barbarian philosophy' of van Heurn that he did not discern by himself the laws needed to bring a barbarian people to a humane civilization, but had to learn them from the Greeks! For the very same thing is true of the Greeks in relation to the Scythians which we have said of them a while ago [90] in relation to the Egyptians: that by their vanity in giving to their knowledge high-sounding origins of foreign antiquity, they truly deserved the reproof they represented the Egyptian priest as giving to Solon (as related by Critias in the first or second *Alcibiades* of Plato [i.e., in his *Timaeus* 22B]): namely that the Greeks had always been children. And so it must be said that by

this conceit the Greeks, in relation both to the Scythians and to the Egyptians, lost as much in real merit as they gained in vain glory.

XXXIX

[Peloponnesian war. Thucydides, who writes that up to his father's day the Greeks knew nothing of their own antiquities, therefore set himself to write of this war. Year of the world 3530.]

101   Thucydides was a young man at the time when Herodotus, who might have been his father, was already old. He lived in the most glorious time of Greece, which was that of the Peloponnesian war, and since he was a contemporary of this struggle he wrote its history in order to write of true things. By him it was said [1.1.2; 1.20] that down to his father's time, which was also that of Herodotus, the Greeks knew nothing of their own antiquities. What then can we think of the things they wrote of the barbarians? And we know of ancient barbarian history only what they tell us. And what must we think of the antiquities of the Romans, up to the time of the Carthaginian wars, in view of the fact that until then they had been concerned only with agriculture and military affairs, when Thucydides establishes this truth about his own Greeks, who so promptly came forth as philosophers? Unless, perhaps, we are willing to say that the Romans had had a particular privilege from God.

XL

[Socrates originates rational moral philosophy. Plato flourishes in metaphysics. Athens is resplendent with all the arts of the most cultivated humanity. Law of the Twelve Tables. Year of the world 3553, of Rome 303.]

102   At this time there is brought from Athens to Rome the Law of the Twelve Tables, just as uncivil, rude, inhuman, cruel, and savage as it is shown to be in our *Principles of Universal Law* [Op. 2.564–580].

XLI

[Xenophon, carrying the Greek arms into the heart of Persia, is the first to learn of Persian institutions with any certainty. Year of the world 3583, of Rome 333.]

103   Thus St. Jerome observes in his Commentary on Daniel [5.1]. Just as the Greeks had begun under Psammeticus to learn Egyptian institutions by way of commerce (so that Herodotus's more certain accounts of them start from that time [90]), so now, from Xenophon on, they began through the exigencies of war to have more certain acquaintance with those of the Persians. Even Aristotle, who accompanied Alexander the Great into Persia, writes [!] that before that time the Greeks had but told

fables about them, as we have indicated in this Chronological Table. In this way the Greeks began to have certain report of foreign institutions.

XLII
[Publilian Law. Year of the world 3658, of Rome 416.]

104 This law was promulgated in the 416th year of Rome, and contains a most important point of Roman history, for by this law the Roman commonwealth declared that its constitution had been changed from aristocratic to popular. That is why Publilius Philo, who was its author, was called the "people's dictator." This has not been remarked because the language of the law has not been properly understood. We shall later make evident that this was the fact [662ff]. Here it will suffice to give a hypothetical idea of it [415].

105 This law and the subsequent Petelian Law [115], which is of equal importance, were left in obscurity by failure to define the three words "people," "kingdom," and "liberty" [666]. Because of these words it has been commonly but erroneously believed that the Roman people from the time of Romulus had been composed of citizens both noble and plebeian, that the Roman kingdom had been monarchical, and that the liberty instituted by Brutus had been a popular liberty. And these three undefined words have led into error all the critics, historians, political theorists, and jurists, because no present commonwealth could give them any idea of the heroic ones, which were of a most severely aristocratic form and therefore entirely different from those of our time.

106 In an asylum opened in the clearing [564], Romulus founded Rome on the clienteles, or protectorships, under which the fathers of families kept as day laborers in the fields those who had fled to this asylum [561]. These refugees had no privilege of citizenship and thus no share of civil liberty. Since they had taken refuge with the fathers to save their lives, the fathers protected their natural liberty by setting them separately to the cultivation of their several fields. The public domain of the Roman territory must have been made up of these fields, just as Romulus constituted the senate from the fathers themselves.

107 Later, Servius Tullius granted the workers bonitary ownership [266] of the fields that were the property of the fathers and imposed the census [tax] upon them. They were to do their own cultivating under the burden of the census, and with the obligation of serving the fathers in war at their own expense; as in fact the plebeians did serve the patricians under what has hitherto been mistaken for popular liberty. This law of Servius Tullius was the *first* agrarian law of the world [109], and it set up the census as the basic institution of the heroic commonwealths, that is to say of the most ancient aristocracies of all the nations [420, 619ff].

108   Subsequently, Junius Brutus, casting out the Tarquin tyrants, restored the Roman commonwealth to its original form; and by instituting the consuls—as it were, an annual pair of aristocratic kings (as Cicero calls them in his *Laws* [3.2.4]) in place of one king for life—he re-established the liberty of the patricians as against their tyrants, not the liberty of the people as against the patricians [662ff]. But, since the nobles did not keep faith with the plebeians under the agrarian law of Servius Tullius, the plebs brought about the creation of the plebeian tribunes and had them accepted under oath by the nobility. The tribunes were to protect for the people that degree of natural liberty represented by bonitary ownership of the fields. Thus, when the plebeians were wanting to secure civil ownership from the nobles, the plebeian tribunes drove Marcius Coriolanus from Rome because he had said that the plebeians should go and till the soil; that is, since they were not content with the agrarian law of Servius but wanted a fuller and stronger one, they should be reduced again to the day laborers they had been under Romulus. Otherwise [—if this was not his intent—] was it not proud folly for the plebs to disdain agriculture, since we know that even the patricians deemed it honorable work? And would so slight a pretext have occasioned so cruel a war? For Marcius, to avenge his exile, would have brought about the ruin of Rome had it not been for the piteous tears of his mother and his wife which turned him aside from his impious enterprise.

109   In consequence of all this, the nobles proceeding to take back the fields from the plebs after they had cultivated them, and the latter having no civil action for laying claim to them, the plebeian tribunes now demanded the Law of the Twelve Tables (by which, as is demonstrated in the *Principles of Universal Law* [Op. 2.572ff], no other affair than this was settled [422]). By this law the nobles conceded to the plebs the quiritary ownership of the fields [266]. This civil ownership is permitted to foreigners by the natural law of the gentes. And this was the *second* agrarian law of the ancient nations [107].

110   Now when the plebeians saw [on the one hand] that they could not transmit the fields intestate to their kin, because they had no direct heirs, agnates, or gentiles [B4] (to which relations legitimate succession was then confined), since their marriages were not solemnized; and [on the other hand] that they could not even dispose of their fields by testament because they did not have the rights of citizens; they demanded for themselves the *connubium* of the nobles; that is, the right to solemnized marriages (for

this is the meaning of *connubium*). Now the most solemn part of the marriage service was taking the auspices, which only the nobles could do [488, 490]. These auspices, moreover, were the great source of all Roman law, private and public. So, then, the institution of marriage was extended by the fathers to the plebeians. But since marriage is, by the definition of the jurisconsult Modestinus [D. 23.2.1], "the sharing of every divine and human right" (*omnis divini et humani juris communicatio*), and since citizenship itself is nought else, the fathers thereby gave the plebeians the privilege of citizenship [598]. Then, in the course of human desires, the plebeians went on to secure from the fathers the communication of all those institutions of private law which depended upon the auspices: as paternal power, direct heirs, agnates, and gentiles [B4], and, in consequence of these, the further institutions of legitimate succession, the making of testaments, and guardianship [1023]. Then they claimed those institutions of public law which depended likewise upon the auspices, securing the communication first of the *imperium*, by the opening to them of the consulship, and finally of the science of the laws, by the opening to them of priesthood and pontificate.

111   In this way the tribunes of the plebs, by performing the function for which they were created, that of protecting the natural liberty of the plebeians, were gradually led to secure for them the whole range of civil liberty as well. And the census instituted by Servius Tullius—with the subsequent provision that payment should no longer be made to the nobles privately but to the public treasury, so that the treasury might supply to the plebeians the expenses of war—developed naturally from basic institution of aristocratic liberty into basic institution of popular liberty. Further on we shall see the way in which this came about [420, 619ff].

112   By steady steps, the tribunes also progressed in the power of making laws. For the Horatian and Hortensian laws could not grant to the plebs that their plebiscites should be binding upon all the people except in these two particular emergencies. In the first, the plebs had withdrawn to the Aventine in the 304th year of Rome, at which time, as we state here by way of hypothesis and shall later show as a fact, the plebeians were not yet citizens [582–598]. In the second, they withdrew to the Janiculum in the 367th year of Rome, at which time the plebs were still struggling with the nobility for the sharing of the consulate. But on the basis of the two aforesaid laws, the plebs finally reached the point where they could make universal laws [binding on the nobles as well as on themselves]. This gave rise to great agitations and revolts at Rome, so that it became necessary to make Publilius Philo dictator, an office never created save in times of

greatest danger to the commonwealth, such as this was. For it had fallen into such great disorder as to nourish within itself two supreme legislative powers without any distinction of time, scope, or territory, with the result that the commonwealth was on the verge of ruin. Wherefore Philo, to cure the ills of the state, ordained that whatever the plebs enacted by plebiscites in the assembly by tribes (*comitia tributa*) "should be binding on all the Quirites" (*omnes quirites teneret*); that is, should be binding on all the people in the assembly by hundreds (*comitia centuriata*) in which "all the Quirites" (*omnes quirites*) met [624ff]. (For the Romans called themselves Quirites only in public assembly, and Quiris in the singular is never found in common Latin speech.) By this formula Philo meant to signify that laws could not be enacted contrary to the plebiscites. Now the plebs had already been made in all respects equal to the nobles by laws to which the latter had agreed. By this most recent move, to which the nobles could offer no opposition without bringing the commonwealth to ruin, the plebs had become superior to the nobles, for without ratification by the senate the plebs could enact general laws for all the people. The Roman commonwealth had thus naturally become one of popular liberty. Philo accordingly proclaimed it such by this law, and hence was called the people's dictator.

113   In conformity with this change in its nature, he gave the commonwealth two ordinances, which are contained in the other two sections of the Publilian Law. Authorization by the senate had hitherto been ratification by the lords. That is, what the people first decided had afterward to be ratified by the fathers (*deinde patres fierent auctores*) [944]. Thus the electing of consuls and the enacting of laws, as actions taken in the first instance by the people, were but public testimonials of merit and public demands of right. But this dictator ordained that authorization should thenceforth be given by the fathers to the people, now free and sovereign, prior to the deliberations of the assembly (*in incertum comitiorum eventum*) [945]; thus making the people lord of the Roman *imperium*, and the fathers their guardians. If the people wished to enact laws, they were to do so according to the formula presented to them by the senate. If not, they could exercise their sovereign choice and "antiquate" the [proposed] laws; that is, declare they wanted no innovation [945]. Thus all future acts of the senate concerning public affairs would be either instructions given by it to the people or commissions given to it by the people. Finally there remained the census, for, since the treasury had hitherto been the property of the nobles, only nobles had been made censors of it. Since, however, by this law the treasury became the property of the people as a whole, Philo ordered, in the third place, that the censorship, the only magistracy in which the plebs had as yet no share, should also be extended to them.

114 If we read further into the history of Rome in the light of this hypothesis, we shall find by a thousand tests that it gives support and consistency to all the things therein narrated that have hitherto lacked a common foundation and a proper and particular connection among themselves because the three aforesaid words [105] were undefined; wherefore this hypothesis should be received as true. However, if we consider well, this is not so much a hypothesis as a truth meditated in idea which later will be authoritatively shown to be the fact [415]. And—granted Livy's generalization [1.8.5] that the asylums were "an old counsel of founders of cities" (*vetus urbes condentium consilium*), as Romulus founded the city of Rome within the asylum opened in the clearing [17]—this hypothesis gives us also the history of all the other cities of the world in times we have so far despaired of knowing. This then is an instance of an ideal eternal history traversed in time by the histories of all nations [349, 393].

XLIII
[Petelian Law. Year of the world 3661, of Rome 419.]

115 This second law, "on slavery for debt" (*de nexu*), was enacted in the year of Rome 419 (and thus three years after the Publilian Law) by the consuls Caius Poetelius and Lucius Papirius Mugillanus. It contains another point of the greatest importance in [the history of] Roman institutions, for by this law the plebeians were released from the feudal liability of becoming liege vassals of the nobles on account of debts, for which the nobles used to compel the plebeians to work for them, often for life, in their private prisons [612]. But the senate retained the sovereign dominion it had over the lands of the Roman *imperium*, though the *imperium* itself had already passed to the people. And under the provisions of the *senatus consultum* which was called *ultimum*, of last resort, the senate kept this power for itself by force of arms as long as the Roman commonwealth remained free. Thus whenever the people intended to dispose of these lands by the agrarian laws of the Gracchi, the senate armed the consuls, who proscribed as rebels and executed the plebeian tribunes who had been the authors of these laws. This great effect can be brought about only under a system of sovereign fiefs subject to a higher sovereignty [1065f]. This system is confirmed by a passage in one of Cicero's Catilines [1.1.3] where he affirms that Tiberius Gracchus by his agrarian law was destroying the constitution of the commonwealth, and had hence been rightfully put to death by Publius Scipio Nasica on the ground set forth in the formula by which the consul armed the people against the authors of the aforesaid law: "Whoever is for the safety of the commonwealth, let him follow the consul" (*Qui rempublicam salvam velit consulem sequatur*) [Cicero, *Tusculan Disputations* 4.23.51].

XLIV

[War with Tarentum wherein the Latins and the Greeks begin to know each other. Year of the world 3708, of Rome 489.]

116 The reason for this war was the maltreatment accorded by the Tarentines to the Roman ships which landed on their coasts, and likewise to the Roman ambassadors. Their excuse, as phrased by Florus [1.13(18).5], was that "they did not know who the Romans were or whence they came" (*qui essent aut unde venirent ignorabant*). So well acquainted were the first peoples, even when they were not separated by water and were not far apart by land!

XLV

[Second Carthaginian war, with which Livy begins the certain history of Rome, though he professes to be ignorant of three important circumstances. Year of the world 3849, of Rome 552.]

117 Livy professed to write the history of Rome with more certainty from the period of the second Carthaginian war, and promised to describe the most memorable of all wars fought by the Romans [21.1.1; cf.6.1.3]. And because of its incomparable greatness the chronicles he writes of it should have the greater certainty that belongs to things of greater fame. Yet he did not know, and openly admits he did not know, three most important circumstances [21.15,38]. The first, in whose consulship Hannibal, after the capture of Saguntum, had started on his march from Spain to Italy. The second, over which Alps he had come, the Cottian or the Pennine. And the third, what strength he had with him. On this last matter there was in the ancient annals such a wide diversity of opinion that some had written 6,000 cavalry and 20,000 infantry, others 20,000 cavalry and 80,000 infantry.

[Conclusion]

118 It can be seen from our discussion in these Notes that all that has come down to us from the ancient gentile nations for the times covered by this Table is most uncertain. So that in all this we have entered as it were into a no man's land where the rule of law obtains that "the [first] occupant acquires title" (*occupanti conceduntur*). We trust therefore that we shall offend no man's right if we often reason differently and at times in

direct opposition to the opinions which have been held up to now concerning the principles of the humanity of the nations [J1]. By so doing we shall reduce them to scientific principles, by which the facts of certain history may be assigned their first origins, on which they rest and by which they are reconciled. For until now they have seemed to have no common foundation or continuous sequence or coherence among themselves.

[SECTION II]

ELEMENTS

119 In order to give form to the materials hereinbefore set in order in the Chronological Table, we now propose the following axioms, both philosophical and philological, including a few reasonable and proper postulates and some clarified definitions. And just as the blood does in animate bodies, so will these elements course through our Science and animate it in all its reasonings about the common nature of nations.

I

120 Because of the indefinite nature of the human mind, wherever it is lost in ignorance man makes himself the measure of all things.

121 This axiom explains those two common human traits, on the one hand that rumor grows in its course (*fama crescit eundo*), on the other that rumor is deflated by presence [of the thing itself] (*minuit praesentia famam*). In the long course that rumor has run from the beginning of the world, it has been the perennial source of all the exaggerated opinions which have hitherto been held concerning remote antiquities unknown to us, by virtue of that property of the human mind noted by Tacitus in his *Life of Agricola* [30], where he says that the unknown is always magnified (*omne ignotum pro magnifico est*).

II

122 It is another property of the human mind that whenever men can form no idea of distant and unknown things, they judge them by what is familiar and at hand.

123 This axiom points to the inexhaustible source of all the errors about the principles of humanity [J1] that have been adopted by entire nations and by all the scholars. For when the former began to take notice of them and the latter to investigate them, it was on the basis of their own enlightened, cultivated, and magnificent times that they judged the origins of humanity, which must nevertheless by the nature of things have been small, crude, and quite obscure.

124 Under this head come two types of conceit, one of nations and the other of scholars.

III

125 On the conceit of nations, there is a golden saying of Diodorus Siculus [1.9.3]. Every nation, according to him, whether Greek or barbarian, has had the same conceit that it before all other nations invented the comforts of human life and that its remembered history goes back to the very beginning of the world.

126 This axiom disposes at once of the proud claims of the Chaldeans, Scythians, Egyptians, Chinese, to have been the first founders of the humanity of the ancient world. But Flavius Josephus the Jew [A.A. 1.12] purges his nation [of this vain boast] by the magnanimous confession that the Hebrews had lived cut off from all the gentiles. And sacred history assures us that the world is almost young in contrast to the antiquity with which it was credited by the Chaldeans, Scythians, Egyptians, and in our own day by the Chinese. This is a great proof of the truth of sacred history.

IV

127 To this conceit of nations is added that of scholars, who will have it that what they know is as old as the world [K3].

128 This axiom disposes of all the opinions of the scholars concerning the matchless wisdom of the ancients. It convicts of fraud the oracles of Zoroaster the Chaldean, of Anacharsis the Scythian, which have not come down to us, the *Poimander* of Thrice-great Hermes, the *Orphics* (or verses of Orpheus), and the Golden Verses of Pythagoras, as all the more discerning critics agree. It further condemns as impertinent all the mystic meanings with which the Egyptian hieroglyphs are endowed by the scholars, and the philosophical allegories which they have read into the Greek fables.

V

129 To be useful to the human race, philosophy must raise and direct weak and fallen man, not rend his nature or abandon him in his corruption.

130 This axiom dismisses from the school of our Science the Stoics, who seek to mortify the senses, and the Epicureans, who make them the criterion. For both deny providence, the former chaining themselves to fate, the latter abandoning themselves to chance. The latter, moreover, affirm that the human soul dies with the body. Both should be called monastic, or solitary, philosophers. On the other hand [this axiom] admits to our school the political philosophers, and first of all the Platonists, who agree with all the lawgivers on these three main points: that there is divine providence, that human passions should be moderated and made into human virtues, and that human souls are immortal. Thus from this axiom are derived the three principles of this Science [333, 360].

VI

131   Philosophy considers man as he should be and so can be of service to but very few, those who wish to live in the Republic of Plato and not to fall back into the dregs of Romulus.

VII

132   Legislation considers man as he is in order to turn him to good uses in human society. Out of ferocity, avarice, and ambition, the three vices which run throughout the human race, it creates the military, merchant, and governing classes, and thus the strength, riches, and wisdom of commonwealths. Out of these three great vices, which could certainly destroy all mankind on the face of the earth, it makes civil happiness.

133   This axiom proves that there is divine providence and further that it is a divine legislative mind. For out of the passions of men each bent on his private advantage, for the sake of which they would live like wild beasts in the wilderness, it has made the civil institutions by which they may live in human society.

VIII

134   Things do not settle or endure out of their natural state.

135   In view of the fact that the human race, as far back as memory of the world goes, has lived and still lives conformably in society, this axiom alone decides the great dispute still waged by the best philosophers and moral theologians against Carneades the skeptic and Epicurus—a dispute which not even Grotius could set at rest—namely, whether law exists by nature, or whether man is naturally sociable, which comes to the same thing [309].

136   This same axiom, together with VII and its corollary, proves that man has free choice, however weak, to make virtues of his passions; but that he is aided by God, naturally by divine providence and supernaturally by divine grace [310].

IX

137   Men who do not know what is true of things take care to hold fast to what is certain, so that, if they cannot satisfy their intellects by

knowledge (*scienza*), their wills at least may rest on consciousness (*coscienza*) [F1].

X

138 Philosophy contemplates reason, whence comes knowledge of the true; philology observes that of which human choice is author, whence comes consciousness of the certain [163, 325].

139 This axiom by its second part includes among the philologians all the grammarians, historians, critics, who have occupied themselves with the study of the languages and deeds of peoples: both at home, as in their customs and laws, and abroad, as in their wars, peaces, alliances, travels, and commerce.

140 This same axiom shows how the philosophers failed by half in not giving certainty to their reasonings by appeal to the authority of the philologians, and likewise how the latter failed by half in not taking care to give their authority the sanction of truth by appeal to the reasoning of the philosophers. If they had done this they would have been more useful to their commonwealths and they would have anticipated us in conceiving this Science [F1].

XI

141 Human choice, by its nature most uncertain, is made certain and determined by the common sense of men with respect to human needs or utilities, which are the two sources of the natural law of the gentes.

XII

142 Common sense is judgment without reflection, shared by an entire class, an entire people, an entire nation, or the entire human race [D4].

143 This axiom, with the following definition, will provide a new art of criticism concerning the founders of nations, who must have preceded by more than a thousand years the writers with whom criticism has so far been occupied [392].

XIII

144 Uniform ideas originating among entire peoples unknown to each other must have a common ground of truth [D4].

145 This axiom is a great principle which establishes the common sense of the human race as the criterion taught to the nations by divine providence to define what is certain in the natural law of the gentes [321f]. And the nations reach this certainty by recognizing the underlying agree-

ments which, despite variations of detail, obtain among them all in respect of this law. Thence issues the mental dictionary for assigning origins to all the diverse articulated languages. It is by means of this dictionary that the ideal eternal history is conceived, which gives us the histories in time of all nations. The axioms proper to this dictionary and to this history will shortly be proposed [162; 240, 294].

146 This same axiom does away with all the ideas hitherto held concerning the natural law of the gentes, which has been thought to have come out of one first nation and to have been received from it by the others. This error was encouraged by the bad example of the Egyptians and Greeks in vainly boasting that they had spread civilization throughout the world. It was this error that gave rise to the fiction that the Law of the Twelve Tables came to Rome from Greece [284f]. If that had been the case, it would have been a civil law communicated to other peoples by human provision, and not a law which divine providence instituted naturally in all nations along with human customs themselves. On the contrary, as it will be one of our constant labors throughout this book to demonstrate, the natural law of the gentes had separate origins among the several peoples, each in ignorance of the others, and it was only subsequently, as a result of wars, embassies, alliances, and commerce, that it came to be recognized as common to the entire human race [B6, E6, 550].

XIV

147 The nature of institutions is nothing but their coming into being (*nascimento*) at certain times and in certain guises. Whenever the time and guise are thus and so, such and not otherwise are the institutions that come into being.

XV

148 The inseparable properties of institutions must be due to the modification or guise with which they are born. By these properties we may therefore verify that the nature or birth (*natura o nascimento*) was thus and not otherwise [C1].

XVI

149 Vulgar traditions must have had public grounds of truth, by virtue of which they came into being and were preserved by entire peoples over long periods of time.

150 It will be another great labor of this Science to recover these

grounds of truth—truth which, with the passage of years and the changes in languages and customs, has come down to us enveloped in falsehood.

XVII

151 The vulgar tongues should be the most weighty witnesses concerning those ancient customs of the peoples that were in use at the time the languages were formed.

XVIII

152 A language of an ancient nation, which has maintained itself as the dominant tongue until it was fully developed, should be a great witness to the customs of the early days of the world.

153 This axiom assures us that the weightiest philological proofs of the natural law of the gentes (in the understanding of which the Romans were unquestionably pre-eminent) can be drawn from Latin speech. For the same reason scholars of the German language can do the like, since it retains this same property possessed by the ancient Roman language [110].

XIX

154 If the Law of the Twelve Tables was customs of the peoples of Latium which came into use in the age of Saturn and which, though they never ceased changing elsewhere [in Latium], were set down by the Romans in bronze and guarded with religious care by Roman jurisprudence, then this Law is a great witness of the ancient natural law of the gentes of Latium.

155 That this was true in fact, we showed many years ago in our *Principles of Universal Law* [Op. 2.572ff], and the present work will throw further light upon it.

XX

156 If the poems of Homer are civil histories of ancient Greek customs, they will be two great treasure houses of the natural law of the gentes of Greece [904].

157 What is here merely assumed will later be shown to have been the fact [780–904].

XXI

158 The Greek philosophers hastened the natural course which their nation was to take, for when they appeared the Greeks were still in a crude state of barbarism, from which they advanced immediately to one of the highest refinement while at the same time preserving intact their fables both of gods and of heroes. The Romans, on the other hand, proceeding at an even pace in [the development of] their customs, quite lost sight of the history of their gods (so that the age of the gods, as the Egyptians called it, is called by Varro the dark time of the Romans [52]) but preserved in vulgar speech their heroic history, which extends from the time of Romulus to the Publilian and Petelian laws [104–115], and which will be found to be a perpetual historic mythology of the Greek age of heroes.

159   This nature of human civil institutions is confirmed by the example of the French nation. For in the midst of the barbarism of the twelfth century there was opened the famous Parisian school where Peter Lombard, the celebrated master of the Sentences, began to lecture on the subtlest scholastic theology. And, like a Homeric poem, there still lived on the history of Bishop Turpin of Paris, full of all those fables of the heroes of France called paladins which were later to fill so many romances and poems. And because of this premature passage from barbarism to the subtlest sciences, French remained a language of the greatest refinement. So much so, indeed, that of all living languages it seems most to have restored to our times the atticism of the Greeks, and it is the best of all languages for scientific reasoning, as Greek was. Yet French preserves, as Greek did, many diphthongs, which are natural to a barbarous tongue still stiff and inept at combining consonants with vowels [461].

In confirmation of what we have said of both these languages, we may here add an observation in regard to young people at an age when memory is tenacious, imagination vivid, and invention quick. At this age they may profitably occupy themselves with languages and plane geometry, without thereby subduing that acerbity of minds still bound to the body which may be called the barbarism of the intellect. But if they pass on while yet in this immature stage to the highly subtle studies of metaphysical criticism or algebra, they become overfine for life in their way of thinking and are rendered incapable of any great work.

160   But as we further meditated this work we came upon another cause for the effect in question, and this cause is perhaps more apposite. Romulus founded Rome in the midst of other more ancient cities of Latium, and founded it by opening there the asylum which Livy defines generally as "an old counsel of founders of cities" (*vetus urbes condentium consilium*) [17]; for since violence still reigned he naturally established the city of Rome on the same institution on which the oldest cities of the world had been founded [561]. And so it came about, since Roman customs were developing from such beginnings at a time when the vulgar

tongues of Latium were already well advanced, that Roman civil institutions, the like of which the Greeks had set forth in heroic speech, were set forth by the Romans in vulgar speech. Thus ancient Roman history will be found to be a perpetual mythology of the heroic history of the Greeks. And this must be the reason why the Romans were the heroes of the world. For Rome subdued the other cities of Latium, then Italy, and finally the whole world, because heroism was still young among the Romans, whereas among the other peoples of Latium, from whose conquest all the greatness of Rome sprang, it must already have begun to decay.

XXII

161 There must in the nature of human institutions be a mental language common to all nations, which uniformly grasps the substance of things feasible in human social life and expresses it with as many diverse modifications as these same things may have diverse aspects. A proof of this is afforded by proverbs or maxims of vulgar wisdom, in which substantially the same meanings find as many diverse expressions as there are nations ancient and modern [445].

162 This common mental language is proper to our Science, by whose light linguistic scholars will be enabled to construct a mental vocabulary common to all the various articulate languages living and dead [D6, 482]. We gave a particular example of this in the first edition of the *New Science* [Op. 3.387ff]. There we proved that the names of the first family fathers, in a great number of dead and living languages, were given them because of the various properties which they had in the state of the families and in that of the first commonwealths, at the time when the nations were forming their languages. As far as our small erudition will permit, we shall make use of this vocabulary in all the matters we discuss.

163 Of the propositions so far stated, I–IV give us the basis for refuting all opinions hitherto held about the principles of humanity [J1]. The refutations turn on the improbabilities, absurdities, contradictions, and impossibilities of these opinions. Propositions V–XV, which give us the foundations of the true, will serve for considering this world of nations in its eternal idea, by that property of every science, noted by Aristotle, that science has to do with what is universal and eternal (*scientia debet esse de universalibus et aeternis*) [*Metaphysics* 1003a 15; F2; 332]. Propositions XV[I]–XXII will give us the foundations of the certain. By their use we shall be able to see in fact this world of nations which we have studied in idea, following the best ascertained method of philosophizing, that of Francis Bacon, Lord Verulam, but carrying it over from the institutions of nature, on which he composed his book *Cogitata [et] visa,* to the civil institutions of mankind [137f, 359].

164   The propositions set forth above are general and are the basis of our Science throughout; those which follow are particular and provide more specific bases for the various matters it treats of.

XXIII

165   Sacred history is more ancient than all the most ancient profane histories that have come down to us, for it narrates in great detail and over a period of more than eight hundred years the state of nature under the patriarchs; that is, the state of the families, out of which, by general agreement of political theorists, the peoples and cities later arose [F7]. Of this family state profane history has told us nothing or little, and that little quite confused.

166   This axiom proves the truth of sacred history as against the national conceit pointed out to us by Diodorus Siculus [125], for the Hebrews have preserved their memories in great detail from the very beginning of the world.

XXIV

167   The Hebrew religion was founded by the true God on the prohibition of the divination on which all the gentile nations arose [365, 381].

168   This axiom is one of the principal reasons for the division of the entire world of the ancient nations into Hebrews and gentiles [F7].

XXV

169   That the flood was world-wide is proved, not indeed by the philological evidence of Martin Schoock, for it is far too slight, nor by the astrological evidence of Cardinal Pierre d'Ailly, followed by Giovanni Pico della Mirandola. For this latter evidence is too uncertain, indeed quite false, relying as it does on the *Alphonsine Tables,* which were refuted by the Jews and are now refuted by the Christians, who, having rejected the calculations of Eusebius and Bede, now follow those of Philo the Jew [54]. But our demonstration will be drawn from physical histories discerned in the fables [192–195, 380].

XXVI

170   The giants were by nature of enormous build, like those gross wild creatures which travelers report finding at the foot of America, in the country of the so-called Patagones [Big Feet]. Ignoring the vain, abortive,

and false reasons adduced for these creatures by the philosophers, as collected and followed by Chassanion in his *De gigantibus,* we adduce the causes, partly physical and partly moral, observed by Julius Caesar [G. W. 4.1; 6.1] and Cornelius Tacitus [G. 4] in speaking of the gigantic stature of the ancient Germans. In our view, these causes are to be traced to the bestial education of their children [195].

XXVII

171 Greek history, from which we get all we know about the history of all other ancient gentile nations except the Roman, starts with the flood and the giants.

172 Axioms XXVI–XXVII make it evident that the entire original human race was divided into two species: the one of giants, the other of men of normal stature; the former gentiles, the latter Hebrews. Also that this difference can have come about only as the result of the bestial education of the former and the human education of the latter. Hence that the Hebrews had a different origin from that of the gentiles [369–373].

XXVIII

173 Two great remnants of Egyptian antiquity have come down to us. One of them is that the Egyptians reduced all preceding world time to three ages; namely, the age of gods, the age of heroes, and the age of men. The other is that during these three ages three languages had been spoken, corresponding in order to the three aforesaid ages; namely, the hieroglyphic or sacred language, the symbolic or figurative (which is the heroic) language, and the epistolary or vulgar language of men employing conventional signs for communicating the common needs of their life [52, 432ff].

XXIX

174 Homer, whose own language was certainly heroic, in five passages from his two poems [437] mentions a more ancient language and calls it "the language of the gods."

XXX

175 Varro had the diligence to collcet thirty thousand names of gods—for the Greeks counted that many. These were related to as many needs of the physical, moral, economic, or civil life of the earliest times. [Augustine, C.G. 6.2–9; 4.8.]

176 Axioms XXVIII–XXX establish the fact that the world of peoples began everywhere with religion. This will be the first of the three principles of this Science [333ff].

XXXI

177   Wherever a people has grown savage in arms so that human laws have no longer any place among it, the only powerful means of reducing it is religion.

178   This axiom establishes that divine providence initiated the process by which the fierce and violent were brought from their outlaw state to humanity and by which nations were instituted among them. It did so by awaking in them a confused idea of divinity, which they in their ignorance attributed to that to which it did not belong. Thus through the terror of this imagined divinity, they began to put themselves in some order [377ff].

179   This [providential] principle of institutions Thomas Hobbes failed to see among his own "fierce and violent men," because he went afield in search of principles and fell into error with the "chance" of his Epicurus. He thought to enrich Greek philosophy by adding a great part which it certainly had lacked (as George Pasch observes in his *De eruditis huius saeculi inventis*): the study of man in the whole society of the human race [G2]. But the result was as unhappy as the effort was noble. Nor would Hobbes have conceived this project if the Christian religion had not given him the inspiration for it, though what it commands is not merely justice but charity toward all mankind. From this point begins the refutation of the false dictum of Polybius [6.56.10] that if there were philosophers in the world there would be no need of religions. For without religions no commonwealths can be born, and if there were no commonwealths in the world there would be no philosophers in it.

XXXII

180   When men are ignorant of the natural causes producing things, and cannot even explain them by analogy with similar things, they attribute their own nature to them. The vulgar, for example, say the magnet loves the iron.

181   This axiom is a piece of the first [120], namely, that the human mind, because of its indefinite nature, wherever it is lost in ignorance makes itself the rule of the universe in respect of everything it does not know.

XXXIII

182   The physics of the ignorant is a vulgar metaphysics by which they refer the causes of the things they do not know to the will of God without considering the means by which the divine will operates.

XXXIV

183 That is a true property of the human mind which Tacitus points out where he says "minds once cowed are prone to superstition" (*mobiles ad superstitionem perculsae semel mentes*) [A. 1.28]. Once men are seized by a frightful superstition, they refer to it all they imagine, see, or even do or make [379].

XXXV

184 Wonder is the daughter of ignorance; and the greater the object of wonder, the more the wonder grows [375].

XXXVI

185 Imagination is more robust in proportion as reasoning power is weak.

XXXVII

186 The most sublime labor of poetry is to give sense and passion to insensate things; and it is characteristic of children to take inanimate things in their hands and talk to them in play as if they were living persons.

187 This philologico-philosophical axiom proves to us that in the world's childhood men were by nature sublime poets [376].

XXXVIII

188 That is a golden passage in Lactantius Firmianus [*Divine Institutions* 1.15] where he considers the origins of idolatry, saying: "Rude men at first called [them, i.e., the king and his family,] gods either for their wonderful excellence (wonderful it seemed to men still rude and simple), or, as commonly happens, in admiration of present power, or on account of the benefits by which they had been brought to humanity."

XXXIX

189 Curiosity—that inborn property of man, daughter of ignorance and mother of knowledge—when wonder wakens our minds, has the habit, wherever it sees some extraordinary phenomenon of nature, a comet for example, a sundog, or a midday star, of asking straightway what it means.

XL

190 Witches, who are full of frightful superstitions, are also exceedingly savage and cruel. Indeed, if it is necessary for the solemnizing of their witchcraft, they do not shrink from killing and dismembering tender innocent children.

191   Propositions XXVIII–XXXVIII reveal to us the beginnings of divine poetry, or poetic theology. Those from XXXI on give us the beginnings of idolatry; from XXXIX, the beginnings of divination; and XL finally gives us the beginnings of sacrifice in connection with bloodthirsty religions. These sacrifices began among the first crude savage men with vows and offerings of human victims. These, as we learn from Plautus [Amphitryon 4.2.15f?], were by the Latins vulgarly called Saturn's victims, Saturni hostiae. They were the sacrifices to Moloch among the Phoenicians, who passed through fire the children consecrated to that false divinity. Some of these consecrations were preserved in the Law of the Twelve Tables [4.1]. These things give the right sense to the saying, "Fear first created gods in the world" (Primos in orbe deos fecit timor) [Statius, Thebaid 3.661]: false religions were born not of imposture but of credulity. Likewise the unhappy vow and sacrifice that Agamemnon made of his pious daughter Iphigenia—at which Lucretius [1.102] impiously exclaims, "So great were the evils religion could prompt" (Tantum religio potuit suadere malorum)—derive from the counsel of divine providence. For all this was necessary to tame the sons of the cyclopes and reduce them to the humanity of an Aristides, a Socrates, a Laelius, and a Scipio Africanus.

XLI

192   We postulate, and the postulate is reasonable, that for several hundred years the earth, soaked by the water of the universal flood, sent forth no dry exhalations or matter capable of igniting in the air to produce lightning.

XLII

193   Jove hurls his bolts and fells the giants, and every gentile nation had its Jove.

194   This axiom contains the physical history that the fables have preserved for us: that the universal deluge covered the whole earth.

195   This same axiom with its preceding postulate should make it clear to us that for a long period of time the impious races of the three children of Noah, having lapsed into a state of bestiality, went wandering like wild beasts until they were scattered and dispersed through the great forest of the earth, and that with their bestial education giants had sprung up and existed among them at the time when the heavens thundered for the first time after the flood [369ff].

XLIII

196 Every gentile nation had its Hercules, who was the son of Jove; and Varro, the most learned of antiquarians, numbered as many as forty of them [14].

197 This axiom marks the beginning, among the first peoples, of heroism, which was born of the false opinion that the heroes were of divine origin [666ff].

198 This same axiom and the preceding one, giving us so many Joves and then so many Herculeses among the gentile nations, together show us that these nations could not have been founded without religion and could not grow without valor. Moreover, since in their beginnings these nations were forest-bred and shut off from any knowledge of each other, and since uniform ideas, born among peoples unknown to each other, must have a common ground of truth [144], these axioms give us this great principle as well: that the first fables must have contained civil truths, and must therefore have been the histories of the first peoples [D5].

XLIV

199 The first sages of the Greek world were the theological poets, who undoubtedly flourished before the heroic poets, just as Jove was the father of Hercules.

200 This and the two preceding axioms establish that all the gentile nations, inasmuch as they all had their Joves and their Herculeses, were poetic in their beginnings, and that divine poetry was born first among them, and later heroic poetry.

XLV

201 Men are naturally impelled to preserve the memories of the laws and institutions that bind them in their societies.

XLVI

202 All barbarian histories have fabulous beginnings.

203 Axioms XLII–XLVI give us the beginning of our historical mythology.

XLVII

204 The human mind is naturally impelled to take delight in uniformity.

205 This axiom, as applied to the fables, is confirmed by the custom

the vulgar have when creating fables of men famous for this or that, and placed in these or those circumstances, of making the fable fit the character and condition. These fables are ideal truths suited to the merit of those of whom the vulgar tell them; and such falseness to fact as they contain consists simply in failure to give their subjects their due. So that, if we consider the matter well, poetic truth is metaphysical truth, and physical truth which is not in conformity with it should be considered false. Thence springs this important consideration in poetic theory: the true war chief, for example, is the Godfrey that Torquato Tasso imagines; and all the chiefs who do not conform throughout to Godfrey are not true chiefs of war.

XLVIII

206   The nature of children is such that by the ideas and names of the men, women, and things they have known first, they afterward apprehend and name all the men, women, and things that bear any resemblance or relation to the first.

XLIX

207   A truly golden passage is that of Iamblichus in *On the Mysteries of the Egyptians* [1] to the effect that the Egyptians attributed to Thrice-great Hermes all discoveries useful or necessary to human life.

208   This statement, supported by the preceding axiom, will restore to this divine philosopher all the sublime natural theology that he himself read into the mysteries of the Egyptians.

209   Axioms XLVII–XLIX give us the origin of the poetic characters [412–427] that constitute the essence of the fables. The first of the three shows the natural inclination of the vulgar to create them, and to create them appropriately. The second shows that the first men, the children, as it were, of the human race, not being able to form intelligible class concepts of things, had a natural need to creat poetic characters; that is, imaginative class concepts or universals, to which, as to certain models or ideal portraits, to reduce all the particular species which resembled them. Because of the resemblance, the ancient fables could not but be created appropriately. Just so the Egyptians reduced to the genus "civil sage" all their inventions useful or necessary to the human race which are particular effects of civil wisdom, and because they could not abstract the intelligible genus "civil sage," much less the form of the civil wisdom in which these Egyptians were sages, they imaged it forth as Thrice-great Hermes. So far were the Egyptians, at the time when they were enriching the world with

discoveries useful or necessary to the human race, from being philosophers and understanding universals or intelligible class concepts!

210   The last of these three axioms, when added to the other two, is the principle of the true poetic allegories which gave the fables univocal, not analogical, meanings for various particulars comprised under their poetic genera. They were therefore called *diversiloquia*; that is, expressions comprising in one general concept various species of men, deeds, or things [403].

L

211   In children memory is most vigorous, and imagination is therefore excessively vivid, for imagination is nothing but extended or compounded memory [699, 819].

212   This axiom is the principle of the expressiveness of the poetic images that the world formed in its first childhood [34].

LI

213   In every [other] pursuit men without natural aptitude succeed by obstinate study of technique, but he who is not a poet by nature can never become one by art.

214   This axiom shows that, since poetry founded gentile humanity [376ff], from which alone sprang all the arts, the first poets were such by nature [not by art].

LII

215   Children excel in imitation; we observe that they generally amuse themselves by imitating whatever they are able to apprehend.

216   This axiom shows that the world in its infancy was composed of poetic nations, for poetry is nothing but imitation.

217   This axiom will explain the fact that all the arts of the necessary, the useful, the convenient, and even in large part those of human pleasure [241], were invented in the poetic centuries before the philosophers came; for the arts are nothing but imitations of nature, and in a certain way "real" poems [made not of words but of things] [498, 794ff].

LIII

218   Men at first feel without perceiving, then they perceive with a troubled and agitated spirit, finally they reflect with a clear mind.

219   This axiom is the principle of poetic sentences [703f], which are formed by feelings of passion and emotion, whereas philosophic sentences

are formed by reflection and reasoning. The more the latter rise toward universals, the closer they approach the truth; the more the former descend to particulars, the more certain they become [137f].

LIV

220 Whatever appertains to men but is doubtful or obscure, they naturally interpret according to their own natures and the passions and customs springing from them.

221 This axiom is a great canon of our mythology. According to it, the fables originating among the first savage and crude men were very severe, as suited the founding of nations emerging from a fierce bestial freedom. Then, with the long passage of years and change of customs, they lost their original meanings and were altered and obscured in the dissolute and corrupt times [708] [beginning] even before Homer [814f]. Because religion was important to them, the men of Greece, lest the gods should oppose their desires as well as their customs, imputed these customs to the gods, and gave improper, ugly, and obscene meanings to the fables.

LV

222 Here is a golden passage of Eusebius referring to the wisdom of the Egyptians but applicable to that of all the other gentiles: "The first theology of the Egyptians was simply a history interpolated with fables, to which later generations, growing ashamed of them, gradually attached mystical interpretations" [*Preparation for the Gospel* 2. pr.?]. That is what was done, for instance, by Manethos, or Manetho, the high priest of the Egyptians, when he translated all Egyptian history into a sublime natural theology [46].

223 Axioms LIV–LV are two great proofs of our historical mythology [203], and they are at the same time two great whirlwinds to sweep away all belief in the matchless wisdom of the ancients [128], and two great foundations of the truth of the Christian religion, whose sacred history narrates nothing to be ashamed of.

LVI

224 The first authors among the Orientals, Egyptians, Greeks, and Latins, and, in the recourse of barbarism, the first writers in the modern languages of Europe, were poets [464–471].

LVII

225 Mutes make themselves understood by gestures or objects that have natural relations with the ideas they wish to signify [400ff].

226 This axiom is the principle of the hieroglyphs by which all nations spoke in the time of their first barbarism.

227 It is also the principle of the natural speech which Plato (in the *Cratylus* [425D; 438D]) and after him Iamblichus (*On the Mysteries of the Egyptians* [7]) guessed to have been spoken in the world at one time. Their view was shared by the Stoics and by Origen (*Against Celsus* [1.24; 5.45]); but, since it was but a guess, it was opposed by Aristotle (in his *On Interpretation* [16a 20ff]) and by Galen (in his *Doctrines of Hippocrates and Plato* [2.2]). The dispute is discussed by Publius Nigidius in Aulus Gellius [10.4]. This natural speech was succeeded by the poetic locution of images, similes, comparisons, and natural properties [34].

LVIII

228 Mutes utter formless sounds by singing, and stammerers by singing teach their tongues to pronounce.

LIX

229 Men vent great passions by breaking into song, as we observe in the most grief-stricken and the most joyful.

230 From axioms LVIII–LIX it follows that the founders of the gentile nations, having wandered about in the wild state of dumb beasts and being therefore sluggish, were inexpressive save under the impulse of violent passions, and formed their first languages by singing [461].

LX

231 Languages must have begun with monosyllables, as in the present abundance of articulated words into which children are now born they begin with monosyllables in spite of the fact that in them the fibers of the organ necessary to articulate speech are very flexible [454, 462].

LXI

232 Heroic verse is the oldest of all, and spondaic the slowest; and we shall see later that heroic verse was originally spondaic [449].

LXII

233 Iambic verse is the closest to prose, and the iamb is a "swift foot," as Horace puts it [A.P. 252].

234 Axioms LXI–LXII lead us to conjecture that ideas and language accelerated at the same rate.

235 Axioms XLVII–LXII, together with those previously set forth as

principles for all the rest [I–XXII], cover the divisions of poetic theory: namely, fable [205]; custom and its appropriateness [220f]; sentence [219]; locution [227] and its expressiveness [212]; allegory [210]; song [228ff]; and finally verse [232f]. Axioms LVI–LXII show also that among all nations speech in verse preceded speech in prose [34].

LXIII

236 The human mind is naturally inclined by the senses to see itself externally in the body, and only with great difficulty does it come to understand itself by means of reflection.

237 This axiom gives us the universal principle of etymology in all languages: words are carried over from bodies and from the properties of bodies to signify the institutions of the mind and spirit.

LXIV

238 The order of ideas must follow the order of institutions.

LXV

239 This was the order of human institutions: first the forests, after that the huts, then the villages, next the cities, and finally the academies.

240 This axiom is a great principle of etymology, for this sequence of human institutions sets the pattern for the histories of words in the various native languages. Thus we observe in the Latin language that almost the whole corpus of its words had sylvan or rustic origins. For example, *lex*. First it must have meant a collection of acorns. Thence we believe is derived *ilex*, as it were *illex*, the oak (as certainly *aquilex* means collector of waters); for the oak produces the acorns by which the swine are drawn together. *Lex* was next a collection of vegetables, from which the latter were called *legumina*. Later on, at a time when vulgar letters had not yet been invented for writing down the laws, *lex* by a necessity of civil nature must have meant a collection of citizens, or the public parliament; so that the presence of the people was the *lex*, or "law," that solemnized the wills that were made *calatis comitiis*, in the presence of the assembled *comitia*. Finally, collecting letters, and making, as it were, a sheaf of them for each word, was called *legere*, reading.

LXVI

241 Men first feel necessity, then look for utility, next attend to comfort, still later amuse themselves with pleasure [217], thence grow dissolute in luxury, and finally go mad and waste their substance.

LXVII

242 The nature of peoples is first crude, then severe, then benign, then delicate, finally dissolute [916ff].

LXVIII

243 In the human race first appear the huge and grotesque, like the cyclopes; then the proud and magnanimous, like Achilles; then the valorous and just, like Aristides and Scipio Africanus; nearer to us, imposing figures with great semblances of virtue accompanied by great vices, who among the vulgar win a name for true glory, like Alexander and Caesar; still later, the melancholy and reflective, like Tiberius; finally the dissolute and shameless madmen, like Caligula, Nero, and Domitian.

244 This axiom shows that the first sort were necessary in order to make one man obey another in the family-state and prepare him to be law-abiding in the city-state that was to come; the second sort, who naturally did not yield to their peers, were necessary to establish the aristocratic commonwealths on the basis of the families; the third sort, to open the way for popular liberty; the fourth, to bring in the monarchies; the fifth, to establish them; the sixth, to overthrow them.

245 This, with the preceding axioms [LXV–LXVII] gives a part of the principles of the ideal eternal history traversed in time by every nation in its rise, development, maturity, decline, and fall [294, 349, 393].

LXIX

246 Governments must conform to the nature of the men governed.

247 This axiom shows that by the nature of human civil institutions the public school of princes is the morality of the peoples.

LXX

248 Let that be granted which is not repugnant in nature and which we shall later find to be true in fact: that from the nefarious state of the outlaw world some few of the sturdiest first withdrew and established families, with whom and by whom they brought the fields under cultivation [520ff]; and a long while later the many others also withdrew and took refuge on the lands cultivated by these fathers [553ff].

LXXI

249 Native customs, and above all that of natural liberty [290], do not change all at once but by degrees and over a long period of time.

LXXII

250 Since all nations began with the cult of some divinity, in the family-state the fathers must have been the sages in auspicial divinity, the priests who sacrificed to take the auspices or to make sure of their meaning, and the kings who brought the divine laws to their families.

LXXIII

251 It is a vulgar tradition that the first to govern the world were kings.

LXXIV

252 It is another vulgar tradition that those were created the first kings who were the worthiest by nature.

LXXV

253 It is yet another vulgar tradition that the first kings were sages, wherefore Plato [R. 473CD] expressed the vain wish for those ancient times in which philosophers reigned or kings were philosophers.

254 All these axioms show that in the persons of the first fathers there were united wisdom, priesthood, and kingship, and the kingship and priesthood depended on the wisdom, not indeed the esoteric wisdom of philosophers but the vulgar wisdom of lawgivers. And therefore thenceforward in all nations the priests wore crowns.

LXXVI

255 It is a vulgar tradition that the first form of government in the world was monarchical.

LXXVII

256 But axiom LXVII and those that follow it, and in particular the corollary of LXIX [i.e., 244], show us that in the family-state the fathers must have exercised a monarchical power, subject only to God, over both the persons and the property of their children and to a much greater extent over those of the *famuli* who had taken refuge on their lands [257]. So they were the first monarchs of the world, of whom sacred history must be understood to speak when it calls them patriarchs or father-princes. This monarchical right was preserved to them for the entire period of the Roman Republic by the Law of the Twelve Tables [4.2]: "The family father shall have power of life and death over his children" (*Patrifamilias* *ius vitae et necis in liberos esto*); from which it follows that "whatever the son acquires, he acquires for his father" (*Quicquid filius acquirit, patri acquirit*) [D. 41.2.4].

LXXVIII

257 The families cannot have owed that name, in keeping with their origin, to anything but these *famuli* of the fathers in the then state of nature [552, 555].

LXXIX

258 The first *socii*, who are properly companions associated for mutual advantage, cannot be imagined or understood to have existed in the world previous to these fugitives who sought to save their lives by taking refuge with the aforesaid first fathers and who, having been received for their lives, were obliged to sustain them by cultivating the fields of the fathers [555].

259 These were the true *socii* of the heroes. Later they were the plebeians of the heroic cities and finally the provincials of sovereign peoples [559, 1066].

LXXX

260 Men come naturally to the feudal system [*ragione de' benefizi*] wherever they see a possibility of retaining in it or gaining from it a good and great share of utility, for such are the benefits [*benefizi*] which may be hoped for in civil life.

LXXXI

261 It is a mark of the strong not to lose by sloth what they have gained by valor. Rather do they yield, from necessity or for utility, as little as they can and bit by bit [585].

262 From these two axioms spring the perennial sources of fiefs, which are called, with Roman elegance, benefices (*beneficia*) [1063].

LXXXII

263 In all ancient nations we find everywhere clients and clienteles, which are best understood as vassals and fiefs [556f]. Nor can learned writers on feudal law find apter Latin terms [for the latter] than *clientes* and *clientelae*.

264 These last three axioms, with the preceding twelve, beginning with LXX [i.e., LXVIII], reveal to us the principles of the commonwealths, born of a great necessity (which we shall later [582ff] determine) imposed upon the family fathers by the *famuli*; a necessity such that the commonwealths naturally took the aristocratic form. For the fathers united themselves in orders to resist the *famuli* who had rebelled against them; and, once thus united, to satisfy these *famuli* and reduce them to obedience, they conceded to them a sort of rustic fiefs. The fathers in turn found their own sovereign family powers (which can only be understood on the analogy of noble fiefs) subjected to the sovereign civil authority of the ruling orders [in which they were now united]. The chiefs of the orders were called kings; it was their function, as the most courageous, to lead the fathers in [quelling] the revolts of the *famuli*. If such an origin of cities (which later we find to be the fact) were offered as a hypothesis, it would command acceptance by its naturalness and simplicity and for the infinite number of civil effects which depend upon it as their proper cause. In no other way can we understand how civil power emerged from family power, and the public patrimony from private patrimonies, or how the commonwealths had their elements prepared in the form of an order of few to command and a multitude of plebeians to obey them. These are the two parts which make up the subject matter of politics. It will later be shown that civil states could not thus have been formed from families containing children only [and not *famuli*] [553ff].

LXXXIII

265 This law concerning the fields is established as the first agrarian law of the world [107], and it would be hard to imagine or conceive one more restricted in nature.

266 This agrarian law distinguished the three types of ownership [or domain (*dominium*)] which can obtain in civil nature, attached to three classes of persons: the bonitary, to the plebeians; the quiritary, maintained by arms and consequently noble, to the fathers; and the eminent, to the order itself, which is the Seigniory, or sovereign power, in aristocratic commonwealths [viii, 25].

LXXXIV

267 There is a golden passage in Aristotle's *Politics* [1285b 4ff,20ff] where, in his classification of commonwealths, he includes the heroic kingdoms in which the kings administered the laws at home, conducted wars abroad, and were heads of the state religion.

268 This axiom fits exactly the two heroic kingdoms of Theseus and Romulus, as we may see of the former in Plutarch's *Life* of him, and of the latter in Roman history; supplementing Greek history with Roman, where Tullus Hostilius administers the law in the accusation against Horatius [500]. And the Roman kings were kings also of sacred institutions under the name of *reges sacrorum;* so that when the kings were driven from Rome, for the sake of certainty in the divine ceremonies an officer was created to be called *rex sacrorum,* who was the head of the *fetiales,* or heralds.

LXXXV

269 There is another golden passage in the *Politics* [1268b 39f; 1269a 11f; 1324b 4ff?] where Aristotle states that the ancient commonwealths had no laws to punish private offenses or to right private wrongs, and he says that such are the mores of barbarous peoples, for peoples are in their origins barbarous precisely because they are not yet tamed by laws.

270 This axiom shows the necessity of duels and reprisals in barbarous times because in such times judicial laws are lacking [959–964].

LXXXVI

271 Golden too is that passage in the *Politics* [1310a 9] where Aristotle says that in the ancient commonwealths the nobles swore to be eternal enemies of the plebs.

272 This axiom explains the cause of the haughty, avaricious, and cruel practices of the nobles toward the plebeians, which we see clearly portrayed in Roman history. For, within the bounds of what has hitherto been mistaken for popular liberty, for a long time they compelled the plebeians at the latter's expense to serve them in war, and drowned them in a sea of usury. Then, as the wretched plebeians could not meet their claims, they confined them for life in private prisons to make them pay off their debts by work and toil, and tyrannically beat them with rods on their bare shoulders as if they were the most abject slaves [668].

LXXXVII

273 The aristocratic commonwealths are most cautious about going to war lest they make warriors of the multitude of plebeians [1025].

274 This axiom is the principle of the justice of the Roman arms down to the Punic Wars.

LXXXVIII

275 The aristocratic commonwealths keep the wealth within the order of the nobility, for wealth adds to the power of this order.

276 This axiom is the principle of Roman clemency in victory; for they deprived the vanquished only of their arms, and left them in bonitary ownership of everything [else they had], subject to a tolerable tribute. Here too is the reason why the [Roman] fathers constantly resisted the agrarian laws of the Gracchi, because they did not wish to enrich the plebs.

LXXXIX

277 Honor is the noblest stimulus to military valor.

XC

278 Peoples are likely to conduct themselves heroically in war if in peace they compete among themselves for honors, some to retain them, others to win the merit of attaining them.

279 This axiom is a principle of Roman heroism from the time of the expulsion of the tyrants down to the Punic Wars. Within this period the nobles naturally dedicated themselves to the safeguarding of their country, by which means they kept all civil honors safe within their own order, and the plebs carried out the most noteworthy enterprises to show that they were worthy of the honors held by the nobles.

XCI

280 The contests waged by the orders in the cities for equality of rights are the most powerful means of making the commonwealths great.

281 This is another principle of Roman heroism, implemented by three public virtues: the magnanimity of the plebs in wanting to share the civil rights and laws of the fathers; the strength of the fathers in keeping those rights within their own order; and the wisdom of the jurisconsults in interpreting the laws and extending their utility little by little as new cases demanded adjudication. These are the three proper reasons for the distinction which Roman law attained in the world [999ff].

282 All these axioms, beginning with LXXXIV, set ancient Roman history forth in its proper aspect; the following three serve in part the same purpose.

XCII

283 The weak want laws; the powerful withhold them; the ambitious, to win a following, advocate them; princes, to equalize the strong with the weak, protect them [952f].

284 This axiom, by its first and second clauses, is the torch of the heroic contests in the aristocratic commonwealths, in which the nobles

want to keep the laws a secret monopoly of their order, so that they may depend on their choice and that they may administer them with a royal hand. These are the three causes adduced by Pomponius the jurisconsult where he relates that the Roman people desire the Law of the Twelve Tables, complaining against the burdensomeness of "secret, uncertain law and regal power" (*ius latens, incertum et manus regia*) [D. 1.2.2.1,3,6]. And it is the cause of the reluctance of the fathers to give [these Tables] to the people, insisting that "the customs of the fathers must be preserved" (*mores patrios servandos*) and "the laws must not be published" (*leges ferri non oportere*), as Dionysius of Halicarnassus states [10.3–4]. He was better informed on Roman institutions than Livy, for he wrote of them under the guidance of Marcus Terentius Varro, who was acclaimed "the most learned of the Romans." On this particular matter he is diametrically opposed to Livy [3.31.8!], who in his account of it says that the nobles (to use his words) "did not spurn the petitions of the plebs" (*desideria plebis non aspernari*). Because of this and other greater contradictions observed in our *Principles of Universal Law* [Op. 2.564–580], there being such opposition between the first authors who wrote of this fable almost five hundred years afterwards, it will be better not to believe either of the two. The more so since in the same period it was believed neither by Varro himself, who in his great work [*The Antiquities*] *of Divine and Human Institutions*, gave purely Latin origins to all the divine and human institutions of the Romans [52]; nor by Cicero, who [in *The Making of an Orator* 1.44.197] has the orator Marcus [i.e., Lucius Licinius] Crassus say in the presence of Quintus Mucius Scaevola, the prince of jurisconsults of his day, that the wisdom of the decemvirs surpassed by a great deal that of Draco and Solon, who gave laws to the Athenians, and that of Lycurgus who gave them to the Spartans: which is as much as to say that the Laws of the Twelve Tables did not come to Rome from Athens or Sparta. Here we believe we are getting at the truth. In Cicero's day the fable was too generally accepted among scholars, born as it was of the conceit of the learned in giving wisest origins to the wisdom they profess. This is the point of the words spoken by Crassus himself: "Though all of you grumble, I shall say what I think" (*Fremant omnes, dicam quod sentio*). Cicero's reason, therefore, for having Quintus Mucius present on that first day only, was to remove any objection to his having an orator speak of the history of Roman law, the field of knowledge proper to the jurisconsults. (These were two distinct professions at that time.) For if Crassus had said anything false on the subject, Mucius would certainly have reproved him for it, as, according to Pomponius, he reproved Servius Sulpicius (who is present at this same discussion), saying to him that "it was a disgrace for a nobleman not to know the law which was his profession" (*turpe esse patricio viro ius, in quo versaretur, ignorare*) [D. 1.2.2.43].

285   But, more than Cicero and Varro, Polybius gives us an un-answerable reason for not believing either Dionysius or Livy. And Polybius without doubt knew more of politics than these two and lived some two hundred years nearer the age of the decemvirs than they did. He sets himself (in the sixth book and the fourth and many following sections in the edition of Jakob Gronov [6.4–18,43–58]) to examine carefully the constitutions of the most famous free commonwealths of his time, and he observes that the Roman constitution is quite different from that of Athens or Sparta. He finds it to differ from that of Athens even more than from that of Sparta, though those who compare Attic with Roman law will have it that it was from Athens rather than from Sparta that the laws came to order the popular liberty already founded by Brutus. But Polybius observes, on the other hand, a great similarity between the Roman and the Carthaginian constitutions. Yet no one has ever dreamed that the freedom of the latter was ordered by the laws of Greece; indeed, so far is this from being true that there was a law in Carthage expressly forbidding the Carthaginians to learn Greek. And how is it that such a learned writer on commonwealths does not investigate the reason of this difference and does not raise on this point the very natural and obvious question: How can the Roman and Athenian commonwealths be different and yet ordered by the same laws, and the Roman and Carthaginian commonwealths be similar but ordered by different laws? To absolve him of so flagrant an oversight, we are compelled to say that in the time of Polybius there had not yet been born at Rome this fable that the Greek laws had been brought there from Athens to order free popular government.

286   This same axiom, by its third clause, opens the way for the ambitious in the popular commonwealths to make themselves monarchs by seconding a natural desire of the plebs, who, not understanding universals, want a law for every particular case. Thus Sulla, the head of the party of the nobles, when he had defeated Marius, the head of the party of the plebs, and was reorganizing the popular constitution with an aristocratic ad-ministration [1084], remedied the multitude of laws by the *quaestiones perpetuae* [a permanent tribunal for criminal investigation].

287   And this same axiom, by its last clause, is the hidden reason why, beginning with Augustus, the Roman emperors made innumerable laws for private cases, and why the sovereigns and powers all over Europe received

into their kingdoms and free commonwealths the corpus of Roman civil law and that of canon law [1001f].

XCIII

288 Since the door to honors in the popular commonwealths is wide open by law to the greedy multitude which is in command, in times of peace nothing remains but to struggle for power, not by law but by arms, and use the power to make laws with a view to increase of wealth. Such were the agrarian laws of the Gracchi at Rome. The result is civil wars at home and unjust wars abroad at the same time.

289 In this axiom Roman heroism is confirmed by contrast for the entire period before the Gracchi.

XCIV

290 Natural liberty is fiercer in proportion as property attaches more closely to the persons of its owners; and civil servitude is clapped on with goods of fortune not essential to life.

291 The first part of this axiom is another principle of the natural heroism of the first peoples [666ff]; the second part is the natural principle of monarchies [1007f].

XCV

292 At first men desire to be free of subjection and attain equality; witness the plebs in the aristocratic commonwealths, which finally turn popular. Then they attempt to surpass their equals; witness the plebs in the popular commonwealths, later corrupted into commonwealths of the powerful. Finally they wish to put themselves above the laws; witness the anarchies, or unlimited popular commonwealths, than which there is no greater tyranny, for in them there are as many tyrants as there are bold and dissolute men in the cities. At this juncture the plebs, warned by the ills they suffer, and casting about for a remedy, seek shelter under monarchies. This is the natural royal law [1007f] by which Tacitus [A. 1.1] legitimizes the Roman monarchy under Augustus, "who, when the world was wearied by civil strife, subjected it to empire under the title of Prince" (*qui cuncta, bellis civilibus fessa, nomine "principis" sub imperium accepit*).

XCVI

293 When the first cities were established on the basis of the families, the nobles, by reason of their native lawless liberty, would not tolerate

checks and burdens; witness the aristocratic commonwealths in which the nobles are lords. Later they are forced by the plebs, greatly increased in numbers and trained in war, to submit to laws and burdens equally with their plebeians; witness the nobles in the popular commonwealths. Finally, in order to preserve their comfortable existence, they are naturally inclined to accept the supremacy of one ruler; witness the nobles under the monarchies [582ff, 925ff, 1008].

294   These two axioms, with the others preceding, from LXVI on, are the principles of the ideal eternal history above referred to [145, 245].

XCVII

295   Let it be granted, as a postulate not repugnant to reason, that after the flood men lived first on the mountains, somewhat later came down to the plains, and finally after long ages dared to approach the shores of the sea.

XCVIII

296   In Strabo [13.1.25] there is a golden passage of Plato [L.3.677–684] saying that, after the local Ogygian and Deucalionian floods, men dwelt in caves in the mountains; and he identifies these first men with the cyclopes, in whom elsewhere [in the same passage] he recognizes the first family fathers of the world. Later they dwelt on the mountainsides, and he sees them represented by Dardanus, the builder of Pergamum, which later became the citadel of Troy. Finally they came down to the plains; this he sees represented by Ilus, by whom Troy was moved onto the plain near the sea, and from whom it took the name of Ilium.

XCIX

297   It is also an ancient tradition that Tyre was founded first inland and later was moved onto the coast of the Phoenician sea; as it is certain history that it was transported from the shore onto a close-lying island, from which Alexander the Great reattached it to the mainland [by a causeway].

298   These two axioms and the preceding postulate [295–297] show us that the inland nations were founded first and later the maritime. And they give us a great argument to prove the antiquity of the Hebrew people, which was founded by Noah in Mesopotamia, the country farthest inland of the first habitable world; so it must have been the most ancient of all nations. And this is confirmed by the fact that the first monarchy was

founded there, that of the Assyrians over the Chaldean people, from whom came the first wise men of the world, their prince being Zoroaster.

C

299   Only by extreme necessities of life are men led to abandon their own lands, which are naturally dear to those native to them. Nor do they leave them temporarily, except from greed to get rich by trade, or from anxiety to keep what they have acquired.

300   This axiom is the principle of the migrations of peoples. It is an induction from the heroic maritime colonies, the inundations of the barbarians (of which alone Wolfgang Latius wrote), the latest known Roman colonies [595], and the colonies of Europeans in the Indies.

301   And this same axiom shows us that the lost races of the three sons of Noah must be supposed to have gone off into bestial wandering, fleeing from beasts (of which the great forest of the earth must have held an unhappy abundance), pursuing the shy and indocile women (for in such a savage state they must have been extremely indocile and shy), and then later seeking pastureland and water, in order to account for their being scattered over the whole earth by the time when the heavens first thundered after the flood. It was thus that every gentile nation began with its own Jove. For if these lost races had persisted in humanity as the people of God did, they would, like the latter, have remained in Asia [F7]. For both because of the vastness of that great part of the world and because of the paucity of men in those days, there was no compelling reason for their abandoning it, since it is not a natural custom to abandon one's native land through caprice.

CI

302   The Phoenicians were the first navigators of the ancient world [305].

CII

303   Nations in their barbarous state are impenetrable; they must be either broken into from outside by war or voluntarily opened to strangers for the advantages of trade. Thus Psammeticus opened Egypt to the Ionian and Carian Greeks, whose renown for maritime traffic must have been second to that of the Phoenicians. So great was their wealth that the temple of Samian Juno was founded in Ionia, and the mausoleum of Artemisia was built in Caria; and these were two of the seven wonders of the world. The glory of this trade was inherited by the Rhodians; in the mouth of their port they had erected the great Colossus of the Sun, which was also counted among the above-mentioned wonders. So too the Chinese, with a view to the advantages of trade, have recently opened their country to us Europeans.

304   These three axioms give us the principle of a new etymologicon for words of certainly foreign origin, different from that mentioned above [240] for native words. It can also give us the history of nations carried one after another into foreign lands by colonization. Thus Naples was first called Sirena (siren), a Syriac word; which is evidence that the Syrians, that is, the Phoenicians, had been the first to establish a colony there, for commercial purposes. Later it was called Parthenope, in heroic Greek, and finally Neapolis, in vulgar Greek; names which prove that the Greeks had afterward settled there to establish trading posts. From this succession there was sure to emerge a mixed language of Phoenician and Greek, in which it is said that the emperor Tiberius took greater pleasure than in pure Greek. Thus also on the Gulf of Tarentum there was a Syrian colony called Siris, whose inhabitants were called Sirites. It was later called by the Greeks Polieion, whence the appellation Polias was given to Minerva, who had a temple there.

305   Axiom CII, moreover, gives a scientific foundation to the thesis of Giambullari that the Etruscan language is of Syriac origin. Such a language could have come only from the most ancient Phoenicians, who, by the axiom above laid down [302], were the first navigators of the ancient world. For later this glory belonged to the Carian and Ionian Greeks, and finally to the Rhodians.

CIII

306   The postulate must needs be granted that on the shore of Latium some Greek colony had been set up, which, after conquest and destruction by the Romans, remained buried in the darkness of antiquity [763, 770ff].

307   If this is not granted, anyone who reflects systematically upon antiquities must be baffled by Roman history when it speaks of Hercules and Evander, Arcadians and Phrygians, within the boundaries of Latium, and of Servius Tullius as a Greek, Tarquinius Priscus as son of Demaratus the Corinthian, and Aeneas as the founder of the Roman people [761–773]. Tacitus [A. 11.14] certainly speaks of the resemblance between Roman and Greek letters [440ff]; yet at the time of Servius Tullius, in the opinion of Livy, the Romans never even heard of the famous name of Pythagoras, who was teaching in his most celebrated school at Croton [93], and they did not make the acquaintance of the Greeks in Italy until the occasion of

the war with Tarentum, which led to the later war with Pyrrhus and the Greeks across the sea [116].

CIV

308   The remark of Dio Cassius [i.e., Dio Chrysostom: *Discourse* 76] is worthy of consideration, that custom is like a king and law like a tyrant; which we must understand as referring to reasonable custom and to law not animated by natural reason.

309   This axiom decides by implication the great dispute "whether law resides in nature or in the opinion of men," which comes to the same thing as that propounded in the corollary of axiom VIII [135], "whether man is naturally sociable." In the first place, the natural law of the gentes was instituted by custom (which Dio says commands us by pleasure like a king) and not by law (which Dio says commands us by force like a tyrant). For it began in human customs springing from the common nature of nations (which is the adequate subject of our Science) and it preserves human society. Moreover, there is nothing more natural (for there is nothing more pleasant) than observing natural customs. For all these reasons, human nature, in which such customs have had their origin, is sociable [E4-5].

310   This axiom, with VIII and its corollary [135], shows that man is not unjust by nature in the absolute sense, but by nature fallen and weak. Consequently, it demonstrates the first principle of the Christian religion, which is Adam before the fall, in the ideal perfection in which he must have been created by God. And therefore it demonstrates the Catholic principles of grace: that it operates in man when his condition is one not of negation but of privation of good works, and hence of a potentiality for them which is ineffectual; that it gives effect to this potentiality; and that it therefore cannot act without the principle of free choice, which God aids naturally by His providence [136], with regard to which the Christian religion is in accord with all others. This is what Grotius, Selden, and Pufendorf should have founded their systems upon before everything else, in agreement with the Roman jurisconsults who define the natural law of the gentes as having been instituted by divine providence [342].

CV

311   The natural law of the gentes is coeval with the customs of the nations, conforming one with another in virtue of a common human sense [142, 145], without any reflection and without one nation following the example of another.

312   This axiom, with the saying of Dio quoted in the preceding

axiom [308f], establishes that providence, being sovereign over the affairs of men, is the institutor of the natural law of the gentes [341ff].

313   This same axiom establishes the difference between the natural law of the Hebrews [396], the natural law of the gentes, and the natural law of the philosophers. For besides the ordinary help from providence which was all that the gentiles had, the Hebrews had extraordinary help from the true God, which was their reason for dividing the whole world of nations into Hebrews and gentiles [F5, F7]. And the philosophers give a more perfect form to natural law by reason than the gentiles do by custom, for the philosophers did not appear until some two thousand years after the gentile nations were founded [E8]. On account of their failure to observe these differences between the three [natural laws], the three systems of Grotius, Selden, and Pufendorf must fall.

CVI

314   Doctrines must take their beginning from that of the matters of which they treat [A4].

315   This axiom, placed here for [its application to] the particular matter of the natural law of the gentes, is universally used in all the matters which are herein discussed. It might have been laid down among the general axioms [I–XXII]; but it has been placed here because in this more than any other particular matter its truth and the importance of using it are apparent.

CVII

316   The [first] gentes began before the cities; they were called by the Latins the greater gentes or ancient noble houses, like those of the Roman fathers of whom Romulus constituted the senate and, with the senate, the city of Rome. On the other hand, the new noble houses founded after the cities were called the lesser gentes; those, for example, with whose fathers Junius Brutus, after the expulsion of the kings, replenished the senate when it had been depleted by the deaths of the senators executed by order of Tarquinius Superbus [B2, 631].

CVIII

317   There was a corresponding twofold division of the gods [392, 734]. First, there were those of the greater gentes; that is, gods who were consecrated by the families before the time of the cities. Among the Greeks and Latins these were certainly twelve [642], and among the Greeks their number was so well known that they were called simply "the twelve."

These gods are brought confusedly together in a Latin distich quoted in our *Principles of Universal Law* [Op. 2.413]. Here, however, in Book Two, following a natural theogony, or generation of the gods, framed naturally in the minds of the Greeks, they will be set forth in this order: Jove [502], Juno [511]; Diana [528], Apollo [533]; Vulcan, Saturn, Vesta [549]; Mars, Venus [562]; Minerva [589], Mercury [604]; Neptune [634].) Secondly, there were the gods of the lesser gentes; that is to say, those consecrated later by the peoples; for example Romulus, whom after his death the Roman people called the god Quirinus.

318   By these three axioms the three systems of Grotius, Selden, and Pufendorf are found wanting in their beginnings. For they begin with nations reciprocally related in the society of the entire human race; whereas, among all the first nations, as we shall show, the race began in the time of the families, under the gods of the so-called greater gentes [502–661].

CIX

319   Men of limited ideas take for law what the words expressly say [939].

CX

320   Golden is the definition which Ulpian [?] assigns to civil equity: "a kind of probable judgment, not naturally known to all men" (as natural equity is [951]) "but to those few who, being eminently endowed with prudence, experience, or learning, have come to know what things are necessary for the conservation of human society" [*probabilis quaedam ratio, non omnibus hominibus naturaliter cognita, sed paucis tantum, qui, prudentia, usu, doctrina praediti, didicerunt quae ad societatis humanae conservationem sunt necessaria*] [949]. This is what is nowadays called "reason of state."

CXI

321   The certain in the laws is an obscurity of judgment backed only by authority, so that we find them harsh in application, yet are obliged to apply them just because they are certain. In good Latin *certum* means particularized, or, as the schools say, individuated; so that, in overelegant Latin, *certum* and *commune*, the certain and the common, are opposed to each other [viii, D1, F1].

322   Axiom CIX and the two following definitions [320f] constitute the principle of strict law [999ff]. Its rule is civil equity, by whose certainty,

that is to say by the determinate particularity of whose words, the barbarians, [men] of particular [not universal] ideas, are naturally satisfied, and such is the law they think is their due. So that what Ulpian says in such cases, "The law is harsh, but so it is written" (*Lex dura est, sed scripta est*) [D. 40.9.12.1], may be put in finer Latin and with greater legal elegance, "The law is harsh, but it is certain" (*Lex dura est, sed certa est*).

CXII

323 Intelligent men take for law whatever impartial utility dictates in each case.

CXIII

324 The true in the laws is a certain light and splendor with which natural reason illuminates them; so that jurisconsults are often in the habit of saying *verum est* for *aequum est*.

325 This definition and CXI [321] are particular propositions whose purpose is to apply to the particular matter of the natural law of the gentes the two general definitions [137f] which treat of the true and the certain in general with a view to conclusions in all the matters that are herein treated.

CXIV

326 The natural equity of fully developed human reason [C7, 924] is a practice of wisdom in affairs of utility, since wisdom in its broad sense is nothing but the science of making such use of things as their nature dictates [364].

327 Axiom CXII and the two following definitions [324, 326] constitute the principle of mild law [940]. Its rule is the natural equity which is connatural with civilized nations. This is the public school from which, as we shall show, the philosophers emerged [1040ff].

328 Propositions CIX–CXIV establish that the natural law of the gentes was instituted by providence [312]. In order that the nations might be preserved, and since they had to live for centuries incapable of truth and natural equity (the latter of which the philosophers later clarified), providence permitted them to cleave to certainty and civil equity, which guards scrupulously the words of decrees and laws, and to be led by the words to observe them generally, even in cases where they proved harsh [321f].

329 Now the fact that [Grotius, Selden, and Pufendorf], the three princes of the doctrine of the natural law of the gentes [394], knew nothing of these six propositions, caused all three of them to err in concert in establishing their systems. For they believed that natural equity in its

perfect form had been understood by the gentile nations from their first beginnings; they did not reflect that it took some two thousand years for philosophers to appear in any of them; and they took no account of the particular assistance which a single people received from the true God [F7, 310, 313, 318].

[SECTION III]

PRINCIPLES [I·1–3]

330 Now, in order to make trial whether the propositions hitherto enumerated as elements of this Science can give form to the materials prepared in the Chronological Table at the beginning, we beg the reader to consider what has hitherto been written concerning the principles of any subject in the whole of gentile knowledge, human and divine. Let him then see if it is inconsistent with the above propositions, whether with all or some or one. For inconsistency with one of them would amount to inconsistency with all, since each accords with all. Certainly on making such a comparison he will perceive that all that has so far been written is a tissue of confused memories, of the fancies of a disordered imagination; that none of it is begotten of intelligence, which has been rendered useless by the two conceits enumerated in the Axioms [125, 127]. For on the one hand the conceit of the nations, each believing itself to have been the first in the world, leaves us no hope of getting the principles of our Science from the philologians. And on the other hand the conceit of the scholars, who will have it that what they know must have been eminently understood from the beginning of the world, makes us despair of getting them from the philosophers. So, for purposes of this inquiry, we must reckon as if there were no books in the world.

331 But in the night of thick darkness enveloping the earliest antiquity, so remote from ourselves, there shines the eternal and never failing light of a truth beyond all question: that the world of civil society has certainly been made by men, and that its principles are therefore to be found within the modifications of our own human mind. Whoever reflects on this cannot but marvel that the philosophers should have bent all their energies to the study of the world of nature, which, since God made it, He alone knows; and that they should have neglected the study of the world of nations, or civil world [B8], which, since men had made it, men could come to know [F2–3]. This aberration was a consequence of that infirmity of the human mind by which, immersed and buried in the body, it

naturally inclines to take notice of bodily things, and finds the effort to attend to itself too laborious; just as the bodily eye sees all objects outside itself but needs a mirror to see itself [236].

332 Now since this world of nations has been made by men, let us see in what institutions all men agree and always have agreed. For these institutions will be able to give us the universal and eternal principles (such as every science must have [163]) on which all nations were founded and still preserve themselves [I·2].

333 We observe that all nations, barbarous as well as civilized, though separately founded because remote from each other in time and space, keep these three human customs: all have some religion, all contract solemn marriages, all bury their dead. And in no nation, however savage and crude, are any human actions performed with more elaborate ceremonies and more sacred solemnity than the rites of religion, marriage, and burial. For, by the axiom that "uniform ideas, born among peoples unknown to each other, must have a common ground of truth" [144], it must have been dictated to all nations that from these three institutions humanity began among them all, and therefore they must be most devoutly guarded by them all, so that the world should not again become a bestial wilderness. For this reason we have taken these three eternal and universal customs as three first principles of this Science [D5].

334 Let not our first principle be accused of falsehood by the modern travelers who narrate that peoples of Brazil, South Africa, and other nations of the New World live in society without any knowledge of God, as Antoine Arnauld believes to be the case also of the inhabitants of the islands called Antilles. Persuaded perhaps by them, Bayle affirms in his treatise on comets [*Pensées diverses* (1683) §§ 161, 172] that peoples can live in justice without the light of God. This is a bolder statement than Polybius ventured in the dictum for which he has been acclaimed, that if there were philosophers in the world, living in justice by force of reason and not of laws, there would be no need in the world of religions [179]. These are travelers' tales, to promote the sale of their books by the narration of portents. Certainly Andreas Rüdiger in his *Physics*, pretentiously entitled *divine* [*Physica divina*] and purporting to show the only middle path between atheism and superstition, is gravely reproved for this opinion by the censors of the University of Geneva. They charge that "he states it with too much assurance," which is the same as saying with not a little boldness. (Yet in the Republic of Geneva, as being free and popular, there would be considerable freedom in writing.) For all nations believe in a provident divinity; yet through all the length of years and all the breadth

of this civil world it has been possible to find only four primary religions. The first is that of the Hebrews, whence came that of the Christians, both believing in the divinity of an infinite free mind. The third is that of the gentiles, who believe in the divinity of a plurality of gods, each imagined as composed of body and of free mind. Hence, when they wish to signify the divinity that rules and preserves the world, they speak of *deos immortales*. The fourth and last is that of the Mohammedans, who believe in the divinity of one god, an infinite free mind in an infinite body, for they look forward to pleasures of the senses as rewards in the other life.

335   No nation has believed in a god all body or in a god all mind but not free. And so neither the Epicureans, who attribute to God body alone, and chance together with body, nor the Stoics, who (in this respect the Spinozists of their day) make God an infinite mind, subject to fate, in an infinite body, could reason of commonwealths or laws; and Benedict Spinoza speaks of the commonwealth as if it were a society of hucksters. Cicero [L. 1.7.21] was indeed right when he told the Epicurean Atticus that he could not discuss laws with him unless he first granted the existence of divine providence. Such is the compatibility of these two sects, the Stoic and the Epicurean, with Roman jurisprudence, which takes divine providence for its first principle [979]!

336   In the second place, the opinion that the sexual unions which certainly take place between free men and free women without solemn matrimony are free of natural wickedness [i.e., do not offend the law of nature], all the nations of the world have branded as false by the human customs with which they all religiously celebrate marriages, thereby determining that this sin is bestial, though in venial degree. And for this reason: such parents, since they are held together by no necessary bond of law, will proceed to cast off their natural children. Since their parents may separate at any time, the children, abandoned by both, must lie exposed to be devoured by dogs. If humanity, public or private, does not bring them up, they will have to grow up with no one to teach them religion, language, or any other human custom. So that, as for them, they are bound to cause this world of nations, enriched and adorned by so many fine arts of humanity, to revert to the great ancient forest through which in their nefarious feral wanderings once roamed the foul beasts of Orpheus, among whom bestial venery was practiced by sons with mothers and by fathers with daughters. This [incest] is the infamous *nefas* of the outlaw world, which Socrates [in Xenophon's *Memorabilia* 4.4.19–23] by rather inappropriate physical reasons tried to prove was forbidden by nature, whereas it is human nature that forbids it; for such relationships are abhorred naturally by all nations, nor

were they ever practiced by any save in their last stage of corruption, as among the Persians.

337 Finally [to realize] what a great principle of humanity burial is, imagine a feral state in which human bodies remain unburied on the surface of the earth as food for crows and dogs. Certainly this bestial custom will be accompanied by uncultivated fields and uninhabited cities. Men will go about like swine eating the acorns found amidst the putrefaction of their dead. And so with good reason burials were characterized by the sublime phrase "compacts of the human race" (*foedera generis humani*), and with less grandeur were described by Tacitus as "fellowships of humanity" (*humanitatis commercia*) [A. 6.19]. Furthermore, it is an opinion in which all gentile nations have certainly concurred, that the souls of the unburied remain restless on the earth and go wandering about their bodies, and consequently that they do not die with their bodies but are immortal. (That such was the consensus of the ancient barbarous nations may be inferred from what we are told of the [present] peoples of Guinea by Hugo van Linschooten; of those of Peru and Mexico, by Acosta in his *Natural and Moral History of the Indies*; of the inhabitants of Virginia, by Thomas Harriot; of those of New England, by Richard Whitbourne; of those of the kingdom of Siam, by Joost Schouten.) Thus Seneca concludes: "When we discuss immortality, we are influenced in no small degree by the general opinion of mankind, who either fear or worship the spirits of the lower world. I make the most of this general belief." (*Quum de immortalitate loquimur, non leve momentum apud nos habet consensus hominum aut timentium inferos aut colentium: hac persuasione publica utor* [*Letter* 117.5–6].)

[SECTION IV]

METHOD

338 To complete the establishment of the principles which have been adopted for this Science, it remains in this first book to discuss the method which it should follow. It must begin where its subject matter began, as we said in the Axioms [314]. We must therefore go back with the philologians and fetch it from the stones of Deucalion and Pyrrha, from the rocks of Amphion, from the men who sprang from the furrows of Cadmus [679] or the hard oak of Vergil [A. 8.315]. With the philosophers we must fetch it from the frogs of Epicurus, from the cicadas of Hobbes, from the simpletons of Grotius; from the men cast into this world without care or aid of God, of whom Pufendorf speaks, as gross and wild as the giants called "Big Feet," who are said to be found near the Strait of Magellan [170]; which is as much as to say from the cyclopes of Homer, in whom Plato recognizes the first fathers in the state of the families [296]. (This is the science the philologians and philosophers have given us of the principles of humanity [J1]!) Our treatment of it must take its start from the time these creatures began to think humanly [K7]. In their monstrous savagery and unbridled bestial freedom there was no means to tame the former or bridle the latter but the frightful thought of some divinity, the fear of whom is the only powerful means of reducing to duty a liberty gone wild [177]. To discover the way in which this first human thinking arose in the gentile world, we encountered exasperating difficulties which have cost us the research of a good twenty years [K4]. [We had] to descend from these human and refined natures of ours to those quite wild and savage natures, which we cannot at all imagine and can comprehend only with great effort [H1, K7].

339 By reason of all this, we must start from some notion of God such as even the most savage, wild, and monstrous men do not lack. That notion we show to be this: that man, fallen into despair of all the succors of nature, desires something superior to save him. But something superior to

nature is God, and this is the light that God has shed on all men. Confirmation may be found in a common human custom: that libertines grown old, feeling their natural forces fail, turn naturally to religion.

340 But these first men, who later became the princes of the gentile nations, must have done their thinking under the strong impulsion of violent passions, as beasts do. We must therefore proceed from a vulgar metaphysics [182], such as we shall find the theology of the poets to have been [366], and seek by its aid that frightful thought of some divinity which imposed form and measure on the bestial passions of these lost men and thus transformed them into human passions. From this thought must have sprung the conatus proper to the human will, to hold in check the motions impressed on the mind by the body, so as either to quiet them altogether, as becomes the wise man, or at least to direct them to better use, as becomes the civil man. This control over the motion of their bodies is certainly an effect of the freedom of human choice, and thus of free will, which is the home and seat of all the virtues, and among the others of justice. When informed by justice, the will is the fount of all that is just and of all the laws dictated by justice. But to impute conatus to bodies is as much as to impute to them freedom to regulate their motions, whereas all bodies are by nature necessary agents. And what the theorists of mechanics call powers, forces, conatus, are insensible motions of bodies, by which they approach their centers of gravity, as ancient mechanics had it, or depart from their centers of motion, as modern mechanics has it [viii, 504].

341 But men, because of their corrupted nature, are under the tyranny of self-love, which compels them to make private utility their chief guide. Seeking everything useful for themselves and nothing for their companions, they cannot bring their passions under control to direct them toward justice. We thereby establish the fact that man in the bestial state desires only his own welfare; having taken wife and begotten children, he desires his own welfare along with that of his family; having entered upon civil life, he desires his own welfare along with that of his city; when its rule is extended over several peoples, he desires his own welfare along with that of the nation; when the nations are united by wars, treaties of peace, alliances, and commerce, he desires his own welfare along with that of the entire human race. In all these circumstances man desires principally his own utility. Therefore it is only by divine providence that he can be held within these institutions to practice justice as a member of the society of the family, of the city, and finally of mankind. Unable to attain all the utilities he wishes, he is constrained by these institutions to seek those

which are his due; and this is called just. That which regulates all human justice is therefore divine justice, which is administered by divine providence to preserve human society.

342 In one of its principal aspects, this Science must therefore be a rational civil theology of divine providence [385], which seems hitherto to have been lacking. For the philosophers have either been altogether ignorant of it, as the Stoics and the Epicureans were, the latter asserting that human affairs are agitated by a blind concourse of atoms, the former that they are drawn by a deaf [inexorable] chain of cause and effect; or they have considered it solely in the order of natural things, giving the name of natural theology to the metaphysics in which they contemplate this attribute [i.e., the providence] of God, and in which they confirm it by the physical order observed in the motions of such bodies as the spheres and the elements and in the final cause observed in other and minor natural things. But they ought to have studied it in the economy of civil institutions, in keeping with the full meaning of applying to providence the term "divinity" [i.e., the power of divining], from *divinari*, to divine, which is to understand what is hidden *from* men—the future—or what is hidden *in* them—their consciousness. It is this [divinatory providence] that makes up the first and principal part of the subject matter of jurisprudence, namely the divine institutions [e.g., augury] on which depend the human institutions which make up its other and complementary part [398]. Our new Science must therefore be a demonstration, so to speak, of what providence has wrought in history, for it must be a history of the institutions by which, without human discernment or counsel, and often against the designs of men, providence has ordered this great city of the human race [B9]. For though this world has been created in time and particular, the institutions established therein by providence are universal and eternal [F6].

343 In contemplation of this infinite and eternal providence our Science finds certain divine proofs [349, 630] by which it is confirmed and demonstrated. Since divine providence has omnipotence as minister, it must unfold its institutions by means as easy as the natural customs of men [309]. Since it has infinite wisdom as counselor, whatever it disposes must, in its entirety, be [institutive] order. Since it has for its end its own immeasurable goodness, whatever it institutes must be directed to a good always superior to that which men have proposed to themselves.

344 In the deplorable obscurity of the beginnings of the nations and in the innumerable variety of their customs, for a divine argument which embraces all human institutions, no sublimer proofs can be desired than the [three] just mentioned: the naturalness [of the means], the [unfolding

institutive] order [in which they are employed], and the end [thereby served], which is the preservation of the human race [M9]. These proofs will become luminous and distinct when we reflect with what ease the institutions are brought into being, by occasions arising often far apart and sometimes quite contrary to the proposals of men, yet fitting together of themselves. Such proofs omnipotence affords. Compare the institutions with one another and observe the order by which those are now born in their proper times and places which ought now to be born, and others deferred for birth in theirs (and all the beauty of order, according to Horace [A.P. 42ff], consists in this [348]). Such proofs eternal wisdom provides. Consider, finally, if in these occasions, places, and times we can conceive how other divine benefits could arise by which, in view of the particular needs and ills of men, human society could be better conducted and preserved. Such proofs the eternal goodness of God will give [F6].

345 Thus the proper and continual proof here adduced will consist in comparing and reflecting whether our human mind, in the series of possibilities it is permitted to understand, and so far as it is permitted to do so, can conceive more or fewer or different causes than those from which issue the effects of this civil world [F2]. In doing this the reader will experience in his mortal body a divine pleasure as he contemplates in the divine ideas this world of nations in all the extent of its places, times, and varieties. And he will find that he has thereby proved to the Epicureans that their chance cannot wander foolishly about and everywhere find a way out, and to the Stoics that their eternal chain of causes, to which they will have it the world is chained, itself hangs upon the omnipotent, wise, and beneficent will of the best and greatest God [342].

346 These sublime natural theological proofs will be confirmed for us by the following sorts of logical proofs. In reasoning of the origins of institutions, divine and human, in the gentile world, we reach those first beginnings beyond which it is vain curiosity to demand others earlier; and this is the defining character of [first] principles. We explain the particular ways in which they come into being; that is to say, their nature, the explanation of which is the distinguishing mark of science. And finally [these origins] are confirmed by the eternal properties [the institutions] preserve, which could not be what they are if the institutions had not come into being just as they did, in those particular times, places, and fashions, which is to say with those particular natures [I·2; 147f].

347 In search of these natures of human institutions our Science proceeds by a severe analysis of human thoughts about the human necessities or utilities of social life, which are the two perennial springs of the

natural law of the gentes [141]. In its second principal aspect, our Science is therefore a history of human ideas, on which it seems the metaphysics of the human mind must proceed. This queen of the sciences, by the axiom that "the sciences must begin where their subject matters began" [314], took its start when the first men began to think humanly [338], and not when the philosophers began to reflect on human ideas (as in an erudite and scholarly little book recently published [by Brucker] under the title *Historia philosophica doctrinae de ideis,* which comes down to the latest controversies between the two foremost minds of our age, Leibniz and Newton).

348   To determine the times and places for such a history—that is, when and where these human thoughts were born—and thus to give it certainty by means of its own (so to speak) metaphysical chronology and geography, our Science applies a likewise metaphysical art of criticism with regard to the founders of these same nations, in which it took well over a thousand years to produce those writers with whom philological criticism has hitherto been occupied [392]. And the criterion our criticism employs is that taught by divine providence and common to all nations, namely the common sense of the human race [142], determined by the necessary harmony of human institutions, in which all the beauty of the civil world consists [344]. The decisive sort of proof in our Science is therefore this: that, since these institutions have been established by divine providence, the course of the institutions of the nations had to be, must now be, and will have to be such as our Science demonstrates, even if infinite worlds were born from time to time through eternity, which is certainly not the case [1096].

349   Our Science therefore comes to describe at the same time an ideal eternal history traversed in time by the history of every nation in its rise, development, maturity, decline, and fall [A4, 145, 245, 294, 393]. Indeed, we make bold to affirm that he who meditates this Science narrates to himself this ideal eternal history so far as he himself makes it for himself by that proof "it had, has, and will have to be" [348]. For the first indubitable principle posited above [331] is that this world of nations has certainly been made by men, and its guise must therefore be found within the modifications of our own human mind. And history cannot be more certain than when he who creates the things also narrates them. Now, as geometry, when it constructs the world of quantity out of its elements, or contemplates that world, is creating it for itself, just so does our Science [create for itself the world of nations], but with a reality greater by just so much as the institutions having to do with human affairs are more real

than points, lines, surfaces, and figures are [F3]. And this very fact is an argument, O reader, that these proofs are of a kind divine and should give thee a divine pleasure, since in God knowledge and creation are one and the same thing.

350   By the definitions of the true and the certain proposed above [138], men were for a long period incapable of truth and of reason, which is the fount of that inner justice by which the intellect is satisfied. This justice was practiced by the Hebrews, who, illuminated by the true God, were by his divine law forbidden even to have unjust thoughts, about which no mortal lawgiver ever troubled himself. (For the Hebrews believed in a God all mind who searches the hearts of men, and the gentiles believed in gods composed of bodies and mind who could not do so [F7].) This same inner justice was later reasoned out by the philosophers, who did not arise until two thousand years after the nations were founded. In the meantime the nations were governed by the certainty of authority, that is, by the same criterion which is used by our metaphysical criticism; namely, the common sense of the human race [142], on which the consciences of all nations repose. So that, in this [third] principal regard, our Science comes to be a philosophy of authority [386ff], which is the fount of the outer justice of which the moral theologians speak [964]. Of such authority account should have been taken by the three princes of the doctrine of the natural law of the gentes [394], and not of that drawn from passages in the writers. For the authority of which we speak reigned among the nations well over a thousand years before the writers could arise, and they could have taken no cognizance of it. For that reason Grotius, more learned and erudite than either of the others, combats the Roman jurisconsults in almost every particular detail of this doctrine; but all his blows fall short, for the jurisconsults established their principles of justice on the certainty of the authority of the human race, not on the authority of the learned.

351   These are the philosophic proofs our Science will use, and consequently those which are absolutely necessary for pursuing it. The philological proofs must come last. They all reduce to the following kinds:

352   (1) Our mythologies agree with the institutions under consideration, not by force and distortion, but directly, easily, and naturally. They will be seen to be civil histories of the first peoples, who were everywhere naturally poets [200, 203, 223, 579].

353   (2) The heroic phrases, as here explained in the full truth of the sentiments and the full propriety of the expressions, also agree [34, 219, 411, 456, 825].

354   (3) The etymologies of the native languages also agree, which

tell us the histories of the institutions signified by the words, beginning with their original and proper meanings and pursuing the natural progress of their metaphors according to the order of ideas, on which the history of languages must proceed [151ff, 238ff].

355 (4) The mental vocabulary of human social institutions, which are the same in substance as felt by all nations but are diversely expressed in language according to their diverse modifications, is exhibited to be such as we conceived it [161].

356 (5) Truth is sifted from falsehood in everything that has been preserved for us through long centuries by those vulgar traditions which, since they have been preserved for so long a time and by entire peoples, must have had a public ground of truth [149].

357 (6) The great fragments of antiquity, hitherto useless to science because they lay begrimed, broken, and scattered, shed great light when cleaned, pieced together, and restored.

358 (7) To all these institutions, as to their necessary causes, are traced all the effects narrated by certain history [F2].

359 These philological proofs enable us to see in fact the institutions we have meditated in idea as touching this world of nations, in accordance with Bacon's method of philosophizing, which is "think [and] see" (cogitare videre) [163]. Thus it is that with the help of the preceding philosophical proofs, the philological proofs both confirm their own authority by reason and at the same time confirm reason by their authority.*

360 From all that has been set forth in general concerning the establishment of the principles of this Science, we conclude that, since its principles are (1) divine providence, (2) marriage and therewith moderation of the passions, and (3) burial and therewith immortality of human souls [I·5]; and since the criterion it uses is that what is felt to be just by all men or by the majority must be the rule of social life (and on these principles and this criterion there is agreement between the vulgar wisdom of all lawgivers and the esoteric wisdom of the philosophers of greatest repute)—these must be the bounds of human reason. And let him who would transgress them beware lest he transgress all humanity [130].

---

* The *Cogitata et visa*, referred to here and in 163 above, is translated and more accurately interpreted by Benjamin Farrington, *The Philosophy of Francis Bacon* (Liverpool, 1964), under the title "Thoughts and Conclusions." Cf. 104, 112, 114, 155, 157, 248, 264, 330, above; 415, 420, below.

BOOK TWO

POETIC WISDOM [K1–7]

[PROLEGOMENA]

Introduction

361 We have said above in the Axioms that all the histories of the gentile nations have had fabulous beginnings [202], that among the Greeks (who have given us all we know of gentile antiquity) the first sages were the theological poets [199], and that the nature of everything born or made betrays the crudeness of its origin [239ff]. It is thus and not otherwise that we must conceive the origins of poetic wisdom. And as for the great and sovereign esteem in which it has been handed down to us, this has its origin in the two conceits, that of nations [125] and that of scholars [127], and it springs even more from the latter than from the former. For just as Manetho, the Egyptian high priest, translated all the fabulous history of Egypt into a sublime natural theology [222], so the Greek philosophers translated theirs into philosophy. And they did so not merely for the reason that the histories as they had come down to both alike were most unseemly [221], but for the following five reasons as well.

362 The first was reverence for religion, for the gentile nations were everywhere founded by fables on religion. The second was the grand effect thence derived, namely this civil world, so wisely ordered that it could only be the effect of a superhuman wisdom. The third was the occasions which, as we shall see, these fables, assisted by the veneration of religion and the credit of such great wisdom, gave the philosophers for instituting research and for meditating lofty things in philosophy. The fourth was the ease with which they were thus enabled, as we shall also show farther on, to explain their sublime philosophical meditations by means of the expressions happily left them by the poets. The fifth and last, which is the sum of them all, is the confirmation of their own meditations which the philosophers derived from the authority of religion and the wisdom of the poets. Of these five reasons, the first two and the last contain the praises of the divine wisdom which ordained this world of nations, and the witness the philosophers bore to it even in their errors. The third and fourth are deceptions permitted by divine providence, that thence there might arise philosophers to understand and recognize it for what it truly is, an attribute of the true God.

363   Throughout this book it will be shown that as much as the poets had first sensed in the way of vulgar wisdom, the philosophers later understood in the way of esoteric wisdom; so that the former may be said to have been the sense and the latter the intellect of the human race [779]. What Aristotle [*On the Soul* 432a 7f] said of the individual man is therefore true of the race in general: *Nihil est in intellectu quin prius fuerit in sensu.* That is, the human mind does not understand anything of which it has had no previous impression (which our modern metaphysicians call "occasion") from the senses. Now the mind uses the intellect when, from something it senses, it gathers something which does not fall under the senses; and this is the proper meaning of the Latin verb *intelligere.*

[*Chapter I*]   *Wisdom in General*

364   Now, before discussing poetic wisdom, it is necessary for us to see what wisdom in general is. Wisdom is the faculty which commands all the disciplines by which we acquire all the sciences and arts that make up humanity. Plato [in his *Alcibiades I*, 124Eff?] defines wisdom as "the perfecter of man." Man, in his proper being as man, consists of mind and spirit, or, if we prefer, of intellect and will. It is the function of wisdom to fulfill both these parts in man, the second by way of the first, to the end that by a mind illuminated by knowledge of the highest institutions, the spirit may be led to choose the best. The highest institutions in this universe are those turned toward and conversant with God; the best are those which look to the good of all mankind. The former are called divine institutions, the latter human. True wisdom, then, should teach the knowledge of divine institutions in order to conduct human institutions to the highest good. We believe that this was the plan upon which Marcus Terentius Varro, who earned the title "most learned of the Romans," erected his great work, [*The Antiquities*] of *Divine and Human Institutions*, of which the injustice of time has unhappily bereft us [M4, 990]. We shall treat of these institutions in the present book so far as the weakness of our education and the meagerness of our erudition permit.

365   Wisdom among the gentiles began with the Muse [391, 508], defined by Homer in a golden passage of the *Odyssey* [8.63] as "knowledge of good and evil," and later called divination. It was on the natural prohibition of this practice, as something naturally denied to man, that

God founded the true religion of the Hebrews, from which our Christian religion arose [167]. The Muse must thus have been properly at first the science of divining by auspices, and this was the vulgar wisdom of all nations [342], of which we shall have more to say presently. It consisted in contemplating God under the attribute of his providence, so that from *divinari* his essence came to be called divinity. We shall see presently that the theological poets, who certainly founded the humanity of Greece, were versed in this wisdom, and this explains why the Latins called the judicial astrologers "professors of wisdom." Wisdom was later attributed to men renowned for useful counsels given to mankind, as in the case of the Seven Sages of Greece. The attribution was then extended to men who for the good of peoples and nations wisely ordered and governed commonwealths. Still later the word "wisdom" came to mean knowledge of natural divine things; that is, metaphysics, called for that reason divine science, which, seeking knowledge of man's mind in God [506], and recognizing God as the source of all truth, must recognize him as the regulator of all good. So that metaphysics must essentially work for the good of the human race, whose preservation depends on the universal belief in a provident divinity. It is perhaps for having demonstrated this providence that Plato deserved to be called divine; and that which denies to God this great attribute must be called stupidity rather than wisdom. Finally among the Hebrews, and thence among us Christians, wisdom was called the science of eternal things revealed by God; a science which, among the Tuscans, considered as knowledge of the true good and true evil, perhaps owed to that fact the first name they gave it, "science in divinity" [K7].

366 We must therefore distinguish more truly than Varro did the three kinds of theology. [Augustine, C.G. 6.5.] First, poetic theology, that of the theological poets, which was the civil theology of all the gentile nations. Second, natural theology, that of the metaphysicians. Third, our Christian theology, a mixture of civil and natural with the loftiest revealed theology; all three united in the contemplation of divine providence. (Our third kind takes the place of Varro's poetic theology, which among the gentiles was the same as civil theology, though he distinguished it from both civil and natural theology because, sharing the vulgar common error that the fables contained high mysteries of sublime philosophy, he believed it to be a mixture of the two.) Divine providence has so conducted human institutions that, starting from the poetic theology which regulated them by certain sensible signs believed to be divine counsels sent to man by the gods, and by means of the natural theology which demonstrates providence by eternal reasons which do not fall under the senses, the nations were

disposed to receive revealed theology in virtue of a supernatural faith, superior not only to the senses but to human reason itself.

[Chapter II]   Exposition and Division of Poetic Wisdom

367   But because metaphysics is the sublime science which distributes their determinate subject matters to all the so-called subaltern sciences; and because the wisdom of the ancients was that of the theological poets, who without doubt were the first sages of the gentile world [199]; and because the origins of all things must by nature have been crude: for all these reasons we must trace the beginnings of poetic wisdom to a crude metaphysics. From this, as from a trunk, there branch out from one limb logic, morals, economics, and politics, all poetic; and from another, physics, the mother of cosmography and astronomy, the latter of which gives their certainty to its two daughters, chronology and geography—all likewise poetic. We shall show clearly and distinctly how the founders of gentile humanity by means of their natural theology (or metaphysics) imagined the gods; how by means of their logic they invented languages; by morals, created heroes; by economics, founded families, and by politics, cities; by their physics, established the beginnings of things as all divine; by the particular physics of man, in a certain sense created themselves [C6]; by their cosmography, fashioned for themselves a universe entirely of gods; by astronomy, carried the planets and constellations from earth to heaven; by chronology, gave a beginning to [measured] times; and how by geography the Greeks, for example, described the [whole] world within their own Greece [K5].

368   Thus our Science comes to be at once a history of the ideas, the customs, and the deeds of mankind [347, 391]. From these three we shall derive the principles of the history of human nature, which we shall show to be the principles of universal history, which principles it seems hitherto to have lacked [399, 736ff].

[Chapter III]   The Universal Flood and the Giants [F7, J3]

369   The founders of gentile humanity must have been men of the races of Ham, Japheth, and Shem, which gradually, one after the other,

renounced that true religion of their common father Noah which alone in the family state had been able to hold them in human society by the bonds of matrimony and hence of the families themselves [301]. As a result of this renunciation, they dissolved their marriages and broke up their families by promiscuous intercourse, and began roving wild through the great forest of the earth. The race of Ham wandered through southern Asia, Egypt, and the rest of Africa; that of Japheth through northern Asia or Scythia, and thence through Europe; and that of Shem through all middle Asia toward the east. By fleeing from the wild beasts with which the great forest must have abounded, and by pursuing women, who in that state must have been wild, indocile, and shy, they became separated from each other in their search for food and water. Mothers abandoned their children, who in time must have come to grow up without ever hearing a human voice, much less learning any human custom, and thus descended to a state truly bestial and savage. Mothers, like beasts, must merely have nursed their babies, let them wallow naked in their own filth, and abandoned them for good as soon as they were weaned. And these children, who had to wallow in their own filth, whose nitrous salts richly fertilized the fields, and who had to exert themselves to penetrate the great forest, grown extremely dense from the flood, would flex and contract their muscles in these exertions, and thus absorb nitrous salts into their bodies in greater abundance. They would be quite without that fear of gods, fathers, and teachers which chills and benumbs even the most exuberant in childhood. They must therefore have grown robust, vigorous, excessively big in brawn and bone, to the point of becoming giants. This upbringing of theirs was even more savage than that to which Caesar and Tacitus ascribe the gigantic stature of the ancient Germans [170]; from which was derived that of the Goths whom Procopius mentions [!], and which was like that of the Patagonians supposed to exist today near the strait of Magellan. Philosophers in physics have spoken much nonsense on this subject, collected by Chassanion, who wrote De gigantibus. Of such giants there have been found and are still being found, for the most part in the mountains (a circumstance with an important bearing on what we have to say below [377, 387]), great skulls and bones of an unnatural size which is further exaggerated by vulgar tradition for reasons of which we shall speak in their proper place.

370 Such giants were scattered over the earth after the flood. We have seen them in the fabulous history of the Greeks [193], and the Latin philologians, without being aware of it, have told us of their existence in the ancient history of Italy, where they say that the most ancient peoples

of Italy, the so-called aborigines, claimed to be *autochthones,* which is as much as to say sons of Earth, which among the Greeks and Latins meant nobles. And in the fables the Greeks quite properly called the sons of earth giants, and the Earth mother of giants. The Greek term *autochthones* should be rendered in Latin *indigenae,* that is, properly, those born of a land; thus the native gods of a people or nation were called *dii indigetes,* as if *inde geniti,* or, as we should say more shortly today, *ingeniti.* For the syllable *de* is one of the redundancies of the first languages of the peoples which we shall discuss later. Thus among the Latins we find *induperator* for *imperator,* and in the Law of the Twelve Tables [1.2] *endoiacito* for *iniicito,* whence perhaps it came that armistices were called *induciae,* as if *iniiciae,* because they must have been so called from *icere foedus,* to make a pact of peace. So, in the case in hand, from *indigeni* was derived *ingenui,* whose first and proper meaning was "noble" (whence the term *artes ingenuae,* "noble arts") but which finally came to mean "free" (though *artes libe-rales* kept the meaning "noble arts"). For nobles alone, as will shortly be demonstrated [597], composed the first cities, in which the plebeians were slaves or precursors of slaves.

371   The same Latin philologians observe that all the ancient peoples were called aborigines, and sacred history tells us of whole peoples called *emim* and *zomzommim* [*Genesis* 14.5; *Deuteronomy* 2.10,20–21], which Hebrew scholars take to mean giants, one of whom was Nimrod; and the giants before the flood are described by Scripture [*Genesis* 6.4] as "strong, famous and powerful men of the age." The Hebrews, on account of their cleanly upbringing and their fear of God and of their fathers, continued to be of the proper stature in which God had created Adam and Noah had procreated his three sons; and it was perhaps in abomination of giantism that the Hebrews had so many ceremonial laws pertaining to bodily cleanliness [F7]. The Romans preserved a great vestige of these laws in the public sacrifice intended to purge the city of all the sins of the citizens, which was performed with water and fire. Their solemn nuptials were also celebrated with water and fire, and participation in these two things was even the mark of citizenship, the deprivation of which was called *interdic-tum aqua et igni* [610, 957]. The sacrifice with fire and water was called *lustrum,* which came to mean a period of five years because that was the interval between these sacrifices, much as among the Greeks an Olympiad meant a period of four years. But *lustrum* also meant a den of wild beasts, and the verb *lustrari,* to seek out or to purge, must at first have meant to seek out these dens and purge them of the beasts lurking within; whence the water required for the sacrifice was called *aqua lustralis.* The Greeks

began to count their years from the burning of the Nemean forest by Hercules to clear it for sowing grain, in commemoration of which, as we pointed out in the Idea of the Work [3] and as we shall see fully later [733], he founded the Olympiads. The Romans, with more discernment, began to count their years in *lustra* from the water of the sacred ablutions, because civilization began with water, the need of which was felt before that of fire, as appears from the formulas of marriage and the interdict, in which *aqua* comes before *igni*. This is the origin of the sacred ablutions which must precede sacrifices, a custom which was and is common to all nations. It was by becoming imbued with this cleanliness of body and this fear of gods and of fathers—in both cases a fear we shall find amounting to terror in the earliest times—that the giants diminished to our normal stature. It was perhaps for this reason that from *politeia*, which in Greek means civil government, was derived the Latin *politus*, clean or neat.

372 This diminution of stature must have continued down to the human times of the nations, as is demonstrated by the excessively large weapons of the ancient heroes, which Augustus, according to Suetonius [*The Deified Augustus* 72.3], preserved along with the bones and skulls of the ancient giants in his museum. Thus, as stated in the Axioms [172], the entire first world of men must be divided into two kinds: the first, men of normal size, which includes the Hebrews only; the second, giants, who were the founders of the gentile nations. Of the giants there were in turn two kinds: the first, the sons of Earth, or nobles, from whom, as being giants in the full sense of the term, the age of giants took its name, as we have said (and it is these whom sacred history defines as "strong, famous and powerful men of the age"); the second, less properly so called, those other giants who were subjugated [by the former] [553].

373 The time at which the founders of the gentile nations reached this condition [of giantism] is fixed a century after the flood for the race of Shem, and two centuries for those of Japheth and Ham, as postulated above [62]. Below, presently, will be given the physical history of this matter [387], which, though related to us in the Greek fables, has not hitherto been observed, and which at the same time will give us a new physical history of the universal flood [380].

[SECTION I]

[POETIC METAPHYSICS]

[*Chapter I*] *Poetic Metaphysics as the Origin of Poetry, Idolatry, Divination, and Sacrifices*

374 From these first men, stupid, insensate, and horrible beasts, all the philosophers and philologians should have begun their investigations of the wisdom of the ancient gentiles; that is, from the giants in the proper sense in which we have just taken them. (Father Boulduc in his *De ecclesia ante Legem* says the scriptural names of the giants signify "pious, venerable and illustrious men"; but this can be understood only of the noble giants who by divination founded the gentile religions and gave the age of giants its name.) And they should have begun with metaphysics, which seeks its proofs not in the external world but within the modifications of the mind of him who meditates it. For since this world of nations has certainly been made by men [331], it is within these modifications that its principles should have been sought. And human nature, so far as it is like that of animals, carries with it this property, that the senses are its sole way of knowing things.

375 Hence poetic wisdom, the first wisdom of the gentile world, must have begun with a metaphysics not rational and abstract like that of learned men now, but felt and imagined as that of these first men must have been, who, without power of ratiocination, were all robust sense and vigorous imagination [185]. This metaphysics was their poetry, a faculty born with them (for they were furnished by nature with these senses and imaginations); born of their ignorance of causes, for ignorance, the mother of wonder, made everything wonderful to men who were ignorant of everything [184]. Their poetry was at first divine, because, as we saw in the passage from Lactantius, they imagined the causes of the things they felt and wondered at to be gods [188]. (This is now confirmed by the American Indians, who call gods all the things that surpass their small understanding. We may add the ancient Germans dwelling about the Arctic Ocean, of whom Tacitus [G. 45] tells that they spoke of hearing the sun pass at night from west to east through the sea, and affirmed that they saw the gods. These very rude and simple nations help us to a much better understanding of the founders of the gentile world with whom we are now concerned.) At the same time they gave the things they wondered at substantial being after their own ideas, just as children do, whom we see take inanimate things in their hands and play with them and talk to them as though they were living persons [186].

376 In such fashion the first men of the gentile nations, children of nascent mankind [209], created things according to their own ideas. But this creation was infinitely different from that of God. For God, in his purest intelligence, knows things, and, by knowing them, creates them; but they, in their robust ignorance, did it by virtue of a wholly corporeal imagination. And because it was quite corporeal, they did it with marvelous sublimity; a sublimity such and so great that it excessively perturbed the very persons who by imagining did the creating, for which they were called "poets," which is Greek for "creators" [K4]. Now this is the threefold labor of great poetry: (1) to invent sublime fables suited to the popular understanding, (2) to perturb to excess, with a view to the end proposed: (3) to teach the vulgar to act virtuously, as the poets have taught themselves; as will presently be shown [379]. Of this nature of human institutions it remained an eternal property, expressed in a noble phrase of Tacitus, that frightened men vainly "no sooner imagine than they believe" (fingunt simul creduntque) [A. 6.5.10].

377 Of such natures must have been the first founders of gentile humanity when at last the sky fearfully rolled with thunder and flashed with lightning, as could not but follow from the bursting upon the air for the first time of an impression so violent. As we have postulated [62, 195], this occurred a hundred years after the flood in Mesopotamia and two hundred years after it throughout the rest of the world; for it took that much time to reduce the earth to such a state that, dry of the moisture of the universal flood, it could send up dry exhalations or matter igniting in the air to produce lightning. Thereupon a few giants, who must have been the most robust, and who were dispersed through the forests on the mountain heights where the strongest beasts have their dens, were frightened and astonished by the great effect whose cause they did not know, and raised their eyes and became aware of the sky. And because in such a case the nature of the human mind leads it to attribute its own nature to the effect [180], and because in that state their nature was that of men all robust bodily strength, who expressed their very violent passions by shout-

ing and grumbling, they pictured the sky to themselves as a great animated body, which in that aspect they called Jove, the first god of the so-called greater gentes [317], who meant to tell them something by the hiss of his bolts and the clap of his thunder [C2]. And thus they began to exercise that natural curiosity which is the daughter of ignorance and the mother of knowledge, and which, opening the mind of man, gives birth to wonder. This characteristic still persists in the vulgar, who, when they see a comet or sundog or some other extraordinary thing in nature, and particularly in the countenance of the sky, at once turn curious and anxiously inquire what it means [189]. When they wonder at the prodigious effects of the magnet on iron, even in this age of minds enlightened and instructed by philosophy, they come out with this: that the magnet has an occult sympathy for the iron; and they make of all nature a vast animate body which feels passions and effects [180].

378   But the nature of our civilized minds is so detached from the senses, even in the vulgar, by abstractions corresponding to all the abstract terms our languages abound in, and so refined by the art of writing, and as it were spiritualized by the use of numbers, because even the vulgar know how to count and reckon, that it is naturally beyond our power to form the vast image of this mistress called "Sympathetic Nature." Men shape the phrase with their lips but have nothing in their minds; for what they have in mind is falsehood, which is nothing; and their imagination no longer avails to form a vast false image. It is equally beyond our power to enter into the vast imagination of those first men, whose minds were not in the least abstract, refined, or spiritualized, because they were entirely immersed in the senses, buffeted by the passions, buried in the body. That is why we said above [338] that we can scarcely understand, still less imagine, how those first men thought who founded gentile humanity.

379   In this fashion the first theological poets created the first divine fable, the greatest they ever created: that of Jove, king and father of men and gods, in the act of hurling the lightning bolt; an image so popular, disturbing, and instructive [376] that its creators themselves believed in it, and feared, revered, and worshiped it in frightful religions [517]. And by that trait of the human mind noticed by Tacitus [183] whatever these men saw, imagined, or even made or did themselves they believed to be Jove; and to all of the universe that came within their scope, and to all its parts, they gave the being of animate substance. This is the civil history of the expression "All things are full of Jove" (*Iovis omnia plena*) [Vergil, *Eclogue* 3.60] by which Plato later understood the ether which penetrates and fills everything [*Cratylus* 412D] [398]. But for the theological poets Jove

was no higher than the mountain peaks [712]. The first men, who spoke by signs, naturally believed that lightning bolts and thunderclaps were signs made to them by Jove [C2]; whence from *nuo*, to make a sign, came *numen*, the divine will, by an idea more than sublime and worthy to express the divine majesty. They believed that Jove commanded by signs, that such signs were real words, and that nature was the language of Jove. The science of this language the gentiles universally believed to be divination, which by the Greeks was called theology, meaning the science of the language of the gods. Thus Jove acquired the fearful kingdom of the lightning and became the king of men and gods; and he acquired the two titles, that of best (*optimus*) in the sense of strongest (*fortissimus*) (as by a reverse process *fortis* meant in early Latin what *bonus* did in late), and that of greatest (*maximus*) from his vast body, the sky itself. From the first great benefit he conferred on mankind by not destroying it with his bolts, he received the title *Soter*, or savior. (This is the first of the three principles we have taken for our Science [333ff].) And for having put an end to the feral wandering of these few giants, so that they became the princes of the gentes, he received the epithet *Stator*, stayer or establisher. The Latin philologians explain this epithet too narrowly from Jove, invoked by Romulus, having stopped the Romans in their flight from the battle with the Sabines.

380 Thus the many Joves the philologians wonder at are so many physical histories preserved for us by the fables, which prove the universality of the flood [194]. For every gentile nation had its Jove, and the Egyptians had the conceit to say that their Jove Ammon was the most ancient of them all [47, 62].

381 Thus, in accordance with what has been said about the principles of the poetic characters [209], Jove was born naturally in poetry as a divine character or imaginative universal, to which everything having to do with the auspices was referred by all the ancient gentile nations, which must therefore all have been poetic by nature. Their poetic wisdom began with this poetic metaphysics, which contemplated God by the attribute of his providence; and they were called theological poets, or sages who understood the language of the gods expressed in the auspices of Jove; and were properly called divine in the sense of diviners, from *divinari*, to divine or predict. Their science was called Muse, defined by Homer as the knowledge of good and evil [365]; that is, divination, on the prohibition of which God ordained his true religion for Adam [167]. Because they were versed in this mystic theology, the Greek poets, who explained the divine mysteries of the auspices and oracles, were called *mystae*, which Horace learnedly

renders "interpreters of the gods" [A.P. 391]. Every gentile nation had its own sybil versed in this science, and we find mention of twelve of them. Sybils and oracles are the most ancient institutions of the gentile world [721, 925].

382   All the things here discussed agree with that golden passage of Eusebius [i.e., Lactantius] on the origins of idolatry: that the first people, simple and rough, invented the gods "from terror of present power" [188]. Thus it was fear which created gods in the world; not fear awakened in men by other men, but fear awakened in men by themselves [191]. Along with this origin of idolatry is demonstrated likewise the origin of divination, which was brought into the world at the same birth. The origins of these two were followed by that of the sacrifices made to procure or rightly understand the auspices [250].

383   That such was the origin of poetry is finally confirmed by this eternal property of it: that its proper material is the credible impossibility. It is impossible that bodies should be minds, yet it was believed that the thundering sky was Jove. And nothing is dearer to poets than singing the marvels wrought by sorceresses by means of incantations. All this is to be explained by a hidden sense the nations have of the omnipotence of God. From this sense springs another by which all peoples are naturally led to do infinite honors to divinity. In this manner the poets founded religions among the gentiles.

384   All that has been so far said here upsets all the theories of the origin of poetry from Plato and Aristotle down to Patrizzi, Scaliger, and Castelvetro [807]. For it has been shown that it was deficiency of human reasoning power that gave rise to poetry so sublime that the philosophies which came afterward, the arts of poetry and of criticism, have produced none equal or better, and have even prevented its production. Hence it is Homer's privilege to be, of all the sublime, that is, the heroic poets, the first in the order of merit as well as in that of age. This discovery of the origins of poetry does away with the opinion of the matchless wisdom of the ancients [128], so ardently sought after from Plato to Bacon's *De sapientia veterum*. For the wisdom of the ancients was the vulgar wisdom of the lawgivers who founded the human race, not the esoteric wisdom of great and rare philosophers. Whence it will be found, as it has been in the case of Jove, that all the mystic meanings of lofty philosophy attributed by the learned to the Greek fables and the Egyptian hieroglyphics [435, 437] are as impertinent as the historical meanings they both must have had are natural.

[*Chapter II*]   *Corollaries concerning the Principal Aspects of This
Science* [*I·8*]

I

385 From what has been said up to this point it is concluded that
divine providence, apprehended by such human sense as could have been
possessed by rough, wild, and savage men who in despair of nature's succors
desired something superior to nature to save them (which is the first
principle on which we established the method of this Science [339]),
permitted them to be deceived [916] into fearing the false divinity of Jove
because he could strike them with lightning. Thus, through the thick
clouds of those first tempests, intermittently lit by those flashes, they made
out this great truth: that divine providence watches over the welfare of all
mankind. So that this Science becomes in this principal aspect a rational
civil theology of divine providence [F6, 342], which began in the vulgar
wisdom of the lawgivers, who founded the nations by contemplating God
under the attribute of providence, and which is completed by the esoteric
wisdom of the philosophers, who give a rational demonstration of it in
their natural theology [366].

II

386 Here begins also a philosophy of authority [350], a second principal aspect of this Science, taking the word "authority" in its original
meaning of property. The word is always used in this sense in the Law of
the Twelve Tables [3.7], and the term *auctores* was accordingly applied to
those from whom we derive title to property. *Auctor* certainly comes from
autos (= *proprius* or *suus ipsius*); and many scholars write *autor* and
autoritas, leaving out the aspirate.

387 Authority was at first divine; the authority by which divinity
appropriated to itself the few giants we have spoken of, by properly casting
them into the depths and recesses of the caves under the mountains [C2].
This is the iron ring by which the giants, dispersed upon the mountains,
were kept chained to the earth by fear of the sky and of Jove, wherever they
happened to be when the sky first thundered. Such were Tityus and
Prometheus, chained to a high rock with their hearts being devoured by an
eagle; that is, by the religion of Jove's auspices [719]. Their being rendered

immobile by fear was expressed by the Latins in the heroic phrase *terrore defixi*, and the artists depict them chained hand and foot with such links upon the mountains. Of these links was formed the great chain which Dionysius Longinus [!] admires as the sublimest of all the Homeric fables. Concerning this chain, Jove, to prove that he is king of men and gods, asserts that if all the gods and men were to take hold of one end, he alone at the other end would be able to drag them all [I. 8.18–27]. The Stoics would have the chain represent the eternal series of causes by which their Fate holds the world girdled and bound, but let them look out lest they be entangled in it themselves, because the dragging of men and gods by this chain depends on Jove's choice, yet they would have Jove subject to Fate.

388   Upon this divine authority followed human authority in the full philosophic sense of the term; that is, the property of human nature which not even God can take from man without destroying him. It is in this sense that Terence [*Lady of Andros* 959f] speaks of *voluptates propriae deorum*, meaning that the felicity of God does not depend on others; and Horace [*Odes* 2.2.22] of *propriam virtutis laurum*, meaning that the triumph of virtue cannot be taken away by envy; and Caesar [*Civil Wars* 3.70] of *propriam victoriam*, which Denis Petau [i.e., Voss] erroneously considers bad Latin, whereas it is exceedingly elegant Latin for a victory which could not be snatched from his hands by the enemy. This authority is the free use of the will, the intellect on the other hand being a passive power subject to truth. For from this first point of all human things, men began to exercise the freedom of human choice to hold in check the motions of the body, either to subdue them entirely or to give them better direction (this being the conatus proper to free agents [340]). Hence it was that the giants gave up the bestial custom of wandering through the great forest of the earth and habituated themselves to the quite contrary custom of remaining settled and hidden for a long period in their caves [C2].

389   This authority of human nature was followed by the authority of natural law; for, having occupied and remained settled for a long time in the places where they chanced to find themselves at the time of the first thunderbolts, they became lords of them by occupation and long possession, the source of all dominion in the world. These are those "few whom just Jupiter loved" (*pauci quos aequus amavit/Iupiter*) [Vergil: A. 6.129f] whom the philosophers later metamorphosed into men favored by God with natural aptitudes for science and virtue. But the historical significance of this phrase is that in the recesses and depths [of the caves] they became the princes of the so-called greater gentes, who counted Jove the first god [317]. These were the ancient noble houses, branching out into many

families [433], of which the first kingdoms and the first cities were composed. Their memory was preserved in those fine heroic Latin phrases: *condere gentes, condere regna, condere urbes; fundare gentes, fundare regna, fundare urbes.*

390 This philosophy of authority follows the rational civil theology of providence because, by means of the former's theological proofs, the latter with its philosophical ones makes clear and distinct the philological ones [342–359]; and with reference to the institutions of the most obscure antiquity of the nations it reduces to certainty human choice, which by its nature is most uncertain [141]—which is as much as to say that it reduces philology to the form of a science.

III

391 The third principal aspect is a history of human ideas [347]. These began with divine ideas by way of contemplation of the heavens with the bodily eyes [377]. Thus in their science of augury the Romans used the verb *contemplari* for observing the parts of the sky whence the auguries came or the auspices were taken. These regions, marked out by the augurs with their wands, were called temples of the sky (*templa coeli*), whence must have come to the Greeks their first *theōrēmata* and *mathēmata*, things divine or sublime to contemplate, which eventuated in metaphysical and mathematical abstractions [710]. This is the civil history of the saying "From Jove the muse began" (*A Iove principium musae*) [Vergil, *Eclogue* 3.60]. For we have just seen that Jove's bolts produced the first muse, which Homer defines as "knowledge of good and evil" [365]. At this point it was all too easy for the philosophers later to intrude the dictum that the beginning of wisdom is piety. The first muse must have been Urania, who contemplated the heavens to take the auguries. Later she came to stand for astronomy, as will presently be shown [739]. Just as poetic metaphysics was above divided into all its subordinate sciences, each sharing the poetic nature of their mother [367], so this history of ideas will present the rough origins both of the practical sciences in use among the nations and of the speculative sciences which are now cultivated by the learned [I·8, K7].

IV

392 The fourth aspect is a philosophical criticism which grows out of the aforesaid history of ideas. Such a criticism will render true judgment upon the founders of the nations, which must have taken well over a thousand years to produce the writers who are the subjects of philological

criticism. Beginning with Jove, our philosophical criticism will give us a natural theogony, or generation of the gods, as it took form naturally in the minds of the founders of the gentile world, who were by nature theological poets. The twelve gods of the so-called greater gentes, the ideas of whom were imagined by them from time to time on certain occasions of human necessity or utility, are assigned to twelve short epochs, into which we divide the period in which the fables were born. Thus this natural theogony will give us a rational chronology of poetic history for at least nine hundred years before vulgar history (which came after the heroic period) had its first beginnings [348].

V

393   The fifth aspect is an ideal eternal history traversed in time by the histories of all nations [A4, 349]. Wherever, emerging from savage, fierce, and bestial times, men begin to domesticate themselves by religion, they begin, proceed, and end by those stages which are investigated here in Book Two, to be encountered again in Book Four, where we shall treat of the course the nations run, and in Book Five, where we shall treat of the recourse of human institutions [L1].

VI

394   The sixth is a system of the natural law of the gentes [E1–8]. The three princes of this doctrine, Hugo Grotius, John Selden, and Samuel Pufendorf, should have taken their start from the beginnings of the gentes, where their subject matter begins [314ff]. But all three of them err together in this respect, by beginning in the middle; that is, with the latest times of the civilized nations (and thus of men enlightened by fully developed natural reason), from which the philosophers emerged and rose to meditation of a perfect idea of justice [G3, K3, 310, 313, 318, 329, 493, 972, 974, 1109].

395   First Grotius, just because of the great love he bears the truth, sets aside divine providence and professes that his system will stand even if all knowledge of God be left out of account. Thus all the reproofs which in a great number of matters he brings against the Roman jurists, do not touch them at all, since they took divine providence for their first principle and proposed to treat the natural law of the gentes, not that of the philosophers and moral theologians.

396   Then Selden assumes providence, but without paying any attention to the inhospitableness of the first peoples [303, 637], or to the

division the people of God made of the whole world of nations at that time into Hebrews and gentiles. Or to the fact that, since the Hebrews had lost sight of their natural law during their slavery in Egypt, God himself had to reinstitute it for them by the law he gave Moses on Sinai. Or to the further fact that God in his law forbids even thoughts that are less than just, with which no mortal lawgiver has ever troubled himself. Or to the bestial origins here discussed of all the gentile nations. And although he pretends that the Jews presently taught their natural law to the gentiles, he is entirely unable to prove it, opposed as he is by the magnanimous confession of Josephus seconded by the grave reflection of Lactantius cited above, and by the hostility with which, as we have also observed above, the Jews have always regarded the gentiles, and which they preserve even now when dispersed among all the nations [94f; F7].

397 And finally Pufendorf begins with an Epicurean hypothesis, supposing man to have been cast into this world without any help or care from God. Reproved for this, he defends himself in a special dissertation, but, because he does not admit providence as his first principle, he cannot even begin to speak of law, as we have heard Cicero tell Atticus the Epicurean in his dialogue *On the Laws* [335].

398 For all these reasons, we begin our treatment of law—the Latin for which is *ius*, contraction of the ancient *Ious* (Jove)—at this most ancient point of all times, at the moment when the idea of Jove was born in the minds of the founders of the nations. To the Latin derivation of *ius* from *Ious* there is a striking parallel in Greek; for, as by a happy chance we find Plato observing in the *Cratylus* [412DE], the Greeks called law at first *diaion*. This means pervasive or enduring by a philosophical etymology intruded by Plato himself, whose erudite mythology makes Jove the ether which penetrates and flows through all things [379]. But the historical derivation of *diaion* is from Jove, whom the Greeks called *Dios*, whence the Latin expression *sub dio*, which, equally with *sub Iove*, means "under the open sky." For the sake of euphony, *diaion* came later to be pronounced *dikaion*. This then is our point of departure for the discussion of law, which was originally divine, in the proper sense expressed by divination, the science of Jove's auspices, which were the divine institutions by which the nations regulated all human institutions [M4]. These two classes of institutions taken together make up the adequate subject matter of jurisprudence [342, 379]. Thus our treatment of natural law begins with the idea of divine providence, in the same birth with which was born the idea of law [E7]. For law began naturally to be observed, in the manner examined above, by the founders of the gentes properly so called, those of

the most ancient order, which were called the greater gentes, whose first god was Jove [316ff; B2].

VII

399   The seventh and last of the principal aspects of this Science is that of the principles of universal history. It begins with this first moment of all human institutions of the gentile world, with the first of the three ages of the world which the Egyptians said had elapsed before them; namely, the age of the gods, in which heaven began to reign on earth and to bestow great benefits on men [64]. This is the golden age of the Greeks, in which the gods consorted with men on earth, as we have seen Jove begin to do [377]. Starting with this first age of the world, the Greek poets in their fables have faithfully narrated the universal flood and the existence of giants in nature, and thus have truly narrated the beginnings of profane universal history. Yet later men were unable to enter into the imaginations of the first men who founded the gentile world, which made them think they saw the gods [375]. The verb *atterrare* was no longer understood in its proper sense, to send underground. The giants who lived hidden in the caves under the mountains were metamorphosed in the later traditions of overcredulous peoples, and were supposed to have piled Olympus, Pelion and Ossa one on top of the other to drive the gods from Heaven. Actually, the first impious giants not only did not fight the gods but were not even aware of them until Jove hurled his bolts. And whereas heaven was raised to an enormous height by the much more developed minds of later Greeks, to the first giants it was but the mountain summits [712f]. The fable above mentioned [of the giants storming heaven] must have been invented after Homer and fastened on him by interpolation in the *Odyssey* [11.313ff]; for in his time merely to shake Olympus would have sufficed to dislodge the gods, since in the *Iliad* he always represents them as residing on the summit of Mount Olympus. For all these reasons profane universal history has hitherto lacked its beginning, and, for lack of the rational chronology of poetic history, it has lacked its continuity as well [732ff].

[SECTION II]

[POETIC LOGIC]

[Chapter I]   *Poetic Logic*

400   That which is metaphysics insofar as it contemplates things in all the forms of their being, is logic insofar as it considers things in all the forms by which they may be signified. Accordingly, as poetry has been considered by us above as a poetic metaphysics in which the theological poets imagined bodies to be for the most part divine substances, so now that same poetry is considered as poetic logic, by which it signifies them.

401   "Logic" comes from *logos*, whose first and proper meaning was *fabula*, fable, carried over into Italian as *favella*, speech. In Greek the fable was also called *mythos*, myth, whence comes the Latin *mutus*, mute. For speech was born in mute times as mental [or sign] language, which Strabo in a golden passage [1.2.6] says existed before vocal or articulate [language]; whence *logos* means both word and idea. It was fitting that the matter should be so ordered by divine providence in religious times, for it is an eternal property of religions that they attach more importance to meditation than to speech. Thus the first language in the first mute times of the nations must have begun with signs, whether gestures or physical objects, which had natural relations to the ideas [to be expressed] [225]. For this reason *logos*, or word, meant also deed to the Hebrews and thing to the Greeks, as Thomas Gataker observes in his *De instrumenti stylo*. Similarly, *mythos* came to be defined for us as *vera narratio*, or true speech, the natural speech which first Plato and then Iamblichus said had been spoken in the world at one time [227]. But this was mere conjecture on their part, and Plato's effort to recover this speech in the *Cratylus* was therefore vain, and he was criticized for it by Aristotle and Galen. For that first language, spoken by the theological poets, was not a language in accord with the nature of the things it dealt with (as must have been the sacred language invented by Adam, to whom God granted divine onomathesia, the giving of names to things according to the nature of each), but was a fantastic

speech making use of physical substances endowed with life and most of them imagined to be divine [F7].

402   This is the way in which the theological poets apprehended Jove, Cybele or Berecynthia, and Neptune, for example, and, at first mutely pointing, explained them as substances of the sky, the earth, and the sea, which they imagined to be animate divinities and were therefore true to their senses in believing them to be gods. By means of these three divinities, in accordance with what we have said above concerning poetic characters [205, 209], they explained everything appertaining to the sky, the earth, and the sea. And similarly by means of the other divinities they signified the other kinds of things appertaining to each, denoting all flowers, for instance, by Flora, and all fruits by Pomona. We nowadays reverse this practice in respect of spiritual things, such as the faculties of the human mind, the passions, virtues, vices, sciences, and arts; for the most part the ideas we form of them are so many feminine personifications, to which we refer all the causes, properties, and effects that severally appertain to them [406]. For when we wish to give utterance to our understanding of spiritual things, we must seek aid from our imagination to explain them and, like painters, form human images of them. But these theological poets, unable to make use of the understanding, did the opposite and more sublime thing: they attributed senses and passions, as we saw not long since [377], to bodies, and to bodies as vast as sky, sea, and earth. Later, as these vast imaginations shrank and the power of abstraction grew [185], the personifications were reduced to diminutive signs. Metonymy [406] drew a cloak of learning over the prevailing ignorance of these origins of human institutions, which have remained buried until now. Jove becomes so small and light that he is flown about by an eagle. Neptune rides the waves in a fragile chariot. And Cybele rides seated on a lion.

403   Thus the mythologies, as their name indicates, must have been the proper languages of the fables; the fables being imaginative class concepts, as we have shown, the mythologies must have been the allegories corresponding to them. Allegory is defined as *diversiloquium* [210] insofar as, by identity not of proportion but (to speak scholastically) of predicability, allegories signify the diverse species or the diverse individuals comprised under these genera. So that they must have a univocal signification connoting a quality common to all their species and individuals (as Achilles connotes an idea of valor common to all strong men, or Ulysses an idea of prudence common to all wise men) [205]; such that these allegories must be the etymologies of the poetic languages, which would make their origins all univocal, whereas those of the vulgar languages are more often

analogical. We also have the definition of the word "etymology" itself as meaning *veriloquium*, just as fable was defined as *vera narratio* [401].

[*Chapter II*]   *Corollaries concerning Poetic Tropes, Monsters, and Metamorphoses*

I

404   All the first tropes are corollaries of this poetic logic. The most luminous and therefore the most necessary and frequent is metaphor. It is most praised when it gives sense and passion to insensate things, in accordance with the metaphysics above discussed [402], by which the first poets attributed to bodies the being of animate substances, with capacities measured by their own, namely sense and passion, and in this way made fables of them. Thus every metaphor so formed is a fable in brief. This gives a basis for judging the time when metaphors made their appearance in the languages. All the metaphors conveyed by likenesses taken from bodies to signify the operations of abstract minds must date from times when philosophies were taking shape. The proof of this is that in every language the terms needed for the refined arts and recondite sciences are of rustic origin [240].

405   It is noteworthy that in all languages the greater part of the expressions relating to inanimate things are formed by metaphor from the human body and its parts and from the human senses and passions. Thus, head for top or beginning; the brow and shoulders of a hill; the eyes of needles and of potatoes; mouth for any opening; the lip of a cup or pitcher; the teeth of a rake, a saw, a comb; the beard of wheat; the tongue of a shoe; the gorge of a river; a neck of land; an arm of the sea; the hands of a clock; heart for center (the Latins used *umbilicus*, navel, in this sense); the belly of a sail; foot for end or bottom; the flesh of fruits; a vein of rock or mineral; the blood of grapes for wine; the bowels of the earth.* Heaven or the sea smiles; the wind whistles; the waves murmur; a body groans under a great weight. The farmers of Latium used to say the fields were thirsty, bore fruit, were swollen with grain; and our rustics speak of plants making love, vines going mad, resinous trees weeping. Innumerable other examples could be collected from all languages. All of which is a consequence of our axiom [120] that man in his ignorance makes himself the rule of the

---

* Several of Vico's examples for which there are no common English parallels are here omitted, and substitutions are made for several others.

universe, for in the examples cited he has made of himself an entire world. So that, as rational metaphysics teaches that man becomes all things by understanding them (*homo intelligendo fit omnia*), this imaginative metaphysics shows that man becomes all things by *not* understanding them (*homo non intelligendo fit omnia*); and perhaps the latter proposition is truer than the former, for when man understands he extends his mind and takes in the things, but when he does not understand he makes the things out of himself and becomes them by transforming himself into them.

II

406   In such a logic, sprung from such a metaphysics, the first poets had to give names to things from the most particular and the most sensible ideas. Such ideas are the sources, respectively, of synecdoche and metonymy. Metonymy of agent for act resulted from the fact that names for agents were commoner than names for acts. Metonymy of subject for form and accident was due to inability to abstract forms and qualities from subjects [209]. Certainly metonymy of cause for effect produced in each case a little fable, in which the cause was imagined as a woman clothed with her effects [402]: ugly Poverty, sad Old Age, pale Death.

III

407   Synecdoche developed into metaphor as particulars were elevated into universals or parts united with the other parts together with which they make up their wholes. Thus the term "mortals" was originally and properly applied only to men, as the only beings whose mortality there was any occasion to notice. The use of "head" for man or person, so frequent in vulgar Latin, was due to the fact that in the forests only the head of a man could be seen from a distance. The word "man" itself is abstract, comprehending as in a philosophic genus the body and all its parts, the mind and all its faculties, the spirit and all its dispositions. In the same way, *tignum* and *culmen*, log and top, came to be used with entire propriety when thatching was the practice for rafter and thatch; and later, with the adornment of cities, they signified all the materials and trim of a building. Again, *tectum*, roof, came to mean a whole house because in the first times a covering sufficed for a house. Similarly, *puppis*, poop, for a ship, because it was the highest part and therefore the first to be seen by those on shore; as in the returned barbarian times a ship was called a sail. Similarly, *mucro*, point, for sword, because the latter is an abstract word and as in a genus comprehends pummel, hilt, edge, and point; and it was the point they felt which aroused their fear. Similarly, the material for the formed whole, as

iron for sword, because they did not know how to abstract the form from the material. That bit of synecdoche and metonymy, *Tertia messis erat* ("It was the third harvest"), was doubtless born of a natural necessity, for it took more than a thousand years for the astronomical term "year" to rise among the nations; and even now the Florentine peasantry say, "We have reaped so many times," when they mean "so many years." And that knot of two synecdoches and a metonymy, *Post aliquot, mea regna videns, mirabor, aristas?* ("After a few harvests shall I wonder at seeing my kingdoms?") [Vergil, *Eclogue* 1.69], betrays only too well the poverty of expression of the first rustic times, in which the phrase "so many ears of wheat"—even more particular than harvests—was used for "so many years." And because of the excessive poverty of the expression, the grammarians have assumed an excess of art behind it.

IV

408 Irony certainly could not have begun until the period of reflection, because it is fashioned of falsehood by dint of a reflection which wears the mask of truth. Here emerges a great principle of human institutions, confirming the origin of poetry disclosed in this work: that since the first men of the gentile world had the simplicity of children, who are truthful by nature, the first fables could not feign anything false; they must therefore have been, as they have been defined above, true narrations [401].

V

409 From all this it follows that all the tropes (and they are all reducible to the four types above discussed), which have hitherto been considered ingenious inventions of writers, were necessary modes of expression of all the first poetic nations, and had originally their full native propriety. But these expressions of the first nations later became figurative when, with the further development of the human mind, words were invented which signified abstract forms or genera comprising their species or relating parts with their wholes. And here begins the overthrow of two common errors of the grammarians: that prose speech is proper speech, and poetic speech improper; and that prose speech came first and afterward speech in verse [460].

VI

410 Poetic monsters and metamorphoses arose from a necessity of this first human nature, its inability to abstract forms or properties from subjects [209]. By their logic they had to put subjects together in order to

put their forms together, or to destroy a subject in order to separate its primary form from the contrary form which had been imposed upon it. Such a putting together of ideas created the poetic monsters. In Roman law, as Antoine Favre observes in his *Iurisprudentiae papinianeae scientia*, children born of prostitutes are called monsters because they have the nature of men together with the bestial characteristic of having been born of vagabond or uncertain unions [688]. And it was as being monsters of this sort, we shall find, that children born of noble women without benefit of solemn nuptials were commanded by the Law of the Twelve Tables to be thrown into the Tiber [566].

VII

411   The distinguishing of ideas produced metamorphoses. Among other examples preserved by ancient jurisprudence is the heroic Latin phrase *fundum fieri*, to become ground of, used in place of *auctorem fieri*, to become author of, to authorize, to ratify; the explanation being that, as the ground supports the farm or soil and that which is sown, planted, or built thereon, so the ratifier supports an act which without his ratification would fail; and he does this by quitting the form of a being moving at will, which he is, and taking on the contrary form of a stable thing [353, 491].

[Chapter III]   Corollaries concerning Speech by Poetic Characters among the First Nations

412   The poetic speech which our poetic logic has helped us to understand continued for a long time into the historical period, much as great and rapid rivers continue far into the sea, keeping sweet the waters borne on by the force of their flow [629]. We have cited in the Axioms [207] the statement of Iamblichus that the Egyptians attributed to Thrice-great Hermes all their discoveries useful to human life. And we confirmed this by another axiom [207]: that "children, by the ideas and names of the men, women and things they have seen first, afterwards apprehend and name all the men, women and things that bear any resemblance or relation to the first." This we said was the great natural source of the poetic characters, with which the first peoples naturally thought and spoke [209]. We also remarked that, if Iamblichus had reflected upon this nature of human institutions, bringing into relation with it the habit of the ancient Egyptians which he himself reports, he would certainly not have intruded into the mysteries of the vulgar wisdom of the Egyptians the sublime mysteries of his own Platonic wisdom [208].

413 Now in view of the nature of children [206] and the custom of the first Egyptians [207], we assert that poetic speech, in virtue of the poetic characters it employs [209], can yield many important discoveries concerning antiquity.

I

414 Solon must have been a sage of vulgar wisdom, party leader of the plebs in the first times of the aristocratic commonwealth at Athens. This fact was indeed preserved by Greek history where it narrates that at first Athens was held by the optimates. In this work we shall show that such was universally the case in all the heroic commonwealths. The heroes or nobles, by a certain nature of theirs which they believed to be of divine origin, were led to say that the gods belonged to them, and consequently that the auspices of the gods were theirs also. By means of the auspices they kept within their own orders all the public and private institutions of the heroic cities [110, 490]. To the plebeians, whom they believed to be of bestial origin and consequently men without gods and hence without auspices, they conceded only the uses of natural liberty. (This is a great principle of institutions that are discussed through almost the whole of the present work.) Solon, however, had admonished the plebeians to reflect upon themselves and to realize that they were of like human nature with the nobles and should therefore be made equal with them in civil rights—unless, indeed, Solon was [a poetic character for] the Athenian plebeians themselves, considered under this aspect [of knowing themselves and demanding their rights].

415 The ancient Romans must also have had such a Solon among them. For the plebeians in the heroic struggles with the nobles, as ancient Roman history openly tells us, kept saying that the fathers of whom Romulus composed the Senate (and from whom these patricians were descended) *non esse caelo demissos*, "had not come down from heaven"; that is, that Jove was equal [just] to all. This is the civil history of the expression *Iupiter omnibus aequus*, into which the learned later read the tenet that all minds are equal and that the differences they take on arise from differences in the organization of their bodies and in their civil education. By this reflection the Roman plebeians began to achieve equality with the patricians in civil liberty, until they entirely changed the Roman commonwealth from an aristocratic to a popular form. We proposed this as a hypothesis in the Notes on the Chronological Table, where we considered the Publilian Law in idea [104, 114]; and we shall show that it occurred in fact not only in the Roman but in all the other ancient commonwealths. Both by reasons and by authority we shall demonstrate

that the plebeians of the peoples universally, beginning with Solon's reflection, changed the commonwealths from aristocratic to popular [598, 621].

416 Hence Solon was made the author of that celebrated saying, "Know thyself," which, because of the great civil utility it had had for the Athenian people, was inscribed in all the public places of the city. Later the learned preferred to regard it as having been intended for what in fact it is, a great counsel respecting metaphysical and moral things, and because of it Solon was reputed a sage in esoteric wisdom and made prince of the Seven Sages of Greece. In this way, because from this reflection there sprang up at Athens all the institutions and laws that shape a democratic commonwealth, and because of the first peoples' habit of thinking in poetic characters, these institutions and laws were all attributed by the Athenians to Solon, just as, by the Egyptians, all inventions useful to human civil life were attributed to Thrice-great Hermes.

II

417 In the same way all the laws concerning social classes must have been attributed to Romulus.

III

418 And to Numa, all those concerning sacred institutions and divine ceremonies, for which Roman religion was later conspicuous in its time of greatest pomp.

IV

419 To Tullus Hostilius, all the laws and institutions of military discipline.

V

420 To Servius Tullius, the census [tax], which is the foundation of democratic commonwealths, and other laws in great number having to do with popular liberty, so that he was acclaimed by Tacitus [A. 3.26] as *praecipuus sanctor legum*, "chief ordainer of laws." For the census of Servius Tullius was the basic institution of the aristocratic commonwealths by which the plebeians obtained from the nobles the bonitary ownership of the fields, which gave them occasion later for creating the tribunes of the plebs to defend for them this part of natural liberty, and the tribunes gradually led them to the attainment of full civil liberty. Thus the census of Servius Tullius, by affording the occasions and starting points, developed into a census which was the basic institution of the Roman popular

commonwealth. This was discussed by way of hypothesis in the Notes on the Publilian Law [107, 111], and will later be shown to be true in fact [619ff].

VI

421 To Tarquinius Priscus, all the ensigns and devices with which the majesty of the Roman Empire was later resplendent in the most illustrious times of Rome.

VII

422 In the same way a great many laws enacted in later times were interpolated in the Twelve Tables [1001]. And (as was fully demonstrated in our *Principles of Universal Law* [Op. 2. 564–80]) since the sole purpose for which the decemvirs were created was the law by which the nobles extended quiritary ownership to the plebeians, and since this was the first law to be inscribed on a public tablet, all the laws making for equal liberty which were later inscribed on public tablets were attributed to the decemvirs because of their aspect of popular liberty. Take as a test case Greek luxury in the matter of funerals. Since the decemvirs would not have taught it to the Romans by prohibiting it, the prohibition must have come after the Romans had adopted it. But that cannot have been until after the wars with the Tarentines and with Pyrrhus, in which their acquaintance with the Greeks began. This explains the fact observed by Cicero [L. 2.25.64] that this law translated into Latin the very words in which it had been conceived in Athens.

VIII

423 It is the same with Draco, author of the laws written in blood at the time when Greek history tells us Athens was occupied by the optimates [414]. This was in the time of the heroic aristocracies, in which Greek history also tells us the Heraclids were scattered through all Greece, even into Attica [77]. They finally settled in the Peloponnesus and established their kingdom in Sparta, which was certainly an aristocratic commonwealth. Draco must have been one of the Gorgon's serpents nailed to the shield of Perseus [734], which signifies the rule of the laws. This shield with the frightful penalties it bore turned to stone those who looked upon it; just as in sacred history similar laws were called *leges sanguinis*, laws of blood, because of the exemplary punishments they carried [F7]. Minerva armed herself with this shield and was called Athena. And among the Chinese, who write in hieroglyphics to this day, a dragon is the ensign of the civil power. It is something to wonder at that two nations so distant from each other in space and time should think and express themselves in the same poetic manner. For in all Greek history nothing else is told of this Draco.

IX

424 This discovery of the poetic characters confirms us in placing Aesop considerably earlier than the Seven Sages of Greece [91]. For this philological truth is confirmed for us by the following history of human ideas. The Seven Sages were admired because they began to impart precepts of morality or of civil doctrine in the forms of maxims like the famous "Know thyself" of Solon, who was their prince. This was a precept of civil doctrine, later carried over into metaphysics and morals [414, 416]. But Aesop had previously imparted such counsels in the form of comparisons, which the poets had still earlier used to express themselves. And the order of human ideas is to observe the similarities of things first to express oneself and later for purposes of proof. Proof, in turn, is first by example, for which a single likeness suffices, and finally by induction, for which more are required. Socrates, father of all the sects of philosophers, introduced by induction the dialectic which Aristotle later perfected with the syllogism, which cannot proceed without a universal. But to undeveloped minds it suffices to present a single likeness in order to persuade them; as, by a single fable of the sort invented by Aesop, the worthy Menenius Agrippa reduced the rebellious Roman plebs to obedience [499].

425 That Aesop was a poetic character of the *socii* or *famuli* of the heroes, is revealed to us with prophetic insight by the urbane Phaedrus in one of the prologues of his *Fables* [3]:

> Attend me briefly while I now disclose
> How art of fable telling first arose.
> Unhappy slaves, in servitude confined,
> Dared not to their harsh masters show their mind,
> But under veiling of the fable's dress
> Contrived their thoughts and feelings to express,
> Escaping still their lords' affronted wrath.
> So Aesop did; I widen out his path,*

---

* Nunc fabularum cur sit inventum genus,
  Brevi docebo. Servitus obnoxia,
  Quia, quae volebat, non audebat dicere,
  Affectus proprios in fabellas transtulit.
  Aesopi illius semita feci viam . . .

as is clearly confirmed for us by his fable of the lion's share. For the plebeians were called *socii* of the heroic cities [259], and shared the hardships and dangers of war but not the spoils and the conquests. Hence Aesop was called a slave, because the plebeians were *famuli* of the heroes [555ff]. And he was represented as ugly, because civil beauty was considered to come only from solemnized marriages, and only the heroes contracted such marriages [565ff]. For the same reason Thersites was ugly, for he must have been a character of the plebeians who served the heroes in the Trojan War. He was beaten by Ulysses with the scepter of Agamemnon, just as the ancient Roman plebeians were beaten by the nobles with rods over their bare shoulders—*regium in morem,* in royal fashion, as Sallust puts it in St. Augustine's *City of God* [2.18.1]—until the Porcian Law freed Roman shoulders from the rod.

426 Such counsels, then, dictated by natural reason as useful to free civil life, must have been sentiments cherished by the plebs of the heroic cities. Aesop was made a poetic character of these plebs in this respect. Later, fables having to do with moral philosophy were ascribed to him, and he was turned into the first moral philosopher, just as Solon, who by his laws made Athens a free commonwealth, was turned into a sage [414ff]. And because Aesop counseled in fables, he was supposed to have lived before Solon, who counseled in maxims. These fables must have been conceived originally in heroic verse. There is a later tradition that they were conceived in iambic verse, which the Greek peoples spoke in a transitional period between heroic verse and prose [463]. They were finally written in prose and have reached us in that form.

X

427 In this way the later discoveries of esoteric wisdom were attributed to the first authors of vulgar wisdom; and [poetic characters like] Zoroaster in the East, Thrice-great Hermes in Egypt, Orpheus in Greece, Pythagoras in Italy, originally lawgivers, were finally believed to have been philosophers, as Confucius is today in China. For certainly the Pythagoreans in Magna Graecia were so called in the sense of nobles, who, having tried to reduce all their commonwealths from popular to aristocratic, were all slain [1087]. And the Golden Verses of Pythagoras were an imposture, as were also the Oracles of Zoroaster, the *Poimander* of Thrice-great Hermes, and the *Orphics* or verses of Orpheus [128]. There did not come down to the ancients any book on philosophy written by Pythagoras, and Philolaus was the first Pythagorean to write one, as Scheffer observes in his *De philosophia italica.*

[*Chapter IV*]   *Corollaries concerning the Origins of Languages and Letters; and, Therein, the Origins of Hieroglyphics, Laws, Names, Family Arms, Medals, and Money; and Hence of the First Language and Literature of the Natural Law of the Gentes*

428   Now from the theology of the poets, or poetic metaphysics, by way of the poetic logic sprung from it, we go on to discover the origin of languages and letters. Concerning these there are as many opinions as there are scholars who have written on the subject. So that Gerard Jan Voss says in his *Grammatica:* "With regard to the invention of letters, many authors have brought together many things, in such profusion and confusion that you go away from them more uncertain than you came." And Herman Hugo in his *De prima scribendi origine* observes: "There is no other subject on which more numerous or more conflicting opinions are to be found than in the discussion of the origin of letters and writing. How many conflicts of opinion! What is one to believe? What not believe?" Not without reason, therefore, did Bernard von Mallinckrodt, in his *De natura et usu literarum*, conclude from the impossibility of understanding how they arose that they were divine inventions; in which view he was followed by Ingewald Eling in his *Historia linguae graecae*.

429   But the difficulty as to the manner of their origin was created by the scholars themselves, all of whom regarded the origin of letters as a separate question from that of the origin of languages, whereas the two were by nature conjoined. And they should have made out as much from the words "grammar" and "characters." From the former, because grammar is defined as the art of speaking, yet *grammata* are letters, so that grammar should have been defined as the art of writing. So, indeed, it was defined by Aristotle [*Topics* 142b 31], and so in fact it originally was; for all nations began to speak by writing, since all were originally mute [225ff, 400ff, 435]. "Character," on the other hand, means idea, form, model; and certainly poetic characters came before those of articulate sounds [that is, before alphabetic characters]. Josephus stoutly maintains [66] that at the time of Homer the so-called vulgar letters had not yet been invented. Moreover, if these letters had been shaped to represent articulated sounds instead of being arbitrary signs, they would have been uniform among all nations, as the articulated sounds themselves are. Thus, in their hopeless ignorance of the way in which languages and letters began,

scholars have failed to understand how the first nations thought in poetic characters, spoke in fables, and wrote in hieroglyphs. Yet these should have been the principles, which must by their nature be most certain, of philosophy in its study of human ideas and of philology in its study of human words.

430 Having now to enter upon a discussion of this matter, we shall give a brief sample of the opinions that have been held respecting it— opinions so uncertain, frivolous, inept, pretentious or ridiculous, and so numerous, that we need not relate them. By way of sample, then: because in the returned barbarian times Scandinavia by the conceit of the nations was called *vagina gentium* and was believed to be the mother of all other nations in the world, therefore by the conceit of scholars Johannes and Olaus Magnus were of opinion that their Goths had preserved from the beginning of the world the letters divinely invented by Adam. This dream was laughed at by all the scholars, but this did not keep Johannes van Gorp from following suit and going one better by claiming that his own Dutch language, which is not much different from Saxon, has come down from the Earthly Paradise and is the mother of all other languages. This claim was ridiculed by Joseph Justus Scaliger, Philipp Camerarius, Christian Becman, and Martin Schoock. And yet this conceit swelled to the bursting point in the *Atlantica* of Olof Rudbeck, who will have it that the Greek letters came from the runes; that the Phoenician letters, to which Cadmus gave the order and values of those of the Hebrews, were inverted runes; and that the Greeks finally straightened them here and rounded them there by rule and compass. And because the inventor is called Merkurssman among the Scandinavians, he will have it that the Mercury who invented letters for the Egyptians was a Goth. Such license in rendering opinions concerning the origins of letters should prepare the reader to receive the things we shall say of them here not merely with impartial readiness to see what they bring forward that is new, but with diligence to meditate upon them and to accept them for what they must be: namely, principles of all the human and divine knowledge of the gentile world.

431 The philosophers and philologians should all have begun to treat of the origins of languages and letters from the following principles. (1) That the first men of the gentile world conceived ideas of things by imaginative characters of animate and mute substances. (2) That they expressed themselves by means of gestures or physical objects which had natural relations with the ideas; for example, three ears of grain, or acting as if swinging a scythe three times, to signify three years. (3) That they thus expressed themselves by a language with natural significations. (Plato

and Iamblichus said such a language had once been spoken in the world [207, 401]; it must have been the most ancient language of Atlantis, which scholars would have us believe expressed ideas by the nature of the things, that is, by their natural properties.) It is because the philosophers and philologians have treated separately these two things which are naturally conjoined [—the origins of languages and letters—] that the inquiry into the origins of letters has proved so difficult for them,—as difficult as that into the origins of languages, with which they have been either not at all or very little concerned.

432   At the outset of our discussion, then, we posit as our first principle the philological axiom [173] that according to the Egyptians there had been spoken in their world in all preceding time three languages corresponding in number and order to the three ages that had elapsed in their world: the ages of gods, heroes, and men. The first language had been hieroglyphic, sacred or divine; the second, symbolic, by signs or by heroic devices; the third, epistolary, for men at a distance to communicate to each other the current needs of their lives. [Cf. Clement of Alexandria, *Miscellanies* 5.4.] Concerning these three languages there are two golden passages in Homer's *Iliad*, from which it clearly appears that the Greeks agreed with the Egyptians in this matter. In the first [1.250ff] it is told how Nestor lived through three generations of men speaking different languages. Nestor must therefore have been a heroic character of the chronology determined by the thee languages corresponding to the three ages of the Egyptians; and the phrase "to live the years of Nestor" must have meant "to live the years of the world." The other passage [20.215ff] is that in which Aeneas relates to Achilles that men of different language began to inhabit Ilium after Troy was moved to the seashore and Pergamum became its fortress. To this first principle we join the tradition, also Egyptian, that their Thoth or Mercury invented both law and letters.

433   Around this truth we assemble the following others. Among the Greeks "name" and "character" had the same meaning, so that the Church Fathers used indiscriminately the two expressions *de divinis characteribus* and *de divinis nominibus*. "Name" and "definition" have also the same meaning; thus, in rhetoric, under the head of *quaestio nominis* we find a search for definition of the fact, and in medicine the nomenclature of diseases is the head under which their nature is defined. Among the Romans "names" meant originally and properly houses branching into many families. And that the first Greeks had also used "names" in this sense is shown by the patronymics, or names of fathers, which are so often used by the poets and above all by Homer. (According to Livy [10.8.10], a

tribune of the plebs defined the patricians as those *qui possunt nomine ciere patrem*, "who can use the surnames of their fathers" [that is, who were born in lawful wedlock].) These patronymics later disappeared in the popular liberty of all the rest of Greece, but were preserved by the Heraclids in the aristocratic commonwealth of Sparta. In Roman law *nomen* signifies right. Similarly, in Greek *nomos* signifies law, and from *nomos* comes *nomisma*, money, as Aristotle notes [E. 1133a 30]; and according to etymologists, *nomos* becomes in Latin *nummus* [487]. In French, *loi* means law, and *aloi* means money; and among the second barbarians the term "canon" was applied both to ecclesiastical law and to the annual rent paid by the feudal leaseholder to the lord of the land he held in fief. This uniformity of thinking perhaps explains why the Latins used the term *ius* both for law and for the fat of sacrificed animals, which was Jove's due; for Jove was originally called *Ious*, from which were later derived the genitives *Iovis* and *iuris* [398]. Among the Hebrews also, of the three parts into which they divided the animal sacrificed as a peace offering, the fat was accounted God's due and burned on the altar [F7]. The Latin *praedia*, estates (a term which must have been applied to rustic earlier than to urban estates), were so called because the first cultivated fields were the first booty (*praeda*) in the world [486, 1027f]. The first taming was of such fields, which were therefore in ancient Roman law called *manucaptae* (whence *manceps* for one under real-estate bond to the public treasury); and in Roman law *iura praediorum* remained a term for the so-called real servitudes, which were attached to real estate. And lands referred to as *manucaptae* must at first have been called *mancipia*; and it is certainly in this sense that we must understand the article of the Law of the Twelve Tables [6.1a], *Qui nexum faciet mancipiumque*; that is, "Whoever shall consign a bond, and shall consign thereby his manor . . ." [570, 1031]. The Italians, following the same line of thought as the ancient Romans, called the manors *poderi*, as having been acquired by force. Further evidence: the returned barbarism called the fields with their boundaries *presas terrarum*. The Spaniards call bold enterprises *prendas*. The Italians call family coats of arms *imprese*, and use *termini* in the sense of "words" (a usage surviving in scholastic dialectic). They also call family coats of arms *insegne*, from which is derived the verb *insegnare*, to teach. So Homer, in whose time so-called vulgar letters had not yet been invented, says Proetus's letter to Eureia against Bellerophon was written in *sēmata*, signs [I. 6.168ff].

434   To crown all these things, let the following three incontrovertible truths be added. (1) Since it has been demonstrated that the first gentile nations were all mute in their beginnings, they must have expressed

themselves by gestures or by physical objects having natural relations with their ideas [225ff, 401]. (2) They must have used signs to fix the boundaries of their estates and to have enduring witnesses of their rights [486]. (3) They all made use of money [487]. All these truths will give us the origins of languages and letters, and thereby of hieroglyphs, laws, names, family coats of arms, medals, money, and of the language and writing in which the first natural law of the gentes was spoken and written.

435   In order to establish more firmly the principles of all this, we must here uproot the false opinion held by some of the Egyptians that the hieroglyphs were invented by philosophers to conceal in them their mysteries of lofty esoteric wisdom. For it was by a common natural necessity that all the first nations spoke in hieroglyphs [226, 429]. In Africa, to the case of Egypt already noted we may add, following Heliodorus in his *Aethiopica* [4.8.1; 4.11.4—or rather Diodorus 3.4], the Ethiopians, who used as hieroglyphs the tools of all the mechanical arts. In the East the magic characters of the Chaldeans must have been hieroglyphs. In northern Asia, Idanthyrsus, king of the Scythians (quite late in their extremely long history, in which they had conquered even the Egyptians, who boasted themselves the most ancient of all nations), used five real words to answer Darius the Great, who had declared war on him [Herodotus 4.131]. These five were a frog, a mouse, a bird, a ploughshare, and a bow. The frog signified that he, Idanthyrsus, was born of the earth of Scythia as frogs are born of the earth in summer rains, so that he was a son of that land [535]. The mouse signified that he, like a mouse, had made his home where he was born; that is, that he had established his nation there. The bird signified that there the auspices were his; that is, that he was subject to none but God [488, 490, 604]. The ploughshare signified that he had reduced those lands to cultivation, and thus tamed and made them his own by force [541, 550]. And finally the bow signified that as supreme commander of the arms of Scythia he had the duty and the might to defend her. This explanation, so natural and necessary, is to be set against the ridiculous ones worked out by the counselors of Darius, according to St. Cyril [i.e., Clement of Alexandria in his *Miscellanies* 5.8]. Add to the interpretation of the Scythian hieroglyphics by Darius's counselors the far-fetched, artificial, and contorted interpretations by scholars of the Egyptian hieroglyphics, and it will be evident that in general the true and proper use made of hieroglyphics by the first peoples has hitherto not been understood. As for the Latins, Roman history has not left us without such a tradition; witness the mute heroic answer which Tarquinius Superbus sends to his son in Gabii, when in the presence of the messenger he cuts off the heads of

poppies with the stick he has in his hands. In northern Europe, as Tacitus [G. 19] observes in describing their customs, the ancient Germans were not acquainted with the secrets of letters (*literarum secreta*); that is, they did not know how to write their hieroglyphics. This must have remained the case down to the times of Frederick the Swabian, indeed to those of Rudolph of Hapsburg, when they began to write state papers in vulgar German script. In northern France there was a hieroglyphic speech called rebus of Picardy, which must have been, as in Germany, a speech by physical things; that is, by the hieroglyphics of Idanthyrsus. Even in Ultima Thule, in fact in its remotest part, namely Scotland, as Hector Boece relates in his history of that nation, they wrote in hieroglyphics in ancient times. In the West Indies the Mexicans were found to write in hieroglyphics, and Jan de Laet in his description of the new India describes the hieroglyphics of the Indians as diverse heads of animals, plants, flowers, and fruits, and notes that they distinguish families by their totemic symbols [on boundary posts]; which is the same use that is made of family coats-of-arms in our world [486]. In the East Indies the Chinese still write in hieroglyphics.

436   Thus is deflated the conceit of the scholars who came afterwards, a conceit to which that of the extremely conceited Egyptians dared not swell itself: namely, that the other sages of the world had learned from the Egyptians how to conceal their esoteric wisdom under hieroglyphics.

437   Having posited these principles of poetic logic and dissipated this conceit of the scholars, we return now to the three languages of the Egyptians. The first of these, that of gods, is attested for the Greeks by Homer, who, in five passages of his two poems, makes mention of a language more ancient than his own, which is certainly heroic, and calls it "language of the gods" [174]. Three of the passages are in the *Iliad*: the first [1.403f] where he tells that the creature called Briareus by the gods was called Aegaeon by men; the second [14.291] where he speaks of a bird called chalcis by the gods and cymindis by men; the third [20.74] where he says the river of Troy is called Xanthus by the gods, Scamander by men. [Add 2.811ff.] In the *Odyssey* there are two passages: one [12.61] where he says what men call Scylla and Charybdis the gods call Planctae Petrae; the other [10.305] where Mercury gives Ulysses a secret remedy against the enchantments of Circe, an herb called moly by the gods, knowledge of which is denied to men. Plato has many things to say about these passages [*Cratylus* 391Dff], but to no purpose; so that Dio Chrysostom later [11.22; 10.23f] slanderously accuses Homer of pretending to understand the language of the gods, which naturally is denied to men. But it may be

questioned whether in these Homeric passages we should not take "gods" to mean "heroes"; for the heroes took the name of gods [449] over the plebeians of their cities, whom they called men (as in the returned barbarian times the vassals were called *homines*, to the astonishment of Hotman), and the great lords (as in the recourse of barbarism) made a vaunt of possessing marvelous medical secrets. Thus the differences referred to may have been no more than differences between noble and vulgar speech. Be that as it may, there can be no doubt that among the Latins Varro occupied himself with the language of the gods, for he had the diligence to collect thirty thousand of their names [175], which would have sufficed for a copious divine vocabulary, with which the peoples of Latium might express all their human needs, which in those simple and frugal times must have been few indeed, being only the things that were necessary to life. The Greeks too had gods to the number of thirty thousand [175], for they made a deity of every stone, spring, brook, plant, and offshore rock. Such deities included the dryads, hamadryads, oreads, and napeads. Just so the American Indians make a god of everything that exceeds their limited understanding. Thus the divine fables of the Greeks and Latins must have been the true first hieroglyphs, or sacred or divine characters, corresponding to those of the Egyptians.

438 The second kind of speech, corresponding to the age of heroes, was said by the Egyptians to have been spoken by symbols. To these may be reduced the heroic emblems, which must have been the mute comparisons which Homer calls *sēmata* (the signs in which the heroes wrote) [433]. In consequence they must have been metaphors, images, similitudes, or comparisons, which, having passed into articulate speech, supplied all the resources of poetic expression. For certainly Homer, if we accept the resolute denial of Josephus the Jew [A.A. 1.2.12] that there has come down to us any writer more ancient than he, was the first author of the Greek tongue; and, since we owe to the Greeks all that has reached us of the gentile world, he was the first author of that entire world. Among the Latins the earliest memorials of their tongue are the fragments of the Salian songs, and the first writer of whom there is mention is Livius Andronicus the poet. With the recourse of barbarism in Europe, new languages were born. The first language of the Spaniards was that called "*el romance*," and consequently that of heroic poetry, for the *romanceros* were the heroic poets of the returned barbarian times. In France the first writer in vulgar French was Arnaut Daniel Pacca, the first of all the Provençal poets, who flourished in the eleventh century. And finally the first writers in Italy were the Florentine and Sicilian rhymers.

439 The epistolary speech of the Egyptians, suitable for expressing the needs of common everyday life in communication from a distance, must have been born of the lower classes of a dominant people in Egypt, which must have been that of Thebes (whose king Ramses extended his rule over all that great nation), because for the Egyptians that language corresponds to the age of men, the term used for the plebeians of the heroic peoples to differentiate them from the heroes [437]. This language must be understood as having sprung up by their free consent, by this eternal property, that vulgar speech and writing are a right of the people. When the emperor Claudius found three additional letters necessary to the Latin language, the Roman people would not accept them; nor have the Italians accepted those devised by Giorgio Trissino, though their lack is felt in Italian.

440 The epistolary or vulgar language of the Egyptians must have been written with letters likewise vulgar. Since the vulgar letters of the Egyptians resemble those of the Phoenicians, it is necessary to suppose that one of these peoples borrowed from the other. Those who think that the Egyptians were the first discoverers of all the things necessary or useful to human society, must consequently hold that the Egyptians taught their letters to the Phoenicians. But Clement the Alexandrian, who must have been better informed than any other author in matters Egyptian, relates that Sanchuniathon or Sancuniates the Phoenician (who in the Chronological Table is placed in the heroic age of Greece) had written the history of Phoenicia in vulgar letters; and he therefore proposes him as the first author of the gentile world to have written in vulgar characters [83]. In this connection is has to be said that the Phoenicians, certainly the first merchant people of the world, having entered Egypt for trading purposes, may well have carried thither their vulgar letters. But, entirely apart from argument or conjecture, vulgar tradition assures us that these same Phoenicians brought their letters to Greece. Tacitus [A. 11.14], examining this tradition, suggests that they passed off as their own invention the letters invented by others, meaning the Egyptian hieroglyphics. But, to allow the popular tradition some ground of truth (as we have proved all such traditions must have [144]), let us say that the Phoenicians brought to Greece hieroglyphics received from others, and that these could only have been the mathematical characters or geometric figures which they had received from the Chaldeans. The latter were beyond question the first mathematicians and especially the first astronomers of the nations; whence Zoroaster the Chaldean (whose name means "observer of the stars" according to Bochart) was the first sage of the gentile world [55, 59]. The

Phoenicians used these Chaldean characters as notations for numbers in their mercantile business, in pursuit of which long before Homer's time they frequented the shores of Greece. This is made evident by Homer's own poems, and especially the *Odyssey*. For in Homer's time, as Josephus vigorously maintains against the Greek grammarian Apion, vulgar letters had not yet been invented by the Greeks [66]. But the latter, with supreme genius, in which they certainly surpassed all nations, took over these geometric forms to represent the various articulated sounds, and shaped them into vulgar characters of letters with consummate beauty. These were later adopted by the Latins, whose letters, as Tacitus himself observes, resembled the most ancient Greek ones. Weighty proof of this is the fact that the Greeks for a long period, and the Latins down to their latest times, used capital letters to represent numbers. It must have been these letters that were taught to the Latins by Demaratus the Corinthian and by Carmenta, the wife of Evander the Arcadian [762]. We shall explain later that in ancient times Greek colonies had been taken to Latium by sea and by land [772].

441   There is no merit in the contention of many scholars that, because the Hebrews and the Greeks give almost the same names to their vulgar letters, the Greeks must have got theirs from the Hebrews. It is more reasonable that the Hebrews should have imitated the Greek nomenclature than vice versa. For it is universally agreed that from the time that Alexander the Great conquered the empire of the East (which after his death was divided by his captains) Greek speech spread throughout Egypt and the East. And since it is also generally agreed that grammar was introduced quite late among the Hebrews, it follows necessarily that the Hebrew men of letters called their Hebrew letters by the Greek names. Moreover, since the elements [of anything] are very simple in nature, the Greeks must at first have called their letters by the simplest sounds [e.g., "ah" for α], and it must have been for that reason that the letters were called elements. The Latins, following suit, called them with the same gravity, and also kept the forms of the letters like the most ancient Greek ones. We must therefore conclude that calling the letters by complex names [e.g., "alpha" for α] was introduced late among the Greeks, and later still brought by the Greeks to the Hebrews in the East.

442   These arguments confute the opinion of those who would have it that Cecrops the Egyptian brought vulgar letters to the Greeks. Another opinion, that Cadmus the Phoenician must have brought them from Egypt into Greece because he founded a city there and named it Thebes after the capital of the greatest Egyptian dynasty, will be refuted later by the

principles of Poetic Geography [742ff], by which it will appear that the Greeks who went to Egypt called the Egyptian capital Thebes because it bore a resemblance to their native city of that name. And finally we understand why cautious critics, cited by an anonymous English writer on the uncertainty of the sciences [Thomas Baker, *Reflections on Learning*], conclude from the too early date assigned to Sancuniates [83] that he never existed. We, accordingly, not to put him out of the world entirely, judge that he must be set in a later age, certainly after Homer. And to allow the Phoenicians priority over the Greeks in the invention of the so-called vulgar letters (not failing, however, to take into account that the Greeks had more genius than the Phoenicians), it has to be said that Sancuniates must have lived a little before Herodotus, who was called the father of Greek history, which he wrote in the vulgar speech. For Sancuniates was called the historian of truth; that is, a writer of what Varro in his division of times calls the historic time [52]. In that time, according to the Egyptian division of three languages corresponding to the three ages of the world that had elapsed before them, they spoke in the epistolary language written in vulgar characters [440].

443 Now, as the heroic or poetic language was founded by the heroes, so the vulgar languages were introduced by the vulgar, who were the plebs of the heroic peoples [597f]. By the Latins these languages were properly called vernacular [994]. They could not, however, have been introduced by those *vernae* defined by the grammarians as slaves born at home of enslaved prisoners of war, for these naturally learn the languages of their parents' peoples. But the first and properly so-called *vernae* were the *famuli* of the heroes in the state of the families [556]. These *famuli*, of whom the masses of the first plebs of the heroic cities were later composed, were precursors of the slaves later secured by the cities through war. All this is confirmed by the two languages of which Homer speaks: the one of gods, the other of men, which we have interpreted as the heroic and the vulgar language, respectively [437].

444 The philologians have all accepted with an excess of good faith the view that in the vulgar languages meanings were fixed by convention. On the contrary, because of their natural origins, they must have had natural significations. This is easy to observe in vulgar Latin (which is more heroic than vulgar Greek, and therefore as much more robust as the latter is more refined), which has formed almost all its words by metaphors drawn from natural objects according to their natural properties or sensible effects. And in general metaphor makes up the great body of the language among all nations. But the grammarians, encountering great numbers of

words which give confused and indistinct ideas of things, and not knowing their origins, which had made them at first clear and distinct, have given peace to their ignorance by setting up the universal maxim that articulate human words have arbitrary significations. And they have dragged in Aristotle, Galen, and other philosophers, and armed them against Plato and Iamblichus [227].

445 There remains, however, the very great difficulty: How is it that there are as many different vulgar tongues as there are peoples? To solve it, we must here establish this great truth: that, as the peoples have certainly by diversity of climates acquired different natures, from which have sprung as many different customs, so from their different natures and customs as many different languages have arisen. For by virtue of the aforesaid diversity of their natures they have regarded the same utilities or necessities of human life from different points of view, and there have thus arisen so many national customs, for the most part differing from one another and at times contrary to one another; so and not otherwise there have arisen as many different languages as there are nations. An evident confirmation of this is found in the proverbs, which are maxims of human life, the same in substance but expressed from as many points of view as there are or have been different nations [161]. Thus the same heroic origins, preserved in brief in the vulgar tongues, have given rise to the phenomenon so astonishing to biblical critics: that the names of the same kings appear in one form in sacred and in another in profane history. The reason is that the one perchance considers men with regard to their appearance or power, the other with regard to their customs, undertakings, or whatever else it may have been. In the same way we still find the cities of Hungary given one name by the Hungarians, another by the Greeks, another by the Germans, another by the Turks. The German language, which is a living heroic language, transforms almost all names from foreign languages into its own. We may conjecture that the Latins and Greeks did the same when we find them discussing so many barbarian matters with Greek and Latin elegance. This must be the cause of the obscurity encountered in ancient geography and in the natural history of fossils, plants, and animals. And for this reason we excogitated, in the first edition of this work [Op. 3.387ff], an Idea of a Mental Dictionary for assigning meanings to all the different articulate languages, reducing them all to certain unities of ideas in substance, which, considered from various points of view, have come to be expressed by different words in each [35, 145]. We make continual use of this in working out the argument of our Science. And we gave a very full example of it in which we showed that the fathers of

families, considered from fifteen different points of view in the state of the families and of the first commonwealths, at the time when the languages must have been taking form, were called by an equal number of different names by fifteen nations ancient and modern. (And most weighty are those arguments concerning the institutions of that time which are taken from the original meanings of the words, as set forth in the Axioms [240].) This is one of the three passages on account of which we do not regret the publication of that book [28, 33, 35]. The aforesaid Dictionary develops in a new way the argument presented by Thomas Hayne in his dissertation on the kinship of languages and in his others on languages in general and on the harmony of various languages. From all this we infer the following corollary: that languages are more beautiful in proportion as they are richer in these condensed heroic expressions; that they are more beautiful because they are more expressive; and that because they are more expressive they are truer and more faithful. And that on the contrary, in proportion as they are more crowded with words of unknown origin, they are less delightful, because obscure and confused, and therefore more likely to deceive and lead astray. The latter must be the case with languages formed by the mixture of many barbarous tongues, the history of whose original and metaphorical meanings has not come down to us.

446 To enter now upon the extremely difficult [question of the] way in which these three kinds of languages and letters were formed, we must establish this principle: that as gods, heroes, and men began at the same time (for they were, after all, men who imagined the gods and believed their own heroic nature to be a mixture of the divine and human natures), so these three languages began at the same time, each having its letters, which developed along with it. They began, however, with these three very great differences: that the language of gods was almost entirely mute, only very slightly articulate; the language of heroes, an equal mixture of articulate and mute, and consequently of vulgar speech and of the heroic characters used in writing by the heroes, which Homer calls *sēmata* [433]; the language of men, almost entirely articulate and only very slightly mute, there being no vulgar language so copious that there are not more things than it has words for. Thus necessarily the heroic language was in the beginning disordered in the extreme; and this is a great source of the obscurity of the fables. The fable of Cadmus will serve as a signal example. Cadmus slays the great serpent, sows its teeth, armed men spring up from the furrows, he throws a great rock among them, they fight to the death, and finally Cadmus himself changes into a serpent. So ingenious was this Cadmus, who brought letters to the Greeks, by whom this fable was

transmitted, that, as we shall explain presently, it contains several centuries of poetic history [679]!

447   To follow up what has already been said: at the same time that the divine character of Jove took shape—the first human thought in the gentile world—articulate language began to develop by way of onomato-poeia, through which we still find children happily expressing themselves. By the Latins Jove was at first, from the roar of the thunder, called *Ious*; by the Greeks, from the whistle of the lightning, *Zeus*; by the Easterners, from the sound of burning fire, he must have been called *Ur*, whence came *Urim*, the power of fire; and from this same origin must have come the Greek *ouranos*, sky, and the Latin verb *uro*, to burn. From the whistle of the lightning must also have come the Latin *cel*, one of the monosyllables of Ausonius [12.14.17], pronounced however with the Spanish cedilla (ç), which is required to give point to Ausonius's own jesting line about Venus [19.52]: *Nata salo, suscepta solo, patre edita caelo*, "Born of the sea, adopted by the soil, raised by her father to the sky." With respect to these origins it is to be noted that the same sublimity of invention evinced in the fable of Jove, which we have observed above, marks the beginning of poetic locution in onomatopoeia, which Dionysius Longinus [i.e., Demetrius *On Style* 2.94f] certainly includes among the sources of the sublime, and which he illustrates from Homer, citing the sizzling sound (*siz'*) emitted by the eye of Polyphemus when Ulysses pierces it with the fiery stake [O. 9.394].

448   Human words were formed next from interjections, which are sounds articulated under the impetus of violent passions. In all languages these are monosyllables. Thus it is not beyond likelihood that, when wonder had been awakened in men by the first thunderbolts, these interjec-tions of Jove should give birth to one produced by the human voice: *pa!*; and that this should then be doubled: *pape!* From this interjection of wonder was subsequently derived Jove's title of father of men and gods, and thus it came about presently that all the gods were called fathers, and the goddesses, mothers; whence the Latin names *Iupiter, Diespiter, Mars-piter, Iuno genitrix*. The fables certainly tell us that Juno was sterile; and many other gods and goddesses did not marry among their kind. (Venus was called the concubine, not the wife, of Mars [579].) Nonetheless they were all called fathers. (On this point there are some verses of Lucilius [1.24–27] which we have cited in the Notes to our *Universal Law* [Op. 2.413].) They were called fathers in the sense in which *patrare* originally meant to do or make, which is the prerogative of God. *Patrare* occurs thus even in Scripture, where, in the story of the creation of the world, it is said that on the seventh day God rested *ab opere quod patrarat*, from the work

which he had done. Thence must have been derived the verb *impetrare*, as if for *impatrare*. The form used in the science of augury was *impetrire*, to obtain a good augury, concerning whose origin the Latin grammarians have written so much nonsense. This proves that the first interpretation (*interpretatio*, as if for *interpatratio*) was the interpretation of the divine laws declared by the auspices [938].

449 The strong men in the family state, from a natural ambition of human pride, arrogated to themselves this divine title of fathers (a fact which may have been the ground for the vulgar tradition that the first strong men of the earth had caused themselves to be adored as gods); but, observing the piety they owed to the deities, they called the latter gods. Later, when the strong men of the first cities took the name of gods upon themselves [437], they were moved by the same piety to call the deities immortal gods, to differentiate them from themselves, the mortal gods. But in this may be observed the grossness of these giants, like that which travelers report of the Big Feet [170]. A fair trace of it has remained in the ancient Latin words *pipulum* and *pipare*, in the sense of complaint and to complain, which must be derived from the interjection of lament, *pi, pi*. *Pipulum* in this sense in Plautus is generally interpreted as synonymous with *obvagulatio* in the Twelve Tables [2.3], which must come from *vagire*, which is properly the crying of children. A similar origin from the interjection of fear must be assigned to the Greek word *paian*, which begins with *pai*. Concerning this the Greeks have a very ancient golden tradition to the effect that when they were terrified by the great serpent called Python they invoked the aid of Apollo with the words *iō paiān*. Dazed with fear, they first pronounced them slowly three times, but then, when Apollo had slain the Python, they jubilantly pronounced them another three times quickly, dividing the omega into two omicrons and the diphthong *ai* into two syllables. Thus naturally was Greek heroic verse at first spondaic and then dactylic, and it has retained this eternal property, that it gives preference to the dactyl in every foot except the last. Song arose naturally, in the measure of heroic verse, under the impulse of most violent passions, even as we still observe men sing when moved by great passions, especially extreme happiness or grief [229]. What has been said here will shortly be of much use when we discuss the origins of song and verse [463].

450 They went on to form pronouns; for interjections give vent to one's own passions, a thing which one can do even by oneself, but pronouns serve in sharing our ideas with others concerning things which we cannot name or whose names another may not understand. Pronouns are likewise in all languages, for the greater part, if not quite all, monosyllables.

The first of them, or at least among the first, must have been the one which occurs in that golden passage of Ennius [Tragedies 351]: *Aspice hoc sublime cadens, quem omnes invocant Iovem* (Behold this sublime over-hanging, which all invoke as Jove), where *hoc*, this, stands for *caelum*, the sky. It occurs also in vulgar Latin: *Luciscit hoc iam*, for *albescit caelum*, the sky grows light. And articles have from their birth this eternal property: that they go before the nouns to which they are attached.

451   Later were formed the particles, of which a great part are the prepositions, which also, in almost all languages, are monosyllables. These preserve in the name they bear this eternal property: that they go before the nouns which require them and the verbs with which they form compounds.

452   Gradually nouns were formed. In the chapter on the Origins of the Latin Language in the first edition of this work [Op. 3.368ff], we listed a great number of nouns which sprang up within Latium, beginning with the sylvan life of the Latins and continuing through their rural into their earliest city life; all of them formed as monosyllables, showing no trace of foreign origin, not even Greek, except for four words: *bous, sūs, mūs*, and *sēps*, the last of which means hedge in Latin and serpent in Greek [550]. This is the second of the three passages in that work which we regard as adequate [445]. It may serve as a model to scholars of other languages in investigating their origins to the great profit of the republic of letters. Certainly in the German language, for instance, which is a mother language (because foreign nations never entered that country to rule over it), the roots are all monosyllabic. And that nouns sprang up before verbs is proved by this eternal property: that there is no statement that does not begin with a noun, expressed or understood, which governs it.

453   Last of all, the authors of the languages formed the verbs, as we observe children expressing nouns and particles but leaving the verbs to be understood. For nouns awaken ideas which leave firm traces; particles, signifying modifications, do the same; but verbs signify motions, which involve past and future, which are measured from the indivisible present, which even philosophers find very hard to understand. Our assertion may be supported by a medical observation. There is a good man living among us who, after a severe apoplectic stroke, utters nouns but has completely forgotten verbs. Even the verbs which are genera of all the others—as *sum* is of being, to which are reduced all essences, which is as much as to say all metaphysical things; *sto* of rest and *eo* of motion, to which are reduced all physical things; *do, dico*, and *facio*, to which are reduced all feasible things, whether moral, economic, or civil—these verbs must have begun as impera-

tives. For in the state of the families, which was extremely poor in language, the fathers alone must have spoken and given commands to their children and *famuli*, who, under the terrors of patriarchal rule, as we shall soon see, must have executed the commands in silence and with blind obsequiousness. These imperatives are all monosyllables, as they have remained: *es, sta, i, da, dic, fac*, be, stand, go, give, say, make.

454 This [theory of the] genesis of languages is in conformity with the principles of universal nature, by which the elements of all things, out of which they are composed and into which they are bound to be resolved, are indivisible; and also with the principles of human nature in particular, according to the axiom that "children, even in the present copiousness of language into which they are born, and in spite of the extreme flexibility of the fibers of their organs for articulating words, begin with monosyllables" [231]. So much the more must we deem the first men of the nations to have done so, for their organs were extremely obdurate, and they had not yet heard a human voice. [Our theory] gives us, moreover, the order in which the parts of speech arose, and consequently the natural causes of syntax.

455 All this seems more reasonable than what Julius Caesar Scaliger and Francisco Sánchez have said with regard to the Latin language, reasoning from the principles of Aristotle, as if the peoples that invented the languages must first have gone to school to him!

[Chapter V]   *Corollaries concerning the Origins of Poetic Style, Digression, Inversion, Rhythm, Song, and Verse*

456 In this way the nations formed the poetic language, composed of divine and heroic characters, later expressed in vulgar speech, and finally written in vulgar characters. It was born entirely of poverty of language and need of expression. This is proved by the first lights of poetic style, which are vivid representations, images, similes, comparisons, metaphors, circumlocutions, phrases explaining things by their natural properties, descriptions gathered from their minuter or their more sensible effects, and, finally, emphatic and even superfluous adjuncts.

457 Digressions were born of the grossness of the heroic minds, unable to confine themselves to those essential features of things that were to the purpose in hand, as we see to be naturally the case with the feeble-minded and above all with women.

458   Inversions arose from the difficulty of completing statements with their verbs, which were the last part of speech to be invented [453]. Thus the Greeks, who were more ingenious, used fewer inversions than the Latins, and the Latins fewer than the Germans.

459   Prose rhythm was understood late by the writers—in Greek by Gorgias of Leontini, and in Latin by Cicero—because earlier (according to Cicero himself [*Orator* 49.166f; *The Making of an Orator* 3.44.173ff]) they had given a rhythmic character to their orations by using certain poetic measures. This fact will presently be very useful when we discuss the origins of song and verse [461ff].

460   From all this it appears to have been demonstrated that, by a necessity of human nature, poetic style arose before prose style; just as, by the same necessity, the fables, or imaginative universals, arose before the rational or philosophic universals, which were formed through the medium of prose speech. For after the poets had formed poetic speech by associating particular ideas, as we have fully shown, the peoples went on to form prose speech by contracting into a single word, as into a genus, the parts which poetic speech had associated. Take for example the poetic phrase "the blood boils in my heart," based on a property natural, eternal, and common to all mankind. They took the blood, the boiling, and the heart, and made of them a single word, as it were a genus, called in Greek *stomachos*, in Latin *ira*, and in Italian *collera* [935]. Following the same pattern, hieroglyphs and heroic letters [or emblems] were reduced to a few vulgar letters, as genera assimilating innumerable diverse articulate sounds; a feat requiring consummate genius. By means of these vulgar genera, both of words and letters, the minds of the peoples grew quicker and developed powers of abstraction, and the way was thus prepared for the coming of the philosophers, who formed intelligible genera. What has here been discussed is a small portion of the history of ideas. To such an extent has it been necessary, in seeking the origins of letters, to deal in the same breath with those of languages!

461   Concerning song and verse, since men are shown to have been originally mute, they must have uttered vowel sounds by singing, as mutes do; and later, like stammerers, they must have uttered articulate consonantal sounds, still by singing [228]. This first singing of the peoples has left a great testimony in the diphthongs surviving in the languages. These must originally have been much more numerous, as the Greeks and the French, who passed prematurely from the poetic to the vulgar age, have left us a great many of them [159]. The reason for this is that the vowels are easy to form and the consonants difficult, and, as has been shown, the first dull-

witted men were moved to utterance only by very violent passions, which are naturally expressed in a very loud voice [230]. And nature brings it about that when man greatly raises his voice, he breaks into diphthongs and song [229]. Thus the first Greeks, in the time of their gods, formed the first spondaic heroic verse with the diphthong *pai*, employing twice as many vowels as consonants [449].

462   Again, this first song of the peoples sprang naturally from the difficulty of the first utterances, which can be demonstrated both from cause and from effect. From cause, since in these men the fibers of the organ for articulating sounds were quite hard, and there were very few sounds they could make; as on the other hand children, with very flexible fibers, born into our present plenty of words, are observed to pronounce consonants only with the greatest difficulty [231]; and the Chinese, whose vulgar language has no more than three hundred articulate vocables, give them various modifications of pitch and time to match their one hundred and twenty thousand hieroglyphs, and thus speak by singing. And from effect, by the contraction of words, of which innumerable examples are observed in Italian poetry (in our "Origins of the Latin Language" [Op. 3.369f] we set forth a great number which must have begun short and been lengthened in the course of time); and on the other hand by redundancies, because stutterers use a syllable which they can more readily utter singing in such a way as to compensate for those they find it difficult to pronounce [228]. Thus there was among us in my time an excellent tenor with this speech defect, who, when he stumbled over a word, would break into the sweetest song and so pronounce it. Certainly the Arabs begin almost all their words with *al-*; and it is said the Huns were so called because they began all theirs with *hun-*. Finally, that languages began with song is shown by what we have just said: that prior to Gorgias and Cicero the Greek and Latin prose writers used certain almost poetic rhythms [459], as in the returned barbarian times the Fathers of the Roman Church did (and, it will be found, those of the Greek Church did too), so that their prose seems made for chanting.

463   The first verse must have sprung up conformably to the language and time of the heroes; that is, it was heroic verse, the grandest of all, and the proper verse for heroic poetry; and it was born of the most violent passions of fear and joy, for heroic poetry has to do only with extremely perturbed passions [449]. However, its spondaic origin was not from the great fear of the Python, as vulgar tradition relates; for such perturbation rather quickens ideas and words then retards them; whence in Latin *festinans* and *solicitus* connote fear. No, it was because of the slowness of

mind and stiffness of tongue of the founders of the nations that heroic verse was born spondaic [454]; and from that origin it retains the characteristic of never admitting anything but a spondee in the last foot [449]. Later, as minds and tongues became quicker, the dactyl was introduced. Then, as both became still more practiced, there arose the iamb, the quick foot, as Horace calls it [232f]. Finally, when mind and tongue had reached the highest degree of celerity, there developed prose, which speaks, as it were, in intelligible genera [460]. Iambic verse comes so near to prose that prose writers have often fallen into it inadvertently. Thus song went on growing swifter in its verse forms in proportion as ideas and tongues became quicker among the nations [234, 240].

464   This philosophy is confirmed by history, which tells us of nothing more ancient than oracles and sybils [381]. Thus, to signify that a thing was very old, there was the saying, "That is older than the sybil"; and the sybils, of whom a good dozen have come down to us, were scattered among all the first nations. There is a vulgar tradition to the effect that the sybils sang in heroic verse, and the oracles of all nations also gave their responses in heroic hexameters. For that reason the Greeks called this verse Pythian from their famous oracle of Pythian Apollo, who must have been so called from his slaying of the serpent called Python, which gave rise to the first spondaic verse [449]. Heroic verse was called Saturnian by the Latins, as Festus attests [s.n. Saturnus]. It must have sprung up in Italy in the age of Saturn, which corresponds to the golden age of the Greeks, in which Apollo, like the other gods, had dealings on earth with men. And Ennius says, again according to Festus, that in this verse the fauns of Italy delivered their prophecies or oracles (which certainly among the Greeks, as we have just said, were delivered in hexameters). But later the term "Saturnian verses" was applied to iambic senarii, perhaps because by then it was as natural to speak in these Saturnian iambic verses as it had previously been to speak in Saturnian heroic verses.

465   Hebraists today are divided in their opinions on the question whether Hebrew poetry is metrical or merely rhythmical. However, Josephus, Philo, Origen, and Eusebius stand as favoring meter, and (what is most to our present purpose) St. Jerome holds [in his preface to it] that the Book of Job, which is older than the books of Moses, was composed in heroic verse from the beginning of the third chapter to the end of the forty-second.

466   The Arabs, ignorant of letters, as related by the anonymous author [Thomas Baker] of [a book on] the uncertainty of the sciences

[442], preserved their language by the oral tradition of their poems until they overran the eastern provinces of the Greek empire.

467 The Egyptians inscribed memorials of their dead in verse on columns called syringes, from *sir*, which means song; whence the name of the Siren, a deity beyond doubt celebrated for her singing. Ovid [in his *Metamorphoses* 1.689ff] says the nymph Syrinx was equally celebrated for beauty and for song. By the same token, the Syrians and Assyrians, whose names are likewise derived from *sir*, must have spoken at first in verse.

468 Certainly the founders of Greek humanity were the theological poets, and these were heroes and sang in heroic verse.

469 The first authors of the Latin language were the Salii [438], who were sacred poets, from whom we have the fragments of the Salian verses, which have an air of heroic verse and are the oldest memorials of Latin speech. The conquering ancient Romans left memorials of their triumphs in a sort of heroic verse, like the *Duello magno dirimendo, regibus subigendis* of Lucius Aemilius Regillus, and the *Fundit, fugat, prosternit maximas legiones* of Acilius Glabrio, and others [in *Grammatici Latini* ed. Keil, 6.265]. In the fragments of the Law of the Twelve Tables, the articles seem upon close examination to end for the most part in Adonic verses, which are the concluding portions of heroic verses. Cicero must have imitated them in his own laws, which begin thus: *Deos caste adeunto. Pietatem adhibento* [L. 2.8.19]. ("They shall approach the gods in purity. They shall bring piety with them.") Whence the Roman custom mentioned by Cicero whereby the children learned the Law of the Twelve Tables by singing it *tanquam necessarium carmen* [L. 2.23.59], as a required song. The Cretan children, we are told by Aelian [*Various History* 2.39], did likewise [with the laws of their country]. Certainly Cicero, famous as the inventor of prose rhythm among the Latins, as Gorgias of Leontini had been among the Greeks [459], must otherwise have shunned in his prose—prose of so weighty an argument—not merely verses so sonorous as these but even iambics (much as they resemble prose), for he guarded himself against the latter even in his familiar correspondence. Hence the vulgar traditions of [laws being given in] this kind of verse must be true [K2]: the first, according to Plato [L. 657AB], that the laws of the Egyptians were poems of the goddess Isis; the second, according to Plutarch [*Lycurgus* 4.2–4], that Lycurgus gave his laws to the Spartans in verse, forbidding them in one particular law to acquire knowledge of letters; the third, according to Maximus of Tyre [6.7; 38.2], that Jove had given the laws to Minos in verse; the fourth and last, cited by Suidas [s.n.], that Draco, who by

another vulgar tradition wrote his laws in blood, proclaimed them to the Athenians in verse [423].

470   We return now from the laws to history. Tacitus in his account of the customs of the ancient Germans [G. 2] relates that they preserved in verse the beginnings of their history, and Lipsius in his notes on this passage says the same of the American Indians. The examples of these two nations, of which the first was known only to the Romans, and to them very late, and the second discovered but two centuries ago by our Europeans, give us a strong argument for conjecturing the same of all other barbarous nations, both ancient and modern; and, conjecture aside, the authorities tell us that the Persians among the ancient nations, and the Chinese among those discovered in modern times, wrote their first histories in verse. And here let this important observation be made: that, if the peoples were established by laws, and if among all these peoples the laws were given in verse, and if the first institutions of these peoples were likewise preserved in verse, it necessarily follows that all the first peoples were poets.

471   We resume now the subject under discussion, concerning the origins of verse. According to Festus [s.n. Saturnus], the wars with Carthage were described in heroic verse by Naevius even before Ennius's time; and Livius Andronicus, the first Latin writer, wrote the *Romanidae*, a heroic poem containing the annals of the ancient Romans. In the returned barbarian times the Latin historians were heroic poets, like Gunther, William of Apulia, and others. The first writers in the modern languages of Europe were versemakers [438]; and in Silesia, a province inhabited almost entirely by peasants, the people are born poets. And generally the German language preserves its heroic origins intact—even to excess—and this is the reason, though Adam Rechenberg is unaware of it, for the fact he attests, that Greek compound words can be happily rendered in German, especially in poetry. Bernegger compiled a catalog of these words and Georg Christoph Peisker has since been at pains to extend it in his *Index . . . pro graecae et germanicae linguae analogia*. The ancient Latin language has also left us many examples of compounds formed by combining whole words; and of these compounds the poets, as of their right, have continued to make use. For it must have been a common property of all the first languages that they were furnished first with nouns and only later with verbs [452f], and so they had supplied the lack of verbs by putting nouns together. These must be the principles of what [G. D.] Morhofen has written in his *Unterricht von der teutschen Sprache und Poesie*. Let this stand as a proof that "if the scholars of the German language apply themselves to

seeking its origins by these principles they will make marvelous discoveries" [I·10; 153].

472 All that has here been reasoned out seems clearly to confute the common error of the grammarians, who say that prose speech came first and speech in verse afterward [409]. And within the origins of poetry, as they have here been disclosed, we have found the origins of languages and letters.

[Chapter VI] The Other Corollaries Announced at the Beginning [of Chapter IV]

I

473 Along with this first birth of characters and languages was also born law, which the Latins called *ious* and the ancient Greeks *diaion*, celestial, from *Dios*, of Zeus or Jove. (Later, as Plato says in the *Cratylus* [412E], *diaion* became *dikaion* for the sake of euphony.) Thence came the Latin phrases *sub dio* and *sub Iove*, both meaning "under the open sky" [398]. For the heavens were observed as the aspect of Jove by all the gentile nations the world over, to receive therefrom their laws in the auspices which they considered to be his divine admonishments or commands. And this shows that all the nations were born in the persuasion of divine providence.

474 To enumerate: (1) For the Chaldeans the sky was Jove in that they believed they could foretell the future by the aspects and movements of the stars. The two sciences of these matters were called astronomy and astrology, the former dealing with the laws of the stars and the latter (in the [restricted] sense of judicial astrology) with their language. In the Roman laws, judicial astrologers were still called Chaldeans [60].

475 (2) For the Persians too the sky was Jove, for it signified for them things hidden from men. Those who were learned in the science of these things were called mages, and the word magic was applied to two sciences, one the legitimate natural science of the marvelous hidden forces of nature, the other the illicit science of the supernatural; in the latter sense a mage was a wizard. The mages used the rod (the *lituus* of the Roman augurs) to describe the circles of the astronomers; later the wizards made use of the rod and circles in their witchcraft. For the Persians the sky was the temple of Jove; and Cyrus, because this was his religion, destroyed the temples built by the Greeks.

476 (3) For the Egyptians too, Jove was the sky, for they believed that the heavens influenced sublunar affairs and announced future events. Hence they believed they could direct celestial influences by casting their images at the right time, and to this day they have preserved a vulgar art of divination.

477 (4) To the Greeks Jove was likewise the sky, for they considered as of celestial origin the theorems and mathemata we have mentioned elsewhere [391]. These they believed to be divine or sublime institutions to be contemplated by the bodily eyes and to be observed (in the sense of obeyed) as laws of Jove. From mathemata comes the term mathematicians as applied in the Roman laws to the judicial astrologers.

478 (5) As for the Romans, the verse of Ennius is well known: Aspice hoc sublime cadens, quem omnes invocant Iovem. The pronoun hoc should here be taken as standing for coelum [450]. The Romans also used the phrase templa coeli for the regions of the sky marked out by the augurs for taking the auspices [391]. Thus the Latin templum came to signify any place which is free on every side and has an unobstructed prospect. Hence extemplo, meaning immediately. It is with this old sense in mind that Vergil calls the sea neptunia templa. [Not Vergil (A. 8.695) but Plautus, Braggart Warrior 413; cf. The Rope 909.]

479 (6) The ancient Germans, as Tacitus narrates [G. 9], worshiped their gods in holy places which he calls luci et nemora. These must have been clearings leveled in the midst of the forest. The Church had great trouble in weaning them from this practice, as we gather from the councils of Nantes and Braga in Burchard's collection of Decreta; and even today traces remain of it in Lapland and Livonia.

480 (7) The Peruvian Indians, it has been learned, called their god simply "the sublime," and their open-air temples were hills up which one climbed on either of two sides by very long stairways; and all their magnificence consists in their height. Thus everywhere the magnificence of temples is measured by their disproportionate height. The pediment of temples we find in Pausanias [10.19.3; cf.1.24.5] was called aetos, which is very much to our purpose, for it means eagle. The forests were cleared to afford a prospect for observing whence came the auspices of the eagles, who fly higher than all other birds. Perhaps for that reason the pediments were called pinnae templorum, which must later have prompted the term pinnae murorum, because on the confines of these first temples of the world the walls of the first cities were erected, as we shall see later. And finally in architecture what we now call the merlons or battlements were called eagles.

481   But the Hebrews worshiped the true All Highest, who is above the heavens, in the enclosure of the tabernacle; and Moses, wherever the people of God extended their conquests, ordered the burning of the sacred groves inclosing the *luci* that Tacitus speaks of [479]. [*Exodus* 40; *Deuteronomy* 7.5; 12.3; 16.21; F7.]

482   From the foregoing we gather that the first laws everywhere were the divine laws of Jove. So ancient in origin is the usage which has come down in the languages of many Christian nations of taking heaven for God. We Italians, for example, say *voglia il cielo*, may heaven please, and *spero al cielo*, I hope to heaven, meaning God in both expressions. The Spanish have the same usage. The French say *bleu* for blue, and since blue is a term of sense perception, they must have meant by *bleu* the sky; and, just as the gentile nations used "sky" for Jove, the French must have used *bleu* for God in that impious oath of theirs, *moure bleu!* [or *morbleu!*], "God's death!"; and they still say *parbleu!* "by God!" And this may serve as an example of our Mental Dictionary [I·9, 162].

II

483   The need for certainty of ownership was a large part of the necessity for the invention of characters and names in the native sense of houses branching into many families, which, with perfect propriety, were called *gentes* [443]. Thus Thrice-great [Hermes or] Mercury, a poetic character of the first founders of the Egyptians, was their inventor of laws and letters [209]. From this *Mercury*, who was likewise held to be the god of com*mer*ce, the Italians—by a wonderful parallel in thought and expression lasting to our own time—took the verb *mercare*, to mark, in the sense of branding with letters or insignia the cattle or other *merch*andise they have for sale, to distinguish and identify the owners [606].

III

484   Such are the first origins of family coats of arms and hence of medals and coins. From these devices, employed first for private and later for public needs, came the learned emblems for pleasure's sake. These latter, by a sort of divination [on the part of the scholars], were called heroic; but they have to be explained by mottoes, for their meanings are [now merely] analogical; whereas the natural heroic emblems were such from lack of mottoes, and spoke forth in their very muteness. Hence they were in their own right the best emblems, for they carried their meaning in themselves. For example, three ears of grain, or three scythe-swinging motions, naturally signified three years [407]. And so it came about that

"names" and "characters" were interchangeable, and "names" and "natures" came to mean the same thing [433].

485   Now, beginning all over again with family arms, in the returned barbarian times the nations again became [analphabetic or] mute in vulgar speech [1051]. For this reason no notice has come down to us of the Spanish, French, Italian, or other languages of those times, and Greek and Latin were known only by the priests, so that among the French *clerc* was used in the sense of a learned man, and on the other hand the Italians, as we see from a fine passage in Dante [!], used *laico*, layman, for a man who did not know his letters. Indeed, even among the clergy ignorance was so dense that we read documents signed by bishops with the simple sign of the cross because they did not know how to write their own names. And even the learned prelates could write but little, as is shown by the diligent Father Mabillon in his work *De re diplomatica*, with its copperplate facsimiles of the signatures of bishops and archbishops to the acts of the councils of those barbarous times. They can be seen to have been written with letters more misshapen and clumsy than those of the most untaught simpleton of today. Yet for the most part the chancellors of the realms of Europe were such prelates, as was the case with the three Chancellor Archbishops of the Empire, one each for German, French, and Italian; and from these, because of the way they had of writing their letters with such irregular shapes, must have come the phrase "chancellor's script." Because of this scarcity of educated men an English law was decreed according to which a criminal under sentence of death who knew his letters would be spared as "excelling in art" [*excellens in arte non debet mori*]. Perhaps from this the term literate came later to mean learned.

486   Because of this same scarcity of men who could write, we do not find a single wall in ancient houses without some emblem [*impresa*] carved upon it. [In explanation of the word *impresa* we note that] the barbarous Latins applied the term *terrae presa* to a farm with its boundaries, and the Italians called it *podere* with the same idea the Latins had in calling it *praedium*, for the lands brought under cultivation were the first prey [or booty] of the world [433]. In the Law of the Twelve Tables estates were called *mancipia*, and those under real-estate bond (principally to the public treasury) were called *praedes* or *mancipes*, and the so-called real servitudes were referred to as *iura praediorum*. The Spanish, moreover, used the word *prenda* for bold enterprises, because the first bold enterprises of the world were the taming and cultivation of the land, the greatest of all the labors of Hercules [540f]. Again, a coat of arms was called by the Italians *insegna*, an ensign in the sense of a thing signifying, whence the Italian verb *insegnare*,

to teach. They also call it *divisa*, device, because the ensigns were used as signs of the first division of the fields, which had previously been used in common by all mankind [434]. The originally real terms [or boundary posts] of these fields later became the vocal terms of the scholastics; that is, significant words serving as terms of propositions [433]. Among the American Indians, the [totems or] hieroglyphs for distinguishing their families have a similar use as [real] terms [435].

487 The conclusion to be drawn from the foregoing is that in the time of mute nations the great need answered by the ensigns was that for certainty of ownership. Later they became public ensigns in time of peace, and from these were derived the medals, which, with the introduction of warfare, were found suitable for military insignia. The latter have their primary use as hieroglyphs, inasmuch as wars are waged for the most part between nations differing in speech and hence mute in relation to each other. Striking confirmation of what has been so far reasoned out is to be found in the example of the eagle on the scepter; for this symbol was used alike by the Egyptians, the Etruscans, the Romans, and the English, who still use it as an ornament of their royal arms. This by a uniformity of ideas, for in all these nations, divided though they are by immense tracts of land and sea, the symbol was meant to signify that the realms had their origins from the first divine kingdoms of Jove by virtue of his auspices. Finally, when commerce by means of coined money was introduced, it was found that these medals were suitable for use as coins, which indeed were for that reason called *monetae*, from *monendo*, warning, by the Latins, just as *insegnare* came from *insegna* among the Italians. In like fashion from the Greek *nomos* came *nomisma*, as Aristotle tells us; and perhaps from it too came the Latin *numus*, which the best authorities write thus with one *m*. In French, too, law is called *loi*, and the metal for coins, *aloi* [433]. These terms can have had no other origin than the law or right signified by the hieroglyph, which is precisely the use of medals. All of which is strikingly confirmed by the following names of coins: ducat from *ducendo*, commanding, which is said of captains; soldo, whence soldier; and scudo, shield, a defensive weapon, which previously meant the ground of family arms, which in the beginning was the tilled land of each father in the time of the families [529, 562ff]. This will shed light on the many ancient medals on which we find an altar, a *lituus* (the augur's rod for taking the auspices), or a tripod (from which the oracle spoke, as is indicated by the phrase *dictum ex tripode* for the word of the oracle).

488 To this sort of medals must have belonged the wings which the Greeks in their fables attached to all the physical objects signifying heroic

institutions founded on the auspices. Thus Idanthyrsus, among the real hieroglyphs with which he answered Darius, sent a bird [435]. And the Roman patricians in all their heroic contests with the plebs (as clearly appears in Roman history [e.g., Livy 6.41.6]) for the preservation of their heroic institutions took the ground that the auspices were theirs: *auspicia esse sua* [490]. Similarly in the recourse of barbarism we find noble arms bearing plumed helmets, and in the West Indies only the nobles are adorned with feathers.

IV

489   The name *Ious*, Jove, when contracted to *ius*, must have meant first of all the fat of the victims owed to Jove [433]. Similarly in the recourse of barbarism the term "canon" was applied both to ecclesiastical law and to the payment made by the fief holder to his immediate master; perhaps because the first fiefs were introduced by the ecclesiastics, who, not being able to cultivate them themselves, gave the fields of the Church to others to till. These two observations are corroborated by the two mentioned above [487]: the Greek usage by which *nomos* means law and *nomisma* means coin, and the French usage by which *loi* and *aloi* have the same meanings respectively. Precisely in the same way that was called *Ious optimus*, for "Jove most strong," which by the force of the thunderbolt gave a beginning to divine authority in its primary sense, which was that of ownership, as we have said above, for all things were of Jove [379, 387].

490   That truth of rational metaphysics concerning the omnipresence of God, which had been taken in the false sense of poetic metaphysics: *Iovis omnia plena*, "All things are full of Jove" [379], conferred human authority on those giants who had occupied the first vacant lands of the world, in the same sense of ownership [388]. In Roman law this was certainly called *ius optimum*, but its original meaning was quite different from that in which it was used in later times. For it had at first the sense defined by Cicero in a golden passage in his orations: "ownership of real estate subject to no encumbrance private or public" [*On the Agrarian Law* 3.2.7ff]. This *ius* was called *optimum* in the same sense of strongest, as not having been weakened by any extraneous encumbrance [601, 984]. For right was reckoned by strength in the first times of the world [520ff, 582ff]. This ownership must have belonged to the fathers in the family-state, and was consequently the natural ownership which had to precede the civil. As cities were formed by uniting families based on this best ownership (called in Greek *dikaion ariston*), they were originally aristocratic [582ff]. Springing from the same origin among the Latins, the so-called commonwealths of the optimates were also called commonwealths of the few, because they

were made up of those "few whom just Jupiter loved," *pauci quos aequus amavit Iupiter* [389]. In their heroic contests with the plebs, the heroes maintained their heroic institutions by means of the divine auspices [414]. In mute times they signified their institutions by the bird of Idanthyrsus, by the wings of the Greek fables; and finally by the articulate language of the Roman patricians, declaring that "the auspices are ours" [110, 488].

491 Jove with his bolts, from which the most important auspices were drawn, had struck down the first giants and driven them under the earth to live in the caves of the mountains. By striking them down in this fashion he had given them the opportunity of becoming lords of the fields of those lands where they found themselves settled in hiding, and thereby they became the lords in the first commonwealths [387ff]; and because of this ownership [when they approved or authorized anything] each of them was said to become its *fundus* in the sense of its *auctor* [411]. From their private authority within the family came, with the union of the families, the civil or public authority of their ruling heroic senates [584], as set forth in the coin (of which there are so many examples among those of the Greek commonwealths reproduced in Goltz) depicting three human thighs united in the center with the soles of the feet supporting the circumference. This signifies the ownership of the fields of each region or territory or district of each commonwealth. This is now called eminent domain [266] and is signified by the hieroglyph of the pome which today surmounts the crowns of civil powers [548, 602]. The [fact that the legs in the medal are] three [in number] lends particular strength to this interpretation, as the Greeks were accustomed to express the superlative by the number three, as the French now say *très* for very [718]. By the same figure of speech, Jove's thunderbolt was called three-furrowed because it furrowed the air most forcefully. (Thus the idea of furrowing was perhaps first applied to air, then earth, and finally water.) Similarly, Neptune's trident was so called because it was a most powerful hook for biting or grappling ships [634]; and Cerberus was called three-throated as having an enormous gullet [718, 721].

492 What we have said here of family arms is to be preferred to our discussion of their origins in the first edition of this work [Op. 3.330–341], though that is the third passage in that edition on account of which we do not regret its publication [445, 452].

V

493 It follows from all this that Grotius, Selden, and Pufendorf, the three princes of the natural law of the gentes [394], should have begun their expositions from the letters and laws which Thrice-great Hermes

devised for the Egyptians [483], from the "characters" and "names" of the Greeks, and from the names which signify both gentes and laws to the Romans. And they should have gone on to unfold it by a well-informed interpretation of the hieroglyphs and fables as the medals of the times in which the gentile nations were founded [487f]; and thus to ascertain their customs by a metaphysical criticism of the founders of the nations [348], which should have given the first light to the philological criticism of their writers [351ff], who did not come forth until more than a thousand years after the nations had been founded.

[Chapter VII]   *Final Corollaries concerning the Logic of the Learned*

I

494   The results so far reached by the aid of this poetic logic concerning the origins of languages do justice to their first creators. They were rightly regarded as sages in all subsequent times because they gave natural and proper names to things, so that among the Greeks and Latins "name" and "nature" meant the same thing [433].

II

495   The first founders of humanity applied themselves to a sensory topics [K5n], by which they brought together those properties or qualities or relations of individuals and species which were, so to speak, concrete, and from these created their poetic genera [205, 209].

III

496   So that we may truly say that the first age of the world occupied itself with the primary operation of the human mind [699].

IV

497   And first it began to hew out topics, which is an art of regulating well the primary operation of our mind by noting the commonplaces that must all be run over in order to know all there is in a thing that one desires to know well; that is, completely.

V

498   Providence gave good guidance to human affairs when it aroused human minds first to topics rather than to criticism, for acquaintance with

things must come before judgment of them. Topics has the function of making minds inventive, as criticism has that of making them exact. And in those first times all things necessary to human life had to be invented, and invention is the property of genius. In fact, whoever gives the matter some thought will observe that not only the necessaries of life but the useful, comfortable, pleasing, and even luxurious and superfluous had already been invented in Greece before the advent of the philosophers [794ff]. On this point we have set forth an axiom above: namely, that "children are extraordinarily gifted in imitation," that "poetry is nothing but imitation," and that "the arts are only imitations of nature and consequently in a certain sense real poetry" [215ff]. Thus the first peoples, who were the children of the human race, founded the first world of the arts; then the philosophers, who came a long time afterward and so may be regarded as the old men of the nations, founded the world of the sciences, thereby making humanity complete.

VI

499 This history of human ideas is strikingly confirmed by the history of philosophy itself. For the first kind of crude philosophy used by men was *autopsia,* or the evidence of the senses. (This was later used by Epicurus, for he, as a philosopher of the senses, was satisfied with the mere exhibition of things to the evidence of the senses.) And the senses of the first poetic nations were extremely lively [375f]. Then came Aesop, or the moral philosophers whom we would call vulgar. (Aesop preceded the Seven Sages of Greece [424ff].) Aesop taught by example and, since he lived in what was still the poetic age, his examples were invented to suit the case. (The good Menenius Agrippa used one such example [the belly and the members, Livy 2.32] to reduce the rebellious Roman plebs to obedience.) An example of this sort, or better still a true one, is even now more persuasive to the ignorant crowd than the most invincible reasoning from maxims. After Aesop came Socrates, who introduced dialectic, employing induction of several certain things related to the doubtful thing in question [1040]. Before Socrates, medicine, by induction of observations, had given us Hippocrates, prince of all doctors both in merit and in precedence, who earned the immortal eulogy: "He deceives no one nor is deceived by any" (*Nec fallit quenquam, nec falsus ab ullo est*). [Cf. Macrobius: *Commentary on the Dream of Scipio* 1.6.64.] Mathematics by the unitive [inductive] method called synthetic had made, in Plato's time, its greatest progress in the Italian school of Pythagoras, as we can see from the *Timaeus.* Thus by virtue of this unitive method, Athens at the time of

Socrates and Plato was resplendent in all the arts for which human genius can be admired—poetry, eloquence, and history, as well as music, casting in bronze, painting, sculpture, and architecture. Then came Aristotle and Zeno. The former taught the syllogism, a method which deduces particulars from their universals rather than uniting particulars to obtain universals. The latter taught the sorites, which, like the method of modern philosophers, makes minds subtle but not sharp. Neither yielded anything more notable to the advantage of the human race. Hence with great reason Bacon, great alike as philosopher and statesman, proposes, commends, and illustrates the inductive method in his [Novum] Organum, and is still followed by the English with great profit in experimental philosophy.

VII

500   This history of human ideas clearly convicts of their common error all those who, under the influence of the mistaken popular belief in the superlative wisdom of the ancients, have held that Minos, the first lawgiver of the gentile nations, Theseus at Athens, Lycurgus at Sparta, and Romulus and other kings at Rome established universal laws. For the most ancient laws, we observe, were each conceived to command or forbid in but a single case; only later were they given general application (so incapable of universals were the first peoples!); and furthermore they were not conceived at all before the acts occurred that made them necessary. The law of Tullus Hostilius in the case against Horatius is nothing else but the penalty decreed by the duumvirs, appointed for that purpose by the king, against the illustrious culprit. Livy [1.26.6] calls it lex horrendi carminis, a law of dread song [or formula] [1036]; it is one of the laws which Draco wrote in blood, and sacred history calls them leges sanguinis [423]. Livy's observation that the king did not wish to proclaim the law, in order not to be responsible for such a harsh and unpopular verdict, is quite ridiculous. For the king himself prescribed the formula of condemnation to the duumvirs, so that the latter could not have acquitted Horatius even had he been found innocent. Livy is here not at all clear, for he did not understand that in the heroic senates, which were aristocratic, the kings had no other power than that of creating duumvirs to act as commissioners to pronounce judgment in criminal trials, and that the peoples of the heroic cities consisted of nobles only, to whom the condemned could appeal [521].

501   To return now to the point, that law of Tullus is in fact one of the so-called examples, in the sense of exemplary punishments, which must have been the first examples used by human reason. (This agrees with what we learned from Aristotle [269], that "in the heroic commonwealths there

were no laws concerning private wrongs or injuries.") Thus first came real examples and later the reasoned ones of logic and rhetoric. But when intelligible universals had come to be understood, that essential property of law—that it must be universal—was recognized, and the maxim of jurisprudence was established that we must judge by the laws, not by examples (*Legibus, non exemplis, est iudicandum*).

[SECTION III]

[POETIC MORALS]

[Chapter I]   Poetic Morals and the Origins of the Vulgar Virtues Taught by Religion through the Institution of Matrimony

502   The metaphysics of the philosophers, by means of the idea of God, fulfills its first task, that of clarifying the human mind, which needs logic so that with clear and distinct ideas it may shape its reasonings, and descend therewith to cleanse the heart of man with morality. Just so the metaphysics of the poet giants [377ff], who had warred against heaven in their atheism, vanquished them with the terror of Jove, whom they feared as the wielder of the thunderbolt. And it humbled not only their bodies but their minds as well, by creating in them this frightful idea of Jove. (The idea was of course not shaped by reasoning, for they were not yet capable of that, but by the senses, which, however false in the matter, were true enough in their form—which was the logic comformable to such natures as theirs [400].) This idea, by making them god-fearing, was the source of their poetic morality. From this nature [or beginning] of human institutions arose the eternal property that minds to make good use of the knowledge of God must humble themselves, just as on the other hand arrogance will lead them to atheism, for atheists become giants in spirit, ready to say with Horace: *Caelum ipsum petimus stultitia,* "Heaven itself we assail in our folly" [*Odes* 1.3.38].

503   Such god-fearing giants Plato certainly recognized as represented by the Polyphemus of Homer [296]. And we find support in what Homer himself tells of this same giant, in the passage [O. 9.508ff] where he makes him say that an augur who had lived at one time among the cyclopes had predicted to him the woes which he later suffered at the hands of Ulysses; for augurs certainly cannot live among atheists. Thus poetic morality began with piety, which was ordained by providence to found the nations, for among them all piety is proverbially the mother of all the moral, economic, and civil virtues. Religion alone has the power to make us practice virtue,

as philosophy is fit rather for discussing it. And piety sprang from religion, which properly is fear of divinity. The heroic origin of the word "religion" was preserved among the Latins by those who derive it from *religando*, binding, with reference to those fetters with which Tityus and Prometheus were bound on the mountain crags to have their hearts and entrails devoured by the eagle; that is, by the frightful religion of the auspices of Jove [387]. Hence came the eternal property among all nations, that piety is instilled in children by the fear of some divinity.

504 Moral virtue began, as it must, from conatus [340]. For the giants, enchained under the mountains by the frightful religion of the thunderbolts, learned to check their bestial habit of wandering wild through the great forest of the earth, and acquired the contrary custom of remaining hidden and settled in their fields. Hence they later became the founders of the nations and the lords of the first commonwealths [387ff, 553ff]. This has been preserved by vulgar tradition as one of the great benefits conferred on the human race by heaven when it reigned on earth through the religion of the auspices. And hence came Jove's title of stayer or establisher [379]. With this conatus the virtue of the spirit [696] began likewise to show itself among them, restraining their bestial lust from finding its satisfaction in the sight of heaven, of which they had a mortal terror. So it came about that each of them would drag one woman into his cave and would keep her there in perpetual company for the duration of their lives. Thus the act of human love was performed under cover, in hiding, that is to say, in shame; and they began to feel that sense of shame which Socrates described as the color of virtue [in Plato's *Euthyphro* 12CD]. And this, after religion, is the second bond that keeps nations united, even as shamelessness and impiety destroy them.

505 In this guise marriage was introduced [C1–2], which is a chaste carnal union consummated under the fear of some divinity. We made this the second principle of our Science [333], with its source in our first principle, which is divine providence. It arose accompanied by three solemnities.

506 The first of these solemnities was the auspices of Jove, taken from the thunderbolts by which the giants were induced to observe them. From this *sors*, or lot [signified by the auspices], marriage was defined among the Romans as *omnis vitae consortium*, a lifelong sharing of lot, and the husband and wife were called *consortes*, or lot sharers. And to this day Italian girls when they marry are said to take up their lot, *prender sorte*. In this determinate guise and in this first time of the world arose the law of the gentes that the wife adopts the public religion of her husband.

For husbands shared their first human ideas with their wives, beginning with the idea of a divinity of theirs which compelled them to drag their women into their caves; and thus even this vulgar metaphysics began to know the human mind in God [365]. And from this first point of all human institutions gentile men began to praise the gods, in the ancient Roman legal sense of citing or calling them by name; whence the phrase *laudare auctores*, bidding men to cite the gods as authors of whatever they themselves did. Such must have been the praises which men owed to the gods.

507   From this most ancient origin of marriage came the custom by which women enter the families and houses of the men they marry. This natural custom of the gentes was preserved by the Romans, among whom women were regarded as daughters of their husbands and sisters of their children. Thus not merely must marriage have been from the beginning a union with one woman only, as it continued to be among the Romans (a custom Tacitus [G. 17] admires in the ancient Germans, who like the Romans kept intact the first institutions of their nations, and who give us ground for conjecturing similar [monogamous] beginnings for all others), but it must also have been a union to last for life, as indeed remained the custom among a great many peoples. Hence among the Romans marriage was defined, with this property in view, as *individua vitae consuetudo*, unbroken companionship of life [J. 1.9.1]; and divorce was introduced very late among them.

508   Among the auspices thus taken from the thunderbolts of Jove, fabulous Greek history describes Hercules (a [poetic] character of founders of nations [514]) as born of Alcmena by a bolt of Jove. Another great hero of Greece is Bacchus, born of thunderstruck Semele. This was the first reason for which the heroes called themselves sons of Jove; the assertion was a truth of the senses for them, persuaded as they were that all things were the work of the gods [377, 379, 506]. And this is the meaning of that passage of Roman history in which, to the patricians who said in the heroic contests that the auspices were theirs [110, 488], the plebs replied that the fathers of whom Romulus had composed the senate, and from whom the patricians traced their descent, *non esse caelo demissos*, "were not de-scended from heaven"; for if this does not mean that the fathers were not heroes, it is hard to see how the reply is appropriate [415]. Hence, to signify that *connubium*, or the right to contract solemn nuptials, whose chief solemnity was the auspices of Jove, was the prerogative of the heroes, they represented noble Love as winged and blindfolded in token of his modesty, and called him *Eros*, a name similar to *heros*, hero, which was their own.

And they created a winged Hymen too, the son of Urania, whose name is from *ouranos*, heaven, and signifies "she who contemplates the heavens" to take thence the auspices. Urania must have been the first of the Muses; she was defined by Homer as "the science of good and evil" [365]; and she too, like the rest, was conceived as winged because she belonged to the heroes [488]. We have already explained the historic sense of the saying about her: A *Iove principium musae* [391]. She and the other Muses were held to be daughters of Jove (for religion gave birth to all the arts of humanity, of which Apollo, held to be principally the god of divination [533], is the presiding deity), and they "sing" in the sense in which the Latin verbs *canere* and *cantare* mean "foretell."

509   The second solemnity is the requirement that the women be veiled in token of that sense of shame that gave rise to the first marriages in the world. This custom has been preserved by all nations; among the Latins it is reflected in the very name "nuptials," for *nuptiae* is from *nubendo*, which means "to cover." And in the returned barbarian times maidens were called virgins *in capillo*, in [uncovered] hair, in distinction from married women, who go about veiled.

510   The third solemnity—also preserved by the Romans—was a certain show of force in taking a wife, recalling the real violence with which the giants dragged the first wives into their caves. And by analogy with the first lands which the giants had occupied by taking physical possession of them, properly wedded wives were said to be *manucaptae*, taken by force.

511   The theological poets who had created the divine character of Jove now created a second, that of solemn matrimony; namely, Juno, the second divinity of the so-called greater gentes [317]. She is both wife and sister of Jove, because the first lawful or solemn marriages (called lawful from the solemnity of the auspices of Jove [398]) must have taken place between brothers and sisters [526]. She is queen of gods and men because the kingdoms were afterward born of these legitimate marriages. And she is fully clothed as we observe in the statues and medals, to signify modesty.

512   The heroic Venus too, called *pronuba* in her character of patron goddess of solemn marriage, covers her private parts with the girdle, which effeminate poets later embroidered with all the incentives to lust. By that time the austere history of the auspices had become corrupt and Venus was believed to lie with men, even as Jove with women, and to have conceived Aeneas by Anchises, for Aeneas was born under the auspices of this Venus. And to this Venus are attributed the swans—shared by her with Apollo —who sing in that sense in which *canere* or *cantare* means *divinari*, to foretell [508]. Taking the shape of one of these swans, Jove lies with Leda,

signifying that under the auspices of Jove, Leda conceives the egg-born Castor, Pollux, and Helen.

513 Juno is called *jugalis*, "of the yoke," with reference to the yoke of solemn matrimony, for which it was called *conjugium* and the married pair *conjuges*. She is also known as Lucina, who brings the offspring into the light; not natural light, for that is shared by the offspring of slaves, but the civil light by reason of which the nobles are called illustrious. And she is jealous with a political jealousy, that from which the Romans down to the 309th year of Rome excluded the plebs from *connubium*, or lawful marriage [110, 598]. By the Greeks, however, she was called Hera, whence the name the heroes gave themselves, for they were born of solemn nuptials, of which Juno was the goddess, and hence generated by noble Love (which is the meaning of Eros [508]), who was identical with Hymen. And the heroes must have been so called in the sense of "lords of the families" in distinction from the *famuli*, who were in effect slaves [553ff]. *Heri* had this same meaning in Latin, whence *hereditas* for inheritance, for which the native Latin word had been *familia*. With such an origin, *hereditas* must have meant a despotic sovereignty, and by the Law of the Twelve Tables there was reserved to the family fathers a sovereign power of testamentary disposition, in the article: *Uti paterfamilias super pecunia tutelave suae rei legassit, ita ius esto* [5.3]. ("As the family father has disposed concerning his property and the guardianship of his estate, so shall it be binding.") The disposing was generally called *legare*, which is a prerogative of sovereigns; thus the heir becomes a "legate" [legatee] who in inheriting represents the defunct paterfamilias, and the children no less than the slaves came under the terms "estate" and "property." All of which proves only too conclusively the monarchic power that the fathers had had over their families in the state of nature. This they were bound to retain—and did in fact retain—in the state of the heroic cities. These must in origin have been aristocratic, that is, commonwealths of lords, for the fathers still retained their power even in the popular commonwealths. All these matters will later be discussed at length [520–678].

514 The goddess Juno imposes great labors on the Theban, that is the Greek, Hercules. (For every ancient gentile nation had a Hercules as its founder [196].) This signifies that piety and marriage form the school wherein are learned the first rudiments of all the great virtues. And Hercules, with the favor of Jove under whose auspices he was begotten, surmounts all the difficulties. He was therefore called Heracles, that is *Heras kleos*, the glory of [Hera or] Juno. And if glory be properly esteemed, as Cicero defines it [*On Behalf of Marcellus* 8.26], as "widespread fame for

services to mankind," how great a glory must it have been for the Herculeses to have founded the nations by their labors! But when these severe significations had been obscured by time, and customs had become effeminate, Juno's sterility was taken as natural and she was held to be jealous only of an adulterous Jove. Hercules was then made a bastard son of Jove, who by Jove's favor and in despite of Juno had carried out all his labors. Thus he became not Juno's glory but her complete disgrace (by a[n interpretation of his] name quite contrary to the facts), and Juno was made a mortal enemy of virtue. [Originally] the hieroglyph or fable of Juno hanging in the air with a rope around her neck and her hands tied by another rope and with two heavy stones tied to her feet, had signified the sanctity of marriage. (Juno was in the air to signify the auspices essential to solemn nuptials, and for the same reason Iris was made her handmaiden and the peacock with its rainbow tail was assigned to her. She had a rope about her neck to recall the violence used by the giants on the first wives. Her hands were bound in token of the subjection of wives to their husbands, later represented among all nations by the more refined symbol of the wedding ring. The heavy stones tied to her feet denoted the stability of marriage, for which Vergil calls solemn matrimony *conjugium stabile* [A. 1.73; 4.126].) But now this fable was taken as representing a cruel punishment inflicted by an adulterous Jove, and, with the unworthy interpretations bestowed upon it by later times with corrupted customs, it has greatly exercised the mythologists ever since.

515 For these very reasons Plato interpreted the Greek fables as Manetho had the Egyptian hieroglyphs, observing on the one hand the incongruity of gods having such customs, and on the other the congruity [of the fables] with his own ideas. Into the fable of Jove he intruded the idea of his ether which flows and penetrates everywhere, on the strength of the phrase "all things are full of Jove" (*Iovis omnia plena*) [379]. But the Jove of the theological poets dwelt no higher than the mountains and the region of the air in which lightning is generated. Into the fable of Juno he intruded the idea of breathable air; but Juno has no offspring by Jove, whereas ether and air produce everything. (So far were the theological poets from understanding by this fable that truth of physics which teaches that the universe is filled with ether, or that truth of metaphysics which demonstrates the omnipresence attributed to God by the natural theologians!) Above poetic heroism Plato raised his own philosophic heroism, placing the hero above man as well as beast [R. 391D]; for the beast is the slave of his passions, and man, in the middle of the scale, struggles with his passions, while the hero at will commands his passions; and thus the heroic

nature is midway between the human and the divine. And Plato held that the noble Love of the poets (called Eros from the same root as *heros*, hero) was fittingly imagined as winged and blindfolded, and plebeian Love as without wings or blindfold, to set forth the two loves, divine and bestial; the one blind to the things of the senses, the other intent upon them; the one rising on wings to the contemplation of intelligible things, the other, for lack of wings, falling back upon sensible things. Ganymede, borne off to heaven by an eagle of Jove, and thus signifying to the austere poets the contemplator of Jove's auspices, became in corrupt times an ignoble pleasure of Jove; but Plato [i.e., Xenophon *Symposium* 8.30] by a fine conceit took him for the metaphysical contemplative, who through contemplation of supreme being by the method he calls unitive has achieved union with Jove.

516   In this way, piety and religion made the first men naturally (1) prudent, by taking counsel from the auspices of Jove; (2) just both in that first justice toward Jove (who gave his name to the just [398]) and in that toward men, which consists in not meddling in one another's affairs, as Polyphemus tells Ulysses of the giants scattered among the caves of Sicily [O. 9.113f] (and which, though it appears to be justice, was in fact savagery); and moreover (3) temperate, content with one woman for their lifetime. And, as we shall see later [1099], piety and religion likewise made them (4) strong, industrious, and magnanimous. Such were the virtues of the golden age, which was not, as effeminate poets later pictured it, an age in which pleasure was law. For in the golden age of the theological poets, men insensible to every refinement of nauseous reflection took pleasure only in what was permitted and useful, as is still the case, we observe, with peasants. (The heroic origin of the Latin verb *iuvare* is preserved in the expression *iuvat* ["it helps"] for "it is pleasant.") Nor were the philosophers right in imagining it as an age in which men read the eternal laws of justice in the bosom of Jove, for at first they read in the aspect of the sky the laws dictated to them by the thunderbolts. In conclusion, the virtues of that first time were like those admired by the Scythians [100], who would fix a knife in the ground and adore it as a god, and thus justify their killings; that is, they were virtues of the senses, with an admixture of religion and cruelty, whose affinity may still be observed among witches [190].

517   From this early morality of the superstitious and cruel gentile world came the custom of sacrificing human victims to the gods. This we have from the most ancient Phoenicians, among whom, when some great calamity was imminent, such as war, famine, or pestilence, the kings

sacrificed their own children to placate the wrath of heaven, as Philo of Byblus narrates [in a passage quoted by Eusebius in his *Preparation for the Gospel* 1.10.40cd]. Such sacrifices of children were regularly offered to Saturn, according to Quintus Curtius [4.3.23]. Justin [18.5.12; 19.1.11] says the custom was continued by the Carthaginians, a people undoubtedly of Phoenician origin [660], and was practiced by them down to their latest times. This is confirmed by Ennius [*Annals* 237] in the verse: *Et Poinei solitei sos sacruficare puellos*, "and the Phoenicians [i.e., Carthaginians] were accustomed to sacrifice their own children." After their defeat at the hands of Agathocles, they sacrificed two hundred noble children to placate their gods. The Greeks fell in with this impiously pious custom of the Phoenicians and Carthaginians in the votive sacrifice Agamemnon made of his daughter Iphigenia. This should cause no surprise to anyone who reflects upon the cyclopean paternal power of the first fathers of the gentile world; a power exercised by the most learned nation, the Greeks, and by the wisest, the Romans. In both these nations down to the times of their most cultivated humanity, fathers had the right to kill their newborn children. This consideration will certainly lessen the repugnance our modern mildness makes us feel for the action of Brutus in decapitating his two sons who had plotted to restore the tyrant Tarquinius to the rule of Rome; and for that of Manlius, called the Imperious, in cutting off the head of his brave son who had fought and won a battle against his father's orders. Caesar [G.W. 6.16] reports that the Gauls also offered sacrifices of human victims, and Tacitus in the *Annals* [14.30] relates of the Britons that the divine science of the Druids (who, according to the conceit of the scholars, were rich in esoteric wisdom) divined the future from the entrails of human victims. This cruel and frightful religion was prohibited by Augustus to Romans living in Gaul, and it was forbidden to the Gauls themselves by Claudius, according to Suetonius in his life of that emperor [25.5]. Students of oriental languages thus hold that the Phoenicians had spread through the rest of the world the sacrifices of Moloch (identified with Saturn by Mornay, van der Driesche, and Selden), to whom they offered a man burnt alive. Such was the humanity which the Phoenicians, who brought letters to Greece, went about inculcating in the first nations of the most barbarous gentiles! It is said that Hercules had purged Latium of a like fearful custom, that of throwing living men into the Tiber as sacrifices, and that he had introduced instead the practice of throwing in men of straw. But Tacitus [G. 9] tells of solemn human sacrifices among the ancient Germans, who certainly throughout all remembered time were shut off from all foreign nations, so that the Romans with all the strength in the world could not penetrate among them. The Spaniards too found such rites in America, which until two centuries ago was hidden from all the rest of the world. The barbarians there feasted on human flesh (according to Lescarbot, *Histoire de la nouvelle France*), which must have been that of men who had been consecrated and killed by them. (Such sacrifices are described by Oviedo, *Hystoria . . . de las Indias*.) So that, while the ancient Germans were beholding the gods on earth, and the American Indians likewise [375], and while the most ancient Scythians were rich in so many golden virtues as we have heard them praised for by the writers—in these same times they were practicing such inhuman humanity! All these [human sacrifices] were those called in Plautus *Saturni hostiae*, Saturn's victims [191], at a time that writers call the golden age of Latium [73]. Such a mild, benign, sober, decent, and well-behaved time it was!

518   We may conclude from all this how empty has been the conceit of the learned concerning the innocence of the golden age observed in the first gentile nations. In fact, it was a fanaticism of superstition which kept the first men of the gentiles, savage, proud, and most cruel as they were, in some sort of restraint by main terror of a divinity they had imagined. Reflecting on this superstition, Plutarch [*Superstition* 10.169EF] poses the problem whether it was a lesser evil thus impiously to venerate the gods than not to believe in them at all. But he is not just in weighing this cruel superstition against atheism, for from the former arose the most enlightened nations while no nation in the world was ever founded on atheism [333ff].

519   So much may be said of the divine morality of the first peoples of the lost human race. The heroic morality we shall discuss in its place [666ff].

[SECTION IV]

[POETIC ECONOMY]

[Chapter I]   Of Poetic Economy, and Here of the Families Which at First Included Only Children [and Not Famuli*]*

520 The heroes apprehended with human senses those two truths which make up the whole of economic doctrine, and which were preserved in the two Latin verbs *educere* and *educare*. In the prevailing best usage the first of these applies to the education of the spirit and the second to that of the body. The first, by a learned metaphor, was transferred by the natural philosophers to the bringing forth of forms from matter. For heroic education began to bring forth in a certain way the form of the human soul which had been completely submerged in the huge bodies of the giants, and began likewise to bring forth the form of the human body itself in its just dimensions from the disproportionate giant bodies [C6, M7, 524, 692].

521 As regards the first part, the heroic fathers must have been, in the state called that of nature, the wise men in the wisdom of the auspices or vulgar wisdom, and consequently they must have been the priests who, as being more worthy, had the duty of making sacrifices in order to take or understand well the auspices. And finally they must also have been the kings who had the duty of carrying the laws from the gods to their own families [250ff]; that is, they were legislators in the proper sense of the word, bearers of laws, as were later the first kings in the heroic cities. For these carried the laws from the reigning senates to the peoples [67] in the two kinds of heroic assemblies described by Homer, the *boulē* and the *agora*. In the former the heroes decreed the laws orally and in the latter they promulgated them also orally, for letters had not yet been invented. The heroic kings bore the laws from the reigning senates to the peoples in the persons of the duumvirs whom they had appointed to announce the laws, as Tullus Hostilius did in the trial of Horatius. The duumvirs thus came to be living and speaking laws. It is this which Livy does not understand, and hence he does not make himself clear in his account of the trial of Horatius [500].

522   This vulgar tradition [250–255, 521] together with the false belief in the matchless wisdom of the ancients [128] tempted Plato to a vain longing for those times in which philosophers reigned or kings were philosophers [253]. And certainly the fathers must have been monarchic family kings, superior to all other members of their families and subject only to God [256]. Their authority was fortified by frightful religions and sanctioned by dreadful punishments, as must have been that of the cyclopes, in whom Plato recognizes the first family fathers of the world [296]. This tradition, misunderstood, gave rise to that common error of all political theorists, that the first form of civil government in the world was monarchic. They are thus given over to those false principles of evil politics: that civil governments were born either of open violence or of fraud which later broke out into violence [552]. But [the truth is that] in those times, full of arrogance and savagery because of the fresh emergence from bestial liberty [290], in the extreme simplicity and crudeness of a life content with the spontaneous fruits of nature, satisfied to drink the water of the springs and to sleep in the caves, in the natural equality of a state in which each of the fathers was sovereign in his own family, one cannot conceive of either fraud or violence by which one man could subject all the others to a civil monarchy [585].

523   Here we may reflect how much it took for the men of the gentile world to be tamed from their feral native liberty through a long period of cyclopean family discipline to the point of obeying naturally the laws in the civil states which were to come later. Hence there remained the eternal property that happier than the commonwealth conceived by Plato are those where the fathers teach only religion and where they are admired by their sons as their sages, revered as their priests, and feared as their kings. Such and so much divine force was needed to reduce these giants, as wild as they were gross, to human duties. Since they were unable to express this force abstractly, they represented it in concrete physical form as a cord, called *chorda* in Greek and in Latin at first *fides*, whose original and proper meaning appears in the phrase *fides deorum*, force of the gods. From this cord (for the lyre must have begun with the monochord) they fashioned the lyre of Orpheus, to the accompaniment of which, singing to them the force of the gods in the auspices, he tamed the beasts of Greece to humanity. And Amphion raised the walls of Thebes with stones that moved themselves. These were the stones which Deucalion and Pyrrha, standing before the temple of Themis (that is, in the fear of divine justice) with veiled heads (the modesty of marriage), found lying before their feet (for men were at first stupid, and *lapis*, stone, remained Latin for a stupid person) and threw over their shoulders (introducing family institutions by means of household discipline), thus making men of them [79].

524 As for the other part of household discipline, the education of bodies, the fathers with their frightful religions, their cyclopean authority, and their sacred ablutions began to educe, or bring forth, from the giant bodies of their sons the proper human form [371]. And herein is providence above all to be admired, for it ordained that until such times as domestic education should supervene, the lost men should become giants in order that in their feral wanderings they might better endure with their robust constitutions the inclemency of the heavens and the seasons, and that they might with their disproportionate strength penetrate the great forest of the earth (which must have been very dense as a result of the recent flood), so that, fleeing from wild beasts and pursuing reluctant women and thus becoming lost from each other, they might be scattered through it in search of food and water until it should be found in due time fully populated [369]; while after they began to remain in one place with their women, first in caves, then in huts near perennial springs [526] and in the fields which, brought under cultivation, gave them sustenance, providence ordained that, from the causes we are now setting forth, they should shrink to the present proper stature of mankind.

525 In the very birth of [domestic] economy, they fulfilled it in its best idea, which is that the fathers by labor and industry should leave a patrimony to their sons, so that they may have an easy and comfortable and secure subsistence, even if foreign commerce should fail, or even all the fruits of civil life, or even the cities themselves, so that in such last emergencies the families at least may be preserved, from which there is hope that the nations may rise again. And the patrimony they leave should include places with good air, with their own perennial water supply, in situations of natural strength whither withdrawal is possible in case the cities have to be abandoned, and in fields with wide bottom lands on which to maintain the poor peasants taking refuge with them on the downfall of the cities, by whose labor they can maintain themselves as lords [553]. Such were the institutions that providence established for the state of the families, not like a tyrant laying down laws but like the queen it is of human affairs working through customs, according to the saying of Dio [308]. For the strong men were found with their lands on the mountain heights, in air stirred by the wind and hence healthful, and in sites naturally strong, which were the first *arces* in the world, later fortified by the devices of military architecture (as in Italian steep rugged mountains were called *rocce*, whence later the term *rocche* for fortresses), and finally they were found near perennial springs [526ff], which for the most part rise in the mountains. Near such springs the birds of prey make their nests, and consequently in their vicinity hunters set their snares. Perhaps for this reason all birds of prey were called *aquilae* by the Latins, as if for *aquilegae*, for certainly *aquilex* retained the sense of finder or conductor of water [240]. For doubtless those birds whose auspices Romulus observed to fix the site of the new city were vultures, as history tells us, but later became eagles and the protecting deities of all the Roman armies. Thus simple and uncouth men, following the eagles, which they believed to be birds of Jove because they flew high in the heavens, discovered the perennial springs and hence venerated this other great benefit which heaven had bestowed upon them when it reigned on earth. And after the auspices of the lightning, the most august were those of the eagle's flight. These were called by Messala and Corvinus major or public auspices [Aulus Gellius 13.15; 9.11; 568, 598], and it was to them that the Roman patricians referred when in the heroic contests they answered the plebs that the auspices were theirs (*auspicia esse sua*) [110, 488]. All this, ordained by providence to give a beginning to gentile humanity, was regarded by Plato [L. 738BC] as the result of human foresight and precaution on the part of the first founders of the cities. But in the recourse of barbarism which destroyed cities everywhere, it was in just this way that the families were preserved whence sprang the new nations of Europe. And all the new seigniories which then arose were called *castella* by the Italians, for we may observe generally that the most ancient cities and almost all the capitals of peoples were placed on the crests of mountains, while the villages on the other hand lie scattered on the plains. Such must be the origin of the Latin phrases *summo loco*, *illustri loco nati*, to signify nobles, and *imo loco*, *obscuro loco nati*, for plebeians; for the heroes dwelt in the cities, the *famuli* in the plains [608].

526   However, above all else, it was with reference to these perennial springs that political theorists asserted that the sharing of water was the occasion for families being brought together in their vicinity. Hence the first communities were called *phratriai* by the Greeks [cf. *phrear*, well, *phreatia*, cistern], and the first lands were called *pagi* by the Latins, like the Dorian Greek for spring, *paga*; that is, water, the first of the two principal solemnities of marriage. For the Romans celebrated marriage *aqua et igni* because the first marriages were naturally contracted between men and women sharing the same water and fire, that is, of the same family; whence marriage must have begun between brothers and sisters [511]. And the lar

of each house was the god of the fire aforesaid; hence *focus laris* for the hearth where the family father sacrificed to the household gods. In the Law of the Twelve Tables, in the article on parricide, according to the reading of Jacob Raewaerd [!], these gods are called *deivei parentum*. A similar expression is frequently found in Holy Scripture: *Deus parentum nostrorum*, the God of our fathers, or, more explicitly, *Deus Abraham, Deus Isaac, Deus Iacob*, the God of Abraham, Isaac, and Jacob [F7]. On this matter there is also the law proposed by Cicero [L. 2.9.22], *Sacra familiaria perpetua manento*, "let sacred family rites be perpetually maintained"; whence the phrase of such frequent occurrence in Roman laws by which a son of a family is said to be *in sacris paternis*, and the paternal power itself is called *sacra patria*, for in the first times, as this work shows [628], all its judgments were believed to be sacred. It must be added that a like custom was observed by the barbarians who came in after; for in Florence in Giovanni Boccaccio's time (as he attests in his *Genealogies of the Gods* [7.65]) it was the custom for the father of a family at the beginning of each year to sit at the hearth and throw incense and sprinkle wine on the end of a log to which he had set fire. And among the lower classes of our own Naples the Christmas Eve custom is observed which calls for the father of the house solemnly to set fire to such a log in the hearth. Indeed, in the Kingdom of Naples families are counted by hearthfires. When cities were later founded the custom became universal of contracting marriages between those of the same city; and there finally remained the rule that when marriages are contracted between those of different cities or countries they should at least have religion in common.

527 To return now from fire to water, the Styx, by which the gods swore, was the source of the springs; hence these gods must have been the nobles of the heroic cities [449], for the sharing of the water had given them dominion over [the plebeians, whom they called] men [437]. Hence down to the 309th year of Rome the patricians excluded the plebs from *connubium* [110, 598]. Apropos of all this, we often read in Holy Writ of [Beer-sheba,] "well of the oath" or "oath of the well" [F7]. Thus the city of Pozzuoli preserves in its name an indication of its great antiquity, for it was called *Puteoli* on account of the number of small wells it united. And it is a reasonable conjecture, based on our Mental Dictionary [162], that the many cities with plural names scattered through the ancient nations received their differently articulated names from what was in substance one and the same [—the union of wells].

528 From this source imagination conceived the third major deity [317], Diana, representing the first human need [—that of water—] which

made itself felt among the giants when they had settled on certain lands and united in marriage with certain women. The theological poets have described the history of these things in two fables of Diana. The first, signifying the modesty of marriage, tells of Diana silently lying with the sleeping Endymion under the darkness of night; so that Diana is chaste with that chastity referred to in a law proposed by Cicero [469], *Deos caste adeunto*, that one should go to the sacrifice only after making the sacred ablutions. The other tells us of the fearful religion of the water springs, to which was attached the perpetual epithet of sacred. It is the tale of Actaeon, who, seeing Diana naked (the living spring) and being sprinkled with water by the goddess (to signify that the goddess cast over him the great awe of her divinity), was changed into a stag (the most timid of animals) and torn to pieces by his dogs (the remorse of his own conscience for the violation of religion). Hence *lymphati* (properly, sprinkled with *lympha* or pure water) must have been originally a term applied to the Actaeons who had been maddened by superstitious terror. This poetic history was preserved by the Latins in their word *latices* (evidently from *latendo*), to which is always added the epithet *puri*, and which means the water gushing from a spring. The *latices* of the Latins must have been identical with the Greek nymphs, handmaidens of Diana, for *nymphai* in Greek meant the same as *lymphae* [in Latin]. The nymphs were so named at a time when all things were apprehended as animate and for the most part human substances [379].

529 Afterward, the god-fearing giants, those settled in the mountains [377], must have become sensible of the stench from the corpses of their dead rotting on the ground near by, and must have begun to bury them; for enormous skulls and bones have been found and are still found, generally on mountaintops, which is a strong indication that the bodies of the impious giants [553] who were scattered everywhere through the valleys and the plains [525] must have rotted unburied and their skulls and bones must have been swept into the sea by the rivers or completely worn away by the rains. And they surrounded these sepulchers with so much religion, or divine terror, that burial grounds were called by the Latins religious places par excellence. Hence emerged the universal belief in the immortality of human souls, which we established as the third of the principles on which our Science is based [337]. The souls of the dead were called *dii manes*, and in the Law of the Twelve Tables in the article on parricide they are spoken of as *deivei parentum* [526]. Furthermore, a stake must have been fixed as a burial marker upon or near the mound, which originally can have been nothing but a slight rounding over of the earth.

(The ancient Germans, according to Tacitus [G. 27], believed that they should not cover the dead with overmuch earth, whence the prayer for the dead, *Sit tibi terra levis*, "May the earth lie light upon thee!" And this German practice permits us to conjecture that the same custom must have prevailed among all the other first barbarous nations.) The grave marker was called by the Greeks the *phylax*, or guardian, because these simple people believed that the post would guard the grave. *Cippus*, the Latin name for the post, came to mean sepulcher, and *ceppo* in Italian means the trunk of a genealogical tree. *Phylax* must accordingly have been the origin of the Greek *phylē*, a tribe [554]. And the Romans set forth their genealogies by placing the statues of their ancestors in rows along the halls of their houses, and these rows were called *stemmata*. (This term must have been derived from *temen*, thread; whence *subtemen* for the thread that is carried under as weft in weaving cloth.) The jurisconsults later called these genealogical rows *lineae*, or lines, and down to our time *stemmata* has kept the meaning of family arms. Thus it is highly probable that the first lands with such buried bodies were the first shields of the families, and the phrase of the Spartan mother, presenting the shield to her son as he goes to war, *aut cum hoc, aut in hoc*, must be understood as meaning "Return with this or on a bier." Even to this day in Naples the bier is called *scudo*, shield. And since the sepulchers were in the ground of the fields, which were at first fields for planting, the shield [or escutcheon] is defined in the science of heraldry as the ground of the field, later called the ground of the arms [487].

530 From the same origin must have come the word *filius*, which, qualified by the name or house of the father, signified noble, precisely as the Roman patrician was defined as one *qui potest nomine ciere patrem*, "who can name his father" [433]. And the names of the Romans were really patronymics, which were so often used by the first Greeks; Homer, for example, calling the heroes *filii Achivorum*, sons of the Achaeans; and in like fashion in Holy Scripture *filii Israel* is used of the nobles of the Hebrew people [F7]. Hence necessarily, if the tribes were originally composed of nobles, the cities must at first have been made up of nobles alone [597].

531 Thus by the graves of their buried dead the giants showed their dominion over their lands, and Roman law called for burial of the dead in a proper place to make it religious [529]. With truth they could pronounce those heroic phrases: we are sons of this earth, we are born from these oaks. Indeed, the heads of families among the Latins called themselves *stirpes* and *stipites*, stems or stocks, and their progeny were called *propagines*, slips

or shoots. In Italian such families were called *legnaggi*, lineages. And the most noble houses of Europe and almost all its reigning families take their names from the lands over which they rule. Thus in Latin and Greek alike "son of the earth" means the same thing as "noble"; and in Latin *ingenui*, the indigenous ones, as if for *indegeniti* or the shorter form *ingeniti*, meant the nobles; as certainly *indigenae* retained the meaning of natives of a country. *Dii indigetes* was the term used for the native gods, who must have been the nobles of the heroic cities, for they were called gods [437], and Earth was thir great mother. Hence from the beginning *ingenuus* and *patricius* meant noble, for the first cities were of nobles only; and these *ingenui* must have been the aborigines, styled, as it were, "without origin," or self-born, to which correspond exactly the Greek *autochthones*. And the aborigines were giants, and the term "giants" properly signifies sons of Earth. Thus, as the fables faithfully tell us, Earth was the mother of gods and giants.

532   These matters [531] have all been set forth above [369–373], but here in their proper place we have repeated them to show that Livy [1.8.5] perverted the heroic phrase of Romulus and the fathers who were his companions where he makes them say to those who had taken refuge in the asylum opened in the clearing that the latter were sons of that earth; and he makes that become in their mouths a barefaced lie which in [reference to themselves as] founders of the first peoples had been a heroic truth [561]. For on the one hand Romulus was recognized as of the royal family of Alba [and therefore noble or son of Earth], and on the other hand their mother [Earth] had been so unjust to them as to give birth only to men, so that they had to carry off the Sabine women to be their wives [510]. We must therefore say that, in the manner the first peoples had of thinking in poetic characters, Romulus, regarded as founder of a city [417], was invested with the qualities proper to the founders of the first cities of Latium, in the midst of a great number of which Romulus founded Rome [160]. Of a piece with the aforesaid error of Livy is the definition he gives of the asylum, that it was *vetus urbes condentium consilium*, an old counsel of founders of cities [106, 114]; for in the first founders of cities, who were simple men, it was not counsel but nature by which providence was served.

533   Imagination here created the fourth divinity of the so-called greater gentes [317]; namely, Apollo, apprehended as god of civil light. Thus the heroes were called *kleitoi*, resplendent, by the Greeks, from *kleos*, glory, and they were called *inclyti* by the Latins, from *cluer*, the splendor of arms [556], and consequently from that light into which Juno Lucina

brought noble offspring [513]. So here, after Urania—the Muse defined by Homer as the Science of good and evil, or of divination [365, 391], in virtue of which Apollo is the god of poetic wisdom or divination [508]—they must have conceived the second of the Muses, Clio, the narrator of heroic history. The first history of this sort must have begun with the genealogies of the heroes, just as sacred history begins with the descendants of the patriarchs [F7]. Apollo begins this history by pursuing Daphne, a vagabond maiden wandering through the forests (in the nefarious life); and she, by the aid she besought of the gods (whose auspices were necessary for solemn nuptials), on standing still is charged to a laurel (a plant which is ever green in its certain and acknowledged offspring), in the same sense in which the Latins use *stipites* for the stocks of families; and the recourse of barbarism brought back the same heroic phraseology, for they call genealogies trees, and the founders they call stocks or stems, and the descendants branches, and the families lineages [531]. Hence the pursuit of Apollo was the act of a god, and the flight of Daphne that of an animal; but later, when the language of this austere history had been forgotten, Apollo's pursuit became a libertine's, and Daphne's flight a woman's.

534   Further, Apollo is the brother of Diana, for the perennial springs made possible the founding of the first nations on the mountaintops [526ff]; wherefore Apollo has his seat on Mount Parnassus, where dwell the Muses (the arts of humanity), near the fount of Hippocrene, whose waters give drink to the swans, birds that sing in that sense in which the Latin verbs *canere* and *cantare* mean "foretell" [508]. Under the auspices of one of these swans, Leda conceives two eggs and from one of them gives birth to Helen and from the other to the twins Castor and Pollux.

535   And Apollo and Diana are children of Latona, so called from *latere*, to hide (the sense which *condere* originally had in the phrases *condere gentes, condere regna, condere urbes*), whence in Italy the name of Latium. And Latona brought forth her children near the waters of the perennial springs [526ff]; and at their birth men became frogs, which in summer rains are born from the earth, called mother of giants, for these are properly sons of Earth [370]. One of these frogs was sent by Idanthyrsus to Darius [435], and it must be three frogs and not three toads that appear in the royal arms of France, later changed to golden lilies. And since the number three was used for the superlative—a usage which persisted in the French *très*—the three frogs mean a big frog, which is to say a great son, and therefore lord, of the earth.

536   Apollo and Diana are both hunters, slaying beasts with uprooted trees, one of which is the club of Hercules. They do this first in defense of

themselves and their families (since they are no longer permitted to save themselves by flight as the vagabonds of the outlaw life had done), and later to provide food. Thus Vergil makes the heroes feast on such game [A. 1.184ff]; and with like purpose, according to Tacitus [G. 46], the ancient Germans and their wives hunted down the beasts.

537   Apollo is also the founding god of humanity and of its arts, the Muses [534]. These arts the Latins call *liberales* in the sense of noble [370, 556]. One of them is the art of riding, whence Pegasus soars over Mount Parnassus armed with wings because he pertains to the nobility [488]. And in the returned barbarism the nobles were called cavaliers by the Spaniards because only they could don armor [for fighting] on horseback. This humanity had its origin in *humare*, to bury (which is the reason we took the practice of burial as the third principle of our Science [337]), and the Athenians, who were the most human of all the nations, were, according to Cicero [L. 2.25.63], the first to bury their dead.

538   Lastly, Apollo is always young (just as the life of Daphne, changed to a laurel, is always verdant), for Apollo, through the names of the great houses [433], makes men eternal in their families. And he wears his hair long as a sign of nobility. The custom of wearing the hair long was preserved by the nobility of many nations, and we read that one of the punishments of nobles among both the Persians and the American Indians was to pull one or several hairs from their heads. And perhaps *Gallia comata*, Long-haired [Transalpine] Gaul, was so called from the nobles who founded that nation; as certainly the slaves in all nations have their heads shaved.

539   Now, however, when the heroes had settled within circumscribed lands and when with the increase of their families the spontaneous fruits of nature were no longer sufficient, while yet they feared to seek for abundance beyond the confines they had set for themselves by those chains of religion by which the giants were chained under the mountains [387, 503], and having been taught by that same religion to set fire to the forests in order to have a prospect of the open sky whence came the auspices [391], they then set about the long, arduous, and heavy task of bringing their lands under cultivation and sowing them with grain, which, roasted among the thorns and briers, they had perhaps discovered to be useful for human nourishment. Hereupon, by a fine natural and necessary metaphor, they called the ears of grain golden apples, transferring the idea of the apples which are fruits of nature gathered in summer, to the ears of grain which human industry gathers likewise in summer.

540   From this labor, the greatest and most glorious of all, the

[poetic] character of Hercules sprang up, reflecting great glory on Juno, who set this task for the nourishment of the families. And, in other metaphors both beautiful and necessary, they imagined the earth in the aspect of a great dragon, covered with scales and spines (the thorns and briers), bearing wings (for the lands belonged to the heroes [488]), always awake and vigilant (thickly grown in every direction). This dragon they made the guardian of the golden apples in the garden of the Hesperides. Because of the wetness from the waters of the flood, the dragon was later believed to have been born in the water. Under another aspect they imagined [the earth as] a hydra (also from *hydōr*, water), which, when any of its heads were cut off, always grew others in their place. It was of three alternating colors: black (the burned-over land), green (the leaf), and gold (the ripe grain). These are the three colors of the serpent's skin, which, when it grows old, is sloughed off for a fresh one. Finally, under the aspect of its fierceness in resisting cultivation, the earth was also imagined as a most powerful beast, the Nemean lion (whence later the name lion was given to the most powerful of the animals), which philologists hold to have been a monstrous serpent. All these beasts vomit forth fire, which is the fire set to the forest by Hercules.

541 These three different stories [of the Hesperides, the hydra, and the Nemean lion], from three different parts of Greece, signify the same thing in substance. In another part of Greece another story grew up, telling of the child Hercules slaying the serpents while yet in his cradle; that is, in the infancy of the heroic age. In yet another, Bellerophon slays the monster called the Chimaera, having the tail of a serpent, the body of a goat (to signify the enforested earth), and the head of a lion belching flames. In Thebes it is Cadmus who slays the great dragon and sows his teeth. (By a fine metaphor they gave the name of serpent's teeth to the curved pieces of hard wood they must have employed to plough the earth before the use of iron was discovered.) Cadmus himself becomes a serpent (the ancient Romans would have said Cadmus *fundus factus est* [411]), as we have indicated above [446] and as we shall explain more fully later on [679], when we shall see that the serpents of Medusa's head [616] and Mercury's staff [604] signified the dominion of the lands. Hence land rent was called *ōpheleia*, from *ophis*, serpent, and was also called the tithe of Hercules [604]. It is in this sense that we read in Homer [I. 2.299ff] of the soothsayer Calchas interpreting the action of the serpent in devouring the eight swallows and their mother as meaning that the land of Troy would fall under the dominion of the Greeks at the end of nine years; so that the Greeks, while fighting the Trojans, when a serpent is slain by an eagle in

the air and falls among them in the midst of the battle, take it for a good augury in conformity with the soothsaying science of Calchas. Hence Proserpine, who was the same as Ceres [716], is depicted in sculpture as being borne off in a chariot drawn by serpents, and hence serpents so often appear on the coins of the Greek commonwealths.

542   Thus, in illustration of the Mental Dictionary [145] (and it is a matter worthy of reflection), the kings of the American Indians, as Fracastoro sings in his *Syphilis* [2.22f], were found to carry a dried snakeskin in place of a scepter [604]. The Chinese too charge their royal arms with a dragon and bear a dragon as the emblem of the civil power. Such must have been the Dragon [Draco] who wrote the Athenian laws in blood; and we remarked above [423] that this Dragon was one of the serpents of the Gorgon, nailed by Perseus to his shield, which later became the shield of Minerva, goddess of the Athenians, and its aspect turned to stone whoever gazed upon it; and this will be found to have been a hieroglyph of the civil power of Athens [616]. Holy Scripture too, in the book of Ezekiel [29.3], bestows on the king of Egypt the title of the great dragon lying in the midst of his rivers [F7], just as the dragons noted above were born in the water and the Hydra took its name from that element. The emperor of Japan has created an order of knights who bear the dragon as their device. And in the returned barbarian times the histories tell us that the house of the Visconti because of its great nobility was called to the duchy of Milan, and this house bears on its arms a dragon devouring a child, which is none other than the Python which devoured the men of Greece and was slain by Apollo [449], the god of nobility [533]. This blazoning may well cause astonishment at the uniformity between the heroic mode of thought of the men of this second barbarism and that of the ancients of the first. Such must be the two winged dragons wearing the necklace of flints by which the fire they vomit forth was kindled; the two guardians, that is, of the Golden Fleece, whose significance Chiflet, who wrote the history of that illustrious order, could not understand, so that Pietrasanta avows its history obscure.

543   As in some parts of Greece it was Hercules who killed the serpents, the lion, the Hydra, or the dragon [540], and in another it was Bellerophon who slew the Chimaera [541], so in yet another it is Bacchus who tames the tigers, which must have been the lands clothed in colors as varied as their skins, and hence the name tiger passed to the animals of this powerful species. The story of Bacchus taming the tigers with wine is a physical history far from the thought of the rustic heroes who founded the nations, nor was it ever related in those times that Bacchus went to Africa

or to Hyrcania to tame them, for the Greeks, as we shall show in our Poetic Geography [747], could not then have known if there was a Hyrcania in the world, much less an Africa, to say nothing of tigers in the forests of Hyrcania or the deserts of Africa.

544   Further, when they called the ears of grain golden apples [539], these must have been the only gold in the world. For at that time metallic gold was still unmined, and they did not know how to extract it in crude masses, to say nothing of shining and burnishing it; nor indeed, when men still drank the water of springs, could the use of gold have been at all prized. It was only later, from the metal's resemblance in color to the most highly prized food of those times, that it was metaphorically called gold. Hence Plautus [*Pot of Gold* 7] was obliged to say *thesaurum auri* to distinguish a hoard of gold from a granary. Certainly Job [31.40], among the great things from which he had fallen, mentions that he had been wont to eat bread made of grain. And in the country districts of our most remote provinces, in place of the juleps of powdered pearls used in cities, they give bread made from grain to the sick, and they say the sick man is eating grain bread when they mean that he is at the point of death.

545   Later, by a further extension of the idea of prizing and cherishing, they must have applied the term golden to fine wool. Hence in Homer Atreus complains that Thyestes has stolen his golden sheep [I. 2.106], and the Argonauts stole from Pontus the Golden Fleece. For this reason Homer gives his kings and heroes the fixed epithet *polymēlos*, rich in flocks [I. 2.605, 705; 14.490]; as the ancient Latins, by uniformity of ideas, called the patrimony *pecunia*, which the Latin grammarians derive from *pecus*, herd or flock. Among the ancient Germans, in Tacitus's account [G. 5], the flocks and herds are their most highly prized, indeed their only wealth (*solae et gratissimae opes sunt*). This custom must also have prevailed among the ancient Romans, whose patrimony was *pecunia*, as the Law of the Twelve Tables attests in the article on testaments [5.3]. And *mēlon* means both apple and sheep to the Greeks, who, perhaps also under the aspect of precious fruit, called honey *meli*; and the Italians call apples *mele*.

546   These ears of grain must then have been the golden apples which Hercules was the first to bring back (or harvest) from Hesperia [540]. The Gallic Hercules, with chains of this gold issuing from his mouth, binds men by the ears; this too is a history of the cultivation of the fields [560]. Hence Hercules was a propitious deity in the search for treasures, of which Dis was the god. Dis is the same as Pluto, who carries Proserpine, who is the same as Ceres (that is, grain), into the underworld of which the poets

tell us. According to them there were three underworlds: the first by the Styx, the second where the dead lay, and the third at the bottom of the furrow [714ff]. From this god Dis the rich are called *dites*, and the rich were the nobles. The Spaniards call their nobles rich men (*ricos hombres*) and among us the nobles were formerly called *benestanti*, well off. The ancient Latins called *ditio* what we now call the seigniory of a state, for the cultivated fields make up the true wealth of states; and in like fashion the Latins called the area of a seigniory *ager*, which is properly land which has been put to the plough (*aratro agitur*). So it must be true that the Nile was called *Chrysorrhoas*, flowing with gold, because it overflows the wide fields of Egypt and its inundations are the source of the great abundance of the harvests. So too the Pactolus, the Ganges, the Hydaspes, and the Tagus are called rivers of gold because they make fertile the fields of grain. Vergil must have had these golden apples in mind when, learned in heroic antiquities as he was, he extended the metaphor and created the golden bough that Aeneas carries into the lower world [A. 6.136ff]. This fable we shall explain later in its more proper place [721]. For the rest, metallic gold was not more highly prized than iron in heroic times. Etearchus, for example, king of Ethiopia, replying to the ambassadors of Cambyses who had presented him with many golden vessels in the name of their king, said that he could see no use for them and much less any need, thus refusing them with a magnanimity that was quite natural [Herodotus 2.38; 3.20f]. Tacitus [G. 5] relates the same of the ancient Germans, who in his time were just such ancient heroes as those of whom we are now speaking: "You may see among them vessels of silver, which have been presented to their envoys and chieftains, held as cheap as those of clay." So in Homer [I. 6.235f] we find the armories of the heroes stocked with arms of iron or gold indifferently, for the first world must have abounded in these minerals (as America was found to do on its discovery), which were later to be exhausted by human avarice.

547   From all of which we derive this great corollary: that the division of the four ages of the world—that is, the ages of gold, silver, copper, and iron—was invented by the poets of degenerate times. For it was this poetic gold, namely, grain, that among the Greeks lent its name to the golden age, whose innocence was but the extreme savagery of the Cyclopes (in whom, as we have said several times above [296, 338, 503], Plato recognizes the first fathers of families), who lived separately and alone in their caves with their wives and children, never concerning themselves with one another's affairs, as Polyphemus tells Ulysses in Homer [O. 9.112ff].

548   In confirmation of all we have so far said of the poetic gold, it

may be useful to cite two customs which are still observed and the causes of which can be explained only on these principles. The first is the custom of putting a golden globe [*pomo*, apple] in the hands of the king in the midst of the solemnities of his coronation [602]. This is evidently the same [pome or globe] that they bear in their royal arms, surmounting their crowns. This custom can have no other origin than the golden apples of grain we are here discussing. For here too the apples will be found to be a hieroglyph of the heroes' ownership of their lands (which perhaps the Egyptians too signified by an apple, if it is not an egg, in the mouth of their [god Knuphis or] Knef [605]). And this hieroglyph was carried by the barbarians who invaded all the nations subject to the Roman Empire. The other custom is that of the gold coins which kings give their queen consorts among the other solemnities of their nuptials. These too must go back to the poetic gold or grain of which we are speaking (for the gold coins signify the heroic nuptials of the ancient Romans *coëmptione et farre*, "by mutual mock sale and bread offering"), in conformity with the heroic practice related by Homer [I. 9.146] of buying their wives with a wedding gift [671]. It was in a shower of this gold that Jove must have appeared to Danaë locked in her tower (which must have been the granary), to signify the abundance of this solemnity. In striking agreement is the Hebrew phrase "and abundance in thy towers" (*et abundantia in turribus tuis* [*Psalm* 122.7]). The conjecture is confirmed by the custom of the ancient Britons, among whom grooms, as a part of the wedding ceremony, gave their brides cakes.

549 At the birth of these human institutions, three other deities of the greater *gentes* [317] sprang forth in the imaginations of the Greeks, with this order of ideas, corresponding to the order of the institutions themselves. First Vulcan, then Saturn (so called from *sati*, sown fields, whence the age of Saturn among the Latins corresponds to the golden age of the Greeks), and thirdly Cybele, or Berecynthia, the cultivated land. Cybele is depicted as seated on a lion [402] (the enforested earth which the heroes reduced to tillage [540]) and is called the great mother of the gods and also the mother of the giants (who were properly so called in the sense of sons of Earth [531]). Hence she is the mother of the gods (that is, of the giants, who in the time of the first cities arrogated to themselves the name of gods), and the pine is sacred to her (as a sign of the stability of the founders of peoples, who, remaining settled on the first lands, founded the cities, of which Cybele is the goddess). Among the Romans she was called Vesta, goddess of divine ceremonies, for the lands ploughed at that time were the first altars of the world [774ff]. Here the goddess Vesta,

armed with a fierce religion, watched over fire and spelt, which was the grain of the ancient Romans. Hence too among the Romans nuptials were celebrated *aqua et igni,* with water and fire, and also with spelt (*far*), and were then called *nuptiae confarreatae* [671]. This ceremony was later confined to priests, for the first families had been all of priests [254] (like the kingdoms of the bonzes in the East Indies). And water, fire, and spelt were the elements used in the Roman divine ceremonies. On these first lands Vesta sacrificed to Jove the impious practicers of the infamous promiscuity [of women and things], who violated the first altars (the first fields of grain). These were the first *hostiae,* the first victims of the gentile religions. Plautus called them *Saturni hostiae,* Saturn's victims [191], and they were called *victimae,* from *victi,* as being weak because alone (the Latin *victus* has preserved this meaning of weakness), and they were called *hostes* because such impious men were rightly held to be enemies of the whole human race. And among the Romans it remained the custom to cover with spelt the brow and the horns of sacrificial victims. From the name of Vesta the Romans called Vestal virgins those who guarded the eternal fire, which if extinguished by mishap had to be relighted from the sun, for from the sun Prometheus stole the first fire and brought it to the Greeks on earth, who therewith set fire to the forests and began to cultivate the land [713]. On this account Vesta is the goddess of divine ceremonies among the Romans, for the first *colere,* or cultivating, in the world of the gentiles was the cultivation of the land, and the first cult was raising these altars, setting this first fire to them, and sacrificing upon them the impious men of whom we have just spoken.

550   In this way the boundaries of the fields were fixed and maintained [486]. This division, too generally set forth by Hermogenianus the jurisconsult [D. 1.1.5], has been imagined as taking place by deliberate agreement of men, and carried out with justice and respected in good faith, at a time when there was as yet no armed public force and consequently no civil authority of law. But it cannot be understood save as taking place among men of extreme wildness, observing a frightful religion which had fixed and circumscribed them within certain lands, and whose bloody ceremonies had consecrated their first walls. For even the philologists say the walls were traced by the founders of the cities with the plough, the moldboard of which, by the origins of language above discovered [428ff], must have been first called *urbs,* whence the ancient *urbum,* curved. Perhaps *orbis* is from the same origin, so that at first *orbis terrae* must have meant any fence made in this way, so low that Remus jumped over it to be killed by Romulus and thus, as Latin historians narrate, to consecrate with his blood the first walls of Rome. Such a fence must evidently have been a

hedge (*siepe*) (and among the Greeks *sēps* signifies serpent [452] in its heroic meaning of cultivated land [540]), from which origin must come *munere viam*, to build a road, which is done by strengthening the hedges around the fields. Hence walls are called *moenia*, as if for *munia*, and certainly *munire* kept the sense of fortifying. The hedges must have been of those plants the Latins called *sagmina*, bloodwort or elder, whose use and name still survive. The name *sagmina* was preserved in the sense of the herbs with which the altars were adorned; it must have come from the blood (*sanguis*) of the slain, who, like Remus, had transgressed them. Hence the so-called sanctity of walls, and also of heralds, who, as we shall see later, crowned themselves with these herbs, as certainly the ancient Roman ambassadors did with those plucked on the Capitoline. And hence finally the sanctity of the laws of war and peace of which the heralds were bearers, whence that part of a law which imposes penalties on its transgressors is called its sanction. And here begins what we are demonstrating in this work: that the natural law of the gentes was by divine providence ordained separately for each people, and only when they became acquainted did they recognize it as common to all [146]. For if the Roman heralds consecrated with these herbs were inviolate among the other peoples of Latium, it could only have been because the former, without knowing anything of the latter, observed the same custom.

551 So the family fathers provided for their heroic families through religion a subsistence which it behooved them through religion to maintain. Hence it was the perpetual custom of the nobles to be religious, as Julius Scaliger observes in his *Poetica* [!]. It must then be a strong sign of the downfall of a nation when the nobles disprize their native religion.

552 Philologians and philosophers have commonly supposed that the families in the so-called state of nature included children only; whereas in fact they included *famuli* also, and that was the original reason for their being called families [257, 555]. On this maimed economy a false politics has been erected [522, 585, 662ff, 1009ff], so that our discussion of the *famuli* [553–569], a topic proper to economic theory, will also serve as transition to politics.

[Chapter II]   The Families with Their Famuli, Which Preceded the Cities, and without Which the Cities Could Not Have Been Born

553 Among the impious giants who had continued the infamous promiscuity of things and of women [D2], the quarrels produced by use in

common finally brought it about, at the end of a long period of time, that
(to borrow the language of the jurists) Grotius's simpletons and Pufendorf's abandoned men had recourse to the altars of the strong to save
themselves from Hobbes's violent men [179, 338], even as beasts driven by
intense cold will sometimes seek salvation in inhabited places. Thereupon
the strong, with a fierceness born of their union in the society of families,
slew the violent who had violated their lands, and took under their protection the miserable creatures who had fled from them. And above the
heroism of nature which was theirs as having been born of Jove or engendered under his auspices, there now shone forth preeminently in them the
heroism of virtue. In this heroism the Romans excelled all other peoples of
the earth, practicing precisely these two aspects of it, sparing the submis-
sive and vanquishing the proud: *Parcere subiectis et debellare superbos*
[Vergil, A. 6.854].

554   And here it is worth reflecting how men in the feral state, fierce
and untamed as they were, came to pass from their bestial liberty into
human society. For in order that the first of them should reach that first
kind of society which is matrimony, they had need of the sharp stimulus of
bestial lust, and to keep them in it the stern restraints of frightful religions
were necessary [505ff]. Thus marriage emerged as the first kind of friendship in the world; whence Homer, to indicate that Jove and Juno lay
together, says with heroic gravity that "they celebrated their friendship"
[I. 14.314]. The Greek word for friendship, *philia*, is from the same root as
phileō, to love; and from it is derived the Latin *filius*, son. *Philios* in Ionic
Greek means friend, and mutation to a letter of similar sound yielded the
Greek *phylē*, tribe. We have already seen above that *stemmata* was the
word for the genealogical threads called *lineae* by the jurisconsults [529].
From this nature of human institutions there remained the eternal property
that the true natural friendship is matrimony, in which are realized the
three final goods: the honorable, the useful, and the pleasant. Husband
and wife by nature share the same lot in all the prosperities and adversities
of life, just as by choice friends have all things in common (*amicorum
omnia sunt communia*), and Modestinus therefore defines matrimony as a
lifelong lot sharing (*omnis vitae consortium*) [110].

555   The second comers came into this second society (which had
that name by a certain excellence [558]) only for the ultimate necessities of
life. And here again is a matter worthy of reflection. For the first comers to
human society were driven thereto by religion and by the natural instinct
to propagate the human race (the former a pious motive, the latter in the
strict sense a gentle one [B3]), and thus gave a beginning to noble and

lordly friendship. The second comers, since they came out of a necessity of saving their lives, gave a beginning to society in the proper sense, with a view principally to utility, and consequently base and servile. These refugees were received by the heroes under the just law of protection, by which they sustained their natural lives under the obligation of serving the heroes as day laborers. So from the fame (*fama*) of the heroes (primarily acquired through the practice of the aforesaid two parts of the heroism of virtue [553]) and from the worldly renown which is the *kleos*, or "glory," of the Greeks [533] (called *fama* by the Latins and *phēmē* too by the Greeks), the refugees were called *famuli*, and it was principally from these *famuli* that the families took their name [257, 552]. It is certainly from this fame that sacred history, speaking of the giants before the flood, calls them famous men. Vergil too [A. 4.173ff] similarly describes *Fama* as seated on a high tower (the high-lying lands of the heroes) with her head in the sky (whose vault rises from the mountaintops), having wings (as pertaining to the heroes [488], whence on the battlefield before Troy, Fame flies amid the ranks of the Greek heroes and not amid the masses of their plebeians [I. 2.93]), and with a trumpet (which must be the trumpet of Clio [533]; that is, heroic history) celebrating the names of the great (the founders of nations).

556 In these families before the time of the cities, the *famuli* lived in a state of slavery. (They were the forerunners of the slaves who were captured in the wars which began after the founding of cities. These latter slaves were called *vernae* by the Latins; with them came the languages called vernacular [443].) To distinguish the sons of the heroes from those of the *famuli*, the former were called *liberi*, free. But it was a distinction without a difference. For Tacitus [G. 20] tells us of the ancient Germans (and we may thence conjecture the same custom among all the first barbarous peoples) that the master is not distinguished from the slave by being brought up with greater delicacy (*dominum ac servum nullis educationis deliciis dignoscas*); and certainly among the ancient Romans the family fathers had a sovereign power of life and death over their children and a despotic dominion over the property they acquired, so that down to imperial times there was no difference between sons and slaves as holders of property (*peculium*) [582]. But originally the word *liberi* meant also noble, so that *artes liberales* are noble arts, and *liberalis* kept the meaning well-born, and *liberalitas* that of gentility [370]. From the same ancient origin the noble houses of the Latins were called gentes, for the first gentes were made up of nobles alone, and only nobles were free in the first cities [B3, 597]. Furthermore, the *famuli* were called *clientes*, originally *cluentes*,

from the ancient verb *cluere*, to shine in the light of arms (whose splendor was called *cluer*), for they reflected the light of the arms borne by their respective heroes. The latter were called first *incluti* and later *inclyti*, from the same root [533, 562]. If not thus resplendent they were not noticed, as if they had no place among men [559].

557   Thus began the clienteles and the first intimations of the fiefs [599ff, 1057ff]. In ancient history we read of such clienteles and clients scattered through all nations [263]. Thucydides [1.104–110!] relates that in Egypt, even in his time, the dynasties of Tanis were all divided among family fathers, the shepherd princes of such families; and Homer calls each hero of whom he sings a king, and describes them as shepherds of the peoples, who must have preceded the shepherds of the flocks [607, 1058f]. They are still found in great numbers in Arabia, as they once were in Egypt; and in the West Indies the greater part were found in this state of nature to be governed by such families, surrounded by slaves in such numbers as to cause Charles V, king of Spain, to consider imposing restrictive measures. It must have been with a family such as these that Abraham made war against the gentile kings; and his servants, who aided him [*Genesis* 14.14], are called by a name much to our purpose which Biblical scholars translate *vernaculos* [F7], according well with the *vernae* discussed above [556].

558   With the beginning of these things came the true origin of the famous Herculean knot by which clients were said to be *nexi*, or tied to the lands they had to cultivate for the nobles. Later this became a figurative knot in the Law of the Twelve Tables, which gave form to the civil mancipation by which all the *actus legitimi* of the Romans were solemnized [1030f]. Now at this point, because one cannot conceive an association more restricted from the side of those having abundance of goods nor more necessary for those who need them, the first *socii* in the world must have had their beginning. These were the *socii* of the heroes, received for life, as they had placed their lives in the hands of the heroes [258f, 721]. This explains how Ulysses is on the point of cutting off the head of Antinous [i.e., Eurylochus: O. 10.438ff], the chief of his *socii*, just for a word which, though well meant, does not please him; and the pious Aeneas kills his *socius* Misenus when it is needful for a sacrifice. This episode was preserved in a vulgar tradition, but Vergil [A. 6.149–189], since in the mild days of the Roman people it was too harsh a thing to tell of Aeneas, whom the poet himself celebrates for his piety, discreetly pretends that Misenus was killed by Triton for presuming to rival him on the trumpet. At the

same time he gives clear hints for the right understanding of the story by placing the death of Misenus among the solemnities prescribed to Aeneas by the Sybil. For one of them was that he must bury Misenus before he could make his descent to the lower world; and this is an open acknowledgment that the Sybil had predicted his death.

559 The *socii* shared only the labors of the heroes, not their winnings, and still less their glory. With this last only the heroes shone, and they were therefore called *kleitoi*, or illustrious, by the Greeks and *inclyti* by the Latins [533]. (There was a similar relationship between the Romans and the provinces they called associate.) Aesop complains of this state of affairs in his fable of the lion's partnership [425]. Among the ancient Germans, certainly, as Tacitus [G. 14] tells us (thereby justifying a like conjecture for all other barbarous peoples), the principal oath of these *famuli* or clients or vassals was to guard and defend each his own prince and to assign to his prince's glory his own deeds of valor; which is one of the most impressive characteristics of our own feudalism. Thus and not otherwise must it have come about that under the person or head [407] (which meant the same as mask [1033]) and under the name (or, as we would now say, device [433, 484]) of a Roman *paterfamilias* were counted, in law, all his children and all his slaves. Hence the Romans called *clypea*, or shields, the half busts representing the images of their ancestors, set in the hollow niches of their courtyard walls. And in modern architecture, quite in line with what we have been saying about the origins of medals [487], these shields are called medallions. And thus in the heroic times of the Greeks, Homer could say with perfect truth [O. 11.556] that Ajax was "the tower of the Greeks," as alone he battles with whole battalions of Trojans; as in the heroic times of the Romans, Horatius alone on the bridge holds back an army of Etruscans; for Ajax and Horatius are alone with their vassals. Just so in the history of the returned barbarism forty Norman heroes returning from the Holy Land scatter an army of Saracens besieging Salerno. Whence it must be said that these first ancient examples of protection extended by the heroes over those who had taken refuge on their lands marked the beginning of fiefs in the world. The first were personal rustic fiefs, and the vassals must have been the first *vades*, or implements, obliged to follow their heroes in person wherever they led them to till their fields (whence the term *vades* was later applied to defendants obliged to appear with their attorneys in court). And just as the vassal was called *vas* in Latin and *bas* in Greek, he continued to be called *was* and *wassus* by the barbarian writers on feudal law [1064]. Later the real rustic fiefs must have

developed, under which the vassals must have been the first *praedes* or *mancipes*, under real-estate bond [433]; and *mancipes* remained the proper term for those under bond to the treasury [1065].

560   Here likewise must have been the origin of the first heroic colonies which we call inland [595] to differentiate them from the maritime colonies which came later [300]. The latter were simply bands of refugees who took to the sea and found safety in other lands. For the term "colony" properly signifies merely a crowd of workers who till the soil (as they still do) for their daily sustenance. The histories of these two kinds of colonies are contained in two fables. (1) For the inland colonies, the famous Gallic Hercules who, with the chains of poetic gold (that is, grain [544]) issuing from his mouth, chains by the ears great multitudes of men and leads them after him whither he will [1064]. This has hitherto been taken as a symbol of eloquence, but the fable was born at a time when the heroes had as yet no articulate speech [401f]. (2) For the maritime colonies, the fable of the net with which heroic Vulcan drags plebeian Venus and Mars from the sea (a distinction of which a general explanation will be given later [579ff]), so that the Sun discovers them completely naked (that is, not clothed in the civil light with which the heroes shone [533]) and the gods (the nobles of the heroic cities [437]) laugh them to scorn (as the patricians ridiculed the poor plebs of ancient Rome).

561   And lastly the asylums had here their first origin. Thus Cadmus founds Thebes, the most ancient city of Greece, as an asylum. Theseus founds Athens on the altar of the unhappy, for such was the appropriate epithet for the impious vagabonds who were without all the divine and human blessings that human society had afforded the pious. Romulus founds Rome by opening an asylum in the clearing [106]; or rather, as [poetic character of] founder of new cities, he, with his comrades, founds it on the institution of the asylums from which the ancient cities of Latium had arisen [160]. Livy, in this connection, defines this institution generally as an old counsel of founders of cities [114]. This definition explains his misconstruing the saying of Romulus that he and his comrades were sons of that earth [532]. Yet Livy's phrase is to our purpose in that it shows that the asylums were the origins of the cities, whose eternal property it is that men live secure from violence in them. In this way, from the multitude of impious vagabonds who everywhere repaired to the lands of the pious and strong and found safety there, came Jove's gracious title, the hospitable. For these asylums were the first hospices in the world, and those who were there received were the first guests or strangers of the first cities [611]. And among the many labors of Hercules poetic Greek history preserved these

two: how he went about the world slaying monsters, men in aspect but beasts in their habits, and how he cleansed the filthy Augean stables.

562 In this connection gentile poetic imagination created two other major divinities, Mars and Venus [317]. The former was a [poetic] character of the heroes as first and properly fighting for their altars and hearths, *pro aris et focis*. This sort of fighting was always heroic, for it was fighting for their own religion, to which mankind takes recourse when all natural help is despaired of. Whence the wars of religion are most sanguinary [958]. Libertines, too, as they grow older, turn to religion, for they feel nature failing them [339]. It was for these reasons that we took religion for the first principle of our Science [333ff]. Now Mars fought on truly real fields and behind truly real shields [529, 563], which, from *cluer*, were called by the Romans first *clupei* and later *clypei* [533, 556]; just as from the time of the returned barbarism pastures and enclosed woods have been called defenses. And these shields were charged with true arms, which at first, before there were arms of iron, were simply poles with their ends burned and then tapered to a point and given sharp edges to make them suitable for inflicting wounds. Such were the simple spears, without iron tips, which were given as military prizes to the Roman soldiers for heroic conduct in war. Hence among the Greeks the spear is borne by Minerva, Bellona, and Pallas [Athena] [590]. And among the Latins, from *quiris*, spear, Juno is called Quirina, and Mars, Quirinus; and Romulus, because in life he excelled with the spear, was called Quirinus after his death. Similarly the Roman people, who were armed with javelins (as the Spartans, the heroic people of Greece, were armed with spears), were called Quirites in solemn assembly [112]. But the barbarian nations, Roman history tells us, used to fight with the primitive spears we are speaking of, and it describes them for us as *praeustas sudes*, burned-tip spears, similar to those the American Indians were found to wield. And in our times the nobles are armed with spears in the tournaments, as they formerly used them in war. The invention of this sort of weapon proceeded from a just idea of strength, as it were elongating the arm and thus using the body to ward off harm from the body; whereas the arms that are held close to the body belong rather to beasts.

563 The first shield in the world was the ground of the field where the dead were buried, whence in the science of heraldry the shield is the ground of the arms [487, 529]. The colors of the fields were true colors. The black came from the burned fields to which Hercules had set fire [540]. The green from the fields of grain in leaf. And it was by an error that the gold was taken as a metal, for it was the yellowing of the standing grain as

it ripened that made the third color of the earth [544]. Thus the Romans, among their heroic military prizes, charged with grain the shields of soldiers who had distinguished themselves in battle, and military glory was called *adorea*, from *ador*, the parched grain which was their primitive food. The ancient Latins called it *adur*, from *uro*, to burn, so that perhaps the first adoration in religious times was the burning of grain. Blue was the color of the sky with which these clearings were covered, which is why *bleu* is French for blue, sky, and God [482]. Red was from the blood of the impious thieves slain by the heroes when found in their fields [549, 553]. The noble arms which have come down to us from the returned barbarism are observed to be charged with many lions, black, green, gold, blue, and finally red. These, according to what we have seen above of the fields of grain that later became fields of arms, must be the cultivated lands, viewed under the aspect of the lion overcome by Hercules [540], with their above enumerated colors. Many are charged with vairs, which must be the furrows whence sprang the armed men of Cadmus, sprouting from the dragon's teeth he had sown after slaying the monster [679]. Many are charged with pales, which must be the spears with which the first heroes waged war. And finally many are charged with rakes, which are clearly agricultural implements. From all this we must conclude that agriculture was the first foundation of nobility not only in the first barbarian times, as we ascertain from the Romans, but also in the second.

564   The shields of the ancients were covered with leather, and we learn from the poets that the old heroes wore leather; that is, the hides of the beasts they hunted and killed. On this there is a fine passage in Pausanias [8.1.5] where he says that leather clothing was invented by Pelasgus (an ancient hero of Greece after whom the people of that nation were first called Pelasgians, and whom Apollodorus [3.8.1] calls auto-chthonous or son of earth, or, in a word, a giant [370]). And there is a striking correspondence between the first and second barbarian times, for Dante [*Paradise* 15.112f], speaking of the grand old personages of the second, says they were clothed in leather and bone, and Boccaccio too [i.e., Giovanni Villani 6.69?] relates that they went about wrapped in leather. This must have been the reason for covering the family arms with leather, and the curling into scrolls of the skin of head and feet is an appropriate finishing touch. The shields were round because the cleared and cultivated lands were the first *orbes terrarum* [550]; and this characteristic survived among the Latins, whose clypeus was round, in distinction from their scutum, which had corners. Every clearing was called a *lucus*, in the sense of an eye, as even today we call eyes the openings through which light

enters houses. The true heroic phrase that "every giant had his *lucus*" [clearing or eye] was altered and corrupted when its meaning was lost, and had already been falsified when it reached Homer, for it was then taken to mean that every giant had one eye in the middle of his forehead. With these one-eyed giants came Vulcan to work in the first forges—that is, the forests to which Vulcan had set fire and where he had fashioned the first arms, which were the spears with burned tips [562]—and, by an extension of the idea of arms, to forge bolts for Jove. For Vulcan had set fire to the forests in order to observe in the open sky the direction from which Jove sent his bolts.

565 The other divinity born amid these most ancient human institutions was Venus, a [poetic] character of civil beauty, whence *honestas* had the meanings of nobility, beauty, and virtue. For this is the order in which these three ideas must have been born. The first to be understood was the civil beauty which appertained to the heroes. Then the natural beauty which is apprehended by the human senses, but only by those men of perception and comprehension who know how to discern the parts and grasp their harmony in the body as a whole, in which beauty essentially consists. This is why peasants and men of the squalid plebs understand little or nothing of beauty (which shows the error of the philologians who say that in these simple and stupid times of which we are speaking kings were chosen for their handsome and well-proportioned bodies; for this tradition [252] is to be understood as referring to civil beauty, which was the nobility of the heroes [566]). And lastly the beauty of virtue, which is called *honestas* and is understood only by philosophers. Hence it must have been the civil beauty that was possessed by Apollo, Bacchus, Ganymede, Bellerophon, Theseus, and other heroes, and perhaps on their account Venus was imagined as male [androgynous].

566 The idea of civil beauty must have been engendered in the minds of the theological poets when they saw that the impious creatures who had taken refuge on their lands were men in aspect but brute beasts in their habits [688]. It was this civil beauty and no other that was cherished by the Spartans, the heroes of Greece, who cast down from Mount Taygetus the ugly and deformed offspring; that is, those borne by noble women but without benefit of solemn nuptials. Such too much have been the monsters condemned by the Law of the Twelve Tables [4.1] to be thrown into the Tiber [410]. For it is not at all likely that the decemvirs, in that parsimony of laws proper to the first commonwealths, would have given any thought to natural monsters, because of whose extreme rarity anything rare in nature is called monstrous, when even in the superfluity of laws with which

we are now afflicted, legislators leave to the discretion of judges those cases that seldom present themselves. Such then must have been the monsters which were first and properly called civil. (It is one of these that Pamphilus had in mind when, under the false suspicion that the maiden Philumena was pregnant, he says: *aliquid monstri alunt*, "Something monstrous is a-breeding" [Terence: *Lady of Andros* 250].) And so they continued to be called in the Roman laws, which must have spoken with all propriety, as Antoine Favre observes in his *Iurisprudentiae papinianeae scientia*, and as we have already remarked above in another connection [410].

567   This must be what Livy [4.2.6] has in mind when, with as much good faith as ignorance of the Roman antiquities of which he writes, he says that if the nobles shared *connubium* with the plebeians the resulting offspring would be *secum ipsa discors*, which is as much as to say a monster of mixed and twofold nature, the one heroic, of the nobles, the other feral, of the plebeians, who "practiced marriages like those of wild animals" (*agitabant connubia more ferarum*) [cf. Horace, *Satire* 1.3.107ff]. This phrase [*more ferarum*] Livy took from some ancient writer of annals and used it ignorantly, for he quotes it as if it meant [that such bestial marriages would result] "if the nobles intermarried with the plebeians." But the plebeians in their miserable state of quasi slavery could not ask any such thing of the nobles. What they demanded was the right of contracting solemn nuptials (for such is the meaning of *connubium*), which right was at that time confined to the nobles [598]. But among animals no species has intercourse with another. We must therefore say that [*more ferarum*] was a phrase of insult applied by the nobles to the plebeians in that heroic contest. For inasmuch as the latter did not possess the public auspices, whose solemnities were required to make marriages legitimate, none of them had a certain father (by the well-known definition in Roman law [D. 2.4.5] that *nuptiae demonstrant patrem*, "the marriage ceremony identifies the father"), and with reference to this uncertainty the plebeians were said by the nobles to have intercourse with their mothers and daughters as beasts do.

568   To the plebeian Venus [512, 560, 579], however, were attributed the doves, not to signify passionate love but because they are, as Horace [*Odes* 4.4.31f] describes them, *degeneres*, base birds in comparison with eagles, which Horace calls *feroces*; and thus to signify that the plebeians had private or minor auspices as contrasted with those of the eagles and thunderbolts possessed by the nobles and called by Varro and Messala major or public auspices [525]. On the latter depended all the heroic institutions of the nobles, as Roman history plainly confirms [110]. To the

heroic Venus, or Venus *pronuba*, on the other hand, were attributed the swans, which appertain also to Apollo (the god of the nobility [533]), and under the auspices of one of which Leda conceives the eggs by Jove [512].

569 The plebeian Venus was depicted as naked, whereas Venus *pronuba* wore the girdle [512]. And here we may see how ideas concerning these poetic antiquities have been distorted. For that [nakedness] was later taken as an incentive to lust which in truth had been invented to signify the natural modesty or the punctuality of good faith with which natural obligations were fulfilled among the plebeians. For the plebeians had no part of citizenship in the heroic cities [597], and thus did not contract obligations sanctioned by any bond of civil law to make their fulfillment necessary. Hence to Venus were attributed the Graces, likewise nude; and among the Latins *caussa* and *gratia* meant the same thing, so that the Graces must have signified to the poets the *pacta nuda*, or simple agreements which involve only natural obligation. And thus those pacts which the Roman jurisconsults called *pacta stipulata* were later described by the medieval interpreters as vested. For, understanding by nude pacts those not stipulated, they did not derive *stipulatio* from *stipes* (for such an origin would have yielded *stipatio*), in the forced sense of that which sustains the pacts, but from *stipula* as used by the peasants of Latium for the blade which clothes the grain. On the other hand, the vested pacts of the early writers on feudal law were so called from the same origin from which came the investiture of the fiefs, from which certainly comes *exfestucare*, to divest of [an estate, office, or] dignity. For the reasons set forth, therefore, *gratia* and *caussa* were understood by the poetic Latins as having the same meaning with respect to the contracts observed by the plebeians of the heroic cities. Similarly, with the later introduction of contracts according to the natural law of the gentes (*de iure naturali gentium*, to which Ulpian [D. 1.1.1.4; 990] adds *humanarum*, human [gentes]), *caussa* and *negocium* signified the same thing, for in such kinds of contracts the transactions themselves are almost always *caussae* or *cavissae* or *cautelae* which serve as stipulations to give security to the pacts [1072].

[Chapter III]   Corollaries concerning Contracts Sealed by Simple Consent

570 The most ancient law of the heroic nations could certainly take no cognizance of the contracts which nowadays are said to be sealed by

simple consent. For these peoples were concerned only with the necessities of life. The only fruits they gathered were natural fruits, as they did not yet understand the use of money. They were, so to speak, all body. They were extremely crude and therefore suspicious, for crudeness is born of ignorance and it is a property of human nature that he who does not know is ever doubtful. For all these reasons they did not recognize good faith, and they made sure of all obligations by a real or fictitious physical transfer. Moreover, the transfer was made certain by solemn stipulations in the course of the transaction [1030]. Hence the celebrated article in the Law of the Twelve Tables [6.1a]: *Si quis nexum faciet mancipiumque, uti lingua nuncupassit, ita ius esto* ("If anyone shall make bond or conveyance, as he has declared with his tongue, so shall it be binding") [433, 1031]. And from this nature of human civil institutions the following truths emerge.

I

571   It is [rightly] said that the oldest buying and selling was barter. In the case of real estate, however, the barter must have been of the kind which in the recourse of barbarism [L3] was called *libellus*, or feudal leasehold. Its utility was apparent from the fact that one man had more than enough fields yielding an abundance of fruits which another man lacked, and vice versa [1071].

II

572   The letting of houses could not be practiced as long as cities were quite small and dwellings simple. Landlords must therefore have let out their lands for others to build on; and thus the only rental was ground rent.

III

573   The letting of land must have been by emphyteusis, which the Latins called *clientela*; whence the grammarians, by an inspired guess, said the *clientes* had been so called as being *colentes*, tillers.

IV

574   This must be the reason why, for the recourse of barbarism [L3], the only contracts we find in the old archives are leases for dwellings or farms, in perpetuity or for limited periods of time.

V

575   This is perhaps the reason why emphyteusis [1067] is a contract *de iure civili*; that is, by our principles, *de iure heroico romanorum*. To this

Ulpian [569] opposes the *ius naturale gentium humanarum*, the natural law of human gentes as distinguished from that of the barbarous gentes that had preceded them, not from that of the barbarous gentes outside the Roman Empire in his own day, for their law was of no importance to Roman jurisconsults.

VI

576 Partnerships were unknown, by that cyclopean custom whereby each family father cared only for his own affairs and did not trouble himself with those of others, as Homer gave us to understand by what he has Polyphemus tell Ulysses [516].

VII

577 For the same reason mandates or contracts of agency were unknown. The rule of ancient civil law was: *Per extraneam personam acquiri nemini* ("No one may acquire by a person not under his power") [D. 50.17.11 + 123?].

VIII

578 But when the law of the heroic gentes was succeeded by what Ulpian [569] defines as that of the human gentes, there was a revolutionary change. The contract of purchase and sale, which in ancient times did not guarantee recovery unless double recovery was stipulated in the contract, now became the queen of those contracts called *bonae fidei*, of good faith, and the right of recovery obtained naturally even without stipulation.

[Chapter IV] Mythological Canon

579 Returning now to the three [poetic] characters, Vulcan, Mars, and Venus, it must be noted here (and this must be considered an important canon of our mythology) that there were three divine characters signifying the heroes, distinguished from three others signifying the plebeians. Vulcan splits Jove's head with a hatchet to give birth to Minerva [589], attempts to interfere in a quarrel between Jove and Juno, is kicked out of heaven by Jove, and is left lame. Mars, in a stern reproof reported by Homer [I. 5.890], is called by Jove "The vilest of all the gods," and Minerva in the battle of the gods related by the same poet [I. 21.403] hurls a stone at him and wounds him [781]. (This Vulcan and this Mars must be the

plebeians who served the heroes in war.) And Venus (signifying the natural wives of the plebeians) along with the plebeian Mars is trapped in the net of the heroic Vulcan; and, being discovered naked by the Sun, they are made the butt of the other gods [560]. Hence Venus was erroneously believed to be the wife of Vulcan, but there was no marriage in heaven save that between Jove and Juno [511], and that was sterile [448]. And it was not said that Mars had committed adultery with Venus but that she was his concubine, because among the plebeians there were only natural marriages [683], and these were called by the Latins concubinages.

580 As we have explained these three characters here, so we shall explain others in their proper places. Among them we shall find the plebeian Tantalus who cannot reach the apples (which rise beyond his grasp) nor the water (which sinks beneath the reach of his lips) [583]; the plebeian Midas who dies of hunger because all he touches turns to gold [649]; and the plebeian Linus who contends in song with Apollo and is vanquished and slain by the god [647].

581 Such double fables or characters must have been necessary in the heroic state in which the plebeians, having no names of their own, bore those of their heroes [559]; to say nothing of the extreme poverty of speech that must have prevailed in the first times, since, copious as our present languages are, even in them the same word often signifies different and sometimes contrary things.

[SECTION V]

[POETIC POLITICS]

[Chapter I] Poetic Politics, under Which the First Common-wealths in the World Were Born in a Most Severely Aristocratic Form

582   In this fashion, then [553–569], the families were founded with the *famuli* taken by the heroes under their faith, force, or protection [523]. And these *famuli* were the first *socii* in the world [258, 555, 558]. Their lives were in bail to their lords, and consequently their acquisitions likewise. The heroes, with their cyclopean paternal authority, had the right of life and death over their own children, and, in consequence of this right over their persons, had also a despotic right over all their acquisitions [556]. This was Aristotle's meaning when he defined the children of a family as "animate instruments of their fathers" [E. 1161b 4]. And the Law of the Twelve Tables, even into the period of the most unbounded popular liberty, preserved to the Roman family fathers both these monarchical rights, of power over the persons and dominion over the acquisitions [of their children]. Indeed, until imperial times, sons, like slaves, had only one kind of *peculium*, or private property, namely *peculium profecticium* [that acquired by their father's consent]. In the earliest times the fathers must have had the power of really selling their children as many as three times; for later, with the progressive softening of human times, they made three pretended sales when they wished to free their children from their paternal power. The Gauls and the Celts, however, retained an equal power over slaves and children; and the custom of fathers really selling their children was found in the West Indies, and in Europe they are sold up to four times by the Muscovites and Tartars. So [far from] true is it that other barbarous nations do not have paternal authority *talem qualem habent cives romani*, "such as Roman citizens have" [J. 1.9.2]! This evident falsehood springs from the common vulgar error of which the scholars have been guilty in interpreting this statement; for it was made by the jurisconsults with

209

reference to the nations vanquished by the Roman people. For such nations, deprived of their entire civil law by the right of conquest, had left to them only natural paternal powers and, consequently, natural blood ties called those of cognation; and similarly only the natural property rights called bonitary; and hence on both these accounts only the natural obligations said to be *de iure naturali gentium,* which Ulpian further specified as *humanarum* [575]. But all the institutions these conquered nations had lost were of course still retained under their own civil laws by the peoples outside the Roman Empire, precisely as the Romans themselves retained them [1023].

583   To return to our argument: when the sons of the families were freed by their fathers' death from this private monarchical rule, each son took it up entire for himself, so that every Roman citizen when free of paternal power is called a *paterfamilias* in Roman law. The *famuli* on the other hand went on living in that servile state. After a long period of time they must naturally have chafed under it, by the axiom that "subject man naturally aspires to free himself from servitude" [292]. Such must have been the plebeian Tantalus, striving in vain to reach the fruit (the golden apples of the grain raised on the lands of the heroes), and unable to slake his burning thirst with so much as a mouthful of the water which rises to his lips only to sink away again. Such also were Ixion, forever turning the wheel, and Sisyphus pushing the rock uphill [719]. (Like that thrown by Cadmus, this rock was the hard earth, and its rolling back when it reached the top was preserved in the Latin phrases *vertere terram* for cultivating it and *saxum volvere* for painfully performing a long and arduous task.) For all these reasons the *famuli* must have revolted against the heroes. And this is that "necessity" [261] which we conjectured generally to have been imposed by the *famuli* upon the heroic fathers in the state of the families, as a result of which the commonwealths were born.

584   For at this point, under pressure of the emergency, the heroes must by nature have been moved to unite themselves in orders so as to resist the multitudes of rebellious *famuli*. And they must have chosen as their head a father fiercer than the rest and with greater presence of spirit. Such men were called *reges,* kings, from *regere,* which properly means to sustain or direct. In this fashion, to use the well-known phrase of the jurisconsult Pomponius, "when the institutions themselves dictated it, kingdoms were founded" (*rebus ipsis dictantibus, regna condita*) [D. 1.2.2.11; 1007]; a phrase in keeping with the doctrine of Roman law which declares that the natural law of the gentes was established by divine providence (*ius naturale gentium divina providentia constitutum*) [J.

1.2.11; 328]. Such was the generation of the heroic kingdoms. And since the fathers were sovereign kings of their families, the equality of their state and the fierce nature of the cyclopes [296] being such that no one of them naturally would yield to another, there sprang up of themselves the reigning senates, made up of so many family kings. They found that, without human discernment or counsel, they had united their private interests in a common interest called *patria*, which, the word *res* being understood, means "the interest of the fathers." The nobles were accordingly called patricians, and the nobles must have been the only citizens of the first *patriae*, or fatherlands. In this sense we may regard as truthful the tradition that has come down to us which says that in the earliest times kings were chosen by nature. On this point there are two golden passages in Tacitus's *Germany* [7] which give us ground for conjecturing the same custom for all the other first barbarous peoples. The first is that "their squadrons and their wedges, instead of being formed by chance or by a casual grouping, are composed of families and clans." And the second is that "their chiefs do more by example than by command; as they are energetic and conspicuous, and as they fight in the forefront, they rule by being admired."

585 Evidence that the first kings on earth were of this nature is afforded by the fact that the heroic poets imagined Jove in heaven to have just such kingship over men and gods, as is shown by that golden passage in Homer [I. 1.517] where Jove explains to Thetis that he can do nothing contrary to what the gods have once determined in their great celestial council. Here speaks a true aristocratic king. On this episode the Stoics later erected their dogma of a Jove subject to fate, but in fact Jove and the other gods held council concerning the affairs of men and freely determined them. And the passage we have cited explains two others in Homer which political theorists have erroneously interpreted as Homeric references to monarchy. In one of them [I. 1.287ff] Agamemnon reproves the stubborn Achilles. In the other [I. 2.204] Ulysses persuades the Greeks, mutinous and desirous of returning home, to continue the siege of Troy. In both passages it is said that "one alone is king." But both passages refer to warfare, in which there is but one commander-in-chief, by the maxim quoted by Tacitus [A. 1.6]: "the condition of bearing rule is that an account cannot be balanced unless it is rendered to but one person" (*eam esse imperandi conditionem, ut non aliter ratio constet quam si uni reddatur*). Moreover, Homer himself, as often as he mentions the heroes by name in his two poems, adds the fixed epithet "king." In striking harmony with this is a golden passage in *Genesis* [36.15ff] in which Moses, enumer-

ating the descendants of Esau, calls them all kings, or rather, as the Vulgate has it, *duces*, "captains" [F7]. Likewise the ambassadors of Pyrrhus report having seen in Rome a senate of so many kings. And in fact one cannot conceive in civil nature any reason why the fathers, in such a change of forms of government, should have altered anything of what they had had in the state of nature, save to subject their sovereign family powers to these reigning orders of theirs. For the nature of the strong is to surrender as little as possible of what they have acquired by valor, and only so much as is necessary to preserve their acquisitions [261]. Hence we read so often in Roman history of that heroic disdain of the strong which will not suffer an ignominious surrender of what has been won by valor (*virtute parta per flagitium amittere*). And among all human possibilities, once it is seen that civil governments were not born either of fraud or of the violence of a single man [522], one cannot imagine any way but the one we have described by which civil power could emerge from family authority, or the eminent domain of civil states from the paternal natural domains [266] (which were *ex iure optimo* in the sense of being free of every private or public encumbrance [490]).

586   This development which we have established by reason is strikingly confirmed by the origins of the words relating to it. For on this *dominium optimum*, or unencumbered domain of the fathers (called *dikaion ariston* by the Greeks [490]), were erected the commonwealths called aristocratic by the Greeks, and by the Romans commonwealths of optimates, from Ops, goddess of power [587]. Perhaps for this reason Ops was called Jove's wife (from whom he must have been called *optimus*, for he is *aristos* to the Greeks and hence *optimus* to the Latins), the wife, that is, of the reigning order of those heroes who had arrogated to themselves the name of gods [437]. (For Juno by the law of the auspices was the wife of Jove understood as the thundering sky [511].) Now the mother of these gods was Cybele, also called mother of the giants properly so called in the sense of nobles [549], and she was later taken for the queen of cities [722]. From Ops, then, came the term "optimates," for all such commonwealths are instituted to preserve the power of the nobles, and to preserve it they retain as eternal properties two principal guards, one of the institutions, the other of the confines [981–998]. Under the guarding of the institutions came first the guarding of the families, by which the Romans down to the 309th year of the city excluded the plebs from *connubium* [598]. Then the guarding of the magistracies, by which the patricians so strongly contested the claim of the plebs to the consulship. Then the guarding of the priesthoods, and finally, by its means, the guarding of the laws [999–1003],

which all the first nations regarded as sacred. Whence down to the Law of the Twelve Tables the nobles governed Rome by custom, as we were assured [284] by Dionysius of Halicarnassus [10.3], and for a century afterward the interpretation of that Law was kept within the college of pontiffs, according to the jurisconsult Pomponius [D. 1.2.2.6], because until then that college was open only to nobles. The other principal guard is that of the confines, in which connection the Romans, until their destruction of Corinth, had observed an incomparable justice in war in order not to militarize the plebeians, and an extreme clemency in victory in order not to enrich them [273–276].

587 This great and important tract of poetic history is all contained in the fable of Saturn seeking to devour the infant Jove, and the priests of Cybele concealing him and by the clash of their arms preventing his infant cries from being heard. Here Saturn must be a character of the *famuli*, who as day laborers till the fields of their masters, the heroic fathers, and with ardent longing seek fields from the fathers on which they may find sustenance for themselves. And this Saturn is the father of Jove because from this Saturn, as its occasion, was born the civil government of the fathers which was set forth in the character of that Jove whose wife was Ops [586]. For Jove taken as the god of the auspices, of which the most solemn were the thunderbolt and the eagle—the Jove whose wife was Juno—is the father of the gods; that is, of the heroes. For they believed themselves sons of Jove, as having been engendered under his auspices in solemn nuptials, of which Juno is the goddess, and so they took the name of gods, whose mother is Earth; that is, Ops, the wife of this Jove. And this same Jove was called king of men; that is, of the *famuli* in the state of the families and of the plebeians in that of the heroic cities [437]. These two divine titles [father and king], through ignorance of this poetic history, have been confused, as if Jove were also the father of men. But men [*famuli* and plebeians] down into the days of the ancient Roman republic could not name their fathers (*non poterant nomine ciere patrem*), as Livy says, because they were born of natural marriages and not of solemn nuptials; whence jurisprudence retained the maxim: *Nuptiae demonstrant patrem* ("The marriage ceremony identifies the father") [433, 567].

588 The fable goes on to relate that the priests of Cybele or Ops (for the first kingdoms were everywhere priestly [250]) conceal Jove. (From this concealment Latin philologians guess the name Latium must have come, and the Latin language preserved the history in its phrase *condere regna* [389], for the fathers formed a closed order against the mutinous *famuli*, and the secrecy of this order was the source of what political theorists

called *arcana imperii*.) And by the clash of their arms they prevent Saturn from hearing the wailing of Jove (newly born to the union of that order), and thus they save him. In this way the same thing is distinctly narrated that Plato stated so obscurely [L. 626A], that the commonwealths were born on the basis of arms. To this may be added what Aristotle told us [271], that in the heroic commonwealths the nobles swore eternal enmity against the plebs! And there remained from all this the eternal property expressed in the saying that servants are the paid enemies of their masters. The Greeks preserve this history for us in the etymology of *polemos*, war, from *polis*, city.

589   In this connection the Greek nations imagined the tenth divinity of the greater gentes, namely Minerva [317]. And her birth was fancied in this wild and uncouth fashion: Vulcan, it was said, split with an ax the forehead of Jove, whence sprang Minerva [579]. By this they meant to signify that the multitude of *famuli* practicing servile arts (which came under the poetic genus of the plebeian Vulcan) broke (in the sense of weakening or diminishing) the rule of Jove. (The Latins used for this the expression *minuere caput*, to split the head, because, not being able to express rule as an abstraction, they used the concrete word "head.") For Jove's rule in the family-state had been monarchic, and they changed it to aristocratic in the city-state. Hence it is not an unlikely conjecture that Minerva's name was derived from *minuere*, nor that from this most ancient poetic antiquity came the phrase in Roman law, *capitis deminutio*, in the sense of change of state, as Minerva changed the family-state to the city-state.

590   To this fable [of Minerva's birth] the philosophers later attached the most sublime of their metaphysical meditations: that the eternal idea is generated by God in himself, while created ideas are produced by God in us. But the theological poets contemplated Minerva under the idea of civil order, as "order" was the preferred Latin term for the senate (and this perhaps led the philosophers to consider it an eternal idea of God, who is nought else than eternal order); and thence there remained the eternal property that the order of the best is the wisdom of cities. However, Minerva in Homer is always distinguished by the fixed epithets "warlike" and "predatory," and only twice do we recall having found her called "counselor" [I. 5.260; O. 16.282]. And the owl and the olive were sacred to her not because she spends the night in meditation and reads and writes by the light of the lamp, but rather to signify the dark night of the hiding places in which humanity had its beginnings [387], and perhaps more properly to signify that the heroic senates that composed the cities con-

ceived their laws in secret. Certainly it remained the custom of the Areopagites to give their votes under cover of darkness in the senate of Athens, the city of Minerva, whom the Greeks called Athena. From this heroic custom came the Latin phrase *condere leges*, so that *legum conditores* properly signified the senates that commanded the laws, and *legum latores* those who carried the laws from the senates to the plebs of the various peoples, as we have noted above in the case of Horatius [521]. How far the theological poets were from considering Minerva the goddess of wisdom appears from the statues and medals in which she is always shown as armed, and from the fact that the same goddess was Minerva in the curia, Pallas in the plebeian assemblies (for example in Homer [!] it is Pallas who leads Telemachus, about to depart in search of his father Ulysses, into the assembly of the plebs, whom he calls the "other people" [O. 2.6ff,267ff; cf. I. 2.54f,93f, esp. 191]), and lastly Bellona in warfare.

591 It must be said that the erroneous belief that Minerva was understood as wisdom by the theological poets is of a piece with the other error that the curia was so called from *cura*, care, that is, the care of the commonwealth, at a time when the nations were confused and stupid. The word must rather have been derived by the most ancient Greeks from *cheir*, hand, in the form *kyria*, power, whence *curia* in Latin. We may infer as much from one of the two great fragments of antiquity (entered in the Chronological Table and mentioned in the Notes upon it [77]) which, to our good fortune, Denis Petau found embedded in Greek history before the heroic age of Greece and consequently in what the Egyptians called the age of the gods [52], which we are here investigating.

592 One of these fragments relates that the Heraclids or descendants of Hercules had been scattered through the whole of Greece, even in Attica where Athens was, and had later retired to the Peloponnesus where Sparta was, an aristocratic commonwealth or kingdom under two kings of the race of Hercules, called Heraclids or nobles, who administered laws and conducted wars under the supervision of the ephors. The latter were guardians not of popular but of aristocratic liberty. They had king Agis strangled because he had tried to bring to the people a law wiping out debts, which Livy [32.38.9] calls "a firebrand for inflaming the plebs against the optimates" (*facem ad accendendum adversus optimates plebem*), and another concerning testaments which would have diverted inheritances outside the order of the nobles, within which they had previously been kept by the law of legitimate succession; for only the nobles had had direct heirs, agnates, or gentiles [110]. There had been similar attempts at Rome before the Law of the Twelve Tables, as will be shown

later [598]. And just as men like [Spurius] Cassius, [Manlius] Capitolinus, the Gracchi, and other leading citizens of Rome were declared traitors and executed by the senate for attempting with like laws to raise up a little the poor oppressed plebs of Rome, so Agis was strangled by the ephors. So far were the ephors of Sparta from being, as Polybius [23.11.4f] represents them, guardians of the popular liberty of Lacedaemon. Thus Athens (named for Minerva, whom they called Athena) must have had in its earliest times an aristocratic form of government; and Greek history has faithfully recounted as much, telling us that Draco reigned in Athens at the time when it was occupied by the optimates [423]. And this is confirmed by Thucydides [i.e., by Isocrates in his *Areopagiticus*], who tells us that as long as the city was governed by the severe Areopagites it shone with the finest heroic virtues and carried out the worthiest enterprises, just as Rome did in the time when it was an aristocratic commonwealth. (Juvenal [9.101!] renders their name "judges of Mars" in the sense of armed judges, though Arēs, Mars, + pēgē, in Latin *pagus*, a country or its people, might better have been rendered "the people of Mars," as the Roman people were called; for at their birth the peoples were composed only of nobles, who alone had the right to bear arms.) But Athens was cast down from this lofty state by Pericles and Aristides in favor of popular liberty, and Rome suffered a like fate beginning with Sextius and Canuleius, tribunes of the plebs.

593   The other great fragment tells how the Greeks traveling abroad observed the Curetes or priests of Cybele scattered through Saturnia or ancient Italy, through Crete, and through Asia; so that everywhere among the first barbarous nations there must have prevailed kingdoms of Curetes, corresponding to the kingdoms of the Heraclids scattered through ancient Greece [25, 77]. These Curetes were the armed priests who by the clashing of their arms muffled the cries of the infant Jove whom Saturn sought to devour in the fable we were just explaining [588].

594   It follows from our entire argument that the first *comitia curiata* must have had their origin at this most ancient point of time and in this way. They are the oldest *comitia* we read of in Roman history [624ff]. They were held under arms, and they were continued later for the purpose of dealing with religious institutions, for in the earliest times all secular institutions were seen under this aspect. Livy [21.20.1] wonders that such assemblies were held in Gaul at the time when Hannibal passed through. But Tacitus in his *Germany* [7] tells us that they were also held by priests, who dealt out penalties in the midst of arms as if in the presence of their gods. This showed a just sense of the fitness of things, for the heroic

assemblies were armed for dealing out penalties because the supreme authority of the laws follows the supreme authority of arms. And speaking generally, Tacitus [G. 11] tells us that the Germans conducted all their public affairs under arms and presided over by priests, as we have just said. Hence among the ancient Germans, whose custom allows us to assume the like for all the first barbarous peoples, we find once more the kingdom of the Egyptian priests [605]; we find the kingdoms of the Curetes, or armed priests, which prevailed among the Greeks of Saturnia or ancient Italy, of Crete, and of Asia [591ff]; we find the Quirites of ancient Latium.

595   In view of what has been set forth, the law of the Quirites must have been the natural law of the heroic gentes of Italy, which, to distinguish it from that of the other peoples, was called *ius Quiritium Romanorum*. This did not come about through any pact made between the Sabines and the Romans that they should be called Quirites from Cures, the capital city of the Sabines, for in that case they would have been called Curetes, the name used by the Greeks of Saturnia. And if the capital of the Sabines had been called Ceres (as the Latin grammarians will have it), they should rather have been called (and note the distortion of ideas!) Cerites, a name applied to those Roman citizens who were condemned by the censors to bear the burdens while having no part of civil honors, just as were the plebs who were composed of the *famuli* at the birth of the heroic cities [597]. It was rather with the mass of the plebs that the Sabines were merged in those barbarous times when conquered cities were destroyed and the survivors scattered over the plains and forced to till the fields for the conquering peoples—a fate that the Romans did not spare even their mother city, Alba. Such [conquered neighbor cities] were the first provinces, so called as if for *prope victae*, near conquered (for example, Corioli, for the conquest of which Marcius was called Coriolanus), as on the other hand the last or farthest provinces were so called as being *procul victae*, far conquered. And in such plains were settled the first inland colonies, called in all propriety *coloniae deductae*, that is, bands of peasant day laborers led down from above [1023]; whereas in the case of the last or farthest colonies, *deductae* meant just the opposite, for, from the low and cramped quarters of Rome where the poor plebeians dwelt, they were led to high and strong places in the provinces, to keep the provinces in order, to be lords therein, and to change the existing lords of the fields into poor day laborers [300, 560]. In this way, according to Livy [1.30.1], who saw only the effects, Rome grows on the ruins of Alba, and the Sabines bring to their Roman sons-in-law the wealth of Ceres [i.e., Cures] as the dowry of their abducted daughters, as Florus [1.1.14] vainly remarks. And these are

the colonies before those which came after the agrarian laws of the Gracchi. Livy [6.11.8] says the Roman plebs, in the heroic contests they carried
on with the nobility, disdained, or rather resented, these first colonies
because they were not of the same kind as the last; and because they did
nothing to raise up the Roman plebs—and Livy finds that they even added
fuel to the contests—he offers these vain reflections upon them.

596 Finally, that Minerva had signified armed aristocratic orders is
attested by Homer where he tells of Minerva wounding Mars with a stone
in the course of their contest. (Mars was the [poetic] character of the
plebeians who served the heroes in war [579].) And again where he tells of
Minerva attempting a conspiracy against Jove [I. 8.374ff], which is after the
manner of aristocracies, in which the lords by secret counsels overthrow
their chiefs when the latter affect tyranny. It is only in this time that we
read of statues being erected to the slayers of tyrants; whereas if the latter
had been monarchical kings, as commonly supposed, their slayers would
have been accounted traitors.

597 Thus the first cities were made up solely of nobles, who were in
command. But because they had need of others to serve them, by a
common sense of utility the heroes were constrained to satisfy the multitude of their rebellious clients; hence they sent to them the first embassies,
which by the law of the gentes are sent by sovereigns. And they sent them
with the first agrarian law in the world [265], under which, as the strong
do, they conceded to the clients the least they could [261], which was
bonitary ownership of the fields the heroes might choose to assign to them
[604]. In this sense it may be true that Ceres discovered both grain and
laws. This law was dictated by the following natural law of the gentes:
since ownership follows power, and since the lives of the *famuli* were
dependent on the heroes who had saved them by granting them asylum, it
was lawful and right that they should have a similarly precarious ownership, which they might enjoy as long as it suited the heroes to maintain
them in possession of the fields they had assigned to them. Thus the *famuli*
merged to form the first plebs of the heroic cities, in which they had none
of the privileges of citizenship. It is just like one of these that Achilles
declares he has been treated by Agamemnon when the latter wrongfully
takes Briseis from him, for he says he has suffered an outrage which would
not have been committed against a day laborer without any rights of
citizenship [I. 9.648].

598 Such were the Roman plebeians down to the struggle over *connubium* [110]. For when, by the second agrarian law, conceded to them by
the nobles in the Law of the Twelve Tables, they had gained quiritary

ownership of the fields, as we showed many years ago in our *Principles of Universal Law* [Op. 2.580] (in one of the two passages on whose account we do not regret the publication of that book [29]), yet, because by the law of the gentes aliens were not capable of civil ownership, and the plebeians were not yet citizens, they were still unable to leave their fields intestate to their kin, because they did not have direct heirs, agnates, or gentiles [B4], which relations were all dependent on solemn nuptials. Nor could they even dispose of their fields by testament, for they were not citizens. Hence the lands assigned to them soon returned to the nobles, to whom they owed their titles of ownership. When they had become aware of this, within three short years they demanded the right of *connubium*. In the condition of miserable slaves that Roman history clearly relates that of the plebeians to have been, they did not demand the right of intermarrying with the nobles, for in that case the Latin would have read *connubia cum patribus* [987]. What they did ask was the right to contract solemn nuptials just as the fathers did, and so they demanded *connubia patrum*, the principal solemnity of which was the public auspices called by Varro and Messala major auspices, those meant by the fathers when they said the auspices were theirs [525]. The plebeians, in making this demand, were in effect asking for Roman citizenship, whose natural principle was solemn nuptials, which were therefore defined by the jurisconsult Modestinus as the sharing of every divine and human right (*omnis divini et humani iuris communicatio*), than which no more proper definition can be given of citizenship itself [110].*

[*Chapter II*] *All Commonwealths Are Born from Certain Eternal Principles of Fiefs*

599 In such fashion, in part from the nature of the strong to preserve their acquisitions, and in part from the nature of the benefits which can be looked for in civil life (on which two natures of human institutions the eternal principles of fiefs were founded [260–262]), the commonwealths were born in the world with three kinds of ownership [266] for three kinds of fiefs, which were held by three kinds of persons over three kinds of things.

---

* The steps by which Vico reached the view expressed in this paragraph are traced by M. H. Fisch, "Vico on Roman Law," *Essays in Political Theory presented to George H. Sabine* (Ithaca, N.Y., 1948), pp. 62–88 at 80–82.

600 The first was bonitary ownership [597] of rustic or human fiefs, which the "men" (those whom Hotman is surprised to find called vassals in the feudal laws of the returned barbarism), that is, the plebians, had of the fruits on the farms of their heroes [437].

601 The second was quiritary ownership of noble, heroic, or armed fiefs, nowadays called military; for the heroes, when they united themselves in armed orders, kept their sovereignty over their farms. This was what had been in the state of nature the optimal ownership, which Cicero recognizes in his *Response of the Soothsayers* [7.14] as held over a number of houses still remaining in the Rome of his day, and which he defines as "ownership of real estate free of any real encumbrance whether private or public" [490, 984]. On this there is a golden passage in the Pentateuch [*Genesis* 47.26] where Moses relates that in the time of Joseph the priests of Egypt did not pay the king tribute on their fields. And we have shown that all the heroic kingdoms were priestly [594], and we shall shortly show that at first the Roman patricians did not pay the treasury any tribute on their fields [619]. When the heroic commonwealths were formed, these sovereign private fiefs naturally became subject to the higher sovereignty of the reigning heroic orders (each community of which was called a *patria* with *res* understood, meaning "interest of the fathers" [584]), which was to be defended and maintained because it had preserved their sovereign family powers on a basis of mutual equality; and this means liberty only for lords [105].

602 The third, with full propriety called civil ownership [= eminent domain], was that which the heroic cities, composed in the beginning of heroes only, had over the lands by certain divine fiefs which the family fathers had previously received from the provident divinity [582] (in virtue of which they had found themselves sovereigns in the state of the families, and had united themselves in reigning orders in the state of the cities); and thus they became sovereign civil kingdoms subject to the supreme sovereign God whose providence is recognized by all sovereign civil powers. This is made plain to human understanding by the explicit avowal of sovereign powers in adding to their titles of majesty such phases as "by divine providence" or "by the grace of God," through which they must publicly profess to have received their kingdoms. So that if worship of providence were forbidden, the natural consequence would be their fall, for a nation of fatalists or casualists or atheists never existed in the world, and all the nations of the world, through four primary religions and no more [paganism, Judaism, Christianity, Islam], believe in a provident divinity [334]. So the plebeians swore by the heroes, and such oaths have survived

as *mehercules! mecastor! aedepol!* and *mediusfidius!* "by the god Fidius!" who was the Roman Hercules [658]; but the heroes swore by Jove. For the plebeians were at first in the power of the heroes (the noble Romans, down to the 419th year of the city, exercised the right of private incarceration over their plebeian debtors [115]), while the heroes, who formed the ruling orders, were in the power of Jove by reason of the auspices. If the auspices seemed to permit, the heroes appointed magistrates, enacted laws, and exercised other sovereign rights; if they seemed to forbid, they abstained. All this is that *fides deorum et hominum,* faith of gods and men, to which pertain the Latin phrases *implorare fidem,* to implore help and aid; *recipere in fidem,* to receive under protection or authority; and the exclamation *proh deûm atque hominum fidem imploro!* used by the oppressed to implore on their behalf the "force of gods and men," which the Italians rendered in the human sense "the power of the world" [523]. For this power in virtue of which civil powers are so called, this force, this faith, for which the oaths just quoted attest the veneration of the subjects, and this protection which the powerful must extend over the weak (in which two things lies the essence of feudalism), are the force which sustains and rules this civil world. The center of this force was the ground [or landed estate] of each civil sphere, as was felt if not rationally understood by the Greeks (in the coins of their commonwealths [491]) and by the Latins (in their heroic phrases [389, 411]). Even today the crowns of sovereign powers are surmounted by a sphere, on which is implanted the divine symbol of the cross [1049]. The sphere is the golden apple, signifying the high dominion which sovereign powers have over the lands of which they are lords; and for this reason it is placed in the left hands of sovereigns in the midst of the solemn rites of coronation [548]. This is to say that civil powers are thus masters of the substance of their peoples, which sustains, contains, and maintains all that is above it and rests upon it. In virtue of its being one part of this substance—a part *pro indiviso,* or undivided share (to use the scholastic expression for a part separated from the rest only in reason or law, not in physical fact)—in the Roman laws the patrimony of each family father is called *substantia patris* or *paterna substantia.* This is at bottom the reason why sovereign civil powers may dispose of whatever belongs to their subjects: their persons as well as their acquisitions, their works and their labors, and impose thereon tribute or taxes, whenever they have to exercise that dominion over their lands which, from different points of view but with the same meaning in substance, moral theologians and writers on public law now call eminent domain, just as they now speak of the laws concerning this domain as the fundamental laws of the realm.

Since this dominion is over the lands themselves, sovereigns naturally may not exercise it save to preserve the substance of their states, on whose maintenance or ruin hinges the maintenance or ruin of all the private property of their peoples.

603   The Romans sensed [intuitively], if they did not [rationally] understand [218], the rise of commonwealths from these eternal principles of fiefs. This is shown by the formula they had for laying claim to a piece of land, which has come down to us as follows: *Aio hunc fundum meum esse ex iure quiritium* ("I declare this land to be mine by the law of the Quirites") [961]. By this formula they brought the civil action of vindication for ownership of the land, an ownership vested in the city itself and proceeding from the, so to speak, central power in virtue of which all Roman citizens are certain masters each of his own farm [but] with an ownership *pro indiviso*, or undivided (as a schoolman would phrase what is marked off [not by a fence but] only by reason or law), and for that reason called ownership *ex iure quiritium*, by the law of the Quirites, who, as shown by a thousand proofs already adduced or to be adduced, were originally the Romans armed with lances in public assembly who composed the city [594f, 624ff, 1073]. This is the basic reason why the lands and all goods (for all spring from the land), when they have no owner, revert to the public treasury; for every private patrimony *pro indiviso* is public patrimony, and therefore, in default of private owners, it loses its designation as a part and retains only that of the whole. This must be the reason for the technical legal expression by which inheritances, particularly on the part of legitimate heirs [those entitled at law in the absence of direct heirs], are said to return (*redire*) to the heirs, though in truth they come to them but once. For those who founded Roman law in the process of founding the Roman commonwealth itself instituted all private patrimonies as fiefs, such as writers on feudal law describe as *ex pacto et providentia*, meaning that they all come from the public patrimony and, by pact and providence of the civil laws, devolve from one private owner to another, and in default of private owners must return to the source from which they came. All this that we have been saying is clearly confirmed by the [provisions of the] *Lex Papia Poppaea* concerning lapsed legacies. This law imposed on celibates the just penalty that, because they had neglected to propagate their Roman name through matrimony, if they had made testaments they were to be declared null and void, and further they were to be considered as having no relatives who could inherit in case of intestacy. In both directions, therefore, they were deprived of heirs to preserve their names, and their patrimonies reverted to the public treasury,

in the quality not of an inheritance but of a peculium accruing, in the phrase of Tacitus [A. 3.28], to the people as the parent of all, *tamquam omnium parentem*. By which phrase this profound writer recalls the reason of all the caducary penalties from the most ancient times when the first fathers of the human race occupied the first vacant lands [389]. Such occupation was the original source of all ownership in the world. Later these fathers, uniting in cities, created the civil power out of their paternal powers, and out of their private patrimonies created the public patrimony called the *aerarium*, or public treasury [619ff]. The patrimonies of the citizens pass from one private owner to another in the quality of inheritances, but, on reverting to the public treasury, they resume their ancient original quality of peculium.

604 Here, at the generation of their heroic commonwealths, the hero poets imagined the eleventh major divinity, Mercury [317]. It is he who carries the law to the mutinous *famuli* [597] in his divine rod (a real word [435] for the auspices), the same rod with which, as Vergil tells [A. 4.242f], he brings back souls from Orcus. (That is, he restores to social life the clients who, having left the protection of the heroes, were again being scattered and lost in the lawless state which is the Orcus of the poets, waiting to swallow all men [688, 717].) The rod is described for us as having one or two serpents wound about it. (These were serpent skins, [the female] signifying the bonitary ownership granted to the *famuli* by the heroes, and [the male] the quiritary ownership they reserved for themselves [541f].) There are two wings at the top of the rod (signifying the eminent domain of the [heroic] orders [488, 590, 603], and the cap worn by Mercury is also winged (to confirm their high and free sovereign constitution, as the cap remained a hieroglyph of [lordly] liberty). In addition, Mercury has wings on his heels (signifying that ownership of the fields resided in the reigning senates). He is otherwise naked (because the ownership he carried to the *famuli* was stripped of all civil solemnity and based entirely on the honor of the heroes) just as we have seen Venus and the Graces depicted as naked [569]. Thus from the bird of Idanthyrsus, by which he meant to say to Darius that he was sovereign lord of Scythia in virtue of possessing the auspices there [435], the Greeks took the wings to signify heroic institutions; and finally in articulate speech, the Romans used the abstract expression "The auspices are ours" to show the plebs that all the heroic civil institutions and laws belonged to themselves [110]. So that this winged staff of the Greek Mercury, with the serpents removed, is the eagle-headed scepter of the Egyptians, Etruscans, Romans, and finally the English [487]. The staff was called *kērykeion* by the Greeks because it

carried the agrarian law to the *famuli* of the heroes, called *kērykes* by Homer. It brought also the agrarian law of Servius Tullius ordering the census [107], so that peasants who came under it are spoken of as *censiti* in the Roman laws. By its serpents it brought the bonitary ownership of the fields, and the land rent paid by the plebeians to the heroes was called *ōpheleia*, from *ophis*, serpent [541]. Lastly, it brought the famous Herculean knot [558], by which men paid the tithe of Hercules to the heroes, and plebeian Roman debtors down to the time of the Petelian Law [115] were "bounden" or liege vassals of the nobles. On all these matters we have much to say further on.

605   Here it must be added that this Greek Mercury was the Thoth or Mercury who gives laws to the Egyptians, represented by the hieroglyph of Knef. He is described as a serpent, to denote the cultivated land [541]. He has the head of a hawk or eagle, as the hawks of Romulus later became the Roman eagles, representing the heroic auspices [487]. He is girt by a belt as a sign of the Herculean knot [558], and in his hand he bears a scepter, which signifies the reign of the Egyptian priests [594]. He wears a winged cap, as an indication of their eminent domain over the land [604]. And finally he holds an egg in his mouth, which stood for the sphere of Egypt, if indeed it is not the golden apple which signified the eminent domain the priests held over the lands of Egypt [602]. Into this hieroglyph Manetho **read** the generation of the entire world [733], and the conceit of the learned reached such an absurd extreme that Athanasius Kircher in his *Obeliscus pamphilius* affirms that this hieroglyph signifies the Holy Trinity.

606   Here began the first commerce in the world, from which this Mercury got his name [483]. He was later regarded as the god of merchantry, as from his first mission [604] he was also held to be the god of ambassadors. With a truth [not of the intellect but] of the senses it was said that he had been sent by the gods (as the heroes of the first cities were called) to men (as the vassals of the returned barbarism were called) [437, 587]. The wings, which signified heroic institutions [488, 604], were later thought to have been used by Mercury to fly from heaven to earth and then to fly back from earth to heaven. But, to return to commerce, it dealt first in this kind of immovable goods [or real estate], and the first *mercedes*, or payments, were, as they could not fail to be, of the most simple and natural sort, that is to say in the produce of the land. Similar payments in labor or goods are still customary in the transactions of peasants.

607   All the above history was preserved by the Greeks in the word *nomos*, signifying both law and pasture; for the first law was the agrarian

law [597, 604] in accordance with which the heroic kings were called shepherds of the people [557, 1058f].

608 The plebeians of the ancient Germans were erroneously believed by Tacitus to be slaves because the life of the heroic *socii* was so slavelike [555, 582]. In the fashion reported by him [G. 25] the plebeians of the first barbarous nations were distributed by the heroes about the countryside and dwelt there in their houses in the fields assigned to them, and by the produce of the farms contributed whatever was needful to the sustenance of their masters. And to those conditions we must add the oath also reported by Tacitus requiring them to guard and defend their masters and to serve to their glory [559]. If we look for a legal name to define such relationships, we shall clearly see that there is none that fits them better than our term feudalism.

609 In this fashion the first cities were founded on orders of nobles and troops of plebeians, with two contrary eternal properties emerging from this nature of human civil institutions which we are here investigating: namely, (1) that the plebeians always want to change the form of government, as in fact it is always they who do change it, and (2) that the nobles always want to keep it as it is. Hence, in the agitations of civil governments, all are called optimates who bend their efforts to maintaining the state and the latter is called a state from this property of standing firm and upright.

610 Here appeared two divisions. The first was that between the wise and the vulgar; for the heroes founded their kingdoms on the wisdom of the auspices [250, 365, 521]. As a result of this division the vulgar received the fixed epithet profane, for the heroes or nobles were the priests of the heroic cities, as certainly they were among the Romans as late as a century after the Law of the Twelve Tables [586, 999]. Hence the first peoples when they took away citizenship used a kind of excommunication, such as the interdict of water and fire among the Romans [957]. For the first plebs of the nations were considered foreigners [611], and from this came the eternal property of not granting citizenship to a man of alien religion [526]. And because the plebeians in the first cities had no share in sacred or divine institutions and for many centuries did not contract solemn matrimony [567], the term *vulgo quaesiti* came to be used for illegitimate children.

611 The second division was that between citizen and *hostis*, which meant both guest or stranger and enemy, for the first cities were composed of heroes and of those received in their asylums (and all heroic hospices are to be understood as asylums) [553]. Similarly, the returned barbarian times left in Italian *oste* for innkeeper and for soldiers' quarters, and *ostello* for

inn. Thus Paris was the guest, that is to say enemy, of the royal house of Argos, for he kidnaped noble Argive maidens, represented by the [poetic] character of Helen. Similarly, Theseus was the guest of Ariadne, and Jason of Medea. Both abandoned the women and did not marry them, and their actions were held to be heroic, while to us, with our present feelings, they seem, as indeed they are, the deeds of scoundrels. In like fashion must the piety of Aeneas be defended, for he abandoned Dido after seducing her (to say nothing of the great kindnesses he had received from her and the magnanimous offer she had made of the kingdom of Carthage as dowry for her marriage) in order to obey the fates that had destined Lavinia in Italy, though she too was a stranger, to be his wife. This heroic custom was preserved by Homer [I. 9.364–394] in the person of Achilles, the greatest of the Greek heroes, who refuses to accept any of the three daughters whom Agamemnon offered him in marriage with the royal dowry of seven lands well populated with ploughmen and shepherds, and replies that his wish is to marry whatever woman in his fatherland his father Peleus may give him. In brief, the plebeians were guests in the heroic cities, and against them, to repeat our frequent quotation from Aristotle [271], the heroes swore eternal enmity. The same division is expressed for us in the terms citizen and peregrine, taking the latter in its original and proper sense of a man wandering through the country, as if *peragrinus*, from *ager* in the sense of territory or district (as in such phrases as *ager neapolitanus, ager nolanus*); whereas those foreigners who travel through the world do not wander across fields but hold straight to the public highways.

612   The origins herein set forth of heroic guests shed a great light on Greek history where it relates that the Samians, Sybarites, Troezenians, Amphipolitans, Chalcedonians, Cnidians, and Chians had their commonwealths changed from aristocratic to popular by strangers. And they give the finishing touch to what we printed many years ago in our *Principles of Universal Law* [Op. 2.564–580] concerning the fable that the Law of the Twelve Tables came from Athens to Rome. (This is one of the two passages that permit us to believe that that work was not entirely useless [29].) We proved there that the article *De forti sanate nexo soluto*, "On the strong and sound freed from the bond" [1.5], was the subject of that whole contest [between nobles and plebeians]. The Latin philologians have said that "the strong and sound" were the strangers reduced to obedience. In fact, they were the Roman plebeians who had revolted because they could not obtain from the nobles the certain ownership of the fields. For, as long as the nobles retained the royal power of taking them back again, the ownership could not continue certain unless the law granting it was

fixed eternally on a public tablet, determining the rights that had been uncertain and making manifest those that had been secret. This is the true meaning of what Pomponius tells us [D. 1.2.2.6]. It was on this account that the plebs raised such a turmoil that it was necessary to create the decemvirs. These officials gave a new form to the constitution and brought the rebellious plebs back to obedience by proclaiming them (in the aforesaid article) free from the veritable bond of bonitary ownership by which they had been bound to the soil (*glebae addicti, adscriptitii,* or *censiti* [604]) under the census of Servius Tullius [107, 597], and bound only by the fictitious bond of quiritary ownership. But a vestige of the old bond remained down to the Petelian Law [115] in the right of private imprisonment the nobles had over their plebeian debtors. These were the strangers who under tribunitial incitements, to use Livy's elegant phrase [2.1.4] (incitements recounted in our Note on the Publilian Law [112]), finally changed the Roman constitution from aristocratic to popular.

613 The fact that Rome was not founded on the first agrarian revolts [584f] shows us that it must have been a new city [160], as history tells. It was founded instead on the asylum in which Romulus and his companions, while violence still prevailed everywhere, had first made themselves strong and then received the refugees and founded the clienteles whose nature we have explained above [263f, 556ff, 597]. About two hundred years must have passed before the clients found their condition burdensome, for it was just this length of time that elapsed before King Servius Tullius brought them the first agrarian law [107]. In the old[er] cities this period must have extended to five hundred years, for the reason that they were composed of simpler men and Rome of a more calculating sort. This is the reason why Rome subjugated Latium, then Italy, and then the world, because their heroism was more youthful than that of the other Latins. It is also the primary reason why the Romans wrote their heroic history in the vulgar language, whereas the Greeks had written theirs in fables [158].

614 All that we have thought out concerning the principles of poetic politics and seen illustrated in Roman history is strikingly confirmed by these four heroic characters: first, the lyre of Orpheus or Apollo; second, the head of Medusa; third, the Roman fasces; fourth and last, the struggle of Hercules with Antaeus.

615 First, the lyre was invented by the Greek Mercury, just as law was invented by the Egyptian Mercury. This lyre was given him by Apollo, god of civil light or of the nobility [533], for in the heroic commonwealths the nobles dictated the laws, and with this lyre Orpheus, Amphion, and other theological poets, who professed knowledge of laws, founded and established the humanity of Greece, as we shall later explain at greater length [647, 661]. So that the lyre was the union of the cords or forces of the fathers, of which the public force was composed which is called civil power, which finally put an end to all private force and violence [523]. Hence the law was defined with full propriety by the poets as *lyra regnorum*, "the lyre of kingdoms," in which were brought into accord the family kingdoms of the fathers which had hitherto been in disaccord because they were all isolated and divided from one another in the state of the families, as Polyphemus told Ulysses [516]. This glorious history was later raised to the heavens and described in the constellation of the Lyre; and the kingdom of Ireland, on the arms of the king of England, charges its shield with a harp. The philosophers afterwards took it for the harmony of the spheres attuned by the sun; but it was on earth that Apollo played the harp that Pythagoras not only could but must have heard, or rather played himself, if we take him as a theological poet and nation founder instead of the imposture he has hitherto been accused of being [427].

616   The snakes joined in the head of Medusa, whose temples bear wings, are the high family domains the fathers had in the state of the families, which later went to make up the civil eminent domain. This head was nailed to the shield of Perseus, which is the same as that borne by Minerva, who, among the arms (that is, in the armed assemblies) of the first nations (among which we found that of Rome), dictates the frightful punishments that turn the spectators to stone. One of these snakes was Draco, who is said to have written his laws in blood, because Athens (Athena being [the Greek] Minerva) was armed with them at the time when it was occupied by the optimates [542]. And among the Chinese, who still write in hieroglyphics, the dragon, as we have also seen above, is the sign of civil power [423].

617   The Roman fasces are the *litui* or rods of the fathers in the state of the families. For one such staff in the hand of one of these fathers the pregnant word "scepter" is used by Homer [I. 18.557], and the father is called a king. This is in his description of the shield of Achilles, which contains the history of the world. In this passage the epoch of the families is placed before that of the cities, as will be fully set forth later [683]. Having taken the auspices with these *litui*, the fathers dictated the prescribed punishments to their children, such as that of the impious son which passed into the Law of the Twelve Tables, as we have seen above [526]. Hence the union of these rods or *litui* signifies the generation of the civil power we are here discussing.

618 Finally Hercules (a character of the Heraclids or nobles of the heroic cities [592]) struggles with Antaeus (a character of the mutinous *famuli*) and, by lifting him into the air (leading the *famuli* back into the first cities on the heights), conquers him and binds him to the earth. From this came a Greek game called the knot, after the Herculean knot by which Hercules founded the heroic nations and by reason of which the plebeians paid to the nobles the tithe of Hercules, which must have been the census [tax] which was the basic institution [M5] of the aristocratic commonwealths. Hence the Roman plebeians under the census of Servius Tullius were *nexi* or bondsmen of the nobles and, by the oath Tacitus tells us was sworn by the ancient Germans to their princes [G. 14], they were bound to serve them as impressed vassals at their own expense in war; a duty the Roman plebs still complained of under what has been supposed to have been popular liberty. These must have been the first tribute-payers (*assidui*), who fought at their own expense (*suis assibus militabant*); but they were soldiers not of fortune but of harsh necessity.

[Chapter III] *The Origins of the Census and the Treasury*

619 The plebeians continued to be oppressed by the usurious exactions and the frequent usurpations of their fields by the nobles, to such a point that at the end of the period [Marcius] Philippus, tribune of the plebs, cried out in public that two thousand nobles possessed all the fields that should be divided among a good three hundred thousand citizens, the number counted at Rome in his time. Beginning forty years after the expulsion of Tarquinius Superbus, in the comfortable assurance of his death, the nobility had again begun to be insolent toward the unhappy plebs. The senate of those days had been obliged to put into practice an ordinance requiring the plebeians to pay into the public treasury the census [tax] which previously they had had to pay privately to the nobles, in order that thenceforth the treasury should be able to take care of the costs of war. From this time the census acquires new prominence in Roman history. According to Livy [4.8.7] the nobles disdained the administration of it as something unworthy of their dignity. But Livy failed to understand that the nobles did not want it because it was not the census ordained by Servius Tullius, which had been the basic institution of lordly liberty and

had been paid privately to them; for Livy, like all the other authorities, was under the false impression that the census of Servius Tullius had been the basic institution of popular liberty. For certainly there was no magistracy of greater dignity than the censorship, which from the first year had been administered by the consuls. In this fashion the nobles, through their own avaricious machinations, came themselves to set up the census, which later was the basic institution of popular liberty. So that when the fields had all fallen into their hands in the time of Philippus the tribune, these two thousand nobles had to pay the tribute for three hundred thousand other citizens then counted (just as in Sparta all the land had come into possession of the few), because in the treasury there was a register of the census taxes which the nobles had privately imposed on the fields which, in an uncultivated state, they had of old allotted to the plebeians for cultivation. On account of the inequality referred to there must have been great agitations and revolts among the Roman plebs. These were quelled by Fabius with a most prudent measure which earned him the name Maximus. He ordered that the whole Roman people should be divided into three classes, senators, knights, and plebeians, and that the citizens should be placed in these classes according to their means. This consoled the plebeians, for the senatorial order which previously had consisted solely of nobles and which held all the magistracies, could thenceforward be entered by plebeians of wealth, and thus the regular avenue to all civil honors was open to plebeians.

620   In such wise only is truth given to the tradition that the census of Servius Tullius was the basic institution of popular liberty, for in it the matter was prepared and from it the occasions were born, as we set forth hypothetically above in the Notes on the Chronological Table, in the passage on the Publilian law [112f]. It was the latter legislation, originating in Rome itself, that established the democratic commonwealth there, and not the Law of the Twelve Tables [supposed to have been] brought there from Athens. Indeed, what Aristotle calls a democratic commonwealth is rendered in Tuscan by Bernardo Segni as a commonwealth by census, meaning a free popular commonwealth. This is evident even in Livy [8.12.14ff], for, ignorant as he was of the Roman form of government in those times, he nevertheless states that the nobles complained that by that law they had lost more in the city than they had gained abroad by force of arms in that year, though it was a year of many great victories. And for this reason Publilius, the author of the law, was called the people's dictator.

621   With popular liberty, in which the whole people constitute the city, it came about that civil ownership lost its proper meaning of public

ownership (which had been called civil from the word for city [603]) and was dispersed among all the private ownerships of the Roman citizens who together now made up the Roman city. The *dominium optimum* or best ownership lost its above stated original meaning of strongest ownership, not weakened by any real encumbrance, even public [601], and survived in the meaning of ownership of property free of any private encumbrance. Quiritary ownership no longer signified such ownership of a piece of land that if the client or plebeian lost possession of it the noble from whom he had title to it was obliged to come to his defense. The first *auctores iuris* or lawmakers in Roman law were those whose duty it was, in connection with these clienteles ordained by Romulus and no others, to expound to the plebeians these and no other laws. For indeed what [other] laws could the nobles have been obliged to set forth to the plebeians, since the latter down to the 309th year of Rome had no privilege of citizenship [110, 598], and since the laws themselves down to a century after the Law of the Twelve Tables had been kept hidden from the plebs by the nobles in their college of pontiffs [999]? So in those days the nobles were *auctores iuris* in a sense which survived in the *laudatio auctoritatis* by possessors of purchased lands when they are summoned in a suit for recovery by others and "cite the authors" [from whom they have title and] whom they wish to assist and defend them. Quiritary ownership now meant private civil ownership capable of being defended by the action of *rei vindicatio*, whereas bonitary ownership could be maintained by simple possession.

622 In the same fashion and not otherwise, by the eternal nature of fiefs, these institutions came back in the returned barbarian times. Let us take for example the kingdom of France. Here the various provinces now composing the nation were sovereign seigniories of the princes subject to the king of that realm, and the princes must have held their property without any public encumbrance. Later, through succession, rebellion or failure of heirs, they were incorporated into the kingdom, and all the property *ex iure optimo* of the princes became subject to public exactions. For the lands and houses of the kings, which contained their royal chambers, having passed by marriage or concession to their vassals, are now found subject to taxation and tribute. Thus in hereditary kingdoms ownership *ex iure optimo* was gradually confused with private ownership subject to public charges, just as the fisc, which was the patrimony of the Roman emperor, was gradually confused with the public treasury [1076].

623 Our research into the census and the treasury has been the most difficult of our studies of Roman institutions, as we indicated in the Idea of the Work [25].

[Chapter IV]   The Origins of the Roman Assemblies

624   Our studies show that the *boulē* and the *agora*, the two heroic assemblies of which Homer speaks [67], must have corresponded respectively to the Roman *comitia curiata*, the assembly by *curiae* which we read of as the most ancient under the kings, and the *comitia tributa* or assembly by tribes. The former were called *curiata* from *quir*, spear, whose genitive *quiris* was later used as the nominative, in conformity with what we have set forth in our Origins of the Latin Language [in the first edition of the present work, Op. 3.370]; just as from *cheir*, hand, which among all nations meant power, must have been derived the Greek *kyria*, with the same meaning as the Latin *curia* [591]. Hence came the Curetes, who were priests armed with spears, for all the heroic peoples were composed of priests and only the heroes had the right to bear arms. The Curetes were found by the Greeks in Saturnia or ancient Italy, in Crete, and in Asia [593]. *Kyria* in its ancient sense must have meant seigniory, just as aristocratic commonwealths are now called seigniories. From the *kyria* of these heroic senates came *kyros* for authority, but this authority, as we have observed above and shall observe more closely, was that of ownership [386, 603, 621, 944]. From these origins came the modern *kyrios* for "sir" and *kyria* for "madam." And as the Greek Curetes came from *cheir*, so we saw above that the Roman Quirites came from *quir* [562]. Quirites was the title of Roman majesty given to the people in public assembly, as we have also noted above in a passage in which, comparing [the assemblies of] the Gauls and the ancient Germans with that of the Greek Curetes, we observed that all the first barbarous peoples held their public assemblies under arms [594].

625   Thus the majestic title of Quirites must have been first used at a time when the people consisted entirely of nobles, who alone had the right to arm. Later, when Rome had become a popular commonwealth, the title passed to the people including the plebeians. For the assemblies of the plebs, who at first did not have the right to arm, were called *comitia tributa* from *tribus*, tribe. And among the Romans, just as in the state of the families the latter were so called from the *famuli* [552], so in the later state of the cities the term *tributum*, tribute, came from *tribus*, tribe, because the tribes of the plebeians met to receive the orders of the reigning senate, the chief and most frequent of which were demands upon the plebeians for contributions to the treasury.

626 Subsequently, however, Fabius Maximus introduced the [reformed] census which divided the whole Roman people into three classes according to the patrimonies of the citizens. Before this only the senators had been knights, for in heroic times only nobles had the right to arm, and hence in Roman history we read that the ancient Roman commonwealth was divided into fathers and plebs. Thus in those days senator and patrician had been interchangeable terms, and likewise plebeian and ignoble. And as there had thus been only two classes of the Roman people, so there had been only two kinds of assembly: one the *curiata*, consisting of fathers or nobles or senators, the other the *tributa*, consisting of plebeians or the ignoble. But now that Fabius had divided the citizens according to their means into the three classes of senators, knights, and plebeians, the nobles ceased to be a separate order in the city and were placed in one or another of the three classes according to their wealth. From that time on patricians were distinguished from senators and knights, and plebeians from the baseborn; and plebeians were no longer contrasted with patricians but with knights and senators. A plebeian no longer meant a base-born person but rather a citizen of small patrimony who might well be a noble; and on the other hand a senator no longer meant a patrician but a citizen of ample patrimony who might well be of low birth.

627 Consequently from that time on *comitia centuriata*, the assembly by hundreds, was the term applied to the assemblies in which the entire Roman people of all three classes came together to enact the consular laws among other public business. Those assemblies were still called *comitia tributa* in which the plebs alone enacted tribunitial laws. These were the plebiscites, at first so called in the sense rendered by Cicero [L. 3.3.10; cf. 3.15.33; 3.17.38] as *plebi nota* or laws published to the plebs. (An example cited by Pomponius [D. 1.2.2.3] is Junius Brutus announcing to the plebs that the kings have been forever expelled from Rome.) In monarchies the royal laws might with equal propriety be called *populo nota*, "made known to the people." On this account Baldus, as acute as he was lacking in erudition, expressed surprise that the word *plebiscitum* should have been written with one *s*, since in the sense of a law enacted by the plebs, it should have had two; the *scitum* being in that case from *sciscor*, not *scio* [and taking the genitive *plebis* instead of the dative *plebi*].

628 Lastly, for the certainty of divine ceremonies, there remained the *comitia curiata* or assemblies of the heads of the *curiae* alone, having to do with sacred institutions. For in the time of the kings all profane institutions were regarded as sacred, and the heroes were everywhere Curetes or armed priests [587f, 593]. Hence, down to the last days of Rome, since

paternal power was still viewed as sacred (and its regulations are often called *sacra patria* in the laws [526]), adoptions took place in these assemblies by *leges curiatae*.

[Chapter V] Corollary: It Is Divine Providence That Institutes Commonwealths and at the Same Time the Natural Law of the Gentes

629 We have seen that the generation of commonwealths began in the age of the gods, in which governments were theocratic; that is, divine. Later they developed into the first human, namely the heroic, governments, here called human to distinguish them from the divine [viii, C7, J5]. Within these human governments, even as the mighty current of a kingly river retains far out to sea the momentum of its flow and the sweetness of its waters [412], the age of the gods coursed on, for there persisted still that religious way of thinking according to which it was the gods who did whatever men themselves were doing [922]. Thus, in the state of the families, out of the reigning fathers they made Jove [585]; and out of the same fathers as united in closed orders at the birth of the first cities they made Minerva [579]; out of their ambassadors sent to the rebel clients they made Mercury [604]; and finally, as we shall shortly see, out of the corsair heroes they made Neptune [634]. Herein is divine providence to be supremely admired, for when men's intentions were quite otherwise, it brought them in the first place to fear of the divinity, the cult of which is the first fundamental basis of commonwealths. Their religion in turn led them to remain fixed on the first vacant lands which they occupied before all others; and such occupation is the source of all dominions [389]. When the more robust giants had occupied lands on the mountaintops where the perennial springs arise, providence ordained that thus they should find themselves in healthful and defensible sites and with abundance of water, so that they could safely stop there and cease their wanderings; and these are the three qualities that lands must have in order for cities later to arise upon them [525ff]. Further, again by means of religion, providence led them to unite with certain women in constant and lifelong companionship; hence the institution of matrimony, the recognized source of all authority [506ff]. With these women, as it later turned out, they had founded the families, which are the seed plot of the commonwealths. And finally, it turned out that by opening the asylums [561] they had founded the

clienteles [557]. Thus the *matters* were prepared from which, with the first agrarian law [597], the cities were to be born, based on the two communities of men that composed them, one of nobles to command, the other of plebeians to obey. (The latter are called by Telemachus, in a speech in Homer, the "other people" [590], which is to say a subject people, different from the reigning people which was made up of heroes.) Hence emerges the *matter* of political science, which is nothing other than the science of commanding and obeying in states. And at their very birth providence causes the commonwealths to spring forth aristocratic in *form*, in conformity with the savage and solitary nature of the first men. This *form* consists entirely, as writers on political theory point out, in guarding the confines and the institutions [586, 981–998], so that peoples newly come to humanity might, by the very *form* of their governments, continue for a long time to remain enclosed within these confines and institutions, and so forget the infamous and nefarious promiscuity of the bestial and feral state. But the minds of men were preoccupied with particulars and incapable of understanding a common good; they were accustomed never to concern themselves even with the particular affairs of others, as Homer makes his Polyphemus tell Ulysses [516] (and in this giant Plato recognizes the family fathers in the so-called state of nature preceding the civil state [296]). Providence therefore, by the aforesaid aristocratic *form* of their governments, led them to unite themselves to their fatherlands in order to preserve such great private interests as their family monarchies were (for this was what they were entirely bent upon) [584], and thus, beyond any design of theirs, they were brought together in a universal civil good called commonwealth [I·3].

630 Now here, by those divine proofs propounded above in the Method [343], let us consider and meditate on the simplicity and naturalness with which providence ordered these institutions of men, concerning which they said truly, though in a false sense, that they were all the work of the gods. And let us consider in this connection the immense number of civil effects which may all be traced to these four causes [F2] which, as will be observed throughout this work, are four elements, as it were, of the civil universe; namely, religion, marriage, asylum, and the first agrarian law [I·6; 629]. Then let us ask ourselves if, among all human possibilities, so many and such various and diverse institutions could in any other way have had simpler or more natural beginnings among those very men who are said by Epicurus to have been born of chance and by Zeno to have been creatures of necessity [345]. Yet chance did not divert them nor fate force them out of this natural order. For at the point when the commonwealths were to

spring forth, the matters were all prepared and ready to receive the form, and there issued from them the format of the commonwealths, composed of mind and body. The prepared matters were these men's own religions, their own languages, their own lands, their own nuptials, their own names (clans or houses), their own arms, and hence their own dominions, their own magistrates, and finally their own laws. And because all these were their own they were completely free and therefore constitutive of true commonwealths. And all this came about because all the aforesaid institutions had previously belonged to the family fathers as monarchs in the state of nature. The fathers at this juncture, by uniting themselves in an order, came to produce the sovereign civil power, just as in the state of nature they had held the family powers, subject to no one but God. This sovereign civil person was formed of mind and body. The mind was an order of wise men, with such wisdom as could naturally exist in that time of extreme crudeness and simplicity. Hence the eternal property that without an order of wise men states may present the appearance of commonwealths, but are so many dead and soulless bodies. There was also the body, formed of the head and lesser members. Hence this second eternal property of commonwealths: that some men must employ their minds in the tasks of civil wisdom, and others their bodies in the trades and crafts that are needed in peace as well as in war. And there is a third eternal property: that the mind should always command and the body should have perpetually to obey [597].

631 Yet here is an even greater cause for marveling. By bringing about the birth of the families (all of them born with some awareness of a divinity although, because of their ignorance and disorder, none knew the true one), since each family had its own religion, language, lands, nuptials, name, arms, government, and laws, providence had at the same time brought into being the natural law of the greater gentes, with all the aforesaid properties, to be used later by the family fathers over their clients. In like fashion, in creating the commonwealths, by means of the aristocratic form in which they arose, providence turned the natural law of the greater gentes (or families), which had been formerly observed in the state of nature, into the natural law of the lesser gentes (or peoples), to be observed in the time of the cities [B2, 316]. For the family fathers, who owned all the aforesaid rights over their clients, at the time when they banded themselves together in a natural order against the latter, came to confine all the aforesaid properties within their civil orders against the plebs. In this consisted the severely aristocratic form of the heroic commonwealths.

632   In this way the natural law of the gentes, which is now observed among peoples and nations, was born as a property of the sovereign civil powers at the birth of the commonwealths. So a people or nation that has not within itself a sovereign civil power vested with all the aforesaid properties is not properly a people or nation at all, nor can it exercise abroad in its relations with other peoples or nations the natural law of the gentes, but both the law and its exercise will fall to another people or nation superior to it [E8n].

633   What we have here set forth, along with the fact that the heroes of the first cities called themselves gods [449], will explain the meaning of the phrase *iura a diis posita*, laws laid down by the gods, applied to the institutes of the natural law of the gentes. But when the natural law of human gentes ensued, on which we have more than once cited Ulpian [569, 575, 578, 582], and upon which the philosophers and moral theologians based their understanding of the natural law of fully unfolded eternal reason, the phrase was fitly reinterpreted to mean that the natural law of the gentes was instituted by the true God.

[Chapter VI]   Heroic Politics Resumed

634   The historians all begin the heroic age from the corsair raids of Minos and Jason's naval expedition to Pontus. (They continue it through the Trojan War. Its last phase, the wanderings of the heroes, they bring to an end with the return of Ulysses to Ithaca.) By about that time the last of the major divinities, Neptune, must therefore have been born [317]. For this we have the authority of the historians, which we confirm by a philosophic reason assisted by several golden passages of Homer. The philosophic reason is that the naval and nautical arts were the last inventions of the nations, since it took the flower of genius to invent them; so much so that Daedalus, their inventor, remained a symbol of genius itself, and *daedala tellus* is used by Lucretius [1.7] in the sense of "the ingenious earth." The Homeric passages to which we refer are in the *Odyssey* [e.g., 10.144ff]. Whenever Ulysses makes a landing or is driven ashore by the tempest, he always mounts a hill to look inland for a trace of smoke which will indicate that the land is inhabited by men. These Homeric passages are reinforced by that golden passage in Plato cited by Strabo [296] in which he tells of the horror the first nations long had of the sea. The reason for this was pointed out by Thucydides [1.8] where he says that

through fear of corsair raids the Greek nations were slow to come down and dwell on the coasts. On this account Neptune is portrayed to us as armed with the trident with which he made the earth shake. The trident must have been a great hook for grappling ships. By a fine metaphor the hook is called a tooth, and the "three" in the prefix means the superlative [491]. With this hook he made the lands of men tremble in fear of his raids. Later, already in Homer's day, he was believed to make the physical earth shake, and in this opinion Homer was followed by Plato with his abyss of waters which he placed in the bowels of the earth, with what reason we shall show later [714].

635 Of such nature must have been the bull in the shape of which Jove abducts Europa, and the Minotaur, or bull of Minos, by which he steals youths and maidens from the shores of Attica (on which account "horns of ships" survived in the sense of sails, as used by Vergil [A. 3.549]). Landsmen thus set forth in all truth that the Minotaur had devoured their children, for to their horror and grief they had seen them swallowed up by the ships. Thus too the Orc seeks to devour Andromeda, lashed to the rock and petrified with terror (so Latin kept the phrase *terrore defixus*, rigid with fear); and the winged horse which Perseus rides to her rescue must have been another corsair ship, as the sails were afterward called the wings of ships. Vergil too, who was acquainted with these heroic antiquities, in speaking of Daedalus, inventor of ships, states that he flies with the machine which he calls *alarum remigium*, "the oarage of wings" [A. 6.19]; and Daedalus, we are told, was the brother of Theseus. Thus Theseus must be a [poetic] character of the Athenian youths who, under the law of force practiced on them by Minos, are devoured by his bull or pirate ship. He is taught by Ariadne (seafaring art) by means of the thread (of navigation) to escape from the labyrinth of Daedalus (which, before those labyrinths which are the elegant playthings of royal villas, must have been the Aegean Sea because of the great number of islands it bathes and contains). Then, having learned the art from the Cretans, he abandons Ariadne and returns with Phaedra, her sister (that is, with a similar art). Thus he slays the Minotaur and frees Athens from the cruel tribute imposed by Minos (which is to say, the Athenians in their turn took up piratical raiding). And so, as Phaedra was the sister of Ariadne, Theseus was the brother of Daedalus.

636 Apropos of these matters, Plutarch in his life of Theseus [i.e., of Pompey, 24.2] says that the heroes considered it a great honor and an added prestige to their arms to be called robbers, just as in the returned barbarian times "corsair" was regarded as a title of nobility [1053]. It is said

that the laws of Solon, who lived about that time, permitted associations for purposes of piracy; so well did Solon understand this complete humanity of ours in which pirates are not protected by the natural law of the gentes! What is even more astonishing is that Plato [*Sophist* 222C] and Aristotle [P. 1256a 36] made robbery a species of hunting; and with these great philosophers of a most civilized people the ancient Germans, in their barbarism, are in agreement. For among them, according to Caesar [G.W. 6.23], robbery not only was not regarded as infamous but was reckoned among the exercises of valor by which those who were not brought up to the practice of any art escaped from idleness. This barbarous custom endured for such a long time afterward among the most enlightened nations that, according to Polybius [3.24.4], one of the terms of peace between the Romans and the Carthaginians was that the former were not to pass Cape Pelorum in Sicily either for piracy or for trade. Still the attitude of the Carthaginians and Romans is of minor importance, for they themselves professed to be barbarians in those days, as may be seen from several passages in Plautus in which he says that he has turned the Greek comedies into a "barbarous tongue," meaning Latin [*Comedy of Asses* 11]. What is more remarkable is that the highly civilized Greeks, in the times of their most cultivated humanity, should have practiced such a barbarous custom, which indeed provided them with almost all the subjects of their comedies. It is perhaps because of this custom, still practiced by the inhabitants against the Christians, that the coast of Africa facing us is called Barbary.

637 The principle of this oldest law of war was the inhospitality of the heroic peoples [611], for they looked on aliens as perpetual enemies and rested their own reputation for power on keeping them at the greatest possible distance from their frontiers (as Tacitus [i.e., Caesar, G.W. 4.3] tells us of the Suebi, the nation of most repute among the ancient Germans). They even looked upon aliens as robbers [636]. There is a golden passage of Thucydides on this subject in which he remarks [1.5.2] that down to his time when travelers met on land or sea they would ask one another if they were robbers, meaning foreigners. But as the Greeks became more civilized they soon cast aside that barbarous custom and called barbarous all the nations that retained it. It was in this sense that the name *Barbary* remained in use for the land of the Troglodytes, who were supposed to kill foreigners who crossed their borders, as indeed even today there are barbarous nations in which this is the custom. It is certain that civilized nations do not allow aliens to enter without first asking permission.

638 Among the nations the Greeks called barbarous for this reason was the Roman. This we know from two golden passages in the Law of the Twelve Tables. One is: *Adversus hostem aeterna auctoritas esto* ("Against an alien the right in property shall be everlasting") [3.7]. The other [2.2] is reported by Cicero [*De Officiis* 1.12.37]: *Si status dies sit, cum hoste venito* ("If a day has been appointed, let him appear with the alien"). Here the word *hostis*, on the basis of a conjecture in general terms, is commonly taken as a metaphor for the adversary in the lawsuit. But on this very passage Cicero makes the observation, very much to our point, that the ancients meant by *hostis* what was later meant by *peregrinus*. These two passages taken together give us to understand that the Romans originally regarded aliens as eternal enemies at war. However, the said two passages must be understood as applying to those who were the first *hostes* in the world. These were the aliens received into the asylums, who later took on the quality of plebeians at the formation of the heroic cities [611]. Thus the passage in Cicero means that on the appointed day "the noble shall appear with the plebeian to claim his farm for him." Hence the "everlasting right of property" mentioned in the same law must have been against the plebeians, toward whom, as we learned from Aristotle [271], the heroes swore eternal enmity. This heroic law kept the plebeians, however long in possession, from usucapting any piece of Roman property, for title to such property could pass only from noble to noble. This is a good part of the reason why the Law of the Twelve Tables did not recognize simple possession. Only later, when heroic law was beginning to fall into abeyance and human law was gaining in strength, did the praetors assist the plebeians by [recognizing] simple possessions *extra ordinem*; for neither by express provision nor by any interpretation could they find in the Law [of the Twelve Tables] any basis for ordinary judgments, whether strict or equitable, to this effect. All this was because that law held simple possession by a plebeian to be in every case at the pleasure of the nobles. Moreover, it took no notice of the underhand or violent acts of the nobles because of that other eternal property of the first commonwealths (on which also we cited Aristotle [269]), namely that they had no laws concerning private wrongs or offenses, which were left to the individuals themselves to settle by force of arms, as we shall show fully in Book Four [960f]. Among the formalities of *rei vindicatio* there was a survival of this real force in the feigned [or symbolized] force which Aulus Gellius [20.10.10] called festucary, "exercised with a straw." All this is confirmed by the interdict *Unde vi* granted by the praetor *extra ordinem* because the Law of the Twelve Tables did not take cognizance of private violence or

even mention it; and also by the actions *De vi bonorum raptorum* and *Quod metus caussa*, which came late and were likewise praetorian.

639 Now the heroic custom of holding aliens to be eternal enemies, which was observed by each people privately in peace, when extended abroad took the form recognized as common to all the heroic nations of carrying on eternal wars with each other, with continual looting and raiding. Thus from the cities, which Plato tells us were born on the basis of arms [588], and which began to govern themselves in military fashion before the existence of such wars as are waged between cities, we get the very name of war; for the Greek *polemos*, war, is from *polis*, city.

640 In proof of what we have said we must make this important observation: that the Romans extended their conquests and gained the victories they won throughout the world on the basis of four laws by which [in succession] they governed the plebeians at home. In the barbarian provinces they made use of the clienteles of Romulus, sending Roman colonists into them, who took the place of the previous masters of the fields and made laborers of them. In the civilized provinces they applied the agrarian law of Servius Tullius, granting them bonitary ownership of the fields [107]. In Italy they adopted the agrarian law of the Twelve Tables, granting them the quiritary ownership enjoyed by the lands called *sola italica*. And to the municipia or towns which had earned better treatment they accorded the right of *connubium* and the share in the consulship which had been extended to their own plebs.

641 The eternal enmity between the first cities made declarations of war unnecessary, and indiscriminate pillaging was regarded as lawful. Inversely, when the nations had been weaned away from this barbarous custom, undeclared wars came to be regarded as piracy, no longer recognized by the natural law of the gentes called human by Ulpian [633]. This same eternal enmity of the first peoples may also explain to us that the long time during which the Romans had waged war on the Albans is to be understood as the entire previous period in which each side had subjected the other to the pillaging raids of which we are here speaking. Hence it is more reasonable that Horatius should have killed his sister because she was mourning the Curiatius who had abducted her than that she should have been married to him. For Romulus himself could not take a wife from among these same Albans; it in no way availed him that he was of the royal house of Alba nor that he rendered his city a great service by expelling the tyrant Amulius and restoring the legitimate king Numitor. It is well worth noting that victory or defeat in war is decided by the issue of combat between the parties principally interested. In the case of the Alban War

this lay between the three Horatii and the three Curiatii; in that of the Trojan War, between Paris and Menelaus. When combat between the latter two was indecisive, the Greeks and Trojans carried on the war to the end. In similar fashion in the last barbarian period the princes would decide the quarrels of their kingdoms by personal combat, on the issue of which the fortunes of their peoples depended. Hence it is clear that Alba was the Latin Troy and Horatia the Roman Helen (the Greeks having just the same story, reported by Gerard Jan Voss in his *Rhetorica*); and the ten years of the siege of Troy among the Greeks must correspond to the ten years of the siege of Veii among the Latins. In both cases we have a finite number standing for the infinity of all preceding time during which the cities had practiced eternal hostilities on each other.

642   For the number system, because of its extreme abstractness, was the last thing to be grasped by the nations [713, 1026]. When their minds had further developed, the Latins used "six hundred" for a number beyond reckoning (just as the Italians at first said "a hundred" and later "a hundred and a thousand"), for the idea of the infinite can be entertained only by the mind of a philosopher. Perhaps it is on this account that the first peoples said "twelve" to signify a large number. For such was the number assigned to the gods of the greater gentes [317], though Varro and the Greeks counted thirty thousand of them [175]. Twelve also were the labors of Hercules, which must have been countless. The Latins said there were twelve parts of the *as*, though it can be infinitely divided. This must have been the case also of the Law of the Twelve Tables, because of the infinite number of laws which were subsequently from time to time inscribed on tables.

643   At the time of the Trojan War it must have been that, in that part of Greece in which it was waged, the Greeks were called Achaeans. (They had previously been called Pelasgians, from Pelasgus, one of the most ancient heroes of Greece [564].) The name Achaeans must then have gone on spreading through all Greece (for it lasted down to the time of Lucius Mummius, according to Pliny [the Elder, 35.8.24]), even as through all later time they were called Hellenes. Thus the propagation of the name Achaeans must have led by Homer's time to the supposition that all the Greeks had been allied in that war, just as the name of Germany, according to Tacitus [G. 2], spread ultimately over all that great part of Europe which was thus known by the name of those who had crossed the Rhine, driven out the Gauls, and begun to call themselves Germans. Thus the glory of this people spread their name over Germany, as the report of the Trojan War spread the name Achaeans over all Greece [741ff]. For the

peoples in their first barbarism were so far from knowing anything of alliances that not even the peoples of offended kings would deign to take up arms to avenge them, as we see at the beginning of the Trojan War.

644 Only by understanding this nature of human civil institutions and in no other way can we solve the amazing problem of Spain. For she was the mother of many nations acclaimed by Cicero [*Philippic* 4.5.13] as most powerful and warlike, and Caesar found it so by experience, for in all other parts of the world, in which he was everywhere victorious, he fought for the Empire, but in Spain alone he fought for his life. Why then was it that after the fame of Saguntum (which made Hannibal sweat for eight months on end, though he had at his disposal and still fresh the entire forces of Africa, with which later—though much reduced and exhausted —he won the battle of Cannae and came very close to holding a triumph over Rome on the very Capitoline), and after the renown of Numantia (which shook the glory of Rome, though she had already triumphed over Carthage, and perplexed the valiant and wise Scipio, the conqueror of Africa)—why was it that Spain did not then unite all her peoples in an alliance to set up a world empire on the banks of the Tagus? Her failure gave occasion for the unhappy elogium of Lucius Florus [1.33.4], that she realized her strength only after the whole country had been conquered part by part. (Tacitus, in his life of Agricola [12], making the same observation of the Britons, who at that time were found to be savage fighters, uses the equally apt expression: *dum singuli pugnant, universi vincuntur,* "by fighting singly they let themselves be conquered collectively.") For, so long as they were not attacked, they remained like beasts within the dens of their confines and went on living the savage and solitary life of the cyclopes [296].

645 The historians have been struck by the fame of heroic naval warfare and so blinded by it as not to take note of heroic land warfare, much less of heroic politics, by which in those times the Greeks must have governed themselves. But Thucydides, a most acute and discerning writer, has left us an item of great significance. He tells us [1.2.2] that the heroic cities were all without walls, as Sparta continued to be in Greece, and Numantia, the Spanish Sparta, in Spain. And, with their arrogant and violent natures, the heroes were continually ejecting each other from their seats, as Amulius drove out Numitor and Romulus drove out the former and restored the latter to the kingdom of Alba. So much do the genealogies of the heroic royal houses of Greece and a continuous succession of fourteen Latin kings give assurance to the chronologists in their calculations of time! For in the recourse of barbarism, when it was at its crudest in

Europe, we read of nothing more varying and inconstant than the fortune of kingdoms [76, 1014, 1019]. Indeed, Tacitus most knowingly indicates as much in the opening words of his *Annals*: *Urbem Roman principio reges habuere* ("The city of Rome in the beginning was held by kings"); for he uses the verb for the weakest of the three degrees of possession distinguished by jurisconsults: *habere, tenere, possidere*.

646   The civil institutions in use under such kingdoms are narrated for us by poetic history in the numerous fables that deal with contests of song (taking song in that sense of the verbs *canere* and *cantare* in which they mean to predict) and consequently refer to heroic contests over the auspices [508].

647   Thus the satyr Marsyas (the monster described by Livy as *secum ipse discors* [567]), when overcome by Apollo in a contest of song, is flayed alive by the god (note the savagery of heroic punishments!). Linus, who must be a character of the plebeians [580] (for certainly the other Linus was a poet hero, being numbered with Amphion, Orpheus, Musaeus, and others), is slain by Apollo in a similar contest of song [Pausanias 9.29.6]. In both these fables the contest is with Apollo, the god of divinity, that is, of the science of divination, or of the auspices; and we found above that he was the god of the nobility also, since the science of the auspices, as we have shown by so many proofs, belonged to the nobles alone [508, 533ff].

648   The sirens, who lull sailors to sleep with their song and then cut their throats; the Sphinx, who puts riddles to travelers and slays them on their failure to find the solution; Circe, who by her enchantments turns into swine the comrades of Ulysses (so that *cantare*, singing, was later understood in the sense of practicing witchcraft, as in the phrase *cantando rumpitur anguis*, "the snake is burst by the singing" [Vergil *Eclogue* 8.72]; whence magic, which in Persia must at first have meant wisdom in divination by auspices, remained with the meaning of the art of magicians, and their spells were known as incantations [475]): all these portray the politics of the heroic cities. The sailors, travelers, and wanderers of these fables are the aliens [638], that is, the plebeians who, contending with the heroes for a share in the auspices, are vanquished in the attempt and cruelly punished.

649   In the same way Pan the satyr tries to seize the nymph Syrinx, famous in song [467], and finds himself embracing only reeds; and likewise Ixion, enamored of Juno, goddess of solemn nuptials, attempting to embrace her finds only a cloud in his arms. Here the reeds signify the lightness and the cloud the emptiness of natural marriage; hence from the cloud, the fable tells, were born the centaurs, that is to say the plebeians, who are the

monsters of discordant natures that Livy speaks of, who steal their brides from the Lapithae while the latter are still celebrating their weddings. So too Midas (a plebeian [580]) wears concealed an ass's ears, and the reeds that Pan seizes (that is, natural marriage) reveal them; just as the Roman patricians made out to their plebeians that the latter were all monsters because they practiced marriages like those of wild animals (*agitabant connubia more ferarum* [567, 734].

650   Vulcan (who here must also be plebeian), attempting to interfere in a contest between Jove and Juno, is precipitated from heaven by a kick of Jove and is left lame as a result of it [579]. This must refer to a struggle by the plebeians to secure from the heroes a share in the auspices of Jove and the solemnized marriages of Juno, in which, having been worsted, they came out lamed, that is, humiliated.

651   So Phaethon, of the family of Apollo and hence regarded as a child of the Sun, in attempting to drive his father's golden chariot (the cart of poetic gold, that is, grain [544]), strays from the accustomed paths leading to the granary of the father of his family (that is, lays claim to ownership of the fields), and is precipitated from heaven.

652   Most significant of all is the fall from heaven of the apple of discord (the apple which signifies the ownership of the fields [548], for the first discord arose over the fields which the plebeians wanted to cultivate for themselves), and the quarrel of Venus (who must here be plebeian) with Juno (of solemn nuptials) and Minerva (of authority). For, apropos of the judgment of Paris, by good fortune we have a remark of [pseudo-] Plutarch in his *Life and Poetry of Homer* [1.5] to the effect that the two verses toward the end of the *Iliad* [24.28f] which refer to it, are not Homer's but by a later hand [780].

653   Atalanta, by throwing away the apples of gold, defeats her suitors in the race, just as Hercules, wrestling with Antaeus, overcomes him by lifting him into the air [618]. [The meaning here is that] Atalanta first concedes to the plebeians the bonitary and then the quiritary ownership of the fields while withholding *connubium*; just as the Roman patricians [conceded] the first agrarian law of Servius Tullius and the second agrarian law of the Twelve Tables, yet retained *connubium* as a prerogative of their own order in the [conjectured] article *Connubia incommunicata plebi sunto*, "Solemnized marriages shall be withheld from the plebs," which is a direct consequence of the [conjectured] article *Auspicia incommunicata plebi sunto*, "The auspices shall be withheld from the plebs." Wherefore, three years later, the plebs began to lay claim to *connubium* too, and, after a heroic contest of three years, succeeded in winning it [110, 567, 598].

654 The suitors of Penelope invade the palace of Ulysses (that is the kingdom of the heroes), arrogate to themselves the title of kings, devour the royal substance (having taken over the ownership of the fields), and seek to marry Penelope (claiming the right to *connubium*). In some versions Penelope remains chaste and Ulysses strings up the suitors like thrushes on a net of the sort in which the heroic Vulcan caught the plebeian Mars and Venus. (That is, Ulysses binds them to cultivate the fields like the laborers of Achilles, just as Coriolanus sought to reduce the plebeians who were not satisfied with the agrarian law of Servius Tullius to the condition of the laborers of Romulus, as we have related above.) [But cf. O. 22.1ff.] Again, Ulysses fights Irus, a poor man, and kills him (which must refer to an agrarian contest in which the plebeians were devouring the substance of Ulysses). [But cf. O. 18.1–107,239–242.] In other versions Penelope prostitutes herself to the suitors (signifying the extension of *connubium* to the plebs) and gives birth to Pan,* a monster of two discordant natures, human and bestial. This is precisely the creature *secum ipse discors* of Livy [567], for the Roman patricians told the plebeians that, if they were to share with them the *connubium* of the nobles, the resulting offspring would be like Pan, a monster of two discordant natures brought forth by Penelope who had prostituted herself to the plebeians.

655 From Pasiphaë, who has lain with a bull, is born the minotaur, a monster of two diverse natures. This story must mean that the Cretans extended *connubium* to foreigners, who must have come to Crete in the ship called a bull in which Minos abducted youths and maidens from Attica, and in which Jove had earlier abducted Europa [635].

656 The fable of Io is also to be assigned to this kind of civil history. For Jove falls in love with her (is favorable to her with his auspices), and Juno becomes jealous (with that civil jealousy with which the heroes guarded their solemn nuptials [513]) and has her watched by Argus of the hundred eyes (that is, by the Argive fathers, each with his eye or clearing, that is, his cultivated land [564]). Then Mercury (who must here be a character of the mercenary plebeians), by the sound of his pipe, or rather by his singing, lulls Argus to sleep (overcomes the Argive fathers in the struggle for the auspices, by which the fortunes were sung or divined in solemn nuptials), whereupon Io is changed into a cow and lies with the bull with which Pasiphaë had lain, and goes wandering into Egypt (that is

---

* Vico here follows Bacon's *Wisdom of the Ancients* (*De sapientia veterum*), ch. 6; cf. *De augmentis scientiarum* 2.13 (English translation in *Works*, ed. Spedding *et al.*, 4.318,320). See 80 above. Bacon was one of Vico's "four authors" (*Autobiography*, Eng. trans., 138f, 154f). See 720* below.

among those foreign Egyptians with whom Danaus had driven the Ina-chids from the kingdom of Argos [75]).

657   But Hercules in his old age becomes effeminate and spins at the behest of Iole and Omphale; that is, the heroic right to the fields falls to the plebs. The heroes called themselves *viri*, men, in contrast to the plebeians, and *viri* in Latin has the same meaning as heroes in Greek. Vergil uses the word emphatically in that sense at the beginning of his *Aeneid: Arma virumque cano;* and Horace [A.P. 141] translates the first verse of the *Odyssey: Dic mihi, Musa, virum. Viri* continued among the Romans to signify husbands by solemn matrimony, magistrates, priests, and judges, for, in the poetic aristocracies, solemn matrimony, magistracy, priesthood, and judgeship were all confined to the heroic orders. Thus [the fable relates that] the heroic right to the fields was extended to the plebeians of Greece, just as the Roman patricians conceded to their plebeians the quiritary right by the second agrarian law, which was fought for and won in the Law of the Twelve Tables [598]. Precisely in the same way in the returned barbarian times feudal goods were called goods of the lance, and alodial goods were called goods of the distaff, as we find in the laws of the Angles. Hence the royal arms of France (in signification of the Salic law which excludes women from inheriting that kingdom) are sup-ported by two angels clothed in dalmatics [1048] and armed with spears, and are adorned with the heroic motto: *Lilia non nent,* "The lilies do not spin." So that just as Baldus, to our good fortune, called the Salic Law *ius gentium Gallorum,* the law of the Gallic gentes, so we may apply the term *ius gentium romanorum* to the Law of the Twelve Tables inasmuch as it rigorously confined intestate succession to direct heirs, agnates, and gentiles [110, 988]. For we shall show later [991] how little truth there is in the belief that in the early times of Rome there had existed a custom whereby daughters could succeed to their fathers *ab intestato,* and that this custom had passed into law in the Twelve Tables.

658   Finally Hercules breaks into a fury on being stained by the blood of the centaur Nessus—the same plebeian monster of two discordant natures mentioned by Livy [567]—that is, in the midst of civil fury he extends *connubium* to the plebs and is contaminated by plebeian blood and so dies, even as the god Fidius, the Roman Hercules, dies with the Petelian law called *De nexu* [115]. By this law *vinculum fidei victum est,* the bond of faith was broken, although Livy [8.28.8] connects it with an event occurring a decade later but similar in substance to the event which had given occasion to the Petelian law, an event in which it was necessary that the matter of the aforesaid phrase should be put into execution and

not simply decreed. Livy must have found the phrase in some ancient chronicler whom he follows with as much good faith as ignorance. For when the plebeian debtors were freed from private incarceration by their noble creditors, debtors were still constrained by judicial decisions to pay their debts, but they were released from the feudal law, the law of the Herculean knot [558], which had had its origin in the first asylums of the world, the bond by which Romulus had founded Rome in his asylum [613]. It seems very likely, therefore, that the chronicler had written *vinculum Fidii*, the bond of the god Fidius [602], whom Varro [*On the Latin Language* 5.66] asserts to have been the Roman Hercules, and that later historians, not understanding the phrase, erroneously read the word as *fidei*. The same heroic natural law is found among the American Indians, and in our world it still obtains among the Abyssinians of Africa and the Muscovites and Tartars of Europe and Asia. It was practiced with greater mildness by the Hebrews, among whom debtors served not more than seven years [F7].

659 And, to conclude, in like manner Orpheus, the founder of Greece, with his lyre or cord or force, which signify the same thing as the knot of Hercules (the knot with which the Petelian law was concerned), met his death at the hands of the Bacchantes (the infuriated plebs), who broke his lyre to pieces (the lyre being the law [615]); so that already in Homer's time the heroes were taking foreign women to wife, and bastards were coming into royal successions, showing that Greece had already begun to observe popular liberty [802].

660 From all this we must conclude that these heroic contests gave the name to the heroic age; and that in these contests many chieftains, vanquished and humbled, were obliged to take to the sea with their followers and wander in search of other lands. Some of them finally returned to their native countries, like Menelaus and Ulysses. Others settled in foreign parts, like Cecrops, Cadmus, Danaus, and Pelops, who settled in Greece (for these heroic contests had arisen many centuries earlier in Phoenicia, Egypt, and Phrygia, since humanity had begun earlier in those places). Dido must have been one of the latter sort [78]; fleeing from Phoenicia to escape the faction of her brother by whom she was pursued, she settled in Carthage, which was called *Punica* as if for *Phoenica*. And of the Trojan refugees after the destruction of their city, Capys stopped at Capua, Aeneas landed in Latium, and Antenor reached Padua [770ff].

661 Thus ended the wisdom of the theological poets, the sages or statesmen of the poetic age of the Greeks, such as Orpheus, Amphion, Linus, Musaeus, and others. By singing to the Greek plebs of the force of

the gods in the auspices (which were the praises that such poets must have sung of the gods; that is, the praises of divine providence which it behooved them to sing), they kept the plebs in subjection to their heroic orders. In like fashion Appius [Claudius], the grandson of the decemvir, about the 300th year of Rome, by singing to the Roman plebeians of the force of the gods in the auspices, of which the nobles claimed to have the science, keeps them in obedience to the nobles [81]. And in the same way Amphion, by singing to his lyre, causes the stones to move and the walls of Thebes, which Cadmus had founded three centuries earlier, to rise; that is, he confirms therein the heroic state [K7, 523, 734].

[Chapter VII] *Corollaries concerning Ancient Roman Institutions, and in Particular the Supposedly Monarchic Kingship at Rome and the Supposedly Popular Liberty Instituted by Junius Brutus*

662   The numerous parallels we have cited in human civil institutions between the Romans and the Greeks, by which we have repeatedly shown that ancient Roman history is a perpetual historic mythology of the many various and diverse fables of the Greeks [158ff], must firmly convince anyone of understanding (which is neither memory nor imagination) that from the times of the kings until the extension of *connubium* to the plebs the Roman people (the people of Mars) was composed of nobles alone [598]. To this people of nobles King Tullus, beginning with the case of Horatius, granted the right of persons condemned for crime by the duumvirs or the quaestors to appeal to the entire order. The only orders were the heroic peoples, and the plebs were accessions to these peoples (as later the provinces were accessions to the conquering nations, as Grotius pointed out [L. 1.3.7.3]) and are in fact the "other people," as Telemachus called his plebeians in the assembly we mentioned above [590]. And hence, by virtue of an invincible metaphysical criticism of these founders of nations [348, 493], we are able to uproot the error which asserts that such a mass of base-born laborers, held as slaves, had the right, from the time of Romulus, to elect their kings and have their choice ratified by the fathers. This must be an anachronism of later times when the plebs had a part in the city and shared in the creating of consuls (which was after the extension of *connubium* to the plebs by the fathers), dated back three hundred years to the interregnum of Romulus.

663   Taking the word people in the sense of recent times and applying

it to the earliest times of the world of the cities (because of the inability of philosophers and philologians alike to imagine such severe aristocracies) has led to misunderstandings of the words king and liberty as well. As a result, everyone has believed that the Roman kingdom was monarchic and that the liberty instituted by Junius Brutus was popular. Jean Bodin, however, though he too falls into the common vulgar error of all preceding political theorists that monarchies came first, then tyrannies, then popular common-wealths, and finally aristocracies (what distortions of human ideas can be and are made when true principles are lacking!), nevertheless, observing the effects of an aristocratic commonwealth in the supposedly popular liberty of ancient Rome, props up his system by distinguishing administra-tion from constitution and asserting that in ancient times Rome had a popular constitution but was aristocratically administered. For all that, since the effects turned out otherwise and even with this prop his political machinery would not stand, he was finally constrained by the force of the truth to confess with gross inconsistency that in ancient times the Roman commonwealth was aristocratic in constitution as well as in administration [1004ff, 1084].

664   All this is confirmed by Livy [2.1.7], who, in his account of the instituting of two annual consuls by Junius Brutus, openly states and avows that there was no change in the constitution. And indeed how could a wise Brutus have done otherwise than restore the constitution to its pristine form from the corruption into which it had fallen! By the institution of two annual consuls, says Livy, *nihil quicquam de regia potestate deminu-tum*, no diminution was made in the royal power; for the consuls emerged as two aristocratic annual kings, as indeed Cicero in his *Laws* calls them *reges annuos* [108] (of the same sort as the kings for life at Sparta, which was beyond question an aristocratic commonwealth). And the consuls, as everyone knows, were subject to recall during their period of office (just as the kings of Sparta were subject to correction by the ephors) and at the end of their year's reign could be put on trial (as Spartan kings were condemned to death by the ephors). This one passage of Livy shows both that the Roman kingdom was aristocratic and that the liberty instituted by Brutus was not popular (the freedom of the people from their lords) but lordly (the freedom of the lords from the Tarquin tyrants). Brutus would certainly not have been able to accomplish this had it not been for the affair of the Roman Lucretia, which, being offered him, he turned to advantage; for this occasion was clothed with all the sublime circumstances necessary to arouse the plebs against the tyrant Tarquinius, who had so badly handled the nobility that Brutus found it necessary to reconstruct

the senate, depleted as it was by the execution of so many senators by [Tarquinius] Superbus [316]. In doing this he achieved, by prudent consideration, two public advantages: He strengthened the order of the nobles, which was declining; and he won the favor of the plebs, for from their body he had to choose many, and perhaps he chose the boldest, who would otherwise have opposed the reorganization of the seigniory [624]. These he caused to enter the order of the nobility, and thus he composed the city, the whole of which was at that time divided *inter patres et plebem*, between fathers and plebs.

665 If the precurrence of the many varied and diverse causes here studied from the age of Saturn onward [73], if the succession of the many varied and diverse effects observed by Bodin in the ancient Roman commonwealth, and if the perpetual and continuous influence of these causes on these effects as considered by Livy, do not suffice to establish the conclusion to which the only authority we have would lead us, namely that the Roman kingdom was aristocratic and that the liberty ordered by Brutus was the liberty of the lords, then we must say that the Romans, a rough and barbarous people, had a privilege from God withheld from the Greeks, an acute and highly civilized people, who, according to Thucydides, knew nothing of their own antiquities down to the Peloponnesian war, the most glorious time of Greece as we observed above in the [Notes on the] Chronological Table [101]. There too we showed that the same was true of the Romans down to the second Carthaginian war, from which Livy professes to write the history of Rome with greater certainty, while yet confessing ignorance of three circumstances, the most important in the history [of that war], which we also observed there [117]. But, even if we concede such a privilege to the Romans, what survives is still but an obscure memory, a confused imagination, and so reason cannot reject the conclusions we have drawn concerning these ancient Roman institutions.

[Chapter VIII]   *Corollary concerning the Heroism of the First Peoples*

666 The study of the heroic age of the early world which we have here been making leads us perforce to reflect on the heroism of the first peoples. This heroism, by axioms set forth above [196f] which have their application here, and by the principles herein established for heroic politics [582ff], was a far different thing from what philosophers have hitherto

imagined as a consequence of the matchless wisdom of the ancients [128], misled by the philologians with respect to the three undefined words, "people," "king," and "liberty" [105]. For they have taken the heroic peoples as also including the plebeians; they have taken the kings as monarchs; and they have taken the liberty as popular. On the other hand, they have applied to these matters three ideas proper to their own refined and learned minds: the first, that of a justice reasoned on maxims of Socratic morals; the second, that of a glory which is the fame of benefits to mankind [514]; and the third, the desire for immortality. By following these errors and applying these ideas, they have believed that the kings or other great personages of ancient times consecrated themselves and their families (as well as their entire patrimonies and substance) to bring happiness to the poor, who are always the majority in any city or nation.

667   Yet concerning Achilles, the greatest of the Greek heroes, Homer tells us of three of his qualities which were in complete contrast with the three ideas of the philosophers. As regards justice, in speaking with Hector, who proposes that the victor in the fight shall bury the vanquished, he forgets their equality of rank and the common lot [of men] (two considerations which naturally induce men to recognize justice) and makes the following savage reply: "When have men ever made pacts with lions? And when were wolves and lambs ever of one mind?" On the contrary: "If I kill you, I shall drag you naked, bound to my chariot, three days around the walls of Troy," as indeed he did, "and finally I shall give your body to my hunting dogs to eat" [I. 22.261ff]. This too he would have done if the unhappy father Priam had not himself come to ransom the corpse. And as for glory, this same Achilles, because of a personal grievance (Agamemnon having wrongfully taken his Briseis from him), considers himself badly treated by gods and men alike, demands of Jove that he be restored to honor, withdraws his men from the allied army and his ships from the fleet, and allows Hector to make a slaughter of the Greeks [I. 1.334ff]. Thus in defiance of the devotion that a man owes his fatherland he insists on avenging a personal offense by the ruin of his entire nation. Indeed, he is not ashamed to rejoice with Patroclus over Hector's slaughter of the Greeks [I. 11.599ff], and, what is much graver, this man who carries in his heels the fate of Troy expresses the disgraceful wish to Patroclus that all, Greeks and Trojans alike, may die in the war, leaving only the two of them alive [I. 16.97ff]. And as for the third idea [the desire of immortality], when Achilles in the lower world is asked by Ulysses if he is content there, he answers that he would rather be the meanest slave in the land of the living [O. 11.488ff]. This is the hero that Homer sings of to the Greek peoples as

an example of heroic virtue and to whom he gives the fixed epithet "blameless"! This epithet (if we are to give Homer credit for making the delight he gives a means of instruction, as poets are supposed to do) can be understood only as meaning a man so arrogant that, as we would say nowadays, he will not let a fly pass the end of his nose. What he preaches is thus the virtue of punctiliousness, on which the duelists of the returned barbarian times based their entire morality, and which gave rise to the proud laws, the lofty duties, and the vindictive satisfactions of the knights-errant of whom the romancers sing [920].

668 As against this, let us reflect on the oath of eternal enmity which Aristotle says the heroes swore against the plebs [271]. Let us reflect further on Roman history in the time of Roman virtue, which according to Livy [9.16.19] was the time of the war against Pyrrhus, a time he acclaims in the phrase *nulla aetas virtutum feracior*, "there was never an age more productive of virtues." Following Sallust as quoted in St. Augustine's *City of God* [2.18], we may extend this period from the expulsion of the kings down to the second Carthaginian war. What of the heroes of this time? Brutus, who consecrates his house in the persons of his two sons to the cause of liberty; Scaevola, who terrifies and routs the Etruscan king Porsena by plunging his own right hand into the flames for its failure to kill him; Manlius called the Imperious, who cuts off the head of his own son for a breach of military discipline though it sprang from love of glory and valor and issued in victory; men like Curtius, who throws himself, mounted and armed, into the fatal abyss; like the Decii, who, father and son, sacrifice themselves to save their army; like Fabricius and Curius, who refuse the Samnite gold and the shares of his kingdom offered them by Pyrrhus; like Atilius Regulus, who returns to a certain and most cruel death at Carthage to preserve the sanctity of the Roman oath—what did any of them do for the poor and unhappy Roman plebs? Assuredly they did but increase their burdens by war, plunge them deeper in the sea of usury, in order to bury them to a greater depth in the private prisons of the nobles, where they were beaten with rods on their bare backs like abject slaves. And if anyone in this period of Roman virtue attempted to relieve the lot of the plebs with some sort of agrarian or grain law, he was accused of treason and sent to his death. Such was the fate, to take only one example, of Manlius Capitolinus, though he had saved the capitol from being burned by the ferocious Senonic Gauls. Likewise in Sparta (the city of the heroes of Greece, as Rome was the city of the heroes of the world), the magnanimous King Agis, because of his attempt to relieve the poor Lacedaemonian plebs of usurious oppression at the hands of the nobles, by a law wiping out

debts, and to aid them by another giving them testamentary rights, was strangled by order of the ephors [985]. As the valorous Agis was the Manlius Capitolinus of Sparta, so Manlius Capitolinus was the Agis of Rome, and, on the simple suspicion of being somewhat mindful of the poor oppressed Roman plebs, he was thrown from the Tarpeian rock. So that precisely because the nobles of the first peoples considered themselves heroes and of a nature superior to that of their plebeians [437], they were capable of such misgovernment of the poor masses of the nations. For certainly Roman history will puzzle any intelligent reader who tries to find in it any evidence of Roman virtue where there was so much arrogance, or of moderation in the midst of such avarice, or of justice or mercy where so much inequality and cruelty prevailed.

669   The only principles that can solve the enigma are of necessity the following.

I

670   Following the bestial education of the giants [170, 195, 523f], the [heroic] education of the young was severe, harsh, and cruel, as in the case of the unlettered Lacedaemonians, who were the heroes of Greece. These people, in order to teach their sons to fear neither pain nor death, would beat them within an inch of their lives in the temple of Diana, so that they often fell dead in agonies of pain beneath their fathers' blows. This cyclopean paternal authority survived among both Greeks and Romans, permitting them to kill their innocent newborn babes. Whereas the indulgence with which we now treat our young children produces all the tenderness of our [modern] natures.

II

671   Wives were bought with heroic dowries, a usage which survived as a solemnity in the nuptials of the Roman priests, which were contracted *coëmptione et farre,* "by mutual [mock] sale and spelt" [spelt-bread offering]. (Wife dower was also the custom among the ancient Germans, according to Tacitus [G. 18], and we may therefore assume the same of all the earliest barbarous peoples.) Wives were maintained as a necessity of nature for the procreation of children. In other respects they were treated as slaves, as is [still] the custom of nations in many parts of our [old] world and almost everywhere in the new. When the wife brings the dowry, it purchases the liberty of her husband and is a public confession on his part of inability to bear the expense of marriage, which is perhaps the reason for the many privileges with which the emperors favored dowries.

III

672   Children acquired and wives saved for the benefit of their husbands and fathers; not, as nowadays, just the contrary.

IV

673   Games and pleasures were strenuous, such as wrestling and racing (whence "swift-footed" as a Homeric fixed epithet of Achilles); and often dangerous too, such as jousting and hunting wild game, to accustom men to steel themselves and to risk and disprize their lives.

V

674   Luxury, refinement, and ease were quite unknown.

VI

675   Wars like the ancient heroic ones were all wars of religion [562], which, for the reason we have taken as the first principle of this Science [333], made them always extremely bitter.

VII

676   Heroic enslavement was also prevalent as a consequence of such wars, in which the vanquished were regarded as godless men, so that along with civil liberty they lost natural liberty as well. Here the axiom finds application that "natural liberty is fiercer in proportion as property attaches more closely to our persons, and civil servitude is clapped on with goods of fortune not necessary to life" [290].

VIII

677   Because of all this the commonwealths were by nature aristocratic, consisting of those who were naturally strongest. They confined all civil honors to the few noble fathers. The public good was the family monarchies preserved by the fatherland; for the true fatherland was the interest of the few fathers [584], and hence the citizens were naturally patricians. Given such natures, customs, commonwealths, institutions, and laws, the heroism of the first peoples will flourish. But this heroism is now by civil nature impossible, since its causes, just enumerated, have given place to their contraries, which have produced the other two kinds of civil states, free popular commonwealths and monarchies; both of these (though the latter more than the former) we have shown to be human [629]. For throughout the whole period of Roman popular liberty Cato of

Utica alone was reputed a hero, and his reputation was that of a spirit of the aristocratic commonwealth whom Pompey's fall left as head of the party of the nobility and who, because he could not bear its humiliation by Caesar, killed himself. In the monarchies the heroes are those who sacrifice themselves for the glory and grandeur of their sovereigns. Wherefore we must conclude that such a hero [as devotes himself to justice and the welfare of mankind [666]] is desired by afflicted peoples, conceived by philosophers, and imagined by poets, but is not included among the benefits afforded by civil nature as covered by our axiom [260].

678 All we have here set forth concerning the heroism of the first peoples receives illumination and illustration from the axioms concerning Roman heroism [278–281], which will be found to apply also to the heroism of the ancient Athenians at the time when, as Thucydides [i.e., Isocrates] relates [592], they were governed by the stern Areopagites, an aristocratic senate, and to the heroism of the Spartans, who were a commonwealth of Heraclids or lords, as a thousand proofs above have demonstrated [423].

[SECTION VI]

[Chapter I]   *Epitomes of Poetic History*

I

679   This whole divine and heroic history of the theological poets was only too unhappily described for us in the fable of Cadmus [541]. For first he slays the great serpent (clears the earth of the great ancient forest). Then he sows the teeth (a fine metaphor for his plowing the first fields of the world with curved pieces of hard wood, which, before the use of iron was discovered, must have served as the teeth of the first plows, and teeth they continued to be called). He throws a heavy stone (the hard earth which the clients or *famuli* wished to plow for themselves [583]). From the furrows armed men spring forth (in the heroic contest over the first agrarian law [264f, 597] the heroes come forth from their estates to assert their lordship of them, and unite in arms against the plebs, and they fight not among themselves but with the clients that have revolted against them; the furrows signifying the orders in which they unite and thereby give form and stability to the first cities on the basis of arms, as is all set forth above). And Cadmus is changed into a serpent (signifying the origin of the authority of the aristocratic senates, for which the ancient Latins would have used the phrase *Cadmus fundus factus est,* and the Greeks said Cadmus was changed into Draco, the dragon that wrote the laws in blood [423]). All of which is what we promised [446] to make clear: that the fable of Cadmus contained several centuries of poetic history, and is a grand example of the inarticulateness with which the still infant world labored to express itself, which is one of the seven great sources of the difficulty of the fables [814]. So easy it was for Cadmus to leave a written record of this history in the vulgar characters which he brought to the Greeks from Phoenicia! And Desiderius Erasmus, with a thousand absurdities unworthy of the learned man who was called the Christian Varro, will have it that [the fable] contains the story of the invention of letters by Cadmus.* Thus

---

* Erasmus, *De recta latini graecique sermonis pronunciatione dialogus,* in his *Opera,* vol. I, Leyden, 1703, col. 927.

the illustrious history of such a great benefit to the nations as the invention of letters, which must have made itself known far and wide, is concealed by Cadmus from the human race in Greece under the veil of this fable, which remained obscure down to the time of Erasmus, in order to keep hidden from the vulgar such a great invention of vulgar wisdom that from the vulgar these letters received the name of vulgar letters!

II

680 But with admirable brevity and appropriateness Homer [I. 2.100ff] tells us the same history compressed in the hieroglyph of the scepter bestowed on Agamemnon. Vulcan made it for Jove (as Jove, with the first thunderbolts after the flood [377], founded his kingdom over gods and men, which is to say the divine kingdoms in the state of the families [522]). Then Jove gave it to Mercury (in the form of the caduceus with which Mercury brought the first agrarian law to the plebs, whence were born the heroic kingdoms of the first cities [604]). Then Mercury gave it to Pelops, Pelops to Thyestes, Thyestes to Atreus, and Atreus to Agamemnon (that is, it came down through the line of inheritance of the royal house of Argos).

III

681 More full and detailed, however, is the history of the world described by the same Homer as depicted on the shield of Achilles [I. 18.483ff].

682 (1) At the beginning there could be seen thereon the sky, the earth, the sea, the sun, the moon, and the stars. This is the epoch of the creation of the world.

683 (2) Thereafter were depicted two cities. In the one there were songs, hymeneals and nuptials: the epoch of the heroic families including only children born of solemn nuptials [520ff]. In the other there were no such things to be seen; this represented the epoch of the heroic families with their *famuli* [553ff], who contracted only natural marriages with none of the solemn rites which surrounded heroic nuptials. So that these two cities together represented the state of nature, or of the families. It was to these two cities that Eumaeus, the steward of Ulysses, had reference when he spoke of the two cities in his fatherland, both ruled by his father, between which the citizens had all their property clearly divided [O. 15. 412ff] (meaning that there was no part of citizenship which they shared in common). Hence the city without hymeneals is exactly the "other people," as Telemachus in assembly calls the plebs of Ithaca [590]. This is

Achilles's meaning in complaining of the outrage done him by Agamemnon, who, he says, has treated him as a common laborer with no part in the governing [597].

684   (3) Then, in the aforesaid city of the nuptials, the shield showed parliaments, laws, trials, and punishments. This accords with the answer of the Roman patricians to the plebs in the heroic contests, declaring that nuptials, *imperium*, and priesthoods, on the last of which depended the science of laws and hence judgments, were all their own exclusive institutions since the auspices which constituted the chief solemnity of nuptials were theirs [110]. For this reason *viri*, men (which meant among the Latins the same as heroes among the Greeks), was the term applied to husbands in solemn matrimony, to magistrates, to priests, and finally to judges. This, then, is the epoch of the heroic cities which, on the basis of families of the *famuli*, arose in strictest aristocratic form [597].

685   (4) The other city is under armed siege and the two cities prey on each other by turns; hence the city without nuptials (the plebs of the heroic cities) becomes a separate and hostile city. This affords striking confirmation of what we have argued above: that the first foreigners, the first *hostes*, were the plebs of the heroic peoples [638], against whom, as we have so often quoted Aristotle as saying, the heroes swore eternal enmity [271]. Hence the two cities, regarding each other as alien, carried on eternal hostilities against each other with their heroic raids [636f].

686   (5) And lastly there was portrayed on the shield the history of the arts of humanity, beginning with the epoch of the families. For, first of all, there appeared the father-king, ordering with his scepter that the roasted ox be divided among the harvesters. Then there were planted vineyards; then flocks, shepherds, and huts; and last of all, dances were depicted. This picture, beautifully and truly following the order of human institutions, indicated that first of all the necessary arts were invented, such as agriculture with a view first to bread and then to wine; then the useful arts, such as herding; then the arts of comfort, such as urban architecture; and lastly those of pleasure, such as the dance [239, 241].

[SECTION VII]

[POETIC PHYSICS]

[Chapter I]   *Poetic Physics*

687   Passing now to the other branch of the main trunk of poetic metaphysics, along which poetic wisdom branches off into physics and thence into cosmography and thus into astronomy, whose fruits are chronology and geography [367], we shall begin this remaining part of our discussion with physics.

688   The physics the theological poets considered was that of the world of nations, and therefore in the first place they defined Chaos as confusion of human seeds in the state of the infamous promiscuity of women [B5]. It was thence that the physicists were later moved to conceive the confusion of the universal seeds of nature, and to express it they took the word already invented by the poets and hence appropriate. [The poetic Chaos] was confused because there was no institution of humanity in it, and obscure because it lacked the civil light in virtue of which the heroes were called *incliti*, illustrious [533]. Further they imagined it as Orcus, a misshapen monster which devoured all things, because men in this infamous promiscuity did not have the proper form of men, and were swallowed up by the void because through the uncertainty of offspring they left nothing of themselves. This [chaos] was later taken by the physicists as the prime matter of natural things, which, formless itself, is greedy for forms and devours all forms. The poets, however, gave it also the monstrous form of Pan, the wild god who is the divinity of all satyrs inhabiting not the cities but the forests; a character to which they reduced the impious vagabonds wandering through the great forest of the earth and having the appearance of men but the habits of abominable beasts. Afterward, by forced allegories, the philosophers, misled by the name *pan*, everything, took him as a symbol for the formed universe [910]. Scholars have also held that the poets meant first matter in the fable of Proteus, with whom

Ulysses [i.e., Menelaus, O. 4.455ff] wrestles in Egypt, Proteus in the water and the hero out of it, unable to get a grip on the monster, who keeps assuming new forms. But the scholars thus made sublime learning out of what was doltishness and simplicity on the part of the first men, who (just as children, looking in a mirror, will try to seize their own reflections) thought from the various modifications of their own shapes and gestures that there must be a man in the water, forever changing into different shapes.

689   At length the sky broke forth in thunder, and Jove thus gave a beginning to the world of men [B8] by arousing in them the conatus [504] which is proper to the liberty of the mind, just as from motion, which is proper to bodies as necessary agents, he began the world of nature. For what seems to be conatus in bodies is but insensible motion, as we said above in the Method [340]. From this conatus came the civil light of which Apollo is the character, by which light was discerned the civil beauty with which the heroes were beautiful [533]. And Venus was the character of this civil beauty [565], which the physicists later took for the beauty of nature, and even for the whole of formed nature, as being beautifully adorned with all sensible forms.

690   The world of the theological poets was composed of four sacred elements: the air whence Jove's bolts come [379], the water of the perennial springs whose divinity is Diana [528], the fire with which Vulcan cleared the forests, and the tilled earth of Cybele or Berecynthia [549]. All four are elements in divine ceremonies: auspices, water, fire, and spelt. They are watched over by Vesta, who is the same as Cybele or Berecynthia. She is crowned with the tilled lands protected by hedges and surmounted by the towers of high-placed towns [555] (whence the Latin *extorris*, exiled, as if *exterris*). This crown encloses all that was signified by the *orbis terrarum* [550], which is properly the world of men [B8]. Thence the physicists were later moved to study the four elements of which the world of nature is composed [724].

691   The same theological poets gave living and sensible and for the most part human forms to the elements and to the countless special natures arising from them, and thus created many and various divinities, as we have set forth above in the Metaphysics [375]. This gave Plato [*Cratylus* 404ff] opportunity to intrude his doctrine of minds or intelligences: that Jove was the mind of ether, Vulcan of fire, and the like. But the theological poets understood so little of these intelligent substances that down to Homer's time they did not understand the human mind itself insofar as, by

dint of reflection, it opposes the senses. On this there are two golden passages in the *Odyssey* [18.34,60] in which it is called sacred force or occult vigor, both of which mean the same thing.

[*Chapter II*]   *Poetic Physics concerning Man, or Heroic Nature*

692   But the greatest and most important part of physics is the contemplation of the nature of man. We have set forth above in the Poetic Economy how the founders of gentile humanity in a certain sense generated and produced in themselves the proper human form in its two aspects: that is, how by means of frightful religions and terrible paternal powers and sacred ablutions they brought forth from their giant bodies the form of our just corporature, and how by discipline of their household economy they brought forth from their bestial minds the form of our human mind [C6, M7, 520, 524]. Here is a proper place for calling attention again to that development.

693   Now the theological poets in their extremely crude physics saw in man these two metaphysical ideas: being and subsisting. Certainly the Latin heroes understood being quite grossly in the sense of eating. This must have been the first meaning of the verb *sum*, which later was used in both senses, just as nowadays when our peasants want to say that a sick man lives [i.e., has not died] they say he still eats. For *sum* in the sense of being is most abstract, as transcending all particular beings; most pervasive, as penetrating all beings; most pure, as not being circumscribed by any. They apprehended substance, that which stands beneath and sustains, as residing in the heels because a man stands on the base of his feet. Hence Achilles carried his fate in his heel, since there stood his fate or lot of living or dying.

694   The composition of the body they reduced to solids and liquids. Under the head of solids they included in the first place the viscera or flesh (as among the Romans *visceratio* was the term applied to the distribution by the priests to the people of the flesh of sacrificial victims), so that they used the verb *vesci* for taking nourishment when the food was flesh. Next, bones and joints. The latter were called *artus* from *ars*, which to the ancient Latins meant the force of the body, whence *artitus*, robust of person; later *ars* was applied to any set of precepts which steadies and directs some faculty of the mind. Then, the sinews. When the poets were still mute and spoke by physical things, they took the sinews for forces

(from one of these sinews, called *fides* in the sense of cord, the force of the gods was called their *fides* or faith, and from this sinew or cord or force they later fashioned the lute of Orpheus [523]); and indeed they justly placed their forces in the sinews, for it is the sinews that stretch the muscles, which is necessary to the exercise of force. And lastly the marrow, in which with an equal sense of fitness they placed the essence of life (whence *medulla* was a term applied by the lover to the woman he loved, and *medullitus* was equivalent to our phrase, "with all one's heart," and great love was said to consume the marrow). The liquids, on the other hand, they reduced to blood alone, for the neural or spermatic substance they called also blood (as is shown by the poetic phrase *sanguine cretus* for "begotten"); here too with a just sense, for this substance is the essence of the blood. And again with fine perception they regarded the blood as the juice of the fibers of which the flesh is composed; hence the Latin expression *succiplenus* for fleshy: "steeped in good blood."

695   As for the other part [of our human form], the soul (*anima*), the theological poets placed it in the air (which is also called *anima* by the Latins) and they thought of it as the vehicle of life. (Hence the propriety of the Latin phrase *anima vivimus* and of the poetic locutions *ferri ad vitales auras*, to be born; *ducere vitales auras*, to live; *vitam referri in auras*, to die. And in prose Latin: *animam ducere*, to live; *animam trahere*, to be at the point of death; *animam efflare, emittere*, to die.) Whence perhaps the motive of the physicists for placing the world soul in the air. And the theological poets, again with a just sense, put the course of life in the course of the blood, on whose proper flow our life depends.

696   They must with a sense equally just have felt that spirit (*animus*) is the vehicle of sensation, for in good Latin the phrase survived *animo sentimus*. And again with a just sense they made spirit (*animus*) masculine and soul (*anima*) feminine, for spirit acts on soul (it is the *igneus vigor* of which Vergil speaks [A. 6.730]); so that spirit must have its subject in the nerves and the neural substance, and soul must have its in the veins and the blood. Thus the vehicle of spirit is the ether and that of soul is the air, as accords with the relative swiftness of animal spirits and slowness of vital spirits. And as soul is the agent of motion, so spirit is the agent and therefore the principle of conatus, as the aforesaid *igneus vigor* of Vergil. The theological poets sensed as much, but without understanding it, and after Homer they used such expressions as sacred force, occult vigor, and unknown god [691]; as the Greeks and Latins, when in saying or doing anything they sensed a superior principle within themselves, would say that some god had willed that thing. Such a principle the Latins called

mens animi, the mind of the spirit. Thus in a crude fashion they apprehended the lofty truth that ideas come to man from God, which later the
natural theology of the metaphysicians proved by invincible reasoning
against the Epicureans who would have it that they spring from the body.

697   They understood generation in such a way that we do not know
if later scholars have been able to find a better. The way in which they
understood it is all contained in the word *concipere,* for *concapere,* which
expresses the natural activity of physical forms (which must now be
supplemented by the weight of the air, demonstrated in our times) in
taking from everywhere around them the bodies within their reach, over-
coming their resistance, adapting and assimilating them to their own form.

698   Decay they expressed very sagaciously in the verb *corrumpi,*
signifying the breaking down of all the parts composing a body, as opposed
to *sanum,* for the sound and healthy condition of all the parts in which life
consists. They must accordingly have thought of disease as bringing on
death by corrupting the solids of the body.

699   They reduced all the internal functions of the spirit to three
parts of the body: the head, the breast, and the heart. To the head they
assigned all cognitive functions, and as these all involved imagination, they
located memory (*memoria* being the Latin term for *phantasia,* or imagination) in the head. And in the returned barbarian times *fantasia* was used
for *ingegno,* and an ingenious or inventive man was called a fantastic man.
Cola di Rienzo [819] is so described by the author of a contemporary
biography in barbarous Italian,* a record of natures and customs like those
of the ancient heroes we are discussing, which is a great evidence of the
recourse the nations take in natures and customs [1046ff]. Imagination,
however, is nothing but the springing up again of reminiscences, and
ingenuity or invention is nothing but the working over of what is remembered. Now, since the human mind at the time we are considering had not
been refined by any art of writing or spiritualized by any practice of
counting or reckoning, and had not developed its powers of abstraction by
the many abstract terms in which languages now abound [378], it exercised
all its force in these three excellent faculties which came to it from the
body. All three appertain to the primary operation of the mind, whose
regulating art is topics, just as the regulating art of the second operation of
the mind is criticism; and as the latter is the art of judging, so the former is
the art of inventing [495ff]. And since naturally the discovery or invention
of things comes before criticism of them, it was fitting that the infancy of
the world should concern itself with the first operation of the human mind,

---

* *La vita di Cola Rienzo,* ed. Zefirino Re, Firenze, 1854, pp. 140f.

for the world then had need of all inventions for the necessities and utilities of life, all of which had been provided before the philosophers appeared, as we shall fully show in the Discovery of the True Homer [782ff]. With reason, then, did the theological poets call Memory the mother of the Muses; that is, of the arts of humanity [508, 534].

700   In this connection we must not omit an important observation of great relevance to the statement in the Method [338] that we can now scarcely understand and cannot at all imagine how the first men thought who founded gentile humanity. For their minds were so limited to particulars that they regarded every change of facial expression as a new face, as we observed above in the fable of Proteus [688], and for every new passion they imagined a new heart, a new breast, a new spirit. Hence the poetic plurals, dictated rather by the nature of human institutions than by the requirements of counting; *ora, vultūs, animi, pectora, corda*, for example, being employed for their singulars.

701   They made the breast the seat of all the passions, and with a due sense of fitness they placed beneath it the two fomenting principles: (1) the irascible in the stomach, because there we feel the spreading of the bile expressed from the surrounding biliary vessels by the intensification of the peristaltic action of the stomach; and (2) the concupiscible more than anywhere else in the liver, which is defined as the blood factory. The poets called these organs the *praecordia*. The Titan [Prometheus] implanted therein the passions of the other animals, taking from each species its ruling passion. In a rough way they understood that concupiscence is the mother of all the passions, and that the passions reside in our humors.

702   The heart they made the seat of all counsel, whence the heroes "kept turning over their cares in their hearts" (*agitabant, versabant, volutabant corde curas*); for, being stupid and insensate, they gave no thought to things to be done except when shaken by passions. Hence the Latins called wise men hearted (*cordati*) and simpletons contrariwise heartless (*vecordes*). And their resolutions they called feelings (*sententiae*), because they judged as they felt, whence heroic judgments were always true in form though often false in matter [825].

[Chapter III]   Corollary on Heroic Sentences

703   Now, since the minds of the first men of the gentile world took things one at a time, being in this respect little better than the minds of beasts, for which each new sensation cancels the last one (which is the

cause of their being unable to compare and reason discursively), therefore their sentences must all have been formed in the singular by those who felt them [825]. Hence the sublime sentence admired by Dionysius Longinus [S. 10.1–2] in the ode of Sappho which Catullus later turned into Latin, in which the lover in the presence of his mistress expresses himself by the simile: *Ille mi par esse deo videtur*, "Like a god he seems to me," yet falls short of the highest degree of sublimity, because the lover does not make the sentence singular to himself, as Terence does when he says: *Vitam deorum adepti sumus*, "We have attained the life of the gods" [*The Self-Tormentor* 693]. This sentiment, though proper to him who speaks, still has the air of a common sentiment because of the Latin usage of plural for singular in the first person. However, in another comedy of the same poet, this sentiment is raised to the highest degree of sublimity by being made singular and appropriated to him who expresses it: *Deus factus sum*, "I am become a god" [*The Mother-in-Law* 843].

704   Abstract sentences are the work of philosophers, because they contain universals, and reflections on the passions are the work of false and frigid poets.

[*Chapter IV*]   *Corollary on Heroic Descriptions*

705   Finally they reduced the external functions of spirit to the five senses of the body, but senses keen, vivid, and strong, for these men were all robust imagination with very little or no reason [378, 699]. Evidence of this may be found in the terms they used for the senses.

706   Their word for hearing was *audire*, as if *haurire*, for the ears drink in the air which has been set in motion by other bodies. Seeing distinctly was called *cernere oculis* (whence perhaps the Italian *scernere*), for the eyes are like a sieve and the pupils like two holes, and as from the sieve sticks of dust issue to touch the earth, so from the eyes, through the pupils, sticks of light issue to touch the objects which are distinctly seen. (This is the visual [ray or] stick of which the Stoics later treated, and which in our day has been happily demonstrated by Descartes [*Dioptrics* 1.2]). The general expression for seeing was *usurpare oculis*, as if things seen were actually taken possession of by sight. *Tangere*, to touch, meant also to steal, for to touch a body is to take something away from it, as our more intelligent physicists are just beginning to understand. Smelling they called *olfacere*, as if by smelling odors they created them; as indeed later the

natural philosophers, by sober observations, found it to be true that the senses make the qualities that are called sensible. And lastly they called tasting *sapere*, a word which properly applies to the things which have savor, because they assayed things for the savor proper to them. Hence later, by a fine metaphor, they used the term *sapientia*, wisdom, for the faculty of making those uses of things which they have in nature, not those which opinion supposes them to have.

707   Herein is divine providence to be admired, because, having given us the senses for the guarding of our bodies, at a time when men had fallen into the state of brutes (in whom the senses are keener than in men), providence saw to it that by their brutish nature itself they should have the keenest senses for their self-preservation. Later, when they entered the age of reflection, by which they could take counsel for the protection of their bodies, the senses became less sharp. Because of all this, the heroic descriptions, as we have them in Homer, are so luminously and splendidly clear that all later poets have been unable to imitate them, to say nothing of equaling them [827f, 894].

[Chapter V]   Corollary on Heroic Customs

708   By such heroic natures, furnished with such heroic senses, customs of like kind were formed and fixed. Because of their recent gigantic origin, the heroes were in the highest degree gross and wild, such as we have found the Patagonians described [170, 338], very limited in understanding but endowed with the vastest imaginations and the most violent passions. Hence they must have been boorish, crude, harsh, wild, proud, difficult, and obstinate in their resolves, and at the same time easily diverted when confronted with new and contrary objects; even as we daily observe in our stubborn peasants, who yield to every reasonable argument that is put to them, but, because their powers of reflection are weak, as soon as the argument which has moved them has left their minds, return at once to their original purpose. From this same lack of reflective capacity, the heroes were bluff, touchy, magnanimous, and generous, as Homer portrays Achilles, the greatest of all the Greek heroes [667, 786]. It was with such examples of heroic customs in mind that Aristotle made it a precept of the art of poetry that the heroes who are taken as protagonists in tragedies should be neither very good nor very bad but should exhibit a mixture of great vices and great virtues [*Poetics* 15.11.1454b 10ff]. For that

heroism of virtue which realizes its highest idea belongs to philosophy and not to poetry; and gallant heroism is a creation of post-Homeric poets who either made up fables of a new cast or took the old fables, originally grave and severe as becoming the founders of nations, and altered and finally corrupted them to suit the growing effeminacy of later times [81]. We have a great proof of this—and it may well serve as a leading canon of the historical mythology we are discussing—in the example of Achilles. On account of Briseis, taken from him by Agamemnon, he makes such an outcry as to fill heaven and earth and provide matter for the whole *Iliad*, yet nowhere in that entire epic does he give the faintest indication of amorous passion at being deprived of the girl. Similarly Menelaus, though on Helen's account he stirs all Greece to war against Troy, does not show, throughout that whole long and great war, the slightest sign of amorous distress or jealousy of Paris, who has robbed him of her and is enjoying her.

709   All that we have remarked in these three corollaries on heroic sentences, descriptions, and customs, belongs properly to the discovery of the true Homer which we shall take up in the following book [780–914].

[SECTION VIII]

[*Chapter I*]   *Poetic Cosmography*

710   As the theological poets had set up as principles in physics the substances they imagined to be divine [401f], so they described a cosmography in accord with this physics, regarding the world as composed of gods of the sky, of the underworld (called by the Latins respectively *dii superi* and *dii inferi*), and of gods intermediate between earth and sky (who must have been those whom the Latins at first called *medioxumi*).

711   The first object of their contemplation in the world was the sky, and heavenly things must have been for the Greeks the first *mathēmata*, or sublime things, and the first *theōrēmata*, or divine objects of contemplation [391]. The contemplation of such things was so called by the Latins from the *templa coeli*, the "temples" or regions of the sky marked off by the augurs for taking auspices by divining from the paths of falling stars at night; and in the East, according to Bochart, the name of the Zoroastrians means "contemplators of the stars" [62].

712   For the poets the first sky was no higher than the summits of the mountains, where the giants were halted in their feral wanderings by Jove's first thunderbolts. This is the Heaven that reigned on earth and, from this beginning, conferred great benefits on mankind [379]. Hence they must have imagined the sky to be the mountaintops (from whose sharpness the Latins applied the term *coelum* also to the burin, a tool used in stone or metal engraving), just as children imagine that mountains are the columns that hold up the roof of the sky (and these principles of cosmography the Arabs gave to their Koran [41.9ff; 78.6ff]). Two of these columns continued to be called the Pillars of Hercules [726]. The original meaning of *columen*, as applied to them, must have been prop or stay; rounded columns were introduced later by architecture. It was from such a roof on Olympus, as Thetis tells Achilles in Homer [I. 1.423!], that Jove went with the other gods to feast on [Mt.] Atlas. The fable of the Titans warring with the gods and piling up lofty mountains, Ossa on Pelion and Olympus on Ossa, in order to climb up to heaven and cast out the gods, must have been made up after Homer's time [399], for certainly in the *Iliad* he always speaks of

the gods as residing on the summit of Olympus, so that the shaking of Olympus alone would have sufficed to cause their downfall. Nor does this fable really fit in the *Odyssey*, where it is found [11.313ff]. For in that poem the lower world in which Ulysses sees and speaks with the departed heroes is no deeper than a ditch [11.25,36,42,95]; and since the Homer of the *Odyssey* had such a limited notion of the lower world, his idea of heaven must have been equally simple, in conformity with that of the Homer of the *Iliad* [879ff]. Consequently the fable is not Homer's.

713   It was in this heaven that the gods first reigned on earth and had dealings with the heroes, according to the order of the natural theogony above set forth, beginning with Jove [317]. In this heaven justice was dealt out on earth by Astraea, crowned with ears of grain and holding a balance; for the first human justice was administered by the heroes to men in the first agrarian law [597]; and men first became aware of weight, then of measure, and only very slowly of number, in which reason finally came to rest [642]; so that Pythagoras put the essence of the human soul in numbers because he knew of nothing more abstracted from bodies. Through this heaven the heroes go galloping on horseback, like Bellerophon on Pegasus; and *volitare equo*, to fly by horse, was Latin for going about on horseback. It is in this heaven that Juno whitens the Milky Way with milk, not her own, for she was sterile, but with the milk of the mothers of the families, who suckled the legitimate offspring of the heroic nuptials, of which Juno was the divinity [513]. Over this heaven the gods are carried in carts of the poetic gold or grain after which the golden age was named [539, 542ff]. In this heaven wings were used, not for flight nor even to signify quickness of wit, but to signify heroic institutions, which were all based on the law of the auspices [488]. Of this sort are the wings of Hymen (heroic Love) [513], Astraea, the Muses, Pegasus, Saturn, Fame, Mercury (who bears them on his heels and at his temples, and whose caduceus is likewise winged, for with it he brought down from this heaven the first agrarian law to the rebellious plebs in the valleys) [604], and also the dragon (for the Gorgon also has winged temples, and clearly its wings stand neither for wit nor for flight) [616]. It is in this heaven that Prometheus steals fire from the sun [549], the fire that the heroes kindled with flints and set to the thorny underbrush on the mountaintops, dried out by the hot suns of summer; and this is why the torch of Hymen, as we are faithfully told, was made of thorns. From this heaven Vulcan is precipitated by a kick of Jove [579]; from this heaven Phaethon falls headlong in the chariot of the sun; and from this heaven the apple of discord drops. And finally, it is from this heaven that the ancilia, or sacred shields of the Romans, must have fallen.

714 The first of the deities of the lower world imagined by the theological poets was that of water, and the first water was that of the perennial springs, which they called Styx and by which the gods swore [527]; on which account, perhaps, Plato supposed that the abyss of waters was in the center of the earth [*Phaedo* 111C–112E]. Homer, however, in the contest of the gods, makes Pluto fear that Neptune may open the earth with an earthquake and expose the lower world to the eyes of men and gods [I. 20.61ff]. And if we assumed that the abyss was in the deepest entrails of the earth, the earthquakes of Neptune would have quite the contrary effect, for the lower world would be submerged and completely covered with water. This fulfills our promise to show that the allegory of Plato was ill suited to the fable [634]. From what has been said [712], the first lower world must not have been any deeper than the source of the springs. Its first deity was Diana [528], of whom poetic history says that she was a triformed goddess, for in the heavens she was Diana, on earth the huntress Cynthia and companion to her brother Apollo, and in the underworld Proserpine.

715 With the practice of burial the idea of the underworld was extended, and the poets called the grave the underworld [721] (an expression also found in Holy Scripture) [F7]. Thus the lower world was no deeper than a ditch, like that in which Ulysses, according to Homer [712], sees the underworld and the souls of the dead heroes; for in this lower world were placed the Elysian fields, wherein, by virtue of burial, the souls of the dead enjoy eternal peace; and the Elysian fields are the happy dwelling place of the Manes, or benevolent spirits of the dead.

716 Later the underworld had the depth of a furrow. It is to this underworld that Ceres (the same as Proserpine, the seed of the grain [541]) is carried off by the god Pluto, to remain there six months and then return to behold the light of heaven. By this will be explained the golden bough with which Aeneas descends into the lower world [721]; which was Vergil's continuation of the heroic metaphor of the golden apple, which we have found to be the ears of grain [546].

717 Finally the underworld was taken to be the plains and the valleys, as opposed to the lofty heaven set on the mountaintops [377]. In this underworld the scattered vagrants remained in their infamous promiscuity [533]. The god of this underworld is Erebus, called the son of Chaos; that is, of the confusion of human seeds [688]. He is the father of civil night (in which [family] names are obscured), even as the heaven is illuminated by the civil light with which the heroes are resplendent [513, 689]. Through this underworld runs the river Lethe, the stream of oblivion, for these men

left no name of themselves to their posterity, whereas the glory of heaven eternalizes the names of the illustrious heroes [555]. From this underworld Mercury with his rod bearing the agrarian law summons the souls from Orcus, the all-devouring monster [604]. This is the civil history preserved for us by Vergil in the phrase: *hac ille animas evocat Orco* [A. 4.242]. That is, he redeems the lives of bestial and lawless men from the feral state which swallows up all mankind in that they leave nothing of themselves to their posterity. The rod was later used by the mages in the vain belief that it had power to bring back the dead. The Roman praetor struck slaves on the shoulder with his staff in token of their liberation, as if therewith bringing them back from death to life. Sorcerers also used in their witchcraft the rod which the wise mages of Persia had used for the divination of the auspices. Wherefore divinity was attributed to the rod, and it was held by the nations to be divine and capable of performing miracles, as Trogus Pompeius assures us in Justin's abridgment of his work [43.3.3].

718 This is the underworld guarded by Cerberus, the doglike impudence of copulating shamelessly in public. Cerberus is three-throated; that is, he has an enormous gullet (the three is superlative [491]) because, like Orcus, he devours everything [717]; and when he comes up on the earth the sun goes backward (for when he enters the heroic cities the civil light of the heroes turns again to civil night).

719 At the bottom of this underworld flows the river Tartarus, and there the damned are tormented: Ixion forever turns his wheel, Sisyphus rolls his stone, and Tantalus is forever dying of hunger and thirst [583]. And the river that causes the torment of thirst is the same river "without contentment" which is signified by both Acheron and Phlegethon. Into this underworld Tityus and Prometheus were later cast by the ignorance of the mythologers; but actually it was in heaven that they were chained to the crags, to have their entrails devoured by the mountain eagle (the grievous superstition of the auspices [387]).

720 The philosophers later found all these fables convenient for the meditation and exposition of their moral and metaphysical doctrines. Plato was prompted by them to understand the three divine punishments which only the gods can inflict, and not men: namely, oblivion, infamy, and the remorse of a guilty conscience; and to understand that it is by the *via purgativa*, through which one purges the passions of the spirit which torment mankind (so he interprets the lower world of the theological poets), that one enters upon the *via unitiva*, by which the human mind attains union with God by means of contemplation of eternal divine things

(which he takes the theological poets to have meant by their Elysian fields).*

721 But the theological poets had spoken of the lower world with political ideas, as it was naturally necessary for them to do as founders of nations, and all the gentile founders of peoples descended into the lower world with ideas quite different from these moral and metaphysical ones [720]. Orpheus, who founded the Greek nation [523], made the descent; and, disobeying the injunction not to look back on leaving, he lost his wife, Eurydice (signifying his return to the infamous promiscuity of women). Hercules (and every nation tells of one as its founder [196]) also descended for the purpose of liberating Theseus, the founder of Athens, who had descended to fetch Proserpine (that is, since she is the same as Ceres [716], to bring back the sown seed in the form of ripened grain). But later Vergil, with his profound knowledge of heroic antiquities (singing of the political hero in the first six books of his *Aeneid* and of the military hero in the last six), gives us an account of the descent of Aeneas more detailed than any of the others. Aeneas has the advice and safe-conduct of the Cumean Sybil (that is, since every gentile nation had a sybil and twelve have come down to us by name [381], his descent was made by divination, which was the vulgar wisdom of the gentiles). With the piety of a bloody religion (the piety professed by the ancient heroes in the fierceness and ruthlessness of their recent bestial origin [516ff]) he sacrificed his *socius* Misenus (by the cruel right which the heroes had over their first *socii* [558]). He then enters the ancient forest (such as covered the land everywhere while it was yet uncultivated), throws the soporific sop to Cerberus and puts him to sleep (just as Orpheus had overcome him with the sound of his lyre, which we have previously seen by abundant evidence to signify law [523, 615]; and just as Hercules had tied him up with the knot with which he had bound Antaeus in Greece [618], that is with the first agrarian law [604]). (Because of his insatiable hunger, Cerberus was imagined as three-throated, that is, as having an enormous gullet, the three standing for the superlative [718].) Thus Aeneas descends into the underworld (at first no deeper than a furrow [716]), comes before Dis (the god of heroic riches, poetic gold or grain, being identical with Pluto the abductor of Proserpine or Ceres, the goddess of grain), and presents the golden bough [A. 6.635f]. (Here the great poet takes the metaphor of the golden apple, signifying the ears of

---

Plato is one of Vico's "four authors" (654), but the *Divine Comedy* comes between him and the myths of the *Phaedo* (108ff), *Gorgias* (523ff), and *Republic* (614ff) in a way that J. A. Stewart helps us see in his *Myths of Plato*, 1905, 101–113.

grain, and extends it to the golden bough, signifying the harvest.) When the golden bough is torn from its trunk another grows in its place [A. 6.143f] (because there can be no second harvest until a year after the first has been gathered). And when the gods are well disposed, the bough readily and easily comes off in the hand of him who seizes it, but otherwise no strength in the world is sufficient to pluck it [A. 6.146ff]. (For the grain grows up naturally where God wills it, but where he does not will it no human industry can hope to make it grow.) Aeneas then proceeds through the underworld to the Elysian fields [A. 6.637ff] (for the heroes, having settled in the cultivated fields, enjoyed eternal peace in death if they had proper burial [529]). Here he beholds his ancestors and those who are to come after him (for on the religion of the graves, called the underworld by the poets [715], were founded the first genealogies, from which history took its beginning [533]).

722   The earth was associated by the theological poets with the guarding of the boundaries, and hence it was called *terra*. This heroic origin the Latins preserved in the word *territorium*, which signifies the district within which the *imperium* is exercised. The Latin grammarians erroneously derived *territorium* from the terror of the fasces used by the lictors to disperse the crowds and make way for the Roman magistrates. But at the time when the word *territorium* was born there were no great crowds in Rome, for, according to Varro [i.e., Augustine], in two hundred and fifty years of rule she had subdued more than twenty peoples without extending her *imperium* more than twenty miles [88]. Instead the word originated in the fact that the boundaries of the cultivated fields, within which the civil powers later arose, were guarded by Vesta with bloody rites. The Latin Vesta was the same as the Greek Cybele or Berecynthia, who wears a crown of towers; that is, of strongly situated lands. From this crown the so-called *orbis terrarum* began to take form, signifying the world of the nations, later amplified by the cosmographers and called *orbis mundanus* or, in a word, *mundus*, the world of nature [549, 690].

723   The poetic world was divided into three kingdoms or regions: that of Jove in heaven, that of Saturn on earth, and the underworld kingdom of Pluto, called Dis, god of heroic riches, the first gold or grain, since tilled fields make the true wealth of peoples.

724   Thus the world of the theological poets was formed of four civil elements, later taken by the physicists as natural elements: namely, the element of Jove, the air; that of Vulcan, fire; that of Cybele, earth; and that of the underworld Diana, water [690]. For Neptune was late in coming into the acquaintance of the poets, because the nations were slow

in coming down to the seacoasts [634]. Any sea extending beyond the horizon was called Ocean, and any land it surrounded an island, as Homer [O. 10.1ff] speaks of the island of Aeolia as surrounded by the Ocean [753]. From such an Ocean must have come the horses of Rhesus, which were made pregnant by Zephyr, the west wind of Greece [742]; and on the shores of the same Ocean the horse of Achilles, also begotten by Zephyr, must have been born. Later the geographers, observing that the whole earth, like a great island, was girt by the sea, called Ocean all the waters by which the land is surrounded [753].

725   Finally, beginning with the idea by which every slight slope was called *mundus* (whence the phrases *in mundo est, in proclivi est*, for "it is easy"; and later everything for the embellishment of a woman came to be called *mundus muliebris*), when they came to understand that the earth and the sky were spherical in form, and that from every point of the circumference there is a slope toward every other, and that the ocean bathes the land on every shore, and that the whole of things is adorned with countless varied and diverse sensible forms, the poets called this universe *mundus* as being that with which, by a beautifully sublime metaphor, nature adorns herself [B5].

[SECTION IX]

[POETIC ASTRONOMY]

[Chapter I]   Poetic Astronomy

726   This world system, somewhat further developed, lasted down to the time of Homer, who always speaks of the gods as settled on Mt. Olympus. We have noted that he has Thetis, the mother of Achilles, tell him that the gods had gone from Olympus to feast on [Mt.] Atlas [712]. So that in Homer's time the highest mountains on the earth were evidently regarded as pillars sustaining the heavens [O. 1.52ff], even as Abyla and Calpe on the Straits of Gibraltar continued to be called the Pillars of Hercules because the hero had taken up the burden of Atlas, who had grown tired of supporting the heavens on his shoulders.

[Chapter II]   Astronomical and Physico-philological Demonstration of the Uniformity of the Principles [of Astronomy] among All Ancient Gentile Nations

727   But as the indefinite force of human minds went on developing, and as contemplation of the heavens to take the auspices obliged the peoples to observe the heavens continually, in the minds of the nations the heavens rose ever higher, and with them rose likewise the gods and the heroes. And here for the ascertainment of poetic astronomy it may help us to make use of three items of philological erudition. The first states that astronomy was brought into the world by the Chaldean people; the second, that the Phoenicians carried from the Chaldeans to the Egyptians the use of the quadrant and the knowledge of the elevation of the polestar; and the third, that the Phoenicians, who must have been instructed by the Chaldeans, brought astral theology to the Greeks. To these three bits of philological erudition we may add these two philosophical truths: first, the

civil truth that nations, if not emancipated in the extreme of religious liberty (which only comes in the final stages of decadence), are naturally wary of accepting foreign deities; and second, the physical truth that, by an ocular illusion, the planets seem to us larger than the fixed stars.

728 Having premised these principles, we may now say that among all the gentile nations of the East, of Egypt, and of Greece (and of Latium too, as we shall see), astronomy sprang from uniform vulgar origins, for by a uniform allocation the gods were raised to the planets and the heroes were assigned to the constellations, because the planets appear much larger than the fixed stars. Hence the Phoenicians found among the Greeks that the gods were already prepared to revolve with the planets and the heroes to compose the constellations, even as later the Greeks found the same to be true among the Latins. And from these examples it is safe to say that the Phoenicians found the same readiness among the Egyptians as among the Greeks. In this way the heroes and the hieroglyphs signifying their institutions or their coats of arms, and a goodly number of the major gods, were raised to the heavens and put in readiness for learned astronomy to give to the hitherto nameless heavenly bodies—to their matter, as it were—the form of stars or constellations on the one hand, and of wandering planets on the other.

729 Thus, beginning with vulgar astronomy, the first peoples wrote in the skies the history of their gods and their heroes. Thence there remained this eternal property, that the memories of men full of divinity or of heroism are matter worthy of history, in the one case because of works of genius and of esoteric wisdom, in the other because of works of valor and of vulgar wisdom. And poetic history gave the learned astronomers occasions for depicting the heroes and the heroic hieroglyphs in the sky with one group of stars rather than another, and in one part of the sky rather than another, and for severally placing in one planet rather than another the major gods by whose names the planets have since been called.

730 To speak somewhat more at length of the planets than of the constellations: Certainly Diana, goddess of the chastity preserved in nuptial relations, who lies all quiet in the night with the sleeping Endymion, was attached to the moon, the giver of nocturnal light [528]. Venus, goddess of civil beauty, was attached to the gayest and the brightest of all the planets [565]. Mercury, the divine herald, clothed in civil light, with all the wings (aristocratic hieroglyphs [488]) with which he is adorned (as he bears the agrarian law to the mutinous clients), is lodged in a planet which is so obscured by the rays of the sun as to be rarely visible [604]. Apollo, god of that same civil light (which gave the epithet *incliti* to the heroes),

is placed in the sun, the source of natural light [533]. Bloody Mars dwells in a star of like hue [562]. Jove, king and father of men and gods [379], is placed above all the rest, but beneath Saturn [549], who, since he is the father both of Jove and of Time, has a longer annual course than all the other planets. His wings ill become him if, by a forced allegory, they are taken to mean the swiftness of time, for he runs his year more slowly than any other planet; but he took them to heaven along with his scythe, the latter signifying the reaping not of men's lives but of grain, by the harvests of which the heroes counted the years [407, 431], and the wings signifying that the cultivated fields were the property of the heroes. Finally the planets or wanderers, with the chariots of gold (that is, of grain) with which they went about in heaven when it was on earth [713], now revolve in their appointed orbits.

731   In view of all that has been set forth, it must be affirmed that the predominating influences which the stars and planets are supposed to have over sublunar bodies, have been attributed to them from those which the gods and heroes exercised when they were on earth. So little do they depend on natural causes!

[SECTION X]

[POETIC CHRONOLOGY]

[Chapter I] Poetic Chronology

732   The theological poets gave beginnings to chronology in conformity with their astronomy. For that same Saturn, who was so called by the Latins from *sati*, sown [fields], and who was called Chronos, or Time, by the Greeks, gives us to understand that the first nations (all composed of farmers) began to count their years by their harvests of grain (the sole or at least the chief thing for which the peasants labored all year). And since they were at first mute, they must have held as many ears or straws and made as many reaping motions as the number of years they meant to signify [431]. Thus in Vergil (as learned as ever man was in heroic antiquities) we find two expressions [407]; the first infelicitous and, by supreme imitative art, infelicitously contorted, to express the infelicity of the first ages in expressing themselves: *Post aliquot mea regna videns mirabor aristas*, meaning simply *post aliquot annos*. The second has somewhat more clarity: *Tertia messis erat*. And indeed even nowadays the peasants of Tuscany, the nation most highly regarded for its speech in all Italy, instead of saying "three years," for example, say "we have harvested three times." The Romans preserved this heroic history of the poetic year signified by the harvests, in using the name *annona* for the management of the stores, particularly of grain.

733   Accordingly Hercules has come down to us as the founder of the Olympiads, the celebrated time divisions of the Greeks (from whom we get all we know of gentile antiquities), for it was he who set fire to the forests in order to prepare for sowing the lands whereon were gathered the harvests by which the years were reckoned. The games must have been instituted by the Nemeans in celebration of the hero's victory over the Nemean fire-breathing lion, which we have interpreted above as the great forest of the earth, to which, apprehended under the idea of a very powerful animal, they gave the name lion, because so much labor was

required to tame it. Later the name was applied to the most powerful of animals [540], and the astronomers assigned to the Lion a house in the zodiac, next to that of Astraea, crowned with ears of grain. This is why in the circuses images of lions were often shown, and images of the sun; it is also the reason for the *metae* with eggs on top, which must originally have been *metae* of grain and the clearings, or deforested eyes of the giants [564]. The astronomers later took the egg as signifying the ellipse described by the sun in its annual path through the ecliptic; a meaning that Manetho might more fittingly have given to the egg which Knef holds in his mouth, instead of interpreting it as signifying the generation of the universe [605].

734   The natural theogony above set forth [317] enables us to determine the successive epochs of the age of the gods, which correspond to certain first necessities or utilities of the human race, which everywhere had its beginnings in religion. The age of the gods must have lasted at least nine hundred years from the appearance of the various Joves among the gentile nations, which is to say from the time when the heavens began to thunder after the universal flood. And the twelve major gods, beginning with Jove, successively imagined within this age, serve to divide it into twelve smaller epochs and thus give some certainty to the chronology of poetic history [392]. By way of example, Deucalion, whom fabulous history places immediately after the flood and the giants, and who with his wife, Pyrrha, founds the families by means of matrimony, is born of Greek imaginations in the epoch of Juno, goddess of solemn nuptials [511ff]. Hellen, who founds the Greek language and, through his three sons, divides it into three dialects, is born in the epoch of Apollo [533ff], god of song, in whose time poetic speech in verse must have begun [456ff]. Hercules, who performs the great labor of slaying the Hydra or the Nemean lion (reducing the land to fields for sowing), and who brings back from Hesperia the golden apples (that is, the harvests, an enterprise worthy of history; not pomegranates, an errand for a parasite), distinguished himself in the epoch of Saturn, god of the sown fields [540, 549]. Likewise Perseus [423] must have achieved his fame in the epoch of Minerva [589] when the civil powers were already in existence, since his shield bears the head of Medusa, as does that of Minerva. And finally, Orpheus must have been born after the epoch of Mercury [604], for by singing to the Greek beasts the force of the gods in the auspices, the science of which belonged to the heroes, he re-established the heroic nations of Greece and gave the heroic age its name, for in that age these heroic contests took place. Hence at the same time with Orpheus there flourish such other heroic poets as Linus, Amphion, and Musaeus. Amphion uses stones (in the sense in

which the Latin word for stone, *lapis*, meant a lout, and signifying therefore the simple-minded plebeians) to erect the walls of Thebes three
hundred years after its founding by Cadmus; exactly as, three hundred
years after the founding of Rome, Appius, the grandson of the decemvir,
by singing to the Roman plebs which *agitabat connubia more ferarum*
(practiced marriages like those of the beasts of Orpheus) of the force of
the gods in the auspices (the science of which belonged to the nobles),
reduces them to obedience and establishes the heroic Roman state [K7,
661].

735 We must here take note of four kinds of anachronisms coming
under the familiar general head of placing times too early or too late. The
first is that of times empty of facts which must really have been full of
them. Thus the age of the gods, in which we have found almost all the
origins of civil human institutions, passes with the learned Varro for the
dark time [52]. The second is that of times full of facts which must have
been empty of them. Thus, under the false belief that the fables were
invented by the heroic poets, especially by Homer, the age of the heroes,
which runs for two hundred years, is filled with all the facts belonging to
the age of the gods, and these facts should be put back into the age to
which they belong. The third is that of uniting times which should be
divided, lest, for example, Greece should seem to have passed from a state
of wild beasts to the splendor of the Trojan War within the single life span
of Orpheus. (This is the chronological monstrosity to which we called
attention in our Notes to the Chronological Table [79].) The fourth and
last is that of dividing times which should be united. By such an anachronism the Greek colonies are brought into Sicily and Italy more than three
hundred years after the wanderings of the heroes, whereas they were
brought there in the course and as the result of the wanderings of these
same heroes.

[Chapter II] *Chronological Canon for Determining the Beginnings
of Universal History, Which Must Precede the Monarchy of Ninus,
with Which It [Commonly] Starts*

736 In virtue of the aforesaid natural theogony which has given us
our rational poetic chronology, and taking into consideration the kinds of
anachronisms noted in poetic history [734f], now, in order to determine the
beginnings of universal history, which must precede the monarchy of

Ninus with which it [commonly] starts, we set up this chronological canon: that from the dispersion of fallen mankind through the great forest of the earth, beginning in Mesopotamia (according to our reasonable postulate in the Axioms [298, 301]), a span of only a hundred years of feral wandering was consumed by the impious [part of the] race of Shem in East Asia, and one of two hundred years by the other two races of Ham and Japheth in the rest of the world. At the end of that time, under the religion of Jove (and the many Joves scattered through the first gentile nations gave us evidence above that the flood was universal [193f]), the princes of the nations began to settle down, each in the land where fortune had placed him. Then ensued the nine hundred years of the age of the gods. Towards the end of that age the nations (which had all been founded inland because they had been dispersed through the world in search of food and [fresh] water, which are not found on the seaboard) must have come down to the coasts. Hence there arose in the minds of the Greeks the idea of Neptune, the last of the twelve major divinities [634]. In like fashion, among the Latins, nine hundred years elapsed between the age of Saturn, the golden age of Latium, and the descent of Ancus Marcius to the coast to take Ostia. After this came the two hundred years which the Greeks assign to the heroic age, beginning with the corsair raids of King Minos, continuing with Jason's naval expedition to Pontus and later with the Trojan war, and ending with the wanderings of the heroes and the return of Ulysses to Ithaca. Thus Tyre, capital of Phoenica, must have been brought from inland to the shore, and thence to an island nearby in the Phoenician sea, more than a thousand years after the flood. And inasmuch as before the Greek heroic age Tyre was already a famous city both for navigation and for its colonies scattered through the Mediterranean and even on the Ocean, it is clearly proved that the beginning of the entire human race was in the East, and that first the feral wanderings through the inland parts of the world, then the heroic law by land and sea, and finally the maritime traffic of the Phoenicians scattered the first nations through the remaining parts of the world. These principles of the migration of the peoples (as we set forth in an axiom [299]) seem more reasonable than those imagined by Wolfgang Latius.

737 Now, in virtue of the uniform course run by all the nations, which has been proved above by the uniformity of the gods raised to the stars [728], as brought by the Phoenicians to Egypt and Greece from the East, we must infer that the reign of the Chaldeans in the East covered a like period of time [1100 years], from Zoroaster to Ninus, who founded there the first monarchy in the world, that of Assyria; and correspondingly

[in Egypt] from Thrice-great Hermes to Sesostris, the Ramses of Tacitus [85], who also founded there a great monarchy. And since these were both inland nations, they must have passed through the successive stages of divine and heroic regimes and then of popular liberty in order to reach that of monarchy, which is the last form of human government, if the Egyptian division of the three times of the world that had elapsed before them is to stand [52]. For, as we shall show later [925ff, 1007f], monarchy cannot arise save as a result of the unchecked liberty of the peoples, to which the optimates subject their power in the course of civil wars. When power is thus divided into minimal parts among the peoples, the whole of it is easily taken over by those who, coming forward as partisans of popular liberty, emerge finally as monarchs. Phoenicia, however, as a maritime nation enriched by its commerce, remained in the stage of popular liberty, which is the first form of human government.

738 Thus purely by understanding, without benefit of memory, which has nothing to go on where facts are not supplied by the senses, we seem to have filled in the beginnings of universal history both in ancient Egypt and in the East, which is more ancient than Egypt [54–58; cf. 44–53]; and further, within the East, the beginnings of the Assyrian monarchy. For hitherto this monarchy, for lack of its many and varied antecedent causes, which must have been previously at work in order to produce a monarchy, which is the last of the three forms of civil government, has appeared in history as a sudden birth, as a frog is born of a summer shower.

739 In this way chronology has certainty lent to its successive periods by the progress of customs and deeds through which the human race must have marched. For, by an axiom above stated [314], chronology has here begun her doctrine where her subject matter began: that is, with Chronos or Saturn (after whom time was called *chronos* among the Greeks), the reckoner of the years by the harvests [73]; with Urania, watcher of the skies for the purpose of taking the auspices [391]; and with Zoroaster, contemplator of the stars in order to give his oracles from the paths of falling stars [62]. (For such were the first *mathēmata* and the first *theōrēmata*, the first sublime or divine things contemplated and observed by the nations [711].) Later, when Saturn ascended to the seventh sphere [730], Urania became the contemplator of the stars and planets, and the Chaldeans, with the advantage of their immense open plains, became astronomers and astrologers, measuring the movements and observing the aspects of the heavenly bodies and imagining their influences on so-called sublunar bodies, and even, though vainly, on the free wills of men. This science preserved the first names that had been given to it in full propriety: astronomy, the

science of the laws of the stars, and astrology, the science of the speech of the stars. Both names signified divination, even as from the aforesaid theorems came the term theology for the science of the language of the gods in their oracles, auspices, and auguries [379]. Thence finally mathematics descended to measure the earth, the measurements of which could not be ascertained save by the already demonstrated measurements of the heavens; and the first and principal part of mathematics bears witness to this origin in the proper name geometry by which it is called.

740   Those two marvelous geniuses, Joseph Justus Scaliger and Denis Petau, with their stupendous erudition, the former in his *De emendatione temporum* and the latter in his *De doctrina temporum*, failed to begin their doctrine at the beginning of their subject matter. For they began with the astronomical year, which, as noted above, was unheard of among the nations for a thousand years, and in any case could have assured them only of conjunctions and oppositions of constellations and planets in the heavens, and not of any of the things that had happened here on earth nor of their sequence (on which the noble efforts of Cardinal Pierre d'Ailly had been expended in vain [169]). And on this account their work has shed little light on the beginnings or on the continuation of universal history.

[SECTION XI]

[POETIC GEOGRAPHY]

[Chapter I] *Poetic Geography*

741 It remains for us now to cleanse the other eye of poetic history, namely poetic geography. By the property of human nature that "in describing unknown or distant things, in respect of which they either have not had the true idea themselves or wish to explain it to others who do not have it, men make use of the semblances of things known or near at hand" [122], poetic geography, in all its parts and as a whole, began with restricted ideas within the confines of Greece. Then, as the Greeks went abroad into the world, it was gradually amplified until it reached the form in which it has come down to us. The ancient geographers agree on this truth although they were unable to avail themselves of it, for they affirm that the ancient nations, emigrating to strange and distant lands, gave their own native names to the [new-found] cities, mountains, rivers, hills, straits, isles, and promontories.

742 Within Greece itself, accordingly, lay the original East called Asia or India, the West called Europe or Hesperia, the North called Thrace or Scythia, and the South called Libya or Mauretania. And these names for the regions of the little world of Greece were [later] applied to those of the world [at large] in virtue of the correspondence which the Greeks observed between the two. We have clear proof of this in the cardinal winds, which retain in their geography the names which they must certainly have first had within Greece itself. Thus the mares of Rhesus on the shores of the Ocean (a name, as we shall see in a moment, applied to any sea of unobstructed horizon) must have been impregnated by Zephyr, the west wind of Greece [724]; and likewise on the shores of the Ocean (in the primary sense just noted) the horses of Achilles must have been generated by Zephyr, even as the mares of Erichthonius—as Aeneas tells Achilles [I. 20.221ff]—must have been impregnated by Boreas, the north wind of Greece. This truth concerning the cardinal winds is confirmed by the immense projection to which the Greek mind extended itself in taking from the mountain on which the Homeric gods dwelt and applying to the starry heaven the name Olympus, by which it continued to be known.

743   On these principles, the great peninsula to the east of Greece came to be called Asia Minor when the name Asia was extended to that great eastern part of the world which has continued to be called Asia without qualification. On the other hand, Greece itself, which was to the west of Asia, was called Europe, the Europe which Jove, in the form of a bull, abducted. Later the name was extended to embrace this other great continent as far as the western ocean. They gave the name Hesperia to the western part of Greece, where the evening star Hesperus comes out in the fourth quarter of the horizon. Later they saw Italy in the same quarter much larger than the Hesperia of Greece, and they called it Hesperia Magna. And finally when they reached Spain in the same direction, they called it Hesperia Ultima. Conversely the Greeks of Italy must have called by the name Ionia that part of Greece lying across the sea to the east of them; hence the name Ionian for the sea between the two Greeces [Greece proper and Magna Graecia, the Greek part of southern Italy]. Later, because of the similarity of position of Greece proper and Asiatic Greece, the inhabitants of Greece proper took to calling by the name Ionia the part of Asia Minor to the east of them. It seems reasonable that out of the first Ionia Pythagoras must have come to Italy from Samos [or Cephallenia], one of the islands ruled by Ulysses, and not from the Samos of the second Ionia.

744   From the Thrace within Greece must have come Mars, who was certainly a Greek divinity; and thence too must have come Orpheus, one of the first Greek theological poets.

745   From the Scythia within Greece came Anacharsis, who left the Scythian oracles in Greece [100, 128]. These must have been similar to the oracles of Zoroaster [59] (which must originally have been an oracular history). Anacharsis has been received among the most ancient oracular gods. By imposture, these oracles were later translated into dogmas of philosophy. Similarly the *Orphica* were supposed to be verses of Orpheus, though, like the oracles of Zoroaster, they have no poetic flavor and give forth too distinct an odor of the Platonic and Pythagorean school. So too from this Scythia [within Greece], by way of the original Hyperboreans, the two famous oracles of Delphi and Dodona must have come into Greece, as we suspected in the Notes on the Chronological Table [100]. For in Scythia, that is among these Hyperboreans of Greece proper, Anacharsis, attempting to order humanity by Greek laws, was slain by

Caduidas his brother. So little did he profit by the barbarous philosophy of [which] van Heurn [speaks] that he could not devise such laws for them himself! By the same reasoning, Abaris must have been a Scythian too, for he is said to have written the Scythian oracles, which must have been no other than those of Anacharsis just mentioned. And he wrote them in that Scythia in which Idanthyrsus long afterwards wrote with those physical objects [99]. Whence we must conclude that they were written by an impostor sometime after the introduction of the Greek philosophies. Hence the oracles of Anacharsis were accepted by the conceit of the scholars as oracles of estoteric wisdom, which have not come down to us.

746 Salmoxis, who, according to Herodotus [4.93ff], brought to the Greeks the dogma of the immortality of the soul, was a Getan in the same sense in which Mars was.

747 It was likewise from a Greek India that Bacchus must have come in triumph from the Indian East (that is, from a Greek land rich in poetic gold). He rides triumphant in a golden chariot (a cart of grain [651, 713]). Hence he is also a tamer of serpents and tigers, as Hercules is of hydras and lions [508, 540].

748 Certainly the name Morea, preserved by the Peloponnesus down to our days, is ample proof that Perseus [423], certainly a Greek hero, carried out his enterprises in the Mauretania within Greece; for the Peloponnesus is in the same [geographical] relation to Achaea as Africa is to Europe. Here can be seen how little Herodotus understood of his own antiquities (on which account indeed Thucydides reproves him [101]); for he relates[!] that the Moors were at one time white, as were certainly the Moors of his own Greece, which to this day is called White Morea.

749 It must likewise have been from the pestilence of this Mauretania that Aesculapius saved his island of Cos by his art; for if he had had to save it from the pestilence of the people of Morocco he would have had to save it from all the pestilences in the world.

750 It was in this Mauretania that Hercules must have taken on his shoulders the burden of the sky that old Atlas was tired of bearing [726]; for the name [Atlas] must originally have been used for Mt. Athos, which, on a neck of land later cut through by Xerxes, divides Macedonia from Thrace; and here, as a matter of fact, between Greece and Thrace, there was also a river called Atlas. Later, at the straits of Gibraltar, when it was observed that Mts. Abyla and Calpe on the narrows of the sea similarly separate Africa from Europe, it was said that there Hercules had fixed the columns which support the heavens, and the name Atlas was applied to the nearby mountain in Africa. And in this way we can find some plausibility

in the answer that Thetis gives her son Achilles in Homer: that she cannot carry his complaint to Jove because he and the other gods have gone from Olympus to feast on Atlas (based on the opinion to which we have before alluded that the gods dwelt on the tops of the highest mountains) [712]; for if this reply had referred to Mt. Atlas in Africa it would have been beyond belief, in view of the fact that Homer himself tells us that Mercury, even with wings, found the greatest difficulty in reaching the isle of Calypso in the Phoenician sea, much nearer to Greece than the kingdom we now call Morocco.

751   It was likewise from the Greek Hesperia that Hercules must have brought the golden apples to Attica [734]; and there too dwelt the Hesperides (the daughters of Atlas) who guarded them.

752   In like manner the Eridanus, into which Phaethon fell [651], must have been the Danube in Greek Thrace, which flows into the Euxine. Later, when the Greeks observed that the Po is the other river in the world which flows from west to east like the Danube, they called it the Eridanus, and the mythologists thus had it that Phaethon fell in Italy. But it was only the tales of their own heroic history, not that of other nations, which the Greeks attached to the stars, among which is Eridanus.

753   Finally, when the Greeks reached the Ocean, they expanded the narrow idea of any sea with an unobstructed prospect (in virtue of which Homer said the isle of Aeolia was girt by the Ocean), and along with the idea the name Ocean was also extended to signify the sea that girds the whole earth, which was conceived as a great island [724]. The power of Neptune was thus immensely enlarged, so that from the abyss of the waters, which Plato placed in the very bowels of the earth, he could shake it with his great trident [634]. The crude principles of this physics have been explained above.

754   By these principles of geography Homer can be completely acquitted of the very grave errors which have been wrongfully imputed to him.

755   I. The Lotus Eaters of Homer [O. 9.80ff; 23.311], who ate the bark of a plant called lotus, must have been nearer [than in the usual view]. For he says that it was a nine days' journey for Ulysses from Cape Malea to the Lotus Eaters; and if the latter, as has been held, had dwelt beyond the straits of Gibraltar, it would have been not merely difficult but impossible to believe that the journey was made in nine days. This error is charged against Homer by Eratosthenes. [Cf. Pliny, Natural History 5.7.41.]

756   II. The Laestrygons in Homer's time must have been a people of Greece, and when he says that they have the longest days [O. 10.80ff] he

must mean the longest in Greece and not in the whole world. This passage led [Crates in a scholium on line 62 of] Aratus to locate them under the head of Draco. Certainly Thucydides [6.2.1], a serious and precise writer, speaks of the Laestrygons in Sicily, who must have been the most northerly people of that island.

757 III. By the same reasoning, the Cimmerians had the longest nights of any people [not of the whole world but only] of Greece, because they were situated in its most northerly part. Because of their long nights they were said to dwell near the infernal regions. (Their name was later transferred to the remote inhabitants about the Sea of Azov.) Hence the people of Cumae, since they had their dwelling near the grotto of the Sybil which led to the infernal regions, must have been called Cimmerians because of the supposed similarity of location. For it is not to be believed that Ulysses, sent forth by Circe without any incantation (inasmuch as Mercury had given him a charm against her spells [437]), in one day could have traveled to the latter-day [and remote] Cimmerians [of the Sea of Azov] to visit the lower regions [O. 11.1–22], and on the same day have made his return to Circeii, now Mt. Circello, not far from Cumae.

758 On these principles of poetic Greek geography it is possible to solve many great difficulties in the ancient history of the East, arising from the fact that many peoples who must have been situated in the [Near] East itself have been taken for very distant peoples, particularly toward the north and south.

759 What we have noted of Greek poetic geography is also found to be true of the ancient geography of the Latins. Latium must at first have been a very small country inasmuch as in two hundred and fifty years under the kings Rome subdued a good twenty peoples and yet did not extend her rule more than twenty miles [88]. Italy was certainly bounded by Cisalpine Gaul and Magna Graecia. Roman conquests later extended the name to its present scope. Similarly the Etruscan [or Tyrrhenian] Sea must have been quite small at the time when Horatius Cocles alone withstood all Etruria on the bridge. Roman victories later extended it to include [the waters bathing] all the lower coast of Italy.

760 In precisely the same way the original Pontus, to which Jason made his naval expedition, must have been the land nearest Europe, from which it is divided by the strait called Propontis. This land must have given its name to the sea of Pontus. Thence the name was extended to its farthest shores in Asia, where the kingdom of Mithridates later stood. This same fable [of the Argonauts] tells us that Aeëtes, father of Medea, was born in Chalcis, a city of Euboea, an island within Greece now called

Negropont, which must have given its first name to what is certainly still called the Black Sea. The original Crete must have been an island within the [Greek] archipelago, which contains the labyrinth of islands [the Cyclades] from which Minos must have made his raids on the Athenians [635]. Only later did Crete move out into the Mediterranean, where it still remains.

761   Now, since we have returned from the Latins to the Greeks, we may note that the latter, as they went out over the world, spread everywhere (vainglorious men as they were!) the fame of the Trojan War and the wanderings of the heroes, both those of the Trojans such as Antenor, Capys, and Aeneas, and those of the Greeks such as Menelaus, Diomed, and Ulysses. They observed scattered through the world a type of nation founder like their Theban Hercules, and so they spread abroad the name of their Hercules, so that Varro was able to enumerate a good forty Herculeses among the ancient nations, and affirmed that the Latin Hercules had been called the god Fidius [14, 658]. Thus it came about that, with a vainglory equaling that of the Egyptians (who, erroneously believing themselves to be the oldest nation in the world, said that their Jove, Ammon, was the most ancient Jove in the world and that all the Herculeses of the other nations had taken their name from the Egyptian Hercules), the Greeks had their Hercules wander through all the parts of the earth, freeing it of monsters, to bring home nothing but the glory.

762   They observed everywhere that there had been a poetic character of shepherds speaking in verse, such as their own Arcadian Evander; and so Evander came from Arcadia to Latium, and there gave shelter to his compatriot Hercules, and took to wife Carmenta, so called from *carmina*, verses. She was the Latin inventress of letters; that is, of the forms of the so-called articulated sounds which are the matter of verses. And finally, in confirmation of all we have been saying, the Greeks observed these poetic characters within Latium at the same time that they found their Curetes scattered through Saturnia (ancient Italy), Crete, and Asia [593f].

763   But these Greek words and ideas came to the Latins in extremely barbarous times in which the nations were closed to strangers. Livy denies that even the famous name of Pythagoras, to say nothing of the man himself, could have reached Rome from Croton in the days of Servius Tullius through the many nations on the way, with their diverse languages and customs [93]. To meet this very difficulty we have postulated, as a necessary conjecture, that there had been on the shore of Latium a Greek city, later shrouded in the mists of antiquity, which had taught the Latins their letters [306, 770]. These, as Tacitus relates, were at first like the

earliest Greek ones [440ff], which argues strongly that the Latins received their letters from the Greeks of Latium and not from those of Magna Graecia and much less from those of Greece proper, with whom they had no acquaintance before the war with Tarentum which led into that with Pyrrhus. For otherwise the Latins would have used the latest Greek letters and would not have retained their original letters, which were the ancient Greek ones.

764 Thus the names of Hercules, Evander, and Aeneas came into Latium from Greece in virtue of the following customs of nations:

765 (1) Just as in their barbarism they are enamored of their native customs, so when they begin to become civilized they take pleasure in foreign tongues as well as in foreign wares and fashions. Hence the Latins exchanged their god Fidius for the Greek Hercules, and in place of the native oath *medius fidius* they introduced *mehercule, edepol, mecastor* [602].

766 (2) In virtue of the conceit of nations [125] which makes them boast illustrious foreign origins, particularly when the traditions of their own barbarous times supply some motive for believing in them, the Latins were pleased to disavow Fidius, their true founder, in favor of Hercules, the true founder of the Greeks, and likewise to exchange the character of their own shepherd poets for Evander of Arcadia. (Similarly, in the returned barbarism, Giovanni Villani [*Chronicle* 1.7,18] relates that Fiesole had been founded by Atlas and that a Trojan king, Priam, had reigned in Germany.)

767 (3) When nations observe foreign things which they cannot explain with certainty in their native vocabulary, they must of necessity make use of foreign terms.

768 (4) Lastly, there is the property of the earliest peoples by which they are incapable of abstracting qualities from subjects and therefore can only designate the qualities by naming the subjects to which they belong [410]. We have clear cases of this in Latin.

769 As the Romans did not know what luxury was until they observed it in the Tarentines, they called a perfumed man a Tarentine. As they did not know what military stratagems were until they observed them in the Carthaginians, they called them *punicas artes*, Carthaginian arts. As they did not know what pomp was until they observed it in the Capuans, they used the phrase *supercilium campanicum* for pomp and pride. In like fashion, Numa and Ancus were called Sabine because the Romans could not otherwise express a religiousness such as that for which the Sabines were distinguished. Servius Tullius was called Greek because they had no

word for astuteness, an idea which must have remained unexpressed until they came to know Greeks of the conquered city of which we were just speaking [763]; and he was also called a slave because they could not otherwise express his weakness in yielding bonitary ownership of the fields to the plebeians by bringing them the first agrarian law [107], on which account, perhaps, the fathers had him slain. For astuteness is a property which goes with weakness, and both alike were foreign to Roman straight-forwardness and valor. For those who affirm that Rome did not have within herself heroes worthy of kingship, so that she had to submit to the rule of a lowborn slave, do a great injustice to the origins of Rome and offend overmuch the wisdom of Romulus, her founder. Such is the honor done him by the critics who have occupied themselves with the writers [143, 348, 392]. It is of a piece with the later tribute to the effect that the Romans, having founded a powerful empire in Latium and maintained it against all the power of Etruria, had to seek, like lawless barbarians, through Italy, Magna Graecia, and Greece proper for laws to order their liberty: all to sustain the credit of the fable that the Law of the Twelve Tables came to Rome from Athens.

[*Chapter II*]   *Corollary on the Coming of Aeneas into Italy*

770   In the light of all our previous discussion, it can now be shown how Aeneas came into Italy and founded the Roman nation in Alba, from which the Romans draw their origin. Our Greek city on the shore of Latium [306, 763] must have been a Greek city from Asia, where Troy was, and must have been unknown to the Romans until they extended their conquests from the hinterland down to the nearby sea. This they began to do under Ancus Marcius, third of the Roman kings. He initiated such conquests with Ostia [736], the maritime city so close to Rome that as the latter afterwards expanded immoderately it made Ostia its port. Thus, just as the Romans had received the Latin Arcadians who were fugitives by land, so later they took under their protection the Phrygians who were fugitives by sea, and by heroic right of war they demolished the city. And thus both Arcadians and Phrygians, by two anachronisms, the former by that of postdating and the latter by that of predating, took refuge in the asylum of Romulus.

771   For if this is not the way things went, then the origin of Rome from Aeneas confounds and baffles any understanding, as we pointed out

in the Axioms [307]. In order to avoid such bafflement and confusion, the scholars from Livy on down have treated that origin as fabulous, failing to consider that, as we have said in the Axioms [149], the fables must have had some public ground of truth. For Evander is so powerful in Latium that he receives and shelters Hercules there some five hundred years before the founding of Rome, and Aeneas founds the royal house of Alba, which, under a succession of fourteen kings, so waxes in prestige as to become the capital of Latium; and the Arcadians and Phrygians, after so long a vagabondage, finally repaired to the asylum of Romulus! We may well ask how a shepherd folk knowing nothing of seafaring and coming from Arcadia, an inland part of Greece, could cross such an expanse of water and penetrate into mid-Latium, when Ancus Marcius, third king after Romulus, was the first to take a colony down to the nearby seacoast. And how they got to Latium, along with the dispersed Phrygians, a good two hundred years before the time of which Livy writes when he tells us that not even the name of Pythagoras, so celebrated in Magna Graecia, could reach Rome from Croton through the many intervening nations of diverse languages and customs [93]. And, for that matter, four hundred years before the Tarentines had heard of the Romans, who were already a powerful people in Italy [116].

772   Nevertheless, as we have often stated in conformity with one of the axioms set forth above [149], these vulgar traditions must from the beginning have had great public grounds of truth, since an entire nation has so long preserved them. What then must we say? We must assume that some Greek city had stood on the shore of Latium, just as so many others stood and remained afterward on the shores of the Tyrrhenian Sea. This city must have been conquered by the Romans before the time of the Law of the Twelve Tables, and, by the heroic right of such barbarous victories, the Romans must have demolished it and received the vanquished inhabitants in the quality of heroic socii [558f]. And in the language of poetic characters these Greeks must have called Arcadians the vagabonds who wandered by land through the forests, and Phrygians those who wandered by sea, just as the Romans described as received into the asylum of Romulus the vanquished who surrendered to them and whom they took in as laborers under the clienteles established by Romulus when he opened the asylum in the clearing for those who came thither as refugees. Out of such conquered and surrendered men (whom we may assign to the period between the expulsion of the kings and the Law of the Twelve Tables) the Roman plebeians must have emerged under the agrarian law of Servius Tullius, who had granted them bonitary ownership of

the fields [107]. Because this was not to the liking of Coriolanus, he sought to reduce [the plebeians to their previous condition as] Romulus's laborers [108]. Subsequently, as the Greeks broadcast everywhere the tale of the Trojan War and the wanderings of the heroes, and particularly in Italy the voyage of Aeneas because in that country they had already discovered their Hercules, their Evander, and their Curetes [761f], it thus came about in the course of time that these traditions were altered and finally corrupted on the lips of a barbarous people. So, as we say, Aeneas became the founder of the Roman people in Latium, though according to Bochart he never set foot in Italy, though Strabo [13.1.53] says he never left Troy, and though Homer [I. 20.307f], of more weight here, relates that he died in Troy and left his kingdom to his descendants. Thus, by two different manifestations of the conceit of the nations [125]—that of the Greeks in making such a stir about the Trojan War, and that of the Romans in boasting an illustrious foreign origin—the Greeks foisted their Aeneas upon the Romans and the latter finally accepted him as their founder.

773   This fable could not have arisen before the time of the war with Pyrrhus, for it was only then that the Romans began to find pleasure in Greek things. It is a habit we find nations acquiring only after long and extensive dealings with foreigners.

[Chapter III]   The Denomination and Description of the Heroic Cities

774   Now, since the parts of geography are nomenclature and chorography, that is to say the denomination and description of places, principally of cities, it remains for us to examine these matters in order to complete our discussion of poetic wisdom.

775   We have seen above [525] that the heroic cities were founded by providence in natural strongholds, to which the ancient Latins in their divine age must have given the sacred name *arae*, altars. They must also have called these strong positions *arces*, fortresses; for in the returned barbarian times the seigniories were called [in Italian] *rocche*, from *rocce*, steep and precipitous rocks, and later *castella*. In like manner the name *arae* must have been extended to the whole district held by a heroic city, which was called *ager* when considered with reference to the frontiers dividing it from foreigners [546, 611], and *territorium* when considered with reference to the jurisdiction of the city over its citizens [722]. On all

this there is a golden passage in Tacitus [A. 12.24] describing the *ara maxima* of Hercules in Rome, and because this passage gives strong support to these principles we shall quote it in full: *Igitur a foro boario, ubi aeneum bovis simulacrum adspicimus, quia id genus animalium aratro subditur, sulcus designandi oppidi captus, ut magnam Herculis aram complecteretur, ara Herculis erat*—"From the ox market, then, where we see the brazen statue of a bull because that is the animal commonly yoked to the plough, a furrow was drawn to mark out the town, so as to embrace the great altar of Hercules [and the land itself within that furrowed circuit] was the [original] altar of Hercules." There is another golden passage in Sallust telling of the famous altar of the brothers Philaeni [*Philaenorum Arae*] left as a boundary marker between the Carthaginian and Cyrenaic empires [*War with Jugurtha* 79.10; cf. 19.3].

776 All ancient geography is strewn with such altars. To begin with Asia, Keller in his *Notitia orbis antiqui* states that all the cities of Syria had the word Aram placed before or after their specific designations, whence Syria itself was called Aramea or Aramia. But in Greece Theseus founded the city of Athens on the famous altar of the unhappy [561], properly considering unhappy those lawless and impious men who, from the brawling of their infamous promiscuity, took recourse to the fortified lands of the strong, all solitary, weak, and needful of all the benefits that the pious had derived from their humanity. And thus in Greek the word *ara* also meant vow, because on these first altars of the gentile world the first victims (called *Saturni hostiae* [191, 517, 549])—the first *anathēmata* (translated into Latin as *diris devoti*)—who were the violent and impious men who dared to enter the cultivated fields of the strong in pursuit of the weak who had fled thither to escape them [553] (whence perhaps the use of *campare* in the sense of saving oneself), were consecrated to Vesta and slain. Hence in Latin *supplicium* meant both punishment and sacrifice, as used by Sallust among others [*War with Catiline* 9.2]. To this double meaning in Latin there is a close correspondence in Greek, for the word *ara*, which as we have said means vow, has also the sense of *noxa*, the body that has done the harm, and also that of *dirae*, the Furies; and precisely such were these first *devoti*, the vowed or devoted men of whom we just spoke (and of whom we shall have more to say in Book IV [957f]), for they were consecrated to the Furies and then sacrificed on these first altars of the gentile world. So the word *hara*, which survived in the sense of coop or pen, must have meant to the ancient Latins the victim. From this word, certainly, is derived *aruspex*, he who divines from the entrails of victims slain before the altars.

777   From what we were saying of the *ara maxima* of Hercules, it was on an altar similar to that of Theseus that Romulus must have founded Rome within the asylum opened in the clearing [561]; for it remained true among the Latins that never was there mention of a clearing or a sacred grove without allusion to an altar erected therein to some divinity. So by telling us that in general the asylums were an ancient counsel of founders of cities, *vetus urbes condentium consilium*, Livy discloses to us the reason why in ancient geography we read of so many cities with the name *Arae*. Whence too we must admit that it was with knowledge of this antiquity that Cicero [in his *Second Speech against Verres*, 5.48.126] called the Senate *ara sociorum*, for it was to the Senate that the provinces carried their fiscal complaints against governors that had governed them avariciously, thereby recalling the origin of the provinces from these first *socii* in the world.

778   We have now shown that the heroic cities in Asia and, as regards Europe, in Greece and Italy were called *Arae* or altars. In Africa, according to Sallust, the aforesaid altar of the brothers Philaeni, *Arae Philaenorum*, remained famous [775]. In the north, coming back to Europe, Altars of the Sicilians [Szekelyek Retze] is still the term applied to the cities in Transylvania inhabited by an ancient Hunnish nation made up of noble farmers and shepherds, which, with the Hungarians and the Saxons, compose that province. For Germany, we read of an *Ara Ubiorum* in Tacitus [A. 1.57]. In Spain *ara* is still a part of the names of many cities. But in the Syrian language the word *ari* means lion; and above, in the natural theogony of the twelve major divinities, we showed that from the defense of their altars the Greeks conceived the idea of Mars, whom they called Ares; so that, with the same idea of strength, in the returned barbarian times many cities and noble houses charged their arms with lions [562f, 773]. This word *ara*, uniform in sound and meaning in so many nations widely separated from each other by space, time, and customs, must have been the root of the Latin word *aratrum*, plough, the moldboard of which was called *urbs* [550]. And the Latins must also have derived from *ara* the words *arx*, fortress, and *arceo*, to repel, whence the phrase *ager arcifinius* used by writers on the boundaries of fields. Hence also the words *arma* and *arcus*, arms and bow. For they justly conceived strength to consist in thrusting back harm and holding it at a distance.

[CONCLUSION]

779 We have shown that poetic wisdom justly deserves two great and sovereign tributes. The one, clearly and constantly accorded to it, is that of having founded gentile mankind, though the conceit of nations on the one hand and that of scholars on the other [124ff], the former with ideas of an empty magnificence and the latter with ideas of an impertinent philosophical wisdom, have in effect denied it this honor by their very efforts to affirm it. The other, concerning which a vulgar tradition has come down to us, is that the wisdom of the ancients made its wise men, by a single inspiration, equally great as philosophers, lawmakers, captains, historians, orators, and poets, on which account it has been so greatly sought after. But in fact it made or rather sketched them such as we have found them in the fables. For in these, as in embryos or matrices, we have discovered the outlines of all esoteric wisdom. And it may be said that in the fables the nations have in a rough way and in the language of the human senses described the beginnings of this world of sciences, which the specialized studies of scholars have since clarified for us by reasoning and generalization. From all this we may conclude what we set out to show in this [Second] Book: that the theological poets were the sense and the philosophers the intellect of human wisdom [363].

BOOK THREE

DISCOVERY OF
THE TRUE HOMER

[SECTION I]

[SEARCH FOR THE TRUE HOMER]

[Introduction]

780 Although our demonstration in the preceding book that poetic wisdom was the vulgar wisdom of the peoples of Greece, who were first theological and later heroic poets, should carry as a necessary consequence that the wisdom of Homer was not at all different in kind, yet, as Plato [R. 598ff,606f!] left firmly fixed the opinion that Homer was endowed with sublime esoteric wisdom (and all the other philosophers have followed in his train, with [pseudo -] Plutarch foremost, writing an entire book on the matter [652, 867]*), we shall here examine particularly if Homer was ever a philosopher. On this question another complete book was written by Dionysius Longinus, which is mentioned by Diogenes Laertius in his life of Pyrrho [i.e., by Suidas in the article on Longinus].

[Chapter I]   The Esoteric Wisdom Attributed to Homer

781 Let us concede to Homer what certainly must be granted, that he had to conform to the quite vulgar feelings and hence the vulgar customs of the barbarous Greece of his day, for such vulgar feelings and vulgar customs provide the poets with their proper materials. Let us therefore concede to him what he narrates: that the gods are esteemed according to their strength, as by his supreme strength Jove attempts to show, in the fable of the great chain, that he is the king of men and gods [387]. On the basis of this vulgar opinion he makes it credible that Diomed can wound Venus and Mars [I. 5.334ff,883ff] with the help of Minerva, who, in the

---

* De vita et poesi Homeri, in the Didot edition of Plutarch's works, vol. V, 1855, pp. 100–64; cf. Anton Westermann (ed.), Vitarum scriptores graeci minores, 1845, pp. 21–24.

contest of the gods, despoils Venus and strikes Mars with a rock [I. 21.403ff,423ff] (and Minerva forsooth was the goddess of philosophy in vulgar belief [509ff], and uses weapons so worthy of the wisdom of Jove!). Let us allow him to tell of the inhuman custom (so contrary to what the writers on the natural law of the gentes claim to have been eternally practiced among the nations) which then prevailed among the barbarous peoples of Greece (who are held to have spread humanity through the world): to wit, that of poisoning arrows (for Ulysses goes to Ephyra to seek poisonous herbs for this purpose [O. 1.259ff]), and further, that of denying burial to enemies slain in battle, leaving their unburied bodies instead as a prey to dogs and vultures (on which account the unhappy Priam found so costly the ransom of his son's body, though the naked corpse of Hector had already been dragged by Achilles's chariot three times around the walls of Troy [667]).

782   Nevertheless, if the purpose of poetry is to tame the ferocity of the vulgar whose teachers the poets are, it was not the part of a wise man, versed in such fierce feelings and customs, to arouse admiration of them in the vulgar in order that they should take pleasure in them and be confirmed in them by that pleasure. Nor was it the part of a wise man to arouse pleasure in the villainous vulgar at the villainies of the gods, to say nothing of the heroes. As, for example, we read of Mars in the midst of the contest calling Minerva a dog-fly [I. 21.394], and of Minerva punching Diana (i.e., Venus, I. 21.424), and of Agememnon and Achilles, the latter the greatest of the Greek heroes and the former the head of the Greek league, and both of them kings, calling each other dogs [I. 1.225], as servants in popular comedies would scarcely do nowadays.

783   But what name under heaven more appropriate than sheer stupidity can be given to the wisdom of his captain, Agamemnon? For he has to be compelled by Achilles to do his duty in restoring Chryseis to Chryses, her father, priest of Apollo, the god who, on account of this rape, was decimating the Greek army with a cruel pestilence. And then, holding himself offended, Agamemnon thought to regain his honor by an act of justice of a piece with his wisdom, by wrongfully stealing Briseis from Achilles, who bore in his person the fate of Troy, so that, on his withdrawing in anger with his men and ships, Hector might make short work of the Greeks still surviving the pestilence. Here is the Homer hitherto considered the architect of Greek polity or civility [B8, 899], starting with such an episode the thread with which he weaves the whole *Iliad*, the principal actors of which are such a captain [as Agamemnon] and such a hero as we have shown Achilles to be when we spoke of the Heroism of the First Peoples [667]. Here is the Homer unrivaled in creating poetic characters

[809], the greatest of which are so discordant with this civil human nature of ours, yet perfectly decorous in relation to the punctilious heroic nature [667, 920].

784   What are we then to say of his representing his heroes as delighting so much in wine, and, whenever they are troubled in spirit, finding all their comfort, yes, and above all others the wise Ulysses, in getting drunk? [O. 8.59–95?] Fine precepts for consolation, most worthy of a philosopher!

785   [J. C.] Scaliger [Poetices 5.3] is indignant at finding almost all his comparisons to be taken from beasts and other savage things. But even if we admit that they were necessary to Homer in order to make himself better understood by the wild and savage vulgar, nevertheless to attain such success in them—for his comparisons are incomparable—is certainly not characteristic of a mind chastened and civilized by any sort of philosophy. Nor could the truculent and savage style in which he describes so many, such varied, and such bloody battles, so many and such extravagantly cruel kinds of butchery as make up all the sublimity of the Iliad in particular, have originated in a mind touched and humanized by any philosophy.

786   The constancy, moreover, which is developed and fixed by the study of the wisdom of the philosophers, could not have depicted gods and heroes of such instability. For some, though deeply moved and distressed, are quieted and calmed by the slightest contrary suggestion; others, though boiling with violent wrath, if they chance to recall some sad event, break into bitter tears [I. 24.507ff]. (Just so, in the returned barbarism of Italy, at the end of which came Dante, the Tuscan Homer, who also sang only of history [817], we read of Cola di Rienzo, whose biography we said above exhibited vividly the customs of the Greek heroes as described by Homer [699], that when he spoke of the unhappy Roman state oppressed by the great of that time, both he and his hearers broke down in uncontrollable tears.*) Others, conversely, when deep in grief, if some pleasant diversion offers itself, like the banquet of Alcinous in the case of the wise Ulysses, completely forget their troubles and give themselves over to hilarity [O. 8.59ff]. Others, quiet and calm, at some innocent remark which is not to their humor, react with such violence and fly into such a blind rage as to threaten the speaker with a frightful death. So it is with Achilles when he receives Priam in his tent on the afore-mentioned occasion when the latter, protected by Mercury, has come through the Greek camp by night and all alone in order to ransom the body of Hector. Achilles receives him at dinner and, because of a little phrase that does not please him and which

---

* La vita di Cola Rienzo, ed. Zefirino Re, Firenze, 1854, p. 31.

has fallen inadvertently from the mouth of the unhappy father grieving for such a valorous son, flies into a rage. Forgetting the sacred laws of hospitality, unmindful of the simple faith in which Priam has come all alone to him because he trusts completely in him alone, unmoved by the many great misfortunes of such a king or by pity for such a father or by the veneration due to so old a man, heedless of the common lot which avails more than anything else to arouse compassion, he allows his bestial wrath to reach such a point as to thunder at him that he will cut off his head [I. 24.552ff]. The same Achilles, even while impiously determined not to forgive a private injury at the hands of Agamemnon (which, grave though it was, could not justly be avenged by the ruin of their fatherland and of their entire nation), is pleased—he who carries with him the fate of Troy—to see all the Greeks fall to ruin and suffer miserable defeat at Hector's hands; nor is he moved by love of country or by his nation's glory to bring them any aid. He does it, finally, only to satisfy a purely private grief, the slaying of his friend Patroclus by Hector. And not even in death is he placated for the loss of his Briseis until the unhappy beautiful royal maiden Polyxena, of the ruined house of the once rich and puissant Priam, but now become a miserable slave, has been sacrificed before his tomb, and his ashes, thirsting for vengeance, have drunk up the last drop of her blood [Euripides, *Hecuba* 37,220f]. To say nothing of what is really past understanding: that a philosopher's gravity and propriety of thought could have been possessed by a man who amused himself by inventing so many fables worthy of old women entertaining children, as those with which Homer stuffed his other poem, the *Odyssey*.

787   Such crude, course, wild, savage, volatile, unreasonable or unreasonably obstinate, frivolous, and foolish customs as we set forth in Book Two in the Corollaries on the Heroic Nature [666ff], can pertain only to men who are like children in the weakness of their minds, like women in the vigor of their imaginations, and like violent youths in the turbulence of their passions; whence we must deny to Homer any kind of esoteric wisdom. These are the considerations which first gave rise to the doubts that put us under the necessity of seeking out the true Homer.

[Chapter II]   *Homer's Fatherland*

788   Such was the esoteric wisdom hitherto attributed to Homer; let us now examine his origin. Almost all the cities of Greece claimed to be his birthplace and there were not lacking those who asserted that he was an

Italian Greek. To determine his native land Leo Allacci in his *De patria Homeri* spends much effort in vain. But since there has come down to us no writer more ancient than Homer, as Josephus stoutly maintains against the grammarian Apion [438], and since the writers came long after him, we are obliged to apply our metaphysical criticism [348], treating him as founder of a nation, as he has been held to be of Greece, and to discover the truth, both as to his age and as to his fatherland, from Homer himself.

789   Certainly, as regards the Homer who was author of the *Odyssey*, we are assured that he must have come from the west of Greece and a little toward the south, as evidenced by that golden passage in which Alcinous, king of the Phaeacians in what is now Corfu, offers to Ulysses, who is anxious to be on his way, a well-fitted ship manned by his vassals. These, he says, are expert mariners who could take the hero, if need were, as far as Euboea (now Negropont), which, by the report of those whom chance had taken thither, was a land far away, a sort of Ultima Thule of the Greeks. This passage [O. 7.319ff] shows clearly that the Homer of the *Odyssey* was not the same as the Homer of the *Iliad*, for Euboea was not far from Troy, which was situated in Asia near the shore of the Hellespont, on the narrow strait of which there are now two fortresses called the Dardanelles, a name recalling to this day its origin from that of Dardania, the ancient territory of Troy. And certainly we find in Seneca [*Shortness of Life* 13.2] that there was a celebrated debate among the grammarians as to whether the *Iliad* and the *Odyssey* were by the same author.

790   As for the contest among the Greek cities for the honor of claiming Homer as citizen, it came about because almost all of them observed in his poems words and phrases and bits of dialect that belonged to their own vernaculars.

791   What has been said here will serve for the discovery of the true Homer.

[Chapter III]   The Age of Homer

792   We find evidence regarding the age of Homer in the following passages of his poems.

I

793   For the funeral of Patroclus, Achilles causes to be played almost all the kinds of games that were later played in the Olympics when Greek civilization was at its height [I. 23.257ff].

II

794   The arts of casting in low relief and of engraving on metals had already been invented, as is shown, among other examples, by the shield of Achilles [681ff]. Painting had not yet been invented. For casting abstracts the surfaces of things along with some relief, and engraving does the same with some depth; but painting abstracts the surfaces absolutely, and this is a labor calling for the greatest ingenuity. Hence neither Homer nor Moses ever mentions anything painted, and this is an argument of their antiquity.

III

795   The delights of the gardens of Alcinous, the magnificence of his palace, and the sumptuousness of his banquets [O. 7.81–184] indicate to us that the Greeks had reached the stage of admiring luxury and pomp.

IV

796   The Phoenicians were already bringing to Greek shores ivory, purple, Arabian incense used to perfume the grotto of Venus; further, a linen finer than the outer skin of an onion [O. 19.232ff], embroidered garments, and, among the gifts of the suitors, one [such garment] for the adornment of Penelope, draped on a frame contrived with such delicate springs that they stretched it out in the fuller places and drew it in the slender places [O. 18.292ff]. An invention worthy of the effeminacy of our day!

V

797   The coach of Priam [I. 24.265ff], in which he drives to Achilles, is made of cedar wood, and the cave of Calypso [O. 5.59ff] is fragrant with its perfumes, which betrays a sensuous refinement that was still foreign to the pleasure of the Romans when they were most bent on wasting their substance in luxury in the days of Nero and Heliogabalus.

VI

798   We read of voluptuous baths in the dwelling of Circe [O. 10.360ff].

VII

799   The youthful servants of the suitors [O. 1.144ff] are handsome, graceful, and blond-haired, even as the amenity of our present customs would demand.

VIII

800 The men care for their hair like women; this is a reproach brought against the effeminate Paris by Hector and Diomed [I. 3.54f; 11.385].

IX

801 It is true that Homer describes his heroes as always eating roast meats [R. 404BC]. This is the simplest and easiest way of cooking them, since it requires nothing but live coals. This practice was retained in the case of sacrifices, and the Romans used the term *prosiicia* for the meat of the victims roasted on the altars, which was then cut up and divided among the guests. In later times, however, it was roasted on spits just like unconsecrated meat. So Achilles on the occasion of the dinner he gives Priam [I. 24.621ff] cuts up the lamb and Patroclus [I. 9.201ff!] then roasts it [on a spit], prepares the table and puts bread upon it in the serving baskets; for the heroes celebrated no banquets which were not sacrificial in nature, with themselves in the character of priests. Among the Latins these survived in the *epulae*, sumptuous banquets given usually by the great, in the *epulum*, a public feast for the people, and in the sacred banquet of which the priests called *epulones* partook. Agamemnon himself, accordingly, kills the two lambs whose sacrifice consecrates the terms of the war with Priam [I. 3.271ff]. Such was the magnificence at that time of an idea we would now associate with a butcher! Only after this stage must have come boiled meats, for in addition to fire they require water, a kettle, and along with it a tripod. Vergil has his heroes eat this kind of meat also, and he has them roast meat on spits [A. 1.210ff]. Last of all came seasoned foods, which, besides the things already mentioned, called also for condiments. Now, to get back to the heroic banquets of Homer, though he describes the most delicate food of the Greeks as made of flour, cheese, and honey [I. 11. 628ff,638ff; O. 10.234f; 20.69], yet two of his similes are drawn from fishing [I. 16.406ff,742ff; O. 5.51ff,432ff; 10.124; 12.251ff; 22.384ff]. And Ulysses, when pretending to be poor and asking alms of one of the suitors, tells him that to hospitable kings, that is to those who are charitable to poor wanderers, the gods give seas abounding in fish [O. 19.113f], which are the greatest delight of the table.

X

802 Lastly (and what is more to our purpose), Homer seems to have appeared at a time when heroic law had already decayed in Greece and the

period of popular liberty had begun, for his heroes contract marriages with foreigners, and bastards succeed to kingdoms. And so indeed it must have been, for, long since, Hercules, stained by the blood of the ugly centaur Nessus, had gone forth in madness and died, signifying the end of heroic law.

803   As therefore with regard to the age of Homer we are unwilling to scorn authority altogether, in all these matters gathered and noted from his poems themselves (not as much from the *Iliad* as from the *Odyssey*, which Dionysius Longinus [S. 9.11ff] holds was composed in Homer's old age), we confirm the opinion of those who place him long after the Trojan War. The interval runs to as much as 460 years, or until about the period of Numa [865]. Indeed, we believe we are humoring them in not assigning him to a time even nearer our own. For they say it was after Numa's time that Psammeticus opened Egypt to the Greeks. Yet the Greeks, as appears from numerous passages particularly in the *Odyssey*, had long since opened their own country to commerce with the Phoenicians, whose tales no less than their merchandise the Greek peoples had come to delight in, just as Europeans do now in those of the Indies. There is thus no contradiction between these two facts: on the one hand that Homer never saw Egypt, and on the other that he recounts so many things of Egypt and Libya, of Phoenicia and Asia, and above all of Italy and Sicily; for these things had been related to the Greeks by the Phoenicians.

804   Yet we do not see how to reconcile so many refined customs with the many wild and savage ones which he attributes to his heroes at the same time, and particularly in the *Iliad*. So that, lest barbarous acts be confounded with gentle ones—*ne placidis coëant immitia* [Horace, A.P. 12]—we must suppose that the two poems were composed and compiled by various hands through successive ages.

805   Thus, from what we have here said of the fatherland and of the age of Homer as he has hitherto been held to be, our doubts take courage for the search for the true Homer.

[*Chapter IV*]   *Homer's Matchless Faculty for Heroic Poetry*

806   The complete absence of philosophy which we have shown in Homer, and our discoveries concerning his fatherland and his age, arouse in us a strong suspicion that he may perhaps have been quite simply a man of the people. This suspicion is confirmed by Horace's observation in his *Art*

of Poetry [128ff] concerning the desperate difficulty of creating fresh characters or persons of tragedy after Homer, on account of which he advises poets to take their characters from Homer's poems. Now this grave difficulty must be taken in conjunction with the fact that the personages of the New Comedy are all of artificial creation; indeed, there was an Athenian law requiring the New Comedy to appear on the stage with characters entirely fictitious, and the Greeks managed this so successfully that the Latins, for all their pride, despaired of competing, as Quintilian [12.10.38] acknowledged in saying: *Cum graecis de comoedia non contendimus,* "We do not rival the Greeks in comedy."

807   To Horace's difficulty we must add two others of wider scope. For one thing, how is it that Homer, who came first, was such an inimitable heroic poet, while tragedy, which was born later, began with the crudeness familiar to everybody and which we shall later describe more in detail [910]? And for another, how is it that Homer, who preceded philosophy and the poetic and critical arts, was yet the most sublime of all the sublime poets, and that after the invention of philosophies and of the arts of poetry and criticism there was no poet who could come within a long distance of competing with him? However, putting aside our two difficulties, that of Horace combined with what we have said of the New Comedy should have spurred scholars like Patrizzi, Scaliger, and Castelvetro [384] and other valiant masters of the poetic art to investigate the reason for the difference.

808   The reason cannot be found elsewhere than in the origin of poetry, as discovered above in the Poetic Wisdom, and consequently in the discovery of the poetic characters in which alone consists the essence of poetry itself [376ff]. For the New Comedy portrays our present human customs, on which the Socratic philosophy had meditated, and hence, from the latter's general maxims concerning human morals, the Greek poets, profoundly steeped in that doctrine (as was Menander for example, in comparison with whom Terence was called even by the Latins "half a Menander"), could create certain luminous examples of ideal human types, by the light and splendor of which they might awaken the vulgar, who are as quick to learn from convincing examples as they are incapable of understanding from reasoned maxims. The Old Comedy took arguments or subjects from real life and made plays of them just as they were, as the wicked Aristophanes once did with the good Socrates, thus bringing on his ruin [906, 911]. But tragedy puts on the scene heroic hatred, scorn, wrath, and revenge, which spring from sublime natures which naturally are the source of sentiments, modes of speech, and actions in general that are

wild, crude, and terrible. Such arguments are clothed with an air of marvel, and all these matters are in closest conformity among themselves and uniform in their subjects. Such works the Greeks could produce only in the time of their heroism, at the end of which Homer must have come. This is shown by the following metaphysical criticism. The fables, which at their birth had come forth direct and proper, reached Homer distorted and perverted [221]. As may be seen throughout the Poetic Wisdom above set forth [514, 708], they were all at first true histories, which were gradually altered and corrupted, and in their corrupt form finally came down to Homer. Hence he must be assigned to the third age of the heroic poets [905]. The first age invented the fables to serve as true narratives, the primary and proper meaning of the word *mythos*, as defined by the Greeks themselves, being "true narration" [401, 814]. The second altered and corrupted them. The third and last, that of Homer, received them thus corrupted.

809   But, to return to our purpose, for the reason assigned by us to this effect, Aristotle in his *Poetics* [24.18.1460a 19] says that only Homer knew how to invent poetic falsehoods. For his poetic characters, which are incomparable for the sublime appropriateness which Horace admires in them [806], were imaginative universals, as defined above in the Poetic Metaphysics [381], to which the peoples of Greece attached all the various particulars belonging to each genus [209, 402, 412ff, 934]. To Achilles, for example, who is the subject of the *Iliad*, they attached all the properties of heroic valor, and all the feelings and customs arising from these natural properties, such as those of quick temper, punctiliousness, wrathfulness, implacability, violence, the arrogation of all right to might, as they are summed up by Horace in his description of this character [A.P. 119ff]. To Ulysses, the subject of the *Odyssey*, they attached all the feelings and customs of heroic wisdom; that is, those of wariness, patience, dissimulation, duplicity, deceit, always preserving propriety of speech and indifference of action, so that others may of themselves fall into error and may be the causes of their own deception. And to these two characters, according to kind, they attached those actions of particular men which were conspicuous enough to arouse and move the still dull and stupid Greeks to note them and refer them to their kinds. These two characters, since they had been created by an entire nation, could only be conceived as naturally uniform (in which uniformity, agreeable to the common sense of an entire nation, alone consists the decorum or beauty and charm of a fable); and, since they were created by powerful imaginations, they could not be created as anything but sublime [142, 144]. Hence derive two eternal properties of poetry: one that poetic sublimity is inseparable from popularity, and the other that peoples who have first created heroic characters for

themselves will afterward apprehend human customs only in terms of characters made famous by luminous examples.

[Chapter V] Philosophical Proofs for the Discovery of the True Homer

810   In view of what we have stated, the following philosophical proofs may be assembled.

I

811   First of all, the one numbered above among the axioms [201] which states that men are naturally led to preserve the memories of the institutions and laws that bind them within their societies.

II

812   The truth understood by Castelvetro,* that history must have come first and then poetry, for history is a simple statement of the true but poetry is an imitation besides. Yet this scholar, though otherwise most acute, failed to make use of this clue to discover the true principles of poetry by combining it with the other philosophical proof which follows next.

III

813   Inasmuch as the poets came certainly before the vulgar historians, the first history must have been poetic.

IV

814   The fables in their origin were true and severe narrations, whence *mythos*, fable, was defined as *vera narratio* [401, 808]. But because they were originally for the most part gross, they gradually lost their original meanings, were then altered, subsequently became improbable, after that obscure, then scandalous, and finally incredible [221, 708]. These are the seven sources of the difficulties of the fables, which can all easily be found throughout Book Two.

V

815   And, as we have shown in the same book, they were received by Homer in this corrupt and distorted from [808].

---

* Lodovico Castelvetro, *Poetica d'Aristotile vulgarizzata et sposta*, 1576, pp. 4–6.

VI

816   The poetic characters, in which the essence of the fables consists, were born of the need of a nature incapable of abstracting forms and properties from subjects. Consequently they must have been the manner of thinking of entire peoples, who had been placed under this natural necessity in the times of their greatest barbarism [209]. It is an eternal property of the fables always to enlarge the ideas of particulars. On this there is a fine passage in Aristotle [*Rhetoric* 2.15.139b 1–10] in which he remarks that men of limited ideas erect every particular into a maxim. The reason must be that the human mind, which is indefinite, being constricted by the vigor of the senses, cannot otherwise express its almost divine nature than by thus enlarging particulars in imagination. It is perhaps on this account that in both the Greek and the Latin poets the images of gods and heroes always appear larger than those of men, and that in the returned barbarian times the paintings particularly of the Eternal Father, of Jesus Christ, and of the Virgin Mary are exceedingly large.

VII

817   Since barbarians lack reflection, which, when ill used, is the mother of falsehood, the first heroic Latin poets sang true histories; that is, the Roman wars. And in the returned barbarian times, in virtue of this nature of barbarism, the Latin poets like Gunther, William of Apulia, and others again sang nothing but history [471], and the romancers of the same period thought they were writing true histories. Even Boiardo and Ariosto, who came in an age illuminated by philosophy, took the subjects of their poems from the history of Bishop Turpin of Paris [159]. And in virtue of this same nature of barbarism, which for lack of reflection does not know how to feign (whence it is naturally truthful, open, faithful, generous, and magnanimous [516, 708]), even Dante, though learned in the loftiest esoteric knowledge, filled the scenes of his *Comedy* with real persons and portrayed real events in the lives of the dead [786]. For that reason he gave the name *Comedy* to his poem, for the Old Comedy of the Greeks portrayed real persons in its plays [808]. In this respect Dante was like the Homer of the *Iliad*, which Dionysius Longinus [S. 9.13] says is all dramatic or representative, as the *Odyssey* is all narrative. Francesco Petrarca too, though a most learned man, yet sang in Latin of the second Carthaginian war, and his *Trionfi*, in Tuscan, which have a heroic note, are nothing but a collection of histories. And here we have a luminous proof of the fact that the first fables were histories. For satire spoke ill of persons not only real but well known; tragedy took for its arguments characters of poetic

history; the Old Comedy put into its plots famous living persons; the New Comedy, born in times of the most lively reflection, finally invented characters entirely fictitious (just as in the Italian language the New Comedy came in again only with the marvelously learned Cinquecento): and neither among the Greeks nor among the Latins was an entirely fictitious character ever the protagonist of a tragedy. Strong confirmation of this is found in the popular taste which will not accept musical dramas, the arguments of which are always tragic, unless they are taken from history, whereas it will tolerate fictitious plots in comedies because, since they deal with private life which is not public knowledge, it believes them true.

VIII

818   Since poetic characters are of this nature, their poetic allegories, as we have shown above throughout the Poetic Wisdom, must necessarily contain historical significations referring only to the earliest times of Greece [403].

IX

819   Such histories must naturally have been preserved in the memories of the communities of the peoples, in virtue of our first philosophical proof [811]; for, as the children of the nations, they must have had marvelously strong memories [211]. And this was not without divine providence, for up to the time of Homer and indeed somewhat afterward, common script had not yet been invented, on the authority of Josephus against Apion [66]. In that human indigence, the peoples, who were almost all body and almost no reflection [375], must have been all vivid sensation in perceiving particulars, strong imagination in apprehending and enlarging them, sharp wit in referring them to their imaginative genera, and robust memory in retaining them. It is true that these faculties appertain to the mind, but they have their roots in the body and draw their strength from it. Hence memory is the same as imagination, which for that reason is called *memoria* in Latin. (In Terence [*Lady of Andros* 625], for example, we find *memorabile* in the sense of imaginable, and commonly we find *comminisci* for feigning, which is proper to the imagination, and thence *commentum* for a fiction.) Imagination is likewise taken for ingenuity or invention. (In the returned barbarian times an ingenious man was called imaginative, *fantastico*; so, for example, Cola di Rienzo is described by his contemporary biographer [699].) Memory thus has three different aspects: memory when it remembers things, imagination when it alters or imitates them, and invention when it gives them a new turn or puts them into

proper arrangement and relationship. For these reasons the theological poets called Memory the mother of the Muses.

X

820   The poets must therefore have been the first historians of the nations [464–471]. This is why Castelvetro failed to make use of his dictum for finding the true origins of poetry [812]; for he and all others who have discussed the matter (from Plato and Aristotle on down) could easily have observed that all gentile histories have their beginnings in fables, as we set forth in the Axioms [202] and demonstrated in the Poetic Wisdom.

XI

821   By the very nature of poetry it is impossible for anyone to be at the same time a sublime poet and a sublime metaphysician, for metaphysics abstracts the mind from the senses, and the poetic faculty must submerge the whole mind in the senses; metaphysics soars up to universals, and the poetic faculty must plunge deep into particulars.

XII

822   In virtue of the axiom [213] that he who has not the natural gift may by industry succeed in every [other] capacity, but that in poetry success by industry is completely denied to him who lacks the natural gift, the poetic and critical "arts" serve to make minds cultivated but not great. For delicacy is a small virtue and greatness naturally disdains all small things. Indeed, as a great rushing torrent cannot fail to carry turbid waters and roll stones and trunks along in the violence of its course, so his very greatness accounts for the low expressions we so often find in Homer.

XIII

823   But this does not make Homer any the less the father and prince of all sublime poets.

XIV

824   For we have seen that Aristotle regarded the Homeric lies as without equal, which is equivalent to Horace's opinion that his characters are inimitable [809].

XV

825   He is celestially sublime in his poetic sentences, which must be conceived of true passions, or in virtue of a burning imagination must

make themselves truly felt by us, and they must therefore be individuated in those who feel them. Hence maxims of life, as being general, we defined as sentences of philosophers; and reflections on the passions themselves are the work of false and frigid poets [703f].

XVI

826 The poetic comparisons taken from wild and savage things are certainly incomparable in Homer [785].

XVII

827 The frightfulness of the Homeric battles and deaths gives to the *Iliad* all its marvelousness.

XVIII

828 But these sentences, comparisons, and descriptions could not have been the natural product of a calm, cultivated, and gentle philosopher.

XIX

829 For in their customs the Homeric heroes are like boys in the frivolity of their minds, like women in the vigor of their imaginations, and like turbulent youths in the boiling fervor of their wrath, and therefore it is impossible that a philosopher should have conceived them so naturally and felicitously [786].

XX

830 The ineptitudes and indecencies are effects of the awkwardness with which the Greek peoples had labored to express themselves in the extreme poverty of their language in its formative period [456ff].

XXI

831 And even if the Homeric poems contained the most sublime mysteries of esoteric wisdom, as we have shown in the Poetic Wisdom that they certainly do not, the form in which they are expressed could not have been conceived by a straightforward, orderly, and serious mind such as befits a philosopher [384].

XXII

832 The heroic language was a language of similes, images, and comparisons [456], born of the lack of genera and species, which are

necessary for the proper definition of things, and hence born of a necessity of nature common to entire peoples.

XXIII

833 It was by a necessity of nature that the first nations spoke in heroic verse [463ff]. Here too we must admire the providence which, in the time when the characters of common script were not yet invented, ordained that the nations should speak in verses so that their memories might be aided by meter and rhythm to preserve more easily the histories of their families and cities.

XXIV

834 These fables, sentences, and customs, this language and verse, were all called heroic, and were current in the times to which history has assigned the heroes, as has been fully shown above in the Poetic Wisdom [634ff].

XXV

835 Hence all the aforesaid were properties of entire peoples and consequently common to all the individual men of these peoples.

XXVI

836 In virtue, however, of the very nature from which sprang all the aforesaid properties, which made Homer the greatest of poets, we denied that he was ever a philosopher [787].

XXVII

837 Further we showed above in the Poetic Wisdom that the meanings of esoteric wisdom were intruded into the Homeric fables by the philosophers who came later [515, 720f].

XXVIII

838 But, as esoteric wisdom appertains to but few individual men, so we have just seen that the very decorum of the heroic poetic characters, in which consists all the essence of the heroic fables, cannot be achieved today by men most learned in philosophy, in the art of poetry, and in the art of criticism. It is for this decorum that Aristotle and Horace give the palm to Homer, the former saying that his lies are beyond equal and the latter that his characters are inimitable, which comes to the same thing [809].

[Chapter VI]   Philological Proofs for the Discovery of the True Homer

839   With this great number of philosophical proofs, resulting in large part from the metaphysical criticism of the founders of the gentile nations, among whom we must number Homer, since certainly we have no more ancient profane writer than he (as Josephus the Jew stoutly maintains) [438], we may conjoin the following philological proofs.

I

840   All ancient profane histories have fabulous beginnings [202].

II

841   Barbarous peoples, cut off from all the other nations of the world, as were the Germans and the American Indians, have been found to preserve in verses the beginnings of their history [470].

III

842   It was the poets who began to write Roman history [471, 871].

IV

843   In the returned barbarian times, the histories were written by the poets who wrote in Latin.

V

844   Manetho, high priest of the Egyptians, interpreted the ancient history of Egypt, written in hieroglyphics, as a sublime natural theology [222].

VI

845   In the Poetic Wisdom we showed that the Greek philosophers did the same with the early history of Greece recounted in fables [361f].

VII

846   Wherefore above in the Poetic Wisdom [384, 403] we were obliged to reverse the path of Manetho and, stripping off the mystical interpretations, to restore to the fables their original historical meanings;

and the naturalness and ease, free of violence, subterfuge, or distortion, with which we were able to do so, show that the historical allegories which they contained were proper to them.

VIII

847   All of which strongly confirms the assertion of Strabo, in a golden passage [1.2.6], that before Herodotus, or rather before Hecataeus of Miletus, the history of the peoples of Greece was all written by their poets.

IX

848   And in Book Two we showed that the first writers of both ancient and modern nations were poets [464–471].

X

849   There are two golden passages in the *Odyssey* [11.367ff] in which it is said, in praise of a speaker who has told a story well, that he has told it like a musician or singer. Just such indeed were the Homeric rhapsodes, who were vulgar men, each preserving by memory some part of the Homeric poems.

XI

850   Homer left none of his poems in writing, according to the firm assertion of Flavius Josephus the Jew against Apion the Greek grammarian [66].

XII

851   The rhapsodes went about the cities of Greece singing the books of Homer at the fairs and festivals, some singing one of them, others another.

XIII

852   By the etymology of their name from the two words which compose it, rhapsodes were stitchers-together of songs, and these songs they must certainly have collected from none other than their own peoples. Similarly [the common noun] *homēros* is said to come from *homou*, together, and *eirein*, to link; thus signifying a guarantor, as being one who binds creditor and debtor together. This derivation is as farfetched and forced [when applied to a guarantor] as it is natural and proper when applied to our Homer as a binder or compiler of fables.

XIV

853   The Pisistratids, tyrants of Athens, divided and arranged the poems of Homer, or had them divided and arranged, into [two groups,] the *Iliad* and *Odyssey*. Hence we may understand what a confused mass of material they must have been before, when the difference we can observe between the styles of the two poems is infinite.

XV

854   The Pisistratids also ordered that from that time onward the poems should be sung by the rhapsodes at the Panathenaic festivals, as Cicero writes in his *On the Nature of the Gods* [i.e., *On the Orator* 3.34.137, or rather Plato in his *Hipparchus* 228B], and Aelian also [*Various History* 8.2], who is followed on this point by [his editor, Johann] Scheffer.

XVI

855   But the Pisistratids were expelled from Athens only a few years earlier than the Tarquins were from Rome. So, if we assume that Homer lived as late as the time of Numa [803], a long period must still have ensued after the Pisistratids during which the rhapsodes continued to preserve his poems by memory. This tradition takes away all credit from the other according to which it was at the time of the Pisistratids that Aristarchus purged, divided, and arranged the poems of Homer, for that could not have been done without vulgar writing, and so from then on there would have been no need of rhapsodes to sing the several parts of them from memory.

XVII

856   By this reasoning, Hesiod, who left his works in writing, would have to be placed after the Pisistratids, since we have no authority for supposing that he was preserved by the memory of the rhapsodes as Homer was, though the vain diligence of the chronologists has placed him thirty years before Homer. Like the Homeric rhapsodes, however, were the cyclic poets, who preserved all the fabulous history of Greece from the origins of their gods down to the return of Ulysses to Ithaca. These cyclic poets, so called from *kyklos*, circle, could have been no other than simple men who would sing the fables to the common people gathered in a circle around them on festive days. The circle is precisely the one alluded to by Horace in his *Art of Poetry* [132] in the phrase *vilem patulumque orbem*, "the base and large circle," concerning which Dacier is not at all satisfied with the

commentators who assert that Horace here means long episodes or digressions. And perhaps the reason for his dissatisfaction is this: that it is not necessary that an episode in a plot be base simply because it is long. To cite examples, the episode of the joys of Rinaldo and Armida in the enchanted garden, and that of the conversation of the old shepherd with Erminia, are indeed long but are not therefore base; for the former is ornate and the latter tenuous and delicate, and both are noble. But in our present passage Horace, having advised the tragic poets to take their arguments from the poems of Homer, runs into the difficulty that in that case they would not be [creative] poets, since their plots would be those invented by Homer. So Horace answers them that the epic stories of Homer will become tragic plots of their own if they will bear three things in mind. The first is to refrain from making idle paraphrases, in the way we still see men read the *Orlando furioso* or the [*Orlando*] *innamorato* or some other rhymed romance to the "base and large circles" of idle people on feast days, and, after reciting each stanza, explain it to them in prose with more words. The second is not to be faithful translators. The third and last is not to be servile imitators, but, adhering to the characters that Homer attributes to his heroes, to bring forth from them new sentiments, speeches, and actions in conformity with them; thus on the same subjects they will be new poets in the style of Homer. So, in the same passage, Horace speaks of a "cyclical poet" as a trivial marketplace poet. Authors of this sort are ordinarily called *kyklioi* and *enkyklioi*, and their collective work was called *kyklos epikos*, *kyklia epē*, *poiēma enkyklikon*, and sometimes *kyklos* without qualification, as Gerard Langbaine observes in his preface to Dionysius Longinus. So in this way it may be that Hesiod, who contains all the fables of the gods, is earlier than Homer.

XVIII

857 For this reason the same may be said of Hippocrates, who left many great works, written not indeed in verse but in prose, so that they naturally could not have been preserved by memory; whence he is to be assigned to about the time of Herodotus.

XIX

858 From all this [it is evident that G. J.] Voss placed an excess of good faith in the three heroic inscriptions [reported by Herodotus 5.59ff] with which he thought he could confute Josephus. For these inscriptions, the first of Amphitryon, the second of Hippocoön, and the third of Laome-

don [i.e., Laodamas], are impostures similar to those still committed by falsifiers of medals. Martin Schoock supports Josephus against Voss.

XX

859   We may add that Homer never mentions vulgar Greek letters, and the epistle written by Proetus to Eureia as a trap for Bellerophon is said by Homer to have been written in *sēmata* [433].

XXI

860   Though Aristarchus emended Homer's poems, they still retain a great variety of dialects and many improprieties of speech, which must have been idiomatic expressions of various peoples of Greece, and many licenses in meter besides.

XXII

861   The fatherland of Homer is not known [788ff].

XXIII

862   Almost all the cities of Greece laid claim to him [788].

XXIV

863   Above we have brought forward strong conjectures that the Homer of the *Odyssey* was from the west of Greece and toward the south, and that the Homer of the *Iliad* was from the east and toward the north [789].

XXV

864   Not even Homer's age is known [792ff].

XXVI

865   The opinions on this point are so numerous and so varied that the divergence extends to 460 years, the extreme estimates putting it as early as the Trojan War and as late as the time of Numa [803].

XXVII

866   Dionysius Longinus, being unable to ignore the great diversity in the styles of the two poems, says that Homer composed the *Iliad* in his youth and the *Odyssey* in his old age [803]: a strange detail to be known about a man of whom we do not know the two most important historical

facts, namely when and where he lived, regarding which history has left us in the dark in telling of the greatest luminary of Greece.

XXVIII

867 This consideration should destroy all faith in Herodotus or whoever was the author of the *Life of Homer,* in which so many delightful minor details are narrated as to fill an entire volume, and all trust as well in the *Life* of him written by Plutarch, who, being a philosopher, spoke of him with greater sobriety [780].

XXIX

868 But perhaps Longinus based his conjecture on the fact that in the *Iliad* Homer depicts the wrath and the pride of Achilles, which are properties of youth, while in the *Odyssey* he relates the wiles and stratagems of Ulysses, which are characteristics of the aged.

XXX

869 Tradition says that Homer was blind and that from his blindness he took his name, which in the Ionic dialect means blind.

XXXI

870 Homer himself describes as blind the poets who sing at the banquets of the great, such as the one who sings at the banquet given by Alcinous for Ulysses [O. 8.64], and the one who sings at the feast of the suitors [O. 1.153ff].

XXXII

871 It is a property of human nature that the blind have marvelously retentive memories.

XXXIII

872 And finally [tradition says] that he was poor and wandered through the market places of Greece singing his own poems.

[SECTION II]

DISCOVERY OF THE TRUE HOMER

[*Introduction*]

873 Now all these things reasoned out by us or related by others concerning Homer and his poems, without our having intentionally aimed at any such result—indeed, it had not even entered into our reflections when readers of the first edition of this *New Science* (which was not worked out on the same method as the present), men of acute minds and excelling in scholarship and learning, suspected that the Homer believed in up to now was not real—all these things, I say, now compel us to affirm that the same thing has happened in the case of Homer as in that of the Trojan War, of which the most judicious critics hold that though it marks a famous epoch in history it never in the world took place. And certainly if, as in the case of the Trojan War, there did not remain of Homer certain great vestiges in the form of his poems, the great difficulties would lead us to conclude that he was a purely ideal poet who never existed as a particular man in the world of nature. But the many great difficulties on the one hand, taken together with the surviving poems on the other, seem to force us to take the middle ground that Homer was an idea or a heroic character of Grecian men insofar as they told their histories in song.

[*Chapter I*] *The Improprieties and Improbabilities of the Homer Hitherto Believed in Become Proper and Necessary in the Homer Herein Discovered*

874 In the light of this discovery, all the things in the speeches and in the narrative which are improprieties and improbabilities in the Homer hitherto believed in become proper and necessary in the Homer herein

discovered. And first of all, those most important matters concerning Homer on which we are left in uncertainty compel us to say:

I

875   That the reason why the Greek peoples so vied with each other for the honor of being his fatherland, and why almost all claimed him as citizen, is that the Greek peoples were themselves Homer [788ff, 861f].

II

876   That the reason why opinions as to his age vary so much is that our Homer truly lived on the lips and in the memories of the peoples of Greece throughout the whole period from the Trojan War down to the time of Numa, a span of 460 years [803].

III

877   And the blindness [869ff]

IV

878   and the poverty of Homer [872] were characteristics of the rhapsodes, who, being blind, whence each of them was called *homēros*, had exceptionally retentive memories, and, being poor, sustained life by singing the poems of Homer throughout the cities of Greece; and they were the authors of these poems inasmuch as they were a part of these peoples who had composed their histories in the poems.

V

879   Thus Homer composed the *Iliad* in his youth, that is, when Greece was young and consequently seething with sublime passions, such as pride, wrath, and lust for vengeance, passions which do not tolerate dissimulation but which love magnanimity; and hence this Greece admired Achilles, the hero of violence. But he wrote the *Odyssey* in his old age, that is, when the spirits of Greece had been somewhat cooled by reflection, which is the mother of prudence, so that it admired Ulysses, the hero of wisdom. Thus in the time of Homer's youth the peoples of Greece found pleasure in coarseness, villainy, ferocity, savagery, and cruelty, while in the time of his old age they found delight in the luxury of Alcinous, the joys of Calypso, the pleasures of Circe, the songs of the Sirens, the pastimes of the suitors, and the attempts, nay the siege and the assaults, on the chastity of Penelope: two sets of customs which, conceived above as existing at the same time, seemed to us incompatible [803f, 866]. This difficulty was

enough to cause the divine Plato [780] to declare, in order to solve it, that Homer had foreseen by inspiration these nauseating, morbid, and dissolute customs. Yet in this way he merely made of Homer a stupid founder of Greek civility [R. 606E], for, however much he may condemn, he nevertheless teaches these corrupt and decadent customs which were to come long after the nations of Greece had been founded, to the end that, by an acceleration of the natural course of human institutions, the Greeks might hasten on toward corruption.

VI

880   In this fashion we show that the Homer who was the author of the *Iliad* preceded by many centuries the Homer who was the author of the *Odyssey*.

VII

881   And we show that it was from the northeastern part of Greece that the Homer came who sang of the Trojan War, which took place in his country, and that it was from the southwestern part of Greece that the Homer came who sang of Ulysses, whose kingdom was in that region [789].

VIII

882   Thus Homer, lost in the crowd of the Greek peoples, is justified against all the accusations leveled at him by the critics, and particularly [against those made] on account of his

IX

883   base sentences,

X

884   vulgar customs,

XI

885   crude comparisons,

XII

886   local idioms,

XIII

887   licenses in meter,

XIV

888   variations in dialect,

XV

889   and his having made men of gods and gods of men.

890   These last-mentioned fables Dionysius Longinus does not trust himself to sustain save by the props of philosophical allegories [S. 9.7], which amounts to admitting that, as they sounded when sung to the Greeks, they cannot have brought Homer the glory of having been the founder of Greek civility [899]. The same difficulty recurs in Homer's case which we raised against Orpheus as the founder of Greek humanity [79–81]. But the aforesaid properties and particularly the last all appertained to the Greek peoples themselves. For inasmuch as at their founding they were themselves pious, religious, chaste, strong, just, and magnanimous [516], they made their gods so also, as our natural theogony has demonstrated above; then later, in the long passage of the years, as the fables became obscure and customs decayed, from their own character they judged the gods too to be dissolute, as we have set forth at length in the Poetic Wisdom. This in virtue of the axiom that men naturally bend obscure or dubious laws to their own passions and utilities [220]. For they feared that the gods would not be agreeable to their desires if they were not like them in customs [221].

XVI

891   But more than ever to Homer belong by right the two great pre-eminences which are really one: that poetic falsehoods, as Aristotle says, and heroic characters, as Horace says, could be created only by him [809]. On this account Horace avows himself to be no poet because he lacks the skill or the wit to maintain what he calls the colors of works, colores operum [A.P. 86], which means the same thing as the poetic untruths of Aristotle's phrase, for in Plautus [Braggart Warrior 186 variant] we find obtinere colorem in the sense of telling a lie that under every aspect has the appearance of truth, which is what a good fable must be.

892   In addition to these, all those other pre-eminences fall to him which have been ascribed to him by all the masters of the art of poetry, declaring him incomparable

XVII

893   in his wild and savage comparisons [785, 826],

XVIII

894   in his cruel and fearful descriptions of battles and deaths [827],

XIX

895   in his sentences filled with sublime passions [825],

XX

896   in the expressiveness and splendor of his style. All these were properties of the heroic age of the Greeks, in which and throughout which Homer was an incomparable poet, just because, in the age of vigorous memory, robust imagination, and sublime invention, he was in no sense a philosopher [781–787].

XXI

897   Wherefore neither philosophies, arts of poetry, nor arts of criticism, which came later, could create a poet who could come anywhere near to rivaling Homer.

898   And, what is more, his title is assured to the three immortal eulogies that are given him:

XXII

899   first of having been the founder of Greek polity or civility [B8, 783, 879, 890];

XXIII

900   second, of having been the father of all other poets;

XXIV

901   and third, of having been the source of all Greek philosophies [779]. None of these eulogies could have been given to the Homer hitherto believed in. Not the first, for, counting from the time of Deucalion and Pyrrha [523], Homer comes eighteen hundred years after the institution of marriage had laid the first foundations of Greek civility, as we have shown throughout the Poetic Wisdom. Not the second, for it was certainly before Homer's time that the theological poets flourished, such as Orpheus, Amphion, Linus, Musaeus, and others, among whom the chronologists have placed Hesiod, putting him thirty years before Homer. Cicero affirms in his *Brutus* [18.71] that there were other heroic poets before Homer, and Eusebius mentions some by name in his *Preparation for the Gospel*

[10.11.495bc], such as Philammon, Thamyris, Demodocus, Epimenides, Aristaeus, and others. And, finally, not the third, for, as we have shown fully and at length in the Poetic Wisdom, the philosophers did not discover their philosophies in the Homeric fables but rather inserted them therein. But it was poetic wisdom itself whose fables provided occasions for the philosophers to meditate their lofty truths, and supplied them also with means for expounding them, as we showed throughout Book Two in fulfillment of the promise made at its beginning [361ff, 779].

[Chapter II]   *The Poems of Homer Revealed as Two Great Treasure Stores of the Natural Law of the Gentes of Greece*

902   But above all, in virtue of our discovery we may ascribe to Homer an additional and most dazzling glory:

XXV

903   that of having been the first historian of the entire gentile world who has come down to us.

XXVI

904   Wherefore his poems should henceforth be highly prized as being two great treasure stores of the customs of early Greece. But the same fate has befallen the poems of Homer as the Law of the Twelve Tables; for, just as the latter, having been held to be the laws given by Solon to the Athenians and subsequently taken over by the Romans, has up to now concealed from us the history of the natural law of the heroic gentes of Latium, so the Homeric poems, having been regarded as works thrown off by a particular man, a rare and consummate poet, have hitherto concealed from us the history of the natural law of the gentes of Greece.

[APPENDIX]

RATIONAL HISTORY OF THE

DRAMATIC AND LYRIC POETS

905 We have already shown above that there were three ages of poets before Homer [808]. First came the age of the theological poets, who were themselves heroes and sang true and austere fables; second, that of the heroic poets, who altered and corrupted the fables [901]; and third, the Homeric age, which received them in their altered and corrupted form. Now the same metaphysical criticism of the history of the obscurest antiquity, that is, the explanation of the ideas the earliest nations naturally formed, can illuminate and distinguish for us the history of the dramatic and lyric poets, on which the philosophers have written only in an obscure and confused fashion.

906 The philosophers class among the lyric poets Amphion [i.e., Arion] of Methymna [908], a most ancient poet of heroic times, and affirm that he discovered the dithyramb and therewith the chorus, and that he introduced satyrs singing in verses, and that the dithyramb was a chorus led about singing verses in praise of Bacchus. They say that noteworthy tragic poets flourished within the period of the lyric; and Diogenes Laertius [3.56] affirms that in tragedy the chorus was at first the only actor. They say that Aeschylus was the first tragic poet, and Pausanias [1.21.2] relates that he was commanded by Bacchus to write tragedies (although Horace says that Thespis was their originator, in that passage of his *Art of Poetry* [275ff] where he begins his treatment of tragedy with satire, and that Thespis introduced satire [i.e., the satyr play] on carts at vintage time). Later, they say, came Sophocles, called by Palaemon the Homer of the tragic poets; and the cycle was completed by Euripides, whom Aristotle [*Poetics* 13.10.1453a 29] calls *tragikōtatos*, the most tragic of them all. They say that in the same period came Aristophanes, who invented the Old Comedy and opened the way for the New (which was later traveled by Menander), with his play entitled *The Clouds*, which was the ruin of

Socrates [808, 911]. Then some of them put Hippocrates in the time of the tragic poets, others in the lyric period. But Sophocles and Euripides lived somewhat before the time of the Law of the Twelve Tables, and the lyric poets came even later; which would seem to upset the chronology which puts Hippocrates in the age of the Seven Sages of Greece.

907   To solve this difficulty we must declare that there were two kinds of tragic poets and two kinds of lyric poets.

908   The ancient lyric poets must in the first place have been the authors of hymns in honor of the gods, like those attributed to Homer, composed in heroic verse. They must later have been the poets of that lyric vein in which Achilles sings to his lyre the praises of the heroes who have gone before [I. 9.186ff]. Similarly among the Latins the first poets were the authors of the Salian verses, which were hymns sung by the priests called Salii on the festival days of the gods. (The priests were perhaps so called from *salio*, to leap, even as the first Greek choruses danced in a circle.) The fragments of these verses are the most ancient memorials of the Latin language that have come down to us, and they have an air of heroic verse [438, 469]. All of which is in accord with the beginnings of the humanity of the nations, which in the first, or religious, period must have offered praise only to the gods (even as in the last barbarian times this religious custom returned, and the priests, the only literate men of the time, composed only sacred hymns); whereas later, in the heroic period, they must have admired and celebrated only the great deeds of heroes, such as those sung by Achilles. It is to this kind of sacred lyric poets that Amphion [i.e., Arion] of Methymna must have belonged [906]. He was also the originator of the dithyramb, which was the first rough beginning of tragedy, composed in heroic verse (the first kind of verse in which the Greeks sang [463]). Thus the dithyramb of Amphion was the first satire, and it is with satire that Horace begins his discussion of tragedy [A.P. 220ff].

909   The new lyric poets were the melic poets, whose prince is Pindar, and who wrote in verse what we in Italian call *arie per musica*, airs to be set to music. This sort of verse must have come later than the iambic, which in turn was the kind of verse in which the Greeks commonly spoke after the heroic verse [464]. Thus Pindar came in the times of the pompous bravery of Greece admired at the Olympic games, at which these lyric poets sang. In the same way Horace came in the most sumptuous times of Rome, under the reign of Augustus; and among the Italians the melic period came in the times of the greatest softness and tenderness.

910   The tragic and comic poets ran their course between the following limits. Thespis in one part of Greece and Amphion [i.e., Arion] in

another originated at vintage time the satire, or satyr play, the primitive form of tragedy, with satyrs for its characters. In the rough and simple fashion of those days they must have invented the first mask by covering their feet, legs, and thighs with goat skins which they must have had at hand, and painting their breasts and faces with the lees of wine and fitting their foreheads with horns (on which account, perhaps, in our own day the vintagers are still vulgarly called *cornuti*, horned). In this sense it may well be true that Bacchus, god of the vintage, commanded Aeschylus to compose tragedies. All of which accords well with the times when the heroes were asserting that the plebeians were monsters of two natures, half man, half goat [566f, 906]. Thus there is strong ground for conjecture that tragedy had its beginnings in this chorus of satyrs and that it took its name from the primitive mask we have described, rather than from the award of a *tragos*, or goat, to the winner in a competition in this sort of verse. (Horace [A.P. 220ff] glances at this latter possibility without making anything of it, and calls the goat paltry.) And the satire preserved this eternal property with which it was born: that of expressing invective and insult; for the peasants, thus roughly masked and riding in the carts in which they carried the grapes, had the license—as the vintagers still have in our happy Campania (once called the dwelling of Bacchus)—of hurling abuse at their betters. Hence we may understand with how little truth the learned later inserted into the fable of Pan (since *pan* signifies "all") the philosophical mythology to the effect that he signifies the universe, and that the hairy nether parts mean the earth, the red breast and face the element of fire, and the horns the sun and the moon [688]. The Romans, however, preserved for us the historical mythology concerning him in the word *satyra*, which, according to Festus, was a dish made of various kinds of foods. Hence the later expression *lex per satyram* for an omnibus law. So, in dramatic satire, which we are discussing here, according to Horace [A.P. 225ff] (for no examples of this form have come down to us either from the Greeks or from the Latins), various types of characters made their appearance, such as gods, heroes, kings, artisans, and slaves. But the satire that survived among the Romans does not treat of varied matters, since each poem is devoted to a separate argument.

911 Then Aeschylus brought about the transition from the Old Tragedy, that is, the satyr play, to Middle Tragedy by using human masks and by converting the dithyramb of Amphion [i.e., Arion], which was a chorus of satyrs, into a chorus of men. And Middle Tragedy must have been the origin of Old Comedy, in which great personages were portrayed and the chorus was therefore fitting. Afterward came first Sophocles and

then Euripides, who left us the final form of tragedy. The Old Comedy ended with Aristophanes, because of the bad name it gave Socrates; and Menander bequeathed us the New Comedy, built around private and fictitious personages, who could be fictitious because they were private, and could therefore be believed to be real [806, 808, 906]. Hence there was no longer any room for the chorus, which is a public that comments, and comments only on public matters.

912   In this way the satire was composed in heroic verse, as the Latins afterward preserved it, because the first peoples spoke in heroic verse. Later they spoke in iambic verse, so that tragedy was composed in iambic verse quite naturally, and comedy only by an empty adherence to precedent when the Greek peoples were already speaking in prose. The iambic meter was certainly appropriate to tragedy, for it is a verse born to give vent to anger, and its movement is that of what Horace calls a swift foot [233]. Vulgar tradition says that it was invented by Archilochus to vent his wrath against Lycambes, who had refused to give him his daughter in marriage, and that the bitterness of his verses drove father and daughter to hang themselves in desperation. This must have been a history of the heroic contest over *connubium*, in which the rebellious plebeians must have hanged the nobles along with their daughters [598].

913   So was born that monstrosity of poetic art by which the same violent, rapid, and excited verse is made to fit such grand poetry as that of tragedy, considered by Plato [R. 394C?] even more lofty than the epic, and at the same time such delicate poetry as that of comedy; and the same metric foot, well adapted, as we have said, to express wrath and rage, in which tragedy must break forth so fearfully, is considered equally good as a vehicle for jests, games, and sentimental love affairs, which must make up all the grace and charm of comedy.

914   As a result of the indiscriminate use of the terms "lyric" and "tragic," Hippocrates was placed in the time of the Seven Sages; but he should rather be put about the time of Herodotus, since he came at a time when men still spoke largely in fables (for his own life has a tinge of the fabulous, and Herodotus's *History* is largely narrated in the form of fables), yet not only had speech in prose been introduced but also writing in vulgar characters, in which Herodotus wrote his history and Hippocrates wrote the many works on medicine that have come down to us [857, 906].

BOOK FOUR

THE COURSE
THE NATIONS RUN [L1]

[INTRODUCTION]

915 In virtue of the principles of this Science established in Book One, and of the origins of all the divine and human institutions of the gentile world which we investigated and discovered in Book Two, and of the discovery in Book Three that the poems of Homer are two great treasure stores of the natural law of the gentes of Greece [902ff] (just as we had already found the Law of the Twelve Tables to be a great monument of the natural law of the gentes of Latium [154]), we shall now, by the aid of this philosophical and philological illumination, and relying on the axioms concerning the ideal eternal history [241–245], discuss in Book Four the course the nations run, proceeding in all their various and diverse customs with constant uniformity upon the division of the three ages which the Egyptians said had elapsed before them in their world, namely, the successive ages of gods, heroes, and men [31]. For the nations will be seen to develop in conformity with this division, by a constant and uninterrupted order of causes and effects present in every nation, through three kinds of natures [916ff]. From these natures arise three kinds of customs [919ff]; and in virtue of these customs three kinds of natural laws of the gentes are observed [922ff]; and in consequence of these laws three kinds of civil states or commonwealths are instituted [925ff]. And to the end that men who have come to human society may on the one hand communicate to each other the three kinds of all the aforesaid major institutions, three kinds of languages [928ff] and as many of characters [932ff] are formed; and to the end that they may on the other hand justify them, three kinds of jurisprudence [937ff] assisted by three kinds of authority [942ff] and three kinds of reason [947ff] in as many of judgments [954–974]. The three kinds of jurisprudence prevail in three sects of times [975ff], which the nations profess in the course of their lives. These [eleven] triadic special unities, with many others that derive from them and will also be enumerated in this Book [980–1045], are all embraced by one general unity. This is the unity of the religion of a provident divinity, which is the unity of spirit that informs and gives life to this world of nations. Having discussed these institutions above in widely separate passages, we shall here exhibit the order of their development.

[SECTION I]

THREE KINDS OF NATURES [C7]

916 The first nature, by a powerful deceit [385] of imagination, which is most robust in the weakest at reasoning [185], was a poetic or creative nature [376] which we may be allowed to call divine, as it ascribed to physical things the being of substances animated by gods, assigning the gods to them according to its idea of each [377, 379, 401f]. This nature was that of the theological poets, who were the earliest wise men in all the gentile nations, when all the gentile nations were founded on the belief which each of them had in certain gods of its own. Furthermore it was a nature all fierce and cruel; but, through that same error of their imagination, men had a terrible fear of the gods whom they themselves had created [518]. From this there remained these two eternal properties: one, that religion is the only means powerful enough to restrain the fierceness of peoples; and the other, that religions flourish when they are inwardly revered by those who preside over them.

917 The second was heroic nature, believed by the heroes themselves to be of divine origin [449]; for, since they believed that the gods made and did everything [377, 379, 508, 629], they held themselves to be sons of Jove, as having been generated under his auspices. Being thus of the human [not a bestial] species, they justly regarded their heroism as including the natural nobility in virtue of which they were the princes of the human race. And this natural nobility they made their boast over those who had fled from the infamous and bestial promiscuity to save themselves from the strife it entailed, and had taken refuge in their asylums; for, since they had come thither without gods, the heroes regarded them as beasts. We have discussed these two natures above [553ff].

918 The third was human nature, intelligent and hence modest, benign, and reasonable, recognizing for laws conscience, reason, and duty.

[SECTION II]

THREE KINDS OF CUSTOMS

919 The first customs were all tinged with religion and piety, like those of Deucalion and Pyrrha, fresh from the flood [523].

920 The second were choleric and punctilious, like those related of Achilles [667, 786].

921 The third are dutiful, taught to everyone by his own sense of civil duty.

[SECTON III]

THREE KINDS OF NATURAL LAW

922 The first law was divine, for men believed themselves and all their institutions to depend on the gods, since they thought everything was a god or was made or done by a god [379, 629, 917].

923 The second was heroic law, the law of force, but controlled by religion, which alone can keep force within bounds where there are no human laws or none strong enough to curb it. Hence providence ordained that the first peoples, ferocious by nature, should be persuaded by this their religion to acquiesce naturally in force, and that, being as yet incapable of reason, they should measure right by fortune, with a view to which they took counsel by auspicial divination. This law of force is the law of Achilles, who referred every right to the tip of his spear.

924 The third is the human law dictated by fully developed human reason [C7, 326].

[SECTION IV]

THREE KINDS OF GOVERNMENTS

925 The first were divine, or, as the Greeks would say, theocratic [629], in which men belived that everything was commanded by the gods [379]. This was the age of oracles, which are the earliest institution we read of in history [381].

926 The second were heroic or aristocratic governments, which is as much as to say governments of the optimates in the sense of the most powerful [586]. In Greek they were called governments of Heraclids (men sprung from the race of Hercules), in the sense of nobles; these were scattered throughout early Greece, and survived at Sparta. They were also called governments of Curetes, which the Greeks found scattered in Saturnia (ancient Italy), Crete, and Asia [591ff]; and hence governments of Quirites among the Romans, that is, of armed priests in public assembly [595]. In governments of this kind, in virtue of the distinction of a nobler nature ascribed to divine origin, as we have noted above, all civil rights were confined to the ruling orders of the heroes themselves, and the plebeians, being considered of bestial origin, were only permitted to enjoy life and natural liberty [597].

927 The third are human governments, in which, in virtue of the equality of the intelligent nature which is the proper nature of man [918], all are accounted equal under the laws, inasmuch as all are born free in their cities. This is the case in the free popular cities in which all or the majority make up the just forces of the city, in virtue of which they are the lords of popular liberty. It is also the case in monarchies, in which the monarchs make all their subjects equal under their laws, and, having all the force of arms in their own hands, are themselves the only bearers of any distinction in civil nature [1004–1008].

[SECTION V]

THREE KINDS OF LANGUAGES

928 Three kinds of languages.

929 The first of these was a divine mental language by mute religious acts or divine ceremonies [401ff], from which there survived in Roman civil law the *actus legitimi* which accompanied all their civil transactions [558, 1030f]. This language belongs to religions by the eternal property that it concerns them more to be reverenced than to be reasoned, and it was necessary in the earliest times when men did not yet possess articulate speech.

930 The second was by heroic blazonings, with which arms are made to speak; this kind of speech survived in military discipline [484-488].

931 The third is by articulate speech, which is used by all nations today [448-454].

[SECTION VI]

THREE KINDS OF CHARACTERS

932 Three kinds of characters.

933 The first were divine, properly called hieroglyphics, used, as we have shown above, by all nations in their beginnings [435]. And they were certain imaginative universals, dictated naturally by the human mind's innate property of delighting in the uniform [204, 209]. Since they could not achieve this by logical abstraction, they did it by imaginative representation. To these poetic universals they reduced all the particular species belonging to each genus, as to Jove everything concerning the auspices [379], to Juno everything touching marriage [513], and so on.

934 The second were heroic characters, which were also imaginative universals to which they reduced the various species of heroic things, as to Achilles all the deeds of valiant fighters and to Ulysses all the devices of clever men. These imaginative genera, as the human mind later learned to abstract forms and properties from subjects, passed over into intelligible genera, which prepared the way for the philosophers, from whom the authors of the New Comedy, which came in the most human times of Greece, took the intelligible genera of human customs and portrayed them in their comedies [808f].

935 Finally, there were invented the vulgar characters which went along with the vulgar languages. The latter are composed of words, which are genera, as it were, of the particulars previously employed by the heroic languages; as, to repeat an example cited above [460], out of the heroic phrase "The blood boils in my heart" they made the word "I am angry." In like fashion, of a hundred and twenty thousand hieroglyphic characters (the number still used, for example, by the Chinese) they made a few letters, to which, as to genera, they reduced the hundred and twenty thousand words (of which the Chinese vulgar spoken language is composed) [462]. This invention certainly is the work of a mind more than human, whence Bernard von Mallinckrodt and Ingewald Eling held it to be a divine invention [428]. It is easy to understand how the common sense of marvel led the nations to believe that these letters had been invented for them by men eminent in divinity, as by St. Jerome in the case of the Illyrians, St. Cyril in that of the Slavs, and so on, as Angelo Rocca observes in his *Bibliotheca Vaticana*, where the authors of what we call vulgar letters are depicted along with their alphabets. But such an opinion can be convicted of manifest falsity if we pose the simple question: Why did they not teach letters of their own creation? Cadmus, for example, brought letters from Phoenicia to the Greeks, yet the latter afterward used letters of very different forms from the Phoenician.

936 Such languages and letters were under the sovereignty of the vulgar of the various peoples, whence both are called vulgar [443]. In virtue of this sovereignty over languages and letters, the free peoples must also be masters of their laws, for they impose on the laws the senses in which they constrain the powerful to observe them, even against their will, as we noted in the Axioms [283ff]. It is naturally not in the power of monarchs to deprive the people of this sovereignty, but, in virtue of this very inalienable nature of human civil affairs, such sovereignty, inseparable from the people, contributes largely to the power of the monarchs, for they may issue their royal laws, which the nobles must accept, according to the senses that their peoples give to them. This sovereignty over vulgar letters and languages implies that, in the order of civil nature, the free popular commonwealths preceded the monarchies.

[SECTION VII]

THREE KINDS OF JURISPRUDENCE

937   Three kinds of jurisprudence, or [legal] wisdom.

938   The first was a divine wisdom called mystic theology, which means the science of divine speech or the understanding of the divine mysteries of divination. This science of auspicial divinity was the vulgar wisdom whose sages were the theological poets, who were the first sages of the gentile world. From this mystic theology they were called *mystai*, or mystics, which the well-informed Horace translates as interpreters of the gods [381]. To this first jurisprudence therefore belonged the first and proper interpreting, called *interpretari* for *interpatrari*; that is, "to enter into the fathers," as the gods were at first called [448]. Dante would call it *indiarsi*, to enter into the mind of God [*Paradise* 4.28]. This sort of jurisprudence measured justice only by the solemnity of the divine ceremonies; whence the Romans preserved such a superstitious regard for the *actus legitimi* [929], and they retained in their laws the phrases *iustae nuptiae, iustum testamentum*, for solemnized nuptials and testaments.

939   The second was the heroic jurisprudence, taking precautions by the use of certain proper words. Such is the wisdom of Ulysses, who speaks so adroitly in Homer that he obtains the advantages he seeks while always observing the propriety of his words. Hence all the reputation of the ancient Roman jurisconsults rested in their *cavere*, their taking care or making sure [569]; and their *de iure respondere* was nothing but cautioning clients who had to present their cases in court to set forth the facts to the praetor with such circumstances that the formulae for action would be satisfied and the praetor would be unable to withhold them [965]. Similarly in the returned barbarian times all the reputation of the doctors rested on finding safeguards for contracts and wills and on knowing how to draw pleadings and articles; which correspond exactly to the *cavere* and the *de iure respondere* of the Roman jurisconsults [1072].

940   The third is human jurisprudence, which looks to the truth of the facts themselves and benignly bends the rule of law to all the require-

ments of the equity of the causes [327]. This kind of jurisprudence is observed in the free popular commonwealths and even more under the monarchies, which are both human governments [927].

941 Thus divine and heroic jurisprudence laid hold of the certain when the nations were rude, and human jurisprudence looked to the true when they had become enlightened. All this in consequence of the definitions of the certain and the true, and of the axioms set forth on the matter in our Elements [137f, 321f, 324f].

[SECTION VIII]

THREE KINDS OF AUTHORITY

942 There were three kinds of authority [350, 386–390]. The first is divine, and for this providence is not called to account. The second is heroic, resting entirely on the solemn formulae of the laws. The third is human, based on the trust placed in persons of experience, of singular prudence in practical matters, and of sublime wisdom in intellectual matters.

943 These three kinds of authority employed by jurisprudence in the course the nations run, correspond to three sorts of authority appertaining to senates, which succeed one another in the same course.

944 The first was the authority of property ownership, in virtue of which those from whom we derive title to property were called *auctores*, and such ownership is itself always called *auctoritas* in the Law of the Twelve Tables [386]. This authority had its source in divine governments from the time of the family state, in which divine authority must have been vested in the gods, for it was believed, fairly enough, that everything belonged to the gods [922]. Afterward in the heroic aristocracies in which the senates were the seat of sovereignty (as they are in the aristocracies of our own time), authority quite properly was vested in these reigning senates. Hence the heroic senates gave their approval to that which the peoples had previously devised; as Livy [1.17.9] puts it, *eius, quod populus iussisset, deinde patres fierent auctores* [113]. This does not, however, date from the interregnum of Romulus, as history relates, but from the declining period of the aristocracy when citizenship had been extended to the plebs, as explained above [598, 112f]. This arrangement, as Livy himself says [1.9.6], *saepe spectabat ad vim,* "frequently threatened to issue in revolt"; so that, if the people wanted their proposals confirmed, they had, for example, to nominate for consuls those who were favored by the senate, just as is the case when magistrates are nominated by the people under monarchies.

945 From the time of the law of Publilius Philo, which declared the

Roman people free and absolute master of the *imperium* [112f], the authority of the senate was that of guardianship, just as the approval given by guardians to the transactions of their wards, who are masters of their own patrimonies, is called *auctoritas tutorum*. This [tutorial] authority was conferred by the senate on the people in the formula of the law drafted beforehand in the senate, by which, just as the authority of the guardian has to be conferred on the ward, the senate was to be present in the people, present in the great assemblies, present in the act of decreeing the law if they decided to decree it; otherwise they might "antiquate," or reject it, *probaret antiqua;* that is, declare that they wanted no innovation [113]. All this in order that the people, in decreeing the laws, might not, by reason of their weak counsel, do any harm to the commonwealth, and in order that, in decreeing them, they might be regulated by the senate. Thus the formulae of the laws brought by the senate to the people to be decreed by them are advisedly defined by Cicero [*The Making of an Orator* 3.2.5] as *perscriptae auctoritates:* not personal authorizations, like those of guardians who by their presence approve the acts of their wards, but authorizations written out in full (for such is the sense of *perscriptae*), as distinguished from the formulae of actions, written *per notas* or employing abbreviations which are not understood by the people. This is what was ordained by the Publilian Law: that thenceforth the authority of the senate, in Livy's words [1.17.9], *valeret in incertum comitiorum eventum,* "should be committed while the outcome in the assembly was as yet uncertain" [113].

946   Finally the commonwealth passed from popular liberty to monarchy, and there ensued the third kind of authority, which is that of credit or reputation for wisdom; and hence the authority of counsel, in respect of which the jurisconsults under the emperors were said to be *auctores*. Such also must be the authority of senates under monarchs, who have full and absolute liberty to follow or not to follow the counsel their senates give them.

[SECTION IX]

THREE KINDS OF REASON

[Chapter I] *[Divine Reason and Reason of State]*

947 There were three kinds of reason [or right: divine reason [948], reason of state [949], natural reason [951]].

948 The first is divine and understood only by God; men know of it only what has been revealed to them. To the Hebrews first and then to the Christians, this has been by internal speech to their minds as the proper expression of a God all mind; but [also] by external speech through the prophets and through Jesus Christ to the Apostles, by whom it was declared to the Church. To the gentiles it has been through the auspices, the oracles, and other corporeal signs regarded as divine messages because they were supposed to come from the gods, whom the gentiles believed to be corporeal [F7]. So that in God who is all reason, reason and authority are the same thing; whence in good theology divine authority holds the same place as reason. Here providence is to be admired because, in the earliest times when the men of the gentile world did not understand reason (which must have been the case above all in the family state), it permitted them to fall into the error of following in place of reason the authority of the auspices, and to govern themselves by what they believed to be the divine counsels thereby communicated. This by the eternal property that when men fail to see reason in human institutions, and much more if they see it opposed, they take refuge in the inscrutable counsels hidden in the abyss of divine providence.

949 The second was reason of state, called by the Romans *civilis aequitas*, which Ulpian defined for us as not naturally known to all men but only to the few experts in government who are able to discern what is necessary for the preservation of mankind [320]. In this the heroic senates were naturally wise, and above them all the Roman senate was most wise both in the times of aristocratic liberty, when the plebs was permitted no voice in public institutions, and in the times of popular liberty, so long as

the people were guided by the senate in public affairs, which is to say down to the times of the Gracchi.

[Chapter II]   *Corollary on the Political Wisdom of the Ancient Romans*

950   Here arises a problem which seems very difficult to solve. How is it that the Romans could have been so wise in statecraft in the rude times of Rome, when in their enlightened times Ulpian [320] says that "today only a few experts in government understand statecraft"? The answer is that, by virtue of the same natural causes which produced the heroism of the first peoples [666ff], the ancient Romans, who were the heroes of the world [160], naturally looked to civil equity, which was most scrupulous about the words in which the laws were expressed. By this superstitious observance of their words, they made the laws march straight through all the facts, even where the laws turned out to be severe, harsh, and cruel [322], just as reason of state operates today. Thus civil equity naturally subordinated everything to that law, queen of all others, conceived by Cicero [L. 3.3.8] with a gravity adequate to the matter: *Suprema lex populi salus esto* ("The safety of the people shall be the supreme law"). For in heroic times, in which the states were aristocratic, the heroes each possessed privately a large share of the public utility in the form of the family monarchies preserved for them by the fatherland; and in view of this great particular interest preserved for them by the commonwealth, they naturally subordinated their minor private interests [584]. Hence naturally as magnanimous men they defended the public good, which is that of the state, and as wise men they gave counsel on affairs of state. This was a high counsel of divine providence, for the cyclopean fathers (such as we have found them in Homer and Plato [296, 338]), if they had not had such a great private interest identified with the public interest, could not have been induced to abandon their savage life and cultivate civility.

951   It is quite otherwise in the human times in which free popular states or monarchies develop. In the former the citizens have command of the public wealth, which is divided among them in as many minute parts as there are citizens making up the people who have command of it. In the second the subjects are commanded to look after their own private interests and leave the care of the public interest to the sovereign prince. To this we must add the natural causes which produced these forms of state

(which are quite opposite to those which had produced heroism); namely, as we have shown above, love of ease, tenderness toward children, love of women, and desire of life [670]. By all these causes men are today naturally led to attend to the smallest details which may bring their private utilities into equality with those of others. This is the *aequum bonum* considered by the third kind of reason to be discussed here, namely, natural reason, which is called *aequitas naturalis* by the jurisconsults [326]. This is the only reason of which the multitude are capable, for, when they are themselves involved, they attend to the smallest considerations of the justice which is called for by cases when the facts are fully specified. And in monarchies there are needed a few men skilled in statecraft to give counsel according to civil equity on public emergencies in the cabinets, and a great many jurists of private jurisprudence to administer justice to the peoples by professing natural equity.

[Chapter III]   Corollary: Fundamental History of Roman Law

952 What has here been set forth concerning the three kinds of reason may serve as a foundation on which to establish the history of Roman law. For governments must conform to the nature of the governed, inasmuch as the governments are born of the nature of the governed [246ff]. So too the laws must be administered in conformity with the governments, and on that account must be interpreted according to the form of the governments [925ff]. (This seems not to have been done by any of the jurisconsults or interpreters, who have fallen into the same error into which the historians of Roman affairs had previously fallen. The latter tell of laws decreed at various times in the Roman commonwealth but fail to point out the relations which these laws must have had to the forms of government through which that commonwealth passed. Hence the facts emerge so denuded of the proper causes which must naturally have produced them, that Jean Bodin [1009ff], equally learned as jurist and as statesman, argues that the institutions created by the ancient Romans in the period of the liberty which the historians falsely describe as popular were instead the effects of an aristocratic commonwealth, as in the present work we have shown to be the fact [629ff].) In view of all this, if all the embellishers of the history of Roman law are asked: Why did the old jurisprudence practice such rigors in applying the Law of the Twelve Tables? Why did the middle jurisprudence, by the edicts of the praetors,

begin to exercise a benignity of reason while still respecting that law? Why did the new jurisprudence, without even a pretense of regard for that law, adopt the generous profession of natural equity?—then, in order to give an explanation of some kind, they put forward one which is very offensive to Roman generosity, for they say that the rigors, the solemnities, the scruples, the verbal subtleties, and finally the secrecy of the laws themselves were impostures on the part of the nobles in order to keep the laws in their own hands, for the reason that the laws make up a great part of civil power.

953   Yet these practices were so far from being impostures that they were customs born of their very natures, which through such customs produced such states as naturally dictated such practices and no others. For in the time of the extreme savagery of earliest mankind, when religion was the only means sufficiently powerful to tame it [177f], providence ordained that men should live under divine governments [925] and that the laws everywhere reigning should be sacred, which is as much as to say mysterious and hidden from the masses of the peoples [586]. The laws in the family state were so naturally of this sort that they were safeguarded in mute languages expressed in consecrated solemnities [999f] (which survived in the *actus legitimi*), which those simple minds held necessary to assure one man of the effective will of another in the exchange of utilities [929], whereas now, in the natural intelligence of our minds, it is sufficient to assure oneself by the spoken word or even by mere signs. Then came the human governments of aristocratic civil states [926], and, naturally continuing to practice the religious customs, they religiously continued to keep the laws mysterious and secret (this secrecy being the soul and life of aristocratic commonwealths), and religion insured the strict observance of the laws which is the rigor of civil equity by which aristocracies are principally preserved [320, 949f]. Afterward, when the time came for popular commonwealths, which are naturally open, generous, and magnanimous (being commanded by the multitude, who naturally understand natural equity [951]), the so-called vulgar languages and letters (of which the multitude are masters [946]) developed at the same pace, and in these they enacted and wrote the laws, and naturally went on to make public what had been secret. This is [the history of] the *ius latens* of which Pomponius relates that the Roman plebs would have no more of it [284] and hence insisted that the laws be inscribed on tablets, since vulgar letters had come from the Greeks to Rome [763]. The order of human civil institutions was finally ready for the monarchic states, in which the monarchs wish the laws administered according to natural equity and consequently in harmony

with the understanding of the multitude, and thus make the powerful and the weak equal before the law, which monarchy alone can do [936, 951]. Whereas civil equity, or reason of state, was understood by a few men wise in public reason and, by virtue of its eternal property, was kept secret within cabinets.

[SECTION X]

THREE KINDS OF JUDGMENTS

[Chapter I] *[First Kind: Divine Judgments]*

954 There were three kinds of judgments.

955 The first were divine judgments. In the so-called state of nature (the family state), as there were no civil authorities ruling by law, the family fathers complained to the gods of the wrongs done them (which was the first and proper meaning of the phrase *implorare deorum fidem*) and called the gods to bear witness to the justice of their causes (the first and proper meaning of *deos obtestari*). Such accusations and defenses were the world's first orations, in the primary and proper sense of that word, and *oratio* continued to be used in Latin for accusation or defense. There are fine examples of this usage in Plautus and Terence and the Law of the Twelve Tables preserved two golden passages [1.6; 8.16] in which *furto orare* and *pacto orare* (not *adorare*, which is Lipsius's reading) are used respectively for *agere* and *excipere*, to bring suit and to enter an exception. From these orations the term *oratores* survived in Latin for those who plead cases in court. The original appeals to the gods were made by simple and rude people in the belief that they were heard by the gods, whom they imagined to dwell on the tops of the mountains, as Homer places them on Olympus [712]; and Tacitus [A. 13.57] tells of a war waged between the Hermunduri and the Chatti under the superstition that nowhere except from the mountaintops were mortal prayers more closely heard by the gods—*preces mortalium nusquam propius audiri*—[than at the river between these two peoples].

956 The rights secured by these divine judgments were themselves gods, for in those times the gentiles imagined that all institutions were gods. For example, *Lar* was the ownership of the household; *dii Hospitales*, the right of shelter; *dii Penates*, the paternal power; *deus Genius*, the right of marriage; *deus Terminus*, the ownership of the farm; *dii Manes*, the right of burial. Of the last, a golden vestige survived in the Law of the Twelve Tables [i.e., in Cicero, L. 2.9.22]: *ius deorum manium.*

957 After such orations (or obsecrations or implorations) and after such obtestations, they proceeded to the act of execrating the criminals. Thus among the Greeks, as was certainly the case at Argos, there were temples of execration, and the execrated men were called *anathēmata,* or, as we say, excommunicates. And against them they made vows (this was the first *nuncupare vota,* which means to make solemn vows with consecrated formulae) and they consecrated them to the Furies (who were truly *diris devoti*) and then killed them. (The custom of the Scythians was to fix a knife in the ground, adore it as a god, and then kill the man with it.) This kind of execution the Latins called *mactare,* which remained a sacred term used in sacrifices; this is the source of the Spanish *matar* and the Italian *ammazzare,* to kill. Among the Greeks *ara* remained in the senses of harmful body, vow, and fury, and among the Latins it meant both altar and victim. Some kind of excommunication survived among all nations. Caesar [G.W. 6.13] left us a detailed account of the Gallic ceremony, and the interdict of fire and water was preserved among the Romans [610]. Many of these consecrations passed into the Law of the Twelve Tables [8.9f]; for example, he who violated a tribune of the plebs was "consecrated to Jove"; an impious son was "consecrated to the gods of the fathers"; he who set fire to another's grain was "consecrated to Ceres" and burned alive [1021]. Such must have been those whom Plautus called Saturn's victims, *Saturni hostiae* [191]. It may be seen that the cruelty of these divine punishments was like that of the cruelest witches [190].

958 From the practice of these judgments in private affairs, the peoples went forth to wage wars which were called pure and pious, *pura et pia bella,* and they waged them *pro aris et focis,* for altar and hearth [562], that is, for civil institutions both public and private; for they regarded all human institutions as divine. Hence the heroic wars were all wars of religion, and the heralds, in delivering a declaration of war, called forth the gods from the enemy city, and consecrated the enemy to the gods [550, 1050]. Wherefore defeated kings were presented by the triumphant Romans to Jove Feretrius on the Capitoline and thereafter slain, after the pattern of the impious violent who had been the first hosts, the first victims, which Vesta had consecrated on the first altars of the world [549]. And the surrendered peoples were considered men without gods, after the pattern of the first *famuli;* whence slaves, like inanimate things, were called *mancipia* in the Roman language, and in Roman jurisprudence they were treated [not as persons but] as things, *in loco rerum.*

[*Chapter II*]   *Corollary on Duels and Reprisals*

959   One sort of divine judgment, in the barbarous period of the nations, was duels, which must have begun under the earliest government of the gods and continued for a long time under the heroic commonwealths. Concerning the latter we cited in the axioms the golden passage in Aristotle's *Politics* where he says that these commonwealths had no judiciary laws for punishing private wrongs and making restitution for private injuries [269]. Until now this has not been believed, because of the false opinion hitherto held by the conceit of scholars concerning the philosophic heroism of the first peoples which was supposed to follow from the matchless wisdom of the ancients [666].

960   Certainly among the Romans the interdict *Unde vi* and the actions *De vi bonorum raptorum* and *Quod metus caussa* were introduced late and only by the praetor [638]. And in the recourse of the latest barbarism private reprisals lasted down to the time of Bartolus [1029, 1054]. Such must have been the condictions or personal actions of the ancient Romans, for *condicere*, according to Festus, means to denounce or serve notice. (Thus a family father had to make formal demand for restitution on one who had unjustly taken from him something that belonged to him, in order to proceed to reprisals.) Such a denunciation remained a formality of personal actions, as Ulrich Zasius acutely discerned.

961   But duels contained real judgments, which, because they took place *in re praesenti*, in the presence of the disputed object, had no need of the formal denunciation. From these developed the *vindiciae*, in which a clod taken from the wrongful possessor with a feigned show of force [1032], which Aulus Gellius calls *festucaria*, of straw [638] (but the name *vindiciae* must have come from the real force originally used), was taken to the judge, before whom the claimant spoke over the *gleba*, or clod, the words: *Aio hunc fundum meum esse ex iure quiritium* ("I declare this farm to be mine by the law of the Quirites") [562]. Hence those who write that duels were introduced for lack of proofs are wrong; they should say rather for lack of judiciary laws. For certainly Frotho, king of Denmark, ordered that all disputes should be settled by duels, thereby forbidding their settlement by legitimate judgments. And, to avoid litigation, the laws of the Lombards, Salians, Englishmen, Burgundians, Normans, Danes, and Germans

are all alike full of duels. On this account Cujas in his *De feudis* says: *Et hoc genere purgationis diu usi sunt christiani tam in civilibus quam in criminalibus caussis, re omni duello commissa:* "Christians made use of this sort of purgation for a long time in both civil and criminal cases, everything being settled by duel." From this it came about that the German knights called *Ritter*, or horseback riders, profess the science of dueling and oblige the prospective adversaries to tell the truth; for duels, if witnesses were admitted and consequently judges had to intervene, would turn into either civil or criminal judgments.

962 It has not been believed that the first barbarism practiced dueling, because no record of it has come down to us. But it passes our understanding how the Homeric cyclopes, in whom Plato recognizes the earliest family fathers in the state of nature [296], can have endured being wronged, to say nothing of showing humanity in the matter. Certainly Aristotle [269] tells us that in the earliest commonwealths, not to speak of the still earlier state of the families, there were no laws to right wrongs and punish offenses suffered by private citizens (as we have just proved in the case of the ancient Roman commonwealth [960]); and therefore Aristotle also tells us that this was the custom of barbarous peoples, for peoples are barbarous in their beginnings because they are not yet tamed by laws.

963 However, there are two great vestiges of such duels, one from Greek and one from Roman history, showing that the peoples must have begun their wars (called *duella* by the ancient Latins) with combats between the offended individuals, even if they were kings, waged in the presence of their respective peoples, who wished publicly to defend or avenge their offenses. In this fashion certainly the Trojan War began with the combat of Menelaus and Paris (the former the wronged husband and the latter the seducer of his wife, Helen); and when the duel was indecisive the Greeks and Trojans proceeded to wage war with each other. And we have already noted the same custom among the Latin nations in the war between the Romans and the Albans, which was effectively settled by the combat between the three Horatii and the three Curiatii, one of whom must have abducted Horatia [641]. In such armed judgments right was measured by the fortune of victory. This was a counsel of divine providence, to the end that, among barbarous peoples with little capacity for reason and no understanding of right, wars might not breed further wars, and that they might thus have some notion of the justice or injustice of men from the favor or disfavor of the gods: even as the gentiles scorned the saintly Job when he had fallen from his royal estate because God was against him. And on the same principle in the returned barbarian times the

barbarous custom was to cut off the hand of the loser, however just his cause.

964 From this sort of custom observed by the peoples in private affairs, there emerged what the moral theologians call the external justice of wars, whereby the nations might rest in the certainty of their dominions [350]. In this fashion the auspices which had founded the monarchical paternal authority of the fathers in the state of the families, and had prepared and preserved for them their aristocratic reigns in the heroic cities, and which, when shared with the plebs, produced the free popular commonwealths (as Roman history openly relates), finally legitimized by the fortune of arms the conquests of the lucky victors. All this can have no other source than the innate concept of providence which all nations possess and to which they must bow when they see the just afflicted and the wicked prospering.

[Chapter III]   [Second Kind: Ordinary Judgments]

965 The second kind of judgments, because of their recent origin from divine judgments, were all ordinary, observed with an extreme verbal scrupulousness which must have carried over from the previous divine judgments [953] the name *religio verborum,* even as divine institutions are universally conceived in sacred formulae which cannot be altered by as much as one little letter; whence it was said of the ancient formulae for actions: *Qui cadit virgula, caussa cadit* ("He who drops a comma loses his case"). This is the natural law of the heroic gentes, observed naturally by ancient Roman jurisprudence; and it was the praetor's *fari,* which was an unalterable utterance, from which the days on which he dispensed justice were called *dies fasti.* This justice, because only the heroes shared in it under the heroic aristocracies, must have been the *fas deorum* of the times in which the heroes had taken to themselves the name of gods [449]; whence later the name *Fatum* was given to the ineluctable order of causes producing the institutions of nature, as being the utterance of God. This may also account for the Italian verb *ordinare,* as applied especially to laws, in the sense of giving commands which must necessarily be carried out [M3–4].

966 Because such an order (which in connection with judgments signifies the solemn formula for an action) had dictated the cruel and shameful punishment against the illustrious defendant Horatius, the

duumvirs themselves could not have acquitted him even had he been found innocent, and the people, to whom he appealed, acquitted him, as Livy [1.26.12] tells us, *magis admiratione virtutis quam iure caussae,* "rather out of admiration of his valor than on account of the justice of his cause" [500]. This order of judgments was necessary in the times of Achilles, who measured all right by force [923], in virtue of that property of the powerful described by Plautus [in his *Pot of Gold* 260] with his usual elegance: *Pactum non pactum, non pactum pactum*—"An agreement is no agreement, and no agreement is an agreement"—where promises are not fulfilled to suit their proud desires or where they themselves are not willing to keep their promises. So, in order that they should not break out into disputes, quarrels, and killings, it was a counsel of providence that they should naturally adopt as their notion of justice that precisely such and so much was their right as had been set forth in solemn verbal formulae; whence the reputation of Roman jurisprudence and of our own ancient [i.e., medieval] doctors lay in safeguarding their clients [939]. This natural law of heroic nations provided Plautus with plots for several comedies [such as *The Persian* and *The Little Carthaginian*], in which panders, through deceptions devised against them by young men enamored of their slave girls, are unjustly defrauded of the girls by being innocently found guilty under some legal formula, and not only are they unable to bring an action for fraud, but one of them reimburses the deceitful youth for the price of the slave, another begs another youth to be content with half the penalty he has incurred for theft not proved by direct evidence, another flies the city for fear of being convicted for having corrupted another's slave. Such was the reign of natural equity in the judgments of Plautus's times!

967 Not only was this strict law naturally observed among men, but, judging the gods from their own natures, men thought that they too observed it in their oaths. So Homer relates that Juno swears to Jove, who is not only witness but also judge in the matter of oaths, that she had not urged Neptune to rouse up a tempest against the Trojans, since the god Somnus had acted as her intermediary, and Jove remains satisfied with her oath. So Mercury, disguised as Sosia, swears to the real Sosia, "If I deceive you, let Mercury be against Sosia"; and we can hardly believe that it was Plautus's intention in the *Amphitryon* [392] to bring in the gods to teach perjury to the people in the theater. It is even less credible in the case of Scipio Africanus and Laelius (who was called the Roman Socrates), two most wise princes of the Roman republic with whose collaboration Terence is said to have composed his comedies; yet in *The Lady of Andros* [728f]

Davus is represented as having the baby placed before Simo's door by the hands of Mysis so that if perchance his master should ask him about it, he may with a clear conscience deny having put it there.

968   But a very grave proof is the fact that in Athens, a city of discerning and intelligent men, on hearing the verse of Euripides [*Hippolytus* 612] which Cicero [*De officiis* 3.29.108] rendered in Latin: *Iuravi lingua, mentem iniuratam habui*—"I swore with my tongue, but my mind I kept unsworn"—the spectators in the theater murmured in disgust, for naturally they held the opinion that *uti lingua nuncupassit, ita ius esto*—"as the tongue has declared, so shall it be binding"—as the Law of the Twelve Tables [6.1a] commanded [570, 1031]. And what release could the unhappy Agamemnon find from the rash vow in fulfillment of which he consecrated and slew his innocent and pious daughter Iphigenia? Hence we can understand how denial of providence led Lucretius impiously to exclaim upon this deed of Agamemnon: *Tantum religio potuit suadere malorum!*—"So great were the evils religion could prompt!"[191].

969   In final confirmation of our argument here, we adduce two certain facts from Roman history and jurisprudence: one, that it was in very late [republican] times that Gallus Aquilius introduced the action *de dolo*; and the other, that Augustus gave judges discretion to absolve those who had been tricked or seduced.

970   Being used to this custom in peace, nations defeated in war, according to the terms of surrender, either suffered miserable oppression or by good fortune mocked the wrath of their conquerors.

971   Miserable oppression was the lot of the Carthaginians, who had accepted the Roman peace under the provision that they would have left to them life, their city, and their substance. For they understood by the city its buildings, for which sense the Latin word is *urbs*, but the Romans had used the word *civitas*, which means the community of citizens. So when in fulfillment of the peace terms the Carthaginians were commanded to abandon their city on the coast and retire inland, they refused to obey and took up their arms again in defense. The Romans then declared them rebels, took Carthage, and, by the heroic law of war, barbarously set fire to it. The Carthaginians repudiated the terms of peace granted them by the Romans, which they had not understood in negotiating them; for they had become intelligent before their time, partly through African sharpness and partly through maritime trading, which quickens the wit of nations. But the Romans did not therefore consider that war unjust; for, excepting a few who regard the Romans as having begun to wage unjust wars with that

against Numantia which was brought to an end by Scipio Africanus, all agree that they began with the later one against Corinth.

972 A still better proof of what we are arguing is afforded by the returned barbarian times. When the Emperor Conrad III dictated the terms of surrender to Weinsberg, whose resistance had been fomented by his rival for the empire, he specified that only the women should be allowed to come out of the city with whatever they could carry away on their backs; whereupon the pious women of Weinsberg came out carrying their children, husbands, and fathers. The victorious emperor stood before the city gate, in the very moment of triumph, which is naturally tempting to insolence, and yet restrained his anger (which is terrifying in the great and must be most ominous when caused by impediments to acquiring or retaining their sovereignty). While the army under his command stood by with swords drawn and lances in rest, prepared to slaughter the men of Weinsberg, he looked on and permitted all to pass safely by him whom he had intended to put to the sword. So far was the natural law of the developed human reason of Grotius, Selden, and Pufendorf from being current by nature through all times in all nations [329]!

973 All that we have so far set forth, and all that we shall have to say later, springs from the definitions of the true and the certain in laws and pacts [321, 324]; and [from the fact] that the strict law observed in words, which is properly the *fas gentium*, is as natural in barbarous times as that benign law is in human times which is measured by the equal utility of causes, which should properly be called *fas naturae*, the immutable law of the rational humanity, which is the true and proper nature of man [C7, 326ff].

[Chapter IV] [Third Kind: Human Judgments]

974 Judgments of the third kind are all extraordinary. In these the governing consideration is the truth of the facts, to which, according to the dictates of conscience, the laws benignly give aid when needed in everything demanded by the equal utility of causes. These are all imbued with natural modesty (which is the child of intelligence) and therefore guaranteed by good faith (the daughter of humanity), which is appropriate to the openness of popular commonwealths and much more to the generosity of monarchies, wherein the monarchs, in these judgments, make it their pride

to be above the laws and subject only to God and their conscience. And from these judgments, practiced in modern times during peace, have arisen the three systems of the law of war which we owe to Grotius, Selden, and Pufendorf [329]. And Father Nicola Concina, having observed many errors and defects in them, has constructed another system more in conformity with good philosophy and more useful to human society. This system of his, to the glory of Italy, he still teaches in the illustrious university of Padua, in addition to metaphysics, in which he holds the pricipal chair.

[SECTION XI]

THREE SECTS OF TIMES [viii]

[Chapter I] *[Sects of Religious, Punctilious, and Civil Times]*

975 All the aforesaid institutions have been practiced through three sects of times.

976 The first was that of religious times which was observed under the divine governments [919, 925].

977 The second was that of the punctilious, like Achilles. In the returned barbarian times it was that of the duelists [920, 667].

978 The third was that of civil or modest times, the times of the natural law of those gentes that Ulpian calls distinctively human in his phrase *ius naturale gentium humanarum* [569, 990]. Hence the Latin writers under the emperors call the duty of subjects *officium civile*, and every offense against natural equity in the interpretation of the laws is called *incivile*. It is the last sect of times in Roman jurisprudence, beginning with the time of popular liberty. Hence the praetors, to accommodate the laws to the Roman nature, customs, and government, which had now suffered change, had first of all to soften the severity and temper the rigidity of the Law of the Twelve Tables, which had been decreed when it was natural in the heroic times of Rome. And later the emperors had to remove all the veils in which the praetors had cloaked it and reveal natural equity in all the openness and generosity which was appropriate to the gentleness to which the nations had become accustomed [952].

979 The jurisconsults accordingly justify their views as to what is just by appealing to the sect of their times, as we may observe. For these [three sects of times] are the proper sects of Roman jurisprudence, in which the Romans concurred with all other nations of the world; sects taught them by divine providence, which the Roman jurisconsults set up as the principle of the natural law of the gentes; and not the sects of the philosophers, which some learned interpreters of Roman law have forcibly intruded therein [335]. And the emperors, when they wish to give a reason for their

laws or for other ordinances issued by them, say that they have been guided by the sect of their times, as in the passages collected by Barnabé Brisson in his *De formulis et solemnibus populi Romani verbis.* For the customs of the age are the school of princes [247], to use the term [*seculum,* age] applied by Tacitus [G. 19] to the decayed sect of his own times, where he says, *Corrumpere et corrumpi seculum vocatur*—"They call it the spirit of the age to seduce and be seduced"—or, as we would now say, the fashion [viii].

[SECTION XII]

OTHER PROOFS DRAWN FROM THE

PROPERTIES OF THE HEROIC ARISTOCRACIES

[*Introduction*]

980 Such a constant and perpetual orderly succession of human civil institutions, within the strong chain of so many and such various causes and effects as we have observed in the course the nations run, should constrain our minds to receive the truth of these principles. But, in order to leave no room for doubt, we shall add the explanation of other civil phenomena which can be explained only by the discovery, made above, of the heroic commonwealths [582ff].

[*Chapter I*]   *The Guarding of the Confines*

981 The two greatest eternal properties of the aristocratic common-wealths are the guarding of the confines and the guarding of the institutions [586, 629].

982 The guarding of the confines began to be observed with bloody religions under the divine governments [925], for it was necessary to set up boundaries to the fields in order to put a stop to the infamous promiscuity of things in the bestial state [549f]. On these boundaries were to be fixed the confines first of families, then of gentes or houses, later of peoples, and finally of nations [B2]. Hence the giants, as Polyphemus tells Ulysses, lived separately, each in his own cave with his wife and children, and did not meddle in one another's affairs [516], thus retaining the habits of their recent savage origin; and they savagely slew any who entered within their confines, as Polyphemus attempted to slay Ulysses and his companions. (In this giant Plato discerns the fathers in the state of the families [296].)

From this the custom was derived whereby the cities for a long period of time looked upon each other as enemies [637ff]. So much for the harmonious division of the fields described by Hermogenianus the jurisconsult and received in good faith by all interpreters of Roman law [550]! From this first and most ancient principle of human institutions, with which its subject matter began, it would be reasonable to begin also the doctrine which teaches *De rerum divisione et acquirendo earum dominio* ("Of the kinds of things and of acquiring ownership of them"). This guarding of the confines is naturally practiced in the aristocratic commonwealths, which, as political writers point out, are not established by conquest. But later, when the infamous promiscuity of things had ceased and the confines of the peoples were well fixed, came the popular commonwealths, which are made for the expansion of empires, and finally the monarchies, which are even more efficient in that respect.

983 This and no other must be the reason why the Law of the Twelve Tables did not recognize simple possession, and usucapion in heroic times served to solemnize natural transfers, the best interpreters defining it as *dominii adiectio*, the addition of civil ownership to the natural ownership previously acquired. But afterward in the time of popular liberty the praetors came to the assistance of bare possession with the interdicts, and usucapion began to be *dominii adeptio*, a way of acquiring civil ownership in the first instance; and while cases of possession did not at first come up for judgment because the praetor took extrajudicial cognizance of them [638], today the most certain judgments are those called possessory.

984 Thus there came about in the period of popular liberty at Rome a fading, and under the monarchy a complete disappearance, of the distinction between (1) bonitary, (2) quiritary, (3) optimal, and (4) civil ownership. Originally these terms carried meanings very different from their present ones. The first meant natural ownership, maintained by perpetual physical possession. The second meant ownership that could be vindicated; it was current among the plebeians, having been extended to them by the nobles in the Law of the Twelve Tables, but a plebeian could vindicate it only by calling in as *auctor* the noble from whom he had acquired title [109, 638, 1073]. The third meant ownership free of any encumbrance public or private; it was enjoyed by the patricians among themselves before the establishment of the census which was the basis of popular liberty [619ff]. The fourth and last meant the ownership belonging to the cities themselves, which today is called eminent domain [266].

The difference between optimal and quiritary ownership had already been obscured in the times of liberty, so that the jurisconsults of the latest period took no account of it. But under the monarchy what is called bonitary ownership (born of bare natural transfer) and the so-called quiritary ownership (born of mancipation or civil conveyance) were quite confused by Justinian in the constitutions *De nudo iure quiritium tollendo* [C. 7.25] and *De usucapione transformanda* [C. 7.31], and the famous distinction between *res mancipi* and *res nec mancipi* was completely obliterated. There remained civil ownership in the sense of ownership yielding an action of *rei vindicatio,* and optimal ownership in the sense of ownership not subject to any private encumbrance.

[*Chapter II*]   *The Guarding of the Institutions*

985 The guarding of the institutions began in divine times from jealousy (the jealousy of Juno, the goddess of solemn matrimony [511, 513]) with a view to the certainty of the families as against the nefarious promiscuity of women. Such vigilance is a natural property of the aristocratic commonwealths, desirous of keeping family relationships, successions, and consequently wealth and through it power, within the order of the nobles. On this account testamentary laws were late in appearing among the nations [992]. (Tacitus [G. 20] says that there was no testament among the ancient Germans.) This is the reason why, when King Agis tried to introduce such laws at Sparta, he was strangled by command of the ephors, the guardians of the liberty of the Lacedaemonian nobles [668]. We may understand from this with how much discernment the embellishers of the Law of the Twelve Tables fixed in the eleventh table [cf. 11.1] the article *Auspicia incommunicata plebi sunto*—"The auspices shall be withheld from the plebs"—for on these originally depended all civil institutions both public and private, which were thus all kept within the order of the nobles. The private institutions were solemn matrimony, paternal power, direct heirs, agnates, gentiles, legitimate succession, testaments, and guardianships [110, 598]. Thus, after having extended all these institutions to the plebs in the first tables and thereby established the laws proper to a popular commonwealth, and particularly the testamentary law [513], they proceed by a single article in the eleventh table to give it a completely aristocratic form. However, in such confusion of institutions

they say this too, which, though a guess on their part, is true: that in the last two tables some ancient customs of the Romans passed into law. This statement verifies the aristocratic nature of the ancient Roman state.

986   Now, to come back to the subject, when the human race was everywhere settled by the solemnizing of matrimony, there appeared the popular commonwealths, and much later the monarchies. In these, as a result of intermarriage with the plebs of the peoples and as a result of testamentary successions, the institutions of the nobility were unsettled, and so, little by little, wealth began to pass from the noble houses. For the Roman plebeians contracted only natural marriages down to the 309th year of Rome, when they finally obtained from the patricians the grant of *connubium*, or the right of contracting solemn nuptials; nor in their miserable state, like that of abject slaves, as Roman history represents it to us, could they have made any pretension to intermarriage with the nobles [598]. This is one of the chief reasons why we said in the first edition of this work [Op. 3.185] that unless we assign these principles to Roman jurisprudence, Roman history as hitherto related is more incredible than the fabulous history of the Greeks. For we could not make out what the latter meant, but we find the former contradicted in our own nature by the order of human desires. For it shows us men of the basest condition aspiring first to nobility in the struggle over *connubium*, then to honors in the struggle for the consulate, and finally to wealth by laying claim to the priesthood; whereas, by the eternal common civil nature, men first seek wealth, then honors, and lastly nobility.

987   Thus we are compelled to say that, when the plebeians had won from the nobles the certain ownership of the fields by the Law of the Twelve Tables (the second agrarian law of the world [109]), as they were still aliens [638] (for such ownership can be granted to aliens), they learned by experience that they could not leave their fields intestate to their kin, for, as they could not contract solemn matrimony, they had no direct heirs, agnates, or gentiles; much less could they dispose of them by testament, as they were not citizens [110]. And there is no reason to wonder at this, since they were men of little or no intelligence, as is evident from the Furian, Voconian, and Falcidian laws, which were all plebiscites; for it took all three of them in order that by the Falcidian Law the desired end should finally be achieved; namely, that estates should not be absorbed by legacies. Because the plebeians perceived, in the case of those of their number who died during the three years [following the Law of the Twelve Tables], that the fields which had been assigned to them reverted to the nobles by reason of the aforesaid disabilities, they laid claim to *connubium*

and thereby to citizenship. But the grammarians, confused by all the political writers who imagined Rome to have been founded by Romulus with the form of government which cities now have, did not know that the plebs of the heroic cities had been for several centuries considered as aliens and had therefore contracted only natural marriages among themselves. Hence they did not observe either the factual impropriety or the poor Latinity of taking the historical phrase *plebei tentarunt connubia patrum* as if it read *cum patribus* (after the manner of the marriage laws, such as: *patruus non habet cum fratris filia connubium*). [Cf. Livy 4.1.1; 4.4.5; J. 1.10.3.] For, if they had noticed this, they would certainly have understood that the plebeians did not claim the right of intermarrying with the nobles, but the right, which belonged to the nobles, of contracting solemn nuptials [598].

988 Hence, if we consider legitimate successions as determined by the Law of the Twelve Tables [5.4-5]—that the deceased father of a family should be succeeded in the first place by his direct heirs, in their default by his agnates, and in defect of these by his gentiles [B4]—the Law of the Twelve Tables will seem to have been precisely a Salic Law of the Romans. This law was also observed by Germany in its earliest times (whence we may assume the like for the other first nations of the returned barbarism), and it finally survived in France and Savoy. Baldus, quite agreeably to our thesis, calls this law of succession *ius gentium gallorum* [1077]. By the same token, the Roman law of agnate and gentile successions may rightfully be called *ius gentium romanarum*, with the addition of the epithet *heroicarum*, and, to put it more properly, *romanum*. This would be precisely the *ius quiritium romanorum* which, as we showed above, was the natural law common to all the heroic gentes [595].

989 What we have said here about the Salic Law, so far as it excludes women from the royal succession, is not, as may appear, contradicted by the statement that Tanaquil, a woman, governed the Roman kingdom. For that was a heroic phrase to describe a weak-spirited king who allowed himself to be dominated by the crafty Servius Tullius, who invaded the Roman kingdom with the favor of the plebs, on whom he had bestowed the first agrarian law [107]. Like Tanaquil, in the recourse of the same manner of heroic speech in the returned barbarian times, Pope John [VIII] was called a woman (against which fable Leo Allaci wrote an entire book) because of the great weakness he showed in yielding to Photius, patriarch of Constantinople, as pointed out by Baronio and after him by de Sponde.

990 Having resolved this difficulty, we may now state that in the

same way as the phrase *ius quiritium romanorum* had first been used in the sense of *ius naturale gentium heroicarum romanarum* [988], just so, when Ulpian under the emperors defines the law current in the free common-wealths and much more under the monarchies, he calls it, weighing his words, *ius naturale gentium humanarum* [569]. And in view of all this the title in the *Institutes* [J. 1.2, *De iure naturali, gentium, et civili,* "Of the law of nature, the law of the gentes, and the civil law"] ought to read, it would seem, *De iure naturali gentium civili,* not only removing with Hermann Vulteius the comma between *naturali* and *gentium* (and with Ulpian supplying *humanarum* in place of the second comma) but sup-pressing as well the particle *et* before *civili.* For the Romans must have had reference to their own law as they had preserved it from the time of its introduction in the age of Saturn, first by their customs and later by their legislation, just as Varro in his great work on [the antiquities of] divine and human institutions—[*Antiquitates*] *rerum divinarum et humanarum* —traced Roman institutions to purely native origins, with no admixture of anything foreign [364].

991 Now, returning to heroic Roman successions, we have many strong reasons for doubting that, in ancient Roman times, daughters were exceptions to the exclusion of women. For we have no reason to believe that the hero fathers had any spark of tenderness, but rather many weighty ones to the contrary. The Law of the Twelve Tables [J. 3.1.9; 3.5.5] called an agnate as remote as the seventh degree in order to exclude an emanci-pated son from succeeding to his father. The family fathers had a sovereign right of life and death over their children and hence a despotic dominion over the acquisitions of their sons. They contracted alliances on behalf of their sons in order to bring into their houses women worthy of the family. (This is evidenced by the verb *spondere,* which properly means to promise for another, whence betrothals were called *sponsalia.*) They regarded adoptions in the same light as marriages, as a means of reinforcing decay-ing families by choosing procreant sons from other stocks. They regarded emancipation as chastisement or punishment. They had no notion of legitimation, since concubinage was practiced only with freed slaves and aliens, with whom in heroic times solemn matrimony could not be con-tracted lest the children degenerate from the nobility of their sires [526, 802]. For the most frivolous reasons, testaments were either null or nulli-fied or broken or of no effect, in order to clear the way for legitimate successions. So blinded were they naturally by the brightness of their own private names, and hence so inflamed by nature for the glory of the common name of Roman! All these are customs proper to aristocratic

commonwealths such as the heroic commonwealths were, and they are all properties in accord with the heroism of the first peoples [670ff].

992 A matter worthy of reflection is this glaring error committed by the erudite embellishers of the Law of the Twelve Tables who assert that it was brought from Athens to Rome: namely, that inheritances left intestate by Roman family fathers, during all the time before that law brought in testamentary and legitimate successions, must have gone under the category of the things called *res nullius*. Providence, on the contrary, in order that the world should not relapse into the infamous promiscuity of things, ordained that the certainty of ownership should be preserved by and through the very form of the aristocratic commonwealths. Hence legitimate successions must naturally have been observed by all the first nations before they had any notion of testaments, which are proper to popular commonwealths and much more to monarchies, as indeed Tacitus clearly tells us was the case among the ancient Germans (whose practice gives us reason to assume the same of all the first barbarous peoples) [985]. This was the basis for our conjecture that the Salic Law, which was certainly observed in Germany, was observed universally by the nations in the time of the second barbarism [988].

993 However, the jurisconsults of the last [period of Roman] jurisprudence, by estimating the institutions of the unknown earliest times by those of their own quite late times, which is the source of innumerable errors noted in this work, believed that the Law of the Twelve Tables [5.4] had called the daughters of families to the inheritances of their fathers who had died intestate, in virtue of the word *suus* [in the phrase *suus heres*, own (or direct) heir, self-successor], following the rule that the masculine gender includes women also. But heroic jurisprudence, of which we have had so much to say in this work, took the words of the laws in their strictest meaning, so that the word *suus* meant only the son of a family. Invincible proof of this is afforded by the formula for the institution of posthumous children [M1], introduced many centuries later by Gallus Aquilius [D. 28.2.29.pr.], which is phrased *Si quis . . . natus natave erit* ("If a son *or daughter* shall have been born posthumously"), lest from the word *natus* alone it should not be understood that a posthumous daughter is included. Because of his ignorance of these matters, Justinian in the *Institutes* [3.2.3] affirms that the Law of the Twelve Tables by the use of the word *adgnatus* had called male and female agnates alike, but that later the middle jurisprudence had made the law more rigid by restricting it to sisters of the same blood. What must have happened is just the contrary. The word *suus* must first have been extended to the daughters of the

families, and afterward the word *adgnatus* to sisters of the same blood. Thus it was by chance that this jurisprudence came to be called middle, and yet happily, for the reason that, beginning with these cases, it mitigated the rigors of the Law of the Twelve Tables, whereas the ancient jurisprudence which preceded it had guarded its words with the greatest scrupulousness. Both have been fully described above [33ff, 952].

994 But when sovereignty had passed from the nobles to the people, since the plebs reckoned all its strength, wealth, and power in the multitude of its children, the tenderness of blood ties began to make itself felt. Before that the plebeians of the heroic cities cannot have had this feeling, for they generated children to make them slaves of the nobles, by whom indeed they were bidden to generate at such a time as would result in springtime births so that the young would be born not only healthy but robust. (Hence they were called *vernae*, as the Latin etymologists tell us, and from this name the vulgar tongues were called vernacular [443].) The mothers must have hated rather than loved their children, for they had only the pain of bearing and the trouble of nursing them, without having from them any joy or profit. But the multitude of the plebeians, while it had been dangerous to the aristocratic commonwealths, which are and profess to be the property of the few, added to the greatness of the popular commonwealths and much more to that of the monarchies (which is why the imperial laws are so favorably disposed to women because of the dangers and pains of childbirth). Hence from the times of popular liberty the praetors began to consider the rights of blood and to satisfy them by means of the *bonorum possessiones*. They began with their remedies to repair the faults and shortcomings of testaments in order to facilitate the diffusion of wealth, which alone is admired by the vulgar.

995 Finally came the emperors, who, taking umbrage at the splendor of the nobles, devoted themselves to promoting the rights of human nature, common to plebeian and noble alike. This began with Augustus, who bent his efforts to the protection of trusteeships (by which formerly property had passed to persons incapable of inheritance thanks only to the conscientiousness of the fiduciary heirs) and gave them such great assistance that within his lifetime he endowed them with legal compulsion, obliging the heirs to give effect to them [J. 2.23,25]. A great many senatus-consults followed which placed cognates on a level with agnates. Finally Justinian abolished the distinction between legacies and trusteeships, merged the Falcidian [i.e., Pegasian] fourth [part of an estate reserved to the heir] with the Trebellian, minimized the distinction between testaments and codicils, and put agnates and cognates on precisely the same

footing as regards intestate inheritance. And the latest Roman laws went to such lengths in favor of last wills that, whereas in ancient times they were declared invalid on the slightest pretext, nowadays they must always be interpreted in such a way as to favor their validity.

996 Because of the humanity of the times (as displayed in the affection of popular commonwealths for their sons and the desire of monarchies to see fathers devoted to their sons), since the cyclopean authority of the family fathers over the persons of their children had already vanished, the emperors sought to do away also with the authority they still had over their acquisitions. To this end, they introduced first the *peculium castrense* to attract young men to war, then extended it to the *peculium quasi castrense* to attract them to the imperial service, and finally, to satisfy the sons who were neither soldiers nor clerks, introduced the *peculium adventitium*. They deprived the paternal power of its influence over adoptions, now no longer restricted to a few close relations. They universally encouraged formal adoptions (*adrogationes*), which had been somewhat difficult in that citizens who were family fathers in their own right thereby became subordinate members of others' families. They counted emancipations as benefits. They gave to legitimation by a subsequent marriage all the efficacy of solemn nuptials [991]. But above all, since the *imperium paternum* seemed to detract from their own majesty, they directed that it should be called *patria potestas*. This was in accordance with their own example, introduced with great sagacity by Augustus; for in order not to arouse the jealousy of the people, who might want to take from him some part of his *imperium*, he assumed the *tribunicia potestas*, thus declaring himself the protector of Roman liberty. In the tribunes of the plebs this had been a *de facto* power, for they had never held *imperium* in the republic. Indeed, in the time of Augustus himself, when Labeo was summoned by a tribune of the plebs to appear before him, this prince of one of the two sects of Roman jurisconsults was within his rights in refusing to obey, since the tribunes of the plebs did not have *imperium*. Yet neither grammarians nor jurists nor writers on politics have observed the reason why the patricians, in the contest over extending the consulship to the plebs, in order to satisfy the latter without yielding any part of the *imperium*, hit upon the device of creating the military tribunes, some of them nobles and some of them plebeians, *cum consulari potestate*, as history always puts it [Livy 4.6.7], and not *cum imperio consulari*, of which we never read.

997 Hence the free Roman commonwealth was entirely conceived in the triple formula: *senatus auctoritas, populi imperium, tribunorum plebis*

potestas—the authority of the senate, the *imperium* of the people, the power of the plebeian tribunes. And the two terms *imperium* and *potestas* retained in the laws this original exactness of meaning; the former being ascribed to the major magistrates, such as consuls and praetors, and including the right to impose the death penalty; and the latter being ascribed to the minor magistrates such as the *aediles,* and limited to but modest powers of coercion—*modica coërcitione continetur.*

998 Finally, displaying all their clemency toward humanity, the Roman emperors began to show favor to slaves and to restrain the cruelty of their masters. They extended the efficacy of manumission and diminished its formalities. Citizenship, which had originally been conferred only on distinguished foreigners who had deserved well of the Roman people, was now granted to everyone born in Rome, even if born of a slave father, provided the mother was free by birth or by enfranchisement. It was from the fact that men were thus born free in the cities that the natural law which had previously been called that of the gentes or noble houses (because in heroic times all commonwealths had been aristocratic and such a law was proper to them [990]) was now called the natural law of nations [E8] after the rise of the popular commonwealths (in which the entire nations are masters of the *imperium*) and later of the monarchies (in which the monarchs represent the entire nations subject to them).

[Chapter III]   *The Guarding of the Laws*

999 The guarding of the institutions carries with it that of the magistracies and priesthoods, and hence also that of the laws and of the science of their interpretation. Hence we read in Roman history that in the times of the aristocratic commonwealth *connubia,* consulships, and priesthoods were all confined to the senatorial order (which was then made up entirely of nobles), and the science of their laws was kept sacred or secret (which are the same thing) within the college of pontiffs (to which only patricians were admitted), as in all the other heroic nations [953]. This lasted among the Romans down to a hundred years after the Law of the Twelve Tables, according to the account of the jurisconsult Pomponius [586]. And the name *viri,* men, which among the Romans of those times had the same meaning as *hēroës* among the Greeks, was applied to husbands in solemn wedlock, to magistrates, priests, and judges [684]. Here, however, we shall discuss the guarding of the laws, since that was a principal

property of the heroic aristocracies and hence was the last to be extended by the patricians to the plebs.

1000 In divine times this guard was scrupulously kept, so that the observance of the divine laws is called religion [953]. This was perpetuated through all subsequent governments, in which the divine laws have to be observed with certain unalterable formulae of consecrated words and solemn ceremonies. There is nothing so characteristic of the aristocratic commonwealths as this guarding of the laws. The reason why Athens (and, after her example, almost all the cities of Greece) passed quickly to popular liberty was that, as the Spartans (whose commonwealth was aristocratic) used to say to the Athenians, the many laws at Athens were written and the few laws at Sparta were observed.

1001 In the aristocratic commonwealth the Romans were very strict guardians of the Law of the Twelve Tables [952]. It was called by Tacitus [A. 3.27] *finis omnis aequi iuris*, the consummation of all equitable law, because after these laws which were considered sufficient to equalize liberty (and which must have been enacted after the decemvirs, for whom, in the manner the ancient peoples had of thinking in poetic characters [422], they were named), there were no consular enactments of private law, or very few. For the same reason it was called by Livy [3.34.6] *fons omnis aequi iuris*, the fountainhead of all equitable law; for it must have been the source of all interpretation [500]. The Roman plebs, like the Athenian, passed new laws every day for single occasions, because it was incapable of universals. Sulla, leader of the nobles, when he had defeated Marius, leader of the plebs, repaired the disorder somewhat with the *quaestiones perpetuae*, or permanent courts, but, once he had resigned the dictatorship, singular laws began to multiply again no less than before, as Tacitus [A. 3.27] relates. And, as political writers point out, there is no readier way to arrive at monarchy than through such a multitude of laws. Hence Augustus, for the purpose of establishing it, enacted a great number of them, and succeeding emperors used the senate above all to issue senatusconsults in the field of private law. Nevertheless, even in these times of popular liberty, the formulae for actions were so strictly guarded that it took all the eloquence of Crassus (whom Cicero [*Brutus* 36.138!] called the Roman Demosthenes) to get an expressed pupillary substitution interpreted as containing an unexpressed vulgar or common substitution; and it took all Cicero's eloquence to prevent Sextus Aebutius from keeping a farm of Aulus Caecina's because of the omission of a "d" from the formula [*Defense of Caecina* 18.53; 13.38]. Finally things reached such a point, when Constantine had done away entirely with the formulae, that every particular motive of equity prevailed over the laws; so willing are human minds under human governments to recognize natural equity [927, 940]. Thus, starting from that article of the Law of the Twelve Tables [9.1]: *Privilegia ne irroganto* ("Laws of personal exception shall not be proposed"), observed in the Roman aristocracy, and passing through the great many singular laws enacted under popular liberty, a point was reached under the monarchy where the emperors did nothing but grant privileges, than which, if proportioned to merit, there is nothing more in harmony with natural equity. Indeed, all the exceptions to the laws which are made nowadays can truly be called privileges dictated by the particular merit of the facts, which removes them from the general disposition of the laws.

1002   Hence, as we believe, it came about that in the rude days of the recourse of barbarism the nations forgot the Roman laws, so much so that whoever invoked one on his behalf was severely punished in France, and in Spain even suffered death. Certainly in Italy the nobles counted it a disgrace to regulate their affairs by Roman laws and professed to be subject to those of the Lombards. The plebeians, slow to shake off their old habits, continued to observe some Roman laws which retained the force of customs. This is the reason why the corpus of the laws of Justinian and other monuments of Western Roman law were lost to us in Italy, and the *Basilica* and other monuments of Eastern Roman law fell into oblivion among the Greeks. But later, when the monarchies were reborn and popular liberty reintroduced, the Roman law comprised in the books of Justinian was universally received, so that Grotius declares that it is now a natural law of the gentes of Europe.

1003   The Roman gravity and wisdom is much to be admired in this: that, in these constitutional changes, the praetors and the jurisconsults put forth every effort to insure that the words of the Law of the Twelve Tables should be shifted from their original and proper meanings as little and as slowly as possible [950ff]. Perhaps it was principally for this reason that the Roman Empire grew so great and endured so long; for in its changes of constitution it made every effort to stand firm by its principles, which were the same as those of this world of nations, and all political theorists agree that there is no better policy for making a state endure and grow great. Thus the cause which produced among the Romans the wisest jurisprudence in the world is the same that made the Roman Empire the greatest in the world. And it is the cause of the Roman greatness, which Polybius [6.56.6ff], in too general a sense, attributes to the religion of the nobles; Machiavelli [*Discourses* 1.4; 2.1], on the contrary, to the magnanimity of the plebs; and Plutarch, envious of Roman virtue and wisdom, to their good fortune; this last in his book *The Fortune of the Romans,* to which, in other and more indirect ways [than ours], Torquato Tasso gave answer in his noble *Reply [of Rome to Plutarch].**

---

* *Risposta di Roma a Plutarco, nella quale riprova la sua opinione della fortuna de' Romani* . . . (1590), in *Opere* 13 (Venice, 1738), 274–315; *Opere* 5 (Milan, 1825), 3–79.

[SECTION XIII]

[Chapter I] Other Proofs Taken from [Mixed Commonwealths, that is from] the Tempering of the Constitution of a Succeeding Commonwealth by the Administration of the Preceding One [1084n]

1004 All that we have had to say in this [fourth] book is so much evidence to prove that in the course of the entire lifetime of nations they follow this order through these three kinds of commonwealths or civil constitutions, and no more. They all have their roots in the first, which were the divine administrations, and from this beginning all nations (by the axioms above posited [241–245] as principles of the ideal eternal history) must proceed through this sequence of human institutions: first becoming commonwealths of optimates, later free popular commonwealths, and finally monarchies. Hence Tacitus, though he does not see them in this order, affirms (as we pointed out in the Idea of the Work [29]) that, outside of these three forms of public constitutions, ordained by the nature of peoples, the others compounded of these three by human design are more to be desired of heaven than ever to be attained by effort, and if by chance any such exist they are not enduring. But, to leave no point of doubt concerning this natural succession of political or civil constitutions, we shall find that the succession admits of natural mixtures, not of form with form (for such mixtures would be monsters), but of a succeeding form with a preceding administration. Such mixtures are founded on the axiom that when men change they retain for some time the impression of their previous customs [249].

1005 Hence we say that the first gentile fathers, passing from the bestial life to the human, retained, in the religious times in the state of nature under the divine administrations, much of the savagery and cruelty of their recent origins (so that Plato recognizes in the Cyclopes of Homer the first family fathers of the world [296]); and that likewise in the formation of the first aristocratic commonwealths the private sovereign powers remained intact in the hands of the family fathers, just as they had held them in the previous state of nature. And because they were intensely proud and there was no reason for one to yield to another when all were equal, they made themselves subject under the aristocratic form to the public sovereignty of their own reigning orders. Thus the high private dominion of each family father went to make up the superior high public dominion of the senates, just as out of the private sovereignties which they had over their families they composed the civil sovereignties of their orders themselves. In no other way is it possible to conceive how the cities were composed of the families. The cities must therefore have been born as aristocratic commonwealths with a natural admixture of family sovereignties [584ff].

1006 The commonwealths remained aristocratic as long as the fathers preserved this authority of ownership within their reigning orders, and until the plebs of the heroic peoples had obtained from the fathers themselves laws extending to them the certain ownership of the fields, the right to solemn nuptials, the sovereign powers, the priesthoods, and thereby the science of the laws. But as soon as the plebs of the heroic cities became numerous and inured to war (to the alarm of the fathers, who in the oligarchic commonwealths must have been few), and, with force on their side (the force of their numbers), began to enact laws without the authority of the senates, then the commonwealths changed from aristocratic to popular. For no one of them could have lived for a moment with two supreme legislative powers without distinction of subjects, times, and territories, concerning which, during which, and within which their laws were to be promulgated. Hence the dictator Philo declared by the Publilian Law that the Roman commonwealth had already become popular by nature [112]. In this revolution, in order that the authority of ownership might retain what it could of the form that had suffered change, it naturally became the authority of wardship (just as the power that fathers have over their minor children is transferred, on the death of the fathers, to others in the form of the authority of guardians). In virtue of this authority, the free peoples, lords of their sovereignties, as it were reigning wards, being weak in public counsel, naturally submitted to administration by their guardians, the senates. Thus they were by nature free commonwealths, administered aristocratically. But when the powerful in the popular commonwealths directed this public counsel to the private interests of their power, and the free peoples, for the sake of private utilities, let themselves be seduced by the powerful into subjecting their public liberty to the ambition of the latter, then factions, seditions, and civil wars, ruinous to their very nations, brought on the monarchical form.

[*Chapter II*]   *An Eternal Natural Royal Law by Which the Nations Come to Rest under Monarchies*

1007   The monarchical form was introduced in accordance with this eternal natural royal law, felt by all the nations which recognize in Augustus the founder of the Roman monarchy. This law has escaped the notice of the interpreters of Roman law, preoccupied as they have all been with the fable of the "royal law" of Tribonian, of which he openly professes himself the author in the *Institutes* [J. 1.2.6], but which he attributes to Ulpian at one point in the *Pandects* [D. 1.4.1.pr.]. Yet it was well understood by the Roman jurisconsults, who were well acquainted with the natural law of the gentes. For Pomponius, in his brief history of Roman law [D. 1.2.2.11], discussing the royal law of which we speak, described it for us in the well-considered phrase: *Rebus ipsis dictantibus, regna condita* ("When the institutions themselves dictated it, kingdoms were founded") [584].

1008   This natural royal law is conceived under this natural formula of eternal utility: Since in the free commonwealths all look out for their own private interests, into the service of which they press their public arms at the risk of ruin to their nations, to preserve the latter from destruction a single man must arise, as Augustus did at Rome, and take all public concerns by force of arms into his own hands, leaving his subjects free to look after their private affairs and after just so much public business, and of just such kinds, as the monarch may entrust to them. Thus are the peoples saved when they would otherwise rush to their own destruction. In this truth the professors of modern law concur when they say that *universitates sub rege habentur loco privatorum* ("corporations are treated as private persons under the king"), because the majority of the citizens no longer concern themselves with the public welfare. Tacitus, most learned in the natural law of the gentes, points out as much in his *Annals* [1.4] within the family of the Caesars itself, by this order of human civil ideas: As the death of Augustus became imminent, *pauci bona libertatis incassum disserere* ("a few talked idly of the blessings of liberty"); as soon as Tiberius came, *omnes principis iussa adspectare* ("all looked to the commands of the emperor"); under the three subsequent Caesars first came *incuria*, or indifference, and finally *ignorantia reipublicae tanquam alienae* [H. 1.1], ignorance of politics as of something alien. Thus, as the citizens have become aliens in their own nations, it becomes necessary for the monarchs to sustain and represent the latter in their own persons. Now in free commonwealths if a powerful man is to become monarch the people must take his side, and for that reason monarchies are by nature popularly governed: first through the laws by which the monarchs seek to make their subjects all equal; then by that property of monarchies whereby sovereigns humble the powerful and thus keep the masses safe and free from their oppressions; further by that other property of keeping the multitude satisfied and content as regards the necessaries of life and the enjoyment of natural liberty; and finally by the privileges [1001] conceded by monarchs to entire classes (called privileges of liberty) or to particular persons by awarding extraordinary civil honors to men of exceptional merit (these being singular laws dictated by natural equity). Hence monarchy is the form of government best adapted to human nature when reason is fully developed [292, 924, 927].

[Chapter III] Refutation of the Principles of Political Theory as Represented by the System of Jean Bodin

1009   In the light of what has been set forth up to this point, we can see how much scientific foundation there is for the political theory of Jean Bodin which places the successive forms of civil constitutions in this order: they were first monarchic, then, having passed through a stage of tyranny, became free and popular, and finally became aristocratic [663]. We might here content ourselves with having refuted him completely by the natural succession of political forms which we have established by such numberless proofs, particularly in this [fourth] book. But it pleases us to add, *ad exuberantiam*, a refutation based on the impossibilities and absurdities of his own position.

1010   He certainly admits the truth that the families were the elements of which the cities were composed. However, by a common error which we have corrected above, he has assumed that the families included only the children [552]. How, we ask him, could monarchies have developed from such families?

1011   There are two possible ways: by force or by fraud.

1012   But how could one family father subdue the rest by force? For if in the free commonwealths (which, according to Bodin, came after the tyrannies) the family fathers consecrated themselves and their families to the fatherlands by which their families were preserved to them (and, according to him, these fathers had already been tamed under the monarchies), must we not suppose that the family fathers, when they were still Cyclopes but recently emerged from their savage bestial liberty, would have allowed themselves to be slain along with their entire families rather than endure inequality? [584].

1013   By fraud, then? This is used by those who, aiming at rule in the free commonwealths, offer to those whom they would seduce either liberty or power or wealth. But as for liberty, in the family state the fathers were all sovereigns. Power? But the nature of the Cyclopes was to live apart in their caves and take care of their own families, with no concern for those of others, in accord with the habits of their savage origin. And wealth, in those simple and frugal first times, had no meaning at all [516].

1014   The difficulty grows out of all proportion when we add that in the first barbarian times there were no fortresses, and the heroic cities, made up of families, were for a long time unwalled, as we learned from Thucydides [76, 645]. And in the midst of the jealousies of state, which were all-consuming in the heroic aristocracies as above described, Valerius Publicola, suspected of plotting tyranny because he had built a house on high ground, in order to justify himself had it dismantled in one night, and the next day, calling a public assembly, had his lictors lay the consular fasces at the feet of the people [Livy 2.7]. The custom of leaving cities unwalled lasted longest among the most savage nations; thus we read that Henry the Fowler was the first in Germany to bring in the people from the villages in which they had previously been dispersed, to dwell in cities and to gird them with walls. So much for the notion that the first founders of the cities were those who marked out with the plough the walls and the gates, the name *porta* for gate being derived, according to the Latin etymologists, from their lifting and carrying the plough, *a portando aratro*, over the places where they wanted the gates to be! [550, 778]. Thus between the savagery of the barbarous times and the insecurity of the palaces, at the court of Spain more than eighty persons of royal blood were slain within sixty years, so that the fathers of the Illiberitan council, one of the earliest of the Latin Church, condemned this frequently recurring wickedness under penalty of solemn excommunication.

1015   But the difficulty mounts to infinity if we assume the families to include only the children. For in that case, whether by force or by fraud, the children must have been the instruments of the ambitions of others and have betrayed and slain their own fathers. Thus the first states would not have been monarchies but impious and wicked tyrannies. But when the

young nobles of Rome conspired against their fathers on behalf of the
tyrant Tarquin, it was because of their hatred for the severity of the laws
which is characteristic of aristocratic commonwealths (as benign laws are
of popular commonwealths, clement ones of legitimate kingdoms, and
dissolute ones of tyrannies); a severity of which these young conspirators
made trial at the cost of their lives. The two sons of Brutus, numbered
among the conspirators, were beheaded, their own father dictating the
severe penalty. Thus we may see how monarchic the Roman commonwealth was and how popular the liberty established therein by Brutus!
[662ff].

1016 In face of such and so many difficulties, Bodin (and with him
all other political writers) ought to recognize the family monarchies in the
state of the families as here shown, and to admit that the families included
not only children but *famuli* (after whom they were called families in the
first place). We have seen that these *famuli* foreshadowed the slaves who
appeared after the founding of cities as a result of their wars [556]. In this
way free men and slaves are the matter of commonwealths, as Bodin will
have it, though they cannot be so on his premises.

1017 Because of this difficulty on Bodin's premises of making free
men and slaves the matter of commonwealths, he himself is surprised that
his own people should have been called Franks or freemen, when, as he
observes, in their earliest times they were treated as baseborn slaves. This is
because, from his position, he could not see that the nations were brought
to completion by those who were freed from bondage by the Petelian Law
[658]. Thus the Franks, the source of Bodin's surprise, are the same as the
rustic vassals whom Hotman is surprised to find called *homines* or men
[437], and of whom, as we have shown in this work, the plebs of the first
heroic peoples were composed [597]. It was these masses, as we have also
shown, that moved the aristocracies to popular liberty and finally to
monarchy [1006], and did so in virtue of the vulgar tongue in which, under
these last two constitutions, the laws are conceived [953]. On this account
the vulgar language was called vernacular by the Latins, as being the
tongue of houseborn slaves, for such a houseborn slave, and not one taken
in war, is what is meant by *verna*. And we have shown above that these
houseborn slaves existed among all the ancient nations from the time of
the family state [443, 994]. For this same reason the Greeks ceased to be
called Achaeans (whence the Homeric phrase for the heroes: sons of the
Achaeans) and took the name Hellenes from Hellen who started the
Greek vulgar tongue [643], just as the sons of Israel dropped that name of
their earliest times [530] and took on that of the Hebrew people from

Heber, whom the fathers declare to have been the propagator of the sacred tongue [F7]. So well did Bodin and all the other writers on political theory see this most luminous truth which has been clearly demonstrated throughout this entire work, with particular reference to Roman history: namely, that the plebs of the peoples, always and in all nations, have changed the constitutions from aristocratic to popular and from popular to monarchic, and that by founding the vulgar languages (as fully proved above in the Origins of Languages [443]) they gave their names to the nations, as we have just seen! It was in this way that the ancient Franks, to the surprise of Bodin, gave their name to France.

1018   Finally, to apply the test of present experience, the aristocratic constitutions are very few and are survivals from barbarian times—Venice, Genoa, and Lucca in Italy, Ragusa in Dalmatia, and Nuremberg in Germany. The others are popular constitutions administered aristocratically. Wherefore Bodin—whose theory obliges him to hold that the Roman kingdom was monarchic and that the expulsion of the tyrants was followed by the introduction of popular liberty at Rome—fails to find in the first period of Roman freedom the effects called for by his principles (because the actual effects were those proper to an aristocratic commonwealth), and in order to come creditably out of it, as we observed above, says at first that the Roman constitution was popular but its administration was aristocratic, and then, constrained by the force of the truth, confesses in another passage, with crass inconsistency, that the constitution as well as the administration was aristocratic [663].

1019   Such errors in political theory spring from a failure to define the three terms people, kingdom, and liberty [105, 666]. Thus it has been believed that the first peoples were composed of plebeian as well as noble citizens, whereas we have shown by a thousand proofs that only the nobles were included [597]. The liberty of ancient Rome has been thought to be popular liberty, meaning the freedom of the people from the lords, whereas we have found it to be lordly liberty, that is, freedom of the lords from the tyrant Tarquins; and statues were erected to the slayers of such tyrants because they had acted by order of the reigning senates. The kings, in the savagery of the first peoples and the insecurity of the palaces [1014], were aristocratic, such as the two life-term kings at Sparta (an aristocratic commonwealth beyond doubt, as we have shown), and later the two annual consuls at Rome whom Cicero calls annual kings in his *Laws*. This institution due to Junius Brutus, as Livy plainly declares, entailed no change in the Roman kingdom so far as the royal power was concerned; and we have already observed that there was appeal to the people from these annual kings during their reign, and that when their reign expired, they had to render an accounting of their administration to the people [664]. And we remarked too that in heroic times it was a daily occurrence for one king to drive another from the throne, as Thucydides said; and we noted in this the resemblance to the returned barbarian times, in which we read of nothing more uncertain and variable than the fortune of kingdoms. We pondered the opening words of the *Annals* of Tacitus, who often conveys his views by the propriety and force of the words he chooses. *Urbem Romam principio reges habuere*—"The city of Rome in the beginning was held by kings." This is the weakest of the three degrees of possession distinguished by the jurisconsults, for which the verbs are *habere, tenere,* and *possidere* [645]. And he uses the word *urbem,* which means, strictly speaking, the buildings, in order to signify a physical possession; and not *civitatem,* which is the community of the citizens, all or the majority of whom make up spiritually the public constitution.

[SECTION XIV]

FINAL PROOFS TO CONFIRM

THE COURSE OF NATIONS

[*Chapter I*]　[*Punishments, Wars, Order of Numbers*]

1020　There are other instances of the congruity of effects with the causes assigned to them in the principles of this Science, which confirm the natural course of the lives of nations. We have already mentioned most of them in scattered passages without any order. Here we shall bring them together and arrange them according to the natural succession of human civil institutions.

1021　Punishments, for example, in the time of the families were of a cyclopean cruelty: it is in this [family] state that Marsyas is flayed by Apollo. They continued so in the aristocratic commonwealths; thus the shield of Perseus turned its beholders to stone [423]. Punishments were called *paradeigmata* by the Greeks in the same sense in which the Latins called them *exempla*; that is, exemplary chastisements [501]. And in the returned barbarian times, as we have observed above [!], punishments by death were called ordinary punishments. So the laws of Sparta (a commonwealth we have shown by a thousand proofs to be aristocratic), which were judged savage and cruel by Plato [L. 635B] and Aristotle [P. 1324b 8] alike, required that the illustrious King Agis should be strangled to death [668, 985]. And the laws of Rome, when it was an aristocratic state, condemned the noble and victorious Horatius to be stripped, beaten with rods, and hanged to the unhappy tree [500]. Under the Law of the Twelve Tables, those who had set fire to another's grain were condemned to be burned alive [8.10], false witnesses were cast from the Tarpeian Rock [8.23], and defaulting debtors were torn to pieces while still alive [3.5f] [957]. This last-named punishment Tullus Hostilius did not spare his peer Metius Fufetius, king of Alba, who had failed to keep his pledge of alliance; and Romulus himself, before that time, had been torn to pieces by the

384

fathers on a mere suspicion of treason to the state. Let this suffice for those who contend that such punishments were never dealt out in Rome.

1022   Later came the mild punishments practiced in the popular commonwealths commanded by the multitude, which, being made up of the weak, is naturally inclined to compassion. Thus the Roman people, more from admiration of his valor than from the justice of his cause— *magis admiratione virtutis quam iure caussae,* in the elegant phrase of Livy [966]—absolved Horatius when he was condemned for killing his sister in heroic rage at seeing her weeping over the public good fortune. And just as Plato and Aristotle in the times of Athenian freedom censured the Spartan laws [1021], so in the mildness of Roman popular liberty Cicero protests against the inhuman cruelty of the death penalty in the case of a private Roman knight, Rabirius, who had been found guilty of treason [*Defence of Rabirius Charged with High Treason* 3.10; 4.13]. Finally came the monarchies, in which princes rejoice to receive the grateful title "Clement."

1023   Again, the barbaric wars of the heroic times meant the ruin of conquered cities, and the surrendered foes became herds of laborers scattered over the countryside to cultivate the fields of the victors. (Such were the heroic inland colonies [595].) Then the magnanimity of the popular commonwealths, as long as they were ruled by their senates, took from the vanquished the law of the heroic gentes but left them in free enjoyment of the natural law of the human gentes of which Ulpian speaks [569, 990]. (As conquests were extended, all the institutions later called *propriae civium romanorum* were restricted to Roman citizens. Among these institutions were solemn nuptials, paternal power, direct heirs, agnates, gentiles, quiritary or civil ownership, mancipation, usucapion, stipulation, testaments, guardianship, and inheritance [110]. Until their subjection, the free nations of course possessed all these as civil institutions of their own [582].) Finally came the monarchies, which seek, as under Antoninus Pius [i.e., Caracalla], to make one Rome of all the Roman world. For it is a vow characteristic of great monarchs to make one city of the whole world, as Alexander the Great used to say that for him all the world was a single city of which his phalanx was the citadel. Thus the natural law of nations [E8], developed in the provinces by the Roman praetors, came home at long last to dictate laws in the Romans' own house. The heroic law which the Romans had exercised over the provinces was relinquished, because monarchs desire all their subjects to be made equal by their laws [953]. And Roman jurisprudence, which in heroic times had been based entirely on the Law of the Twelve Tables [952], and which in the times of Cicero (as he notes in his *Laws* [1.5.16]) had begun to follow the edict of the Roman praetor, finally, from the days of the emperor Hadrian on down, concerned itself entirely with the *Edictum perpetuum*, the Perpetual Edict composed and arranged by Salvius Julianus almost wholly from the provincial edicts.

1024   Again, from the little districts which could be well governed by the aristocratic commonwealths, through expansion by the conquests to which the free commonwealths are disposed, we finally arrive at monarchies, which are beautiful and magnificent in proportion as they are big.

1025   From the brooding suspicions of aristocracies, through the turbulence of popular commonwealths, nations come at last to rest under monarchies.

1026   But lastly we wish to show how, on this concrete and complex order of human civil institutions, we may superimpose the order of numbers, which are the simplest abstractions [643, 713]. Governments began with the one, in the family monarchies; passed to the few in the heroic aristocracies; went on to the many and the all in the popular commonwealths, in which all or the majority make up the body politic; and finally in civil monarchies return again to the one. By the nature of numbers we cannot conceive a more adequate division or another order than one, few, many and all, with the few, many and all retaining, each in its kind, the principle of the one; just as numbers consist of indivisibles according to Aristotle [*Metaphysics* 1085b 22], and, when we have passed the all, we must begin again with the one. And thus humanity is all contained between the family monarchies and the civil monarchies.

[Chapter II]   Corollary: That the Ancient Roman Law Was a Serious Poem, and the Ancient Jurisprudence a Severe Kind of Poetry, within Which Are Found the First Outlines of Legal Metaphysics in the Rough; and How, among the Greeks, Philosophy Was Born of the Laws

1027   There are many other great effects, particularly in Roman jurisprudence, which find their causes only in these same principles. Above all, by the axiom that as men are naturally drawn to the pursuit of the true, their desire of it, when they cannot attain it, causes them to cling to the certain [137], mancipations began *vera manu*, with the actual hand, that is with real force, since force is abstract and hand is concrete. Among all nations the hand signified power; hence the *cheirothesiai*, hand placings, and *cheirotoniai*, hand raisings, of the Greeks. In the former, those elected to power had it bestowed upon them by the laying of hands on their heads; in the latter, powers already bestowed were acclaimed by the raising of hands. Such ceremonial gestures are proper to mute times; the election of kings in the returned barbarian times was similarly acclaimed. Such actual mancipation occurs in the case of occupation, the first great natural source of all property rights, of which military occupation, *occupatio bellica*, was a survival among the Romans; hence slaves were called *mancipia*, and the booty and the conquests *res mancipi*, of the Romans, having become by the victory *res nec mancipi* in relation to the vanquished. So [far from] true is it that mancipation began within the walls of the single city of Rome as a way of acquiring civil ownership in private transactions between Romans [582]!

1028 This actual mancipation was accompanied by a correspondingly actual usucapion [983]; that is, acquisition of ownership (for such is the meaning of *capio*) by actual use (in the sense in which *usus* signifies *possessio*). Possession was originally exercised by continuous physical tenure of the thing possessed. *Possessio* must have come from *porro sessio* (as domiciles were called *sedes* in Latin from this continual act of sitting or standing firm) and not from *pedum positio* as the Latin etymologists say, for the praetor assists the former and not the latter kind of possession and upholds it by interdicts. From this tenure, called *thesis* by the Greeks, Theseus must have taken his name, and not from his handsome posture as the Greek etymologists say, for the men of Attica founded Athens by remaining fixed there a long time. This is the usucapion which among all nations legitimizes status [in respect of liberty, citizenship, and family] [1032].

1029 Further, in Aristotle's heroic commonwealths, which had no laws for redress of private wrongs [269], *rei vindicationes* were carried out with real force (such were the first duels or private wars of the world), and *condictiones* were private reprisals, which in the recourse of barbarism lasted down to the times of Bartolus [960f].

1030 As the savagery of the times began to abate, as private violence began to be forbidden by judiciary laws, and all private forces were becoming united in the public force called civil sovereignty [583ff], the first peoples, by nature poets [187, 200], must naturally have imitated [215f] the real forces that they had previously employed to preserve their rights and institutions. And so they made a fable of natural mancipation and created from it the solemn civil conveyance represented by the handing over of a symbolic knot [558] in imitation of the chain whereby Jove had bound the giants to the first unoccupied lands [387, 781], and by which they themselves had later bound thereto their clients or *famuli*. With this symbolic mancipation they consecrated all their civil transactions by *actus legitimi* [558], which must have been solemn ceremonies of peoples still mute. Later (articulate speech having meanwhile been formed), in order to make certain of one another's wills in contracts, they determined that agreements, at the moment of handing over this knot, should be clothed with solemn words in which certain and precise stipulations were conceived [569]. Thus later in war they conceived the terms under which they accepted the surrender of vanquished cities. These were called "peaces," from *pacio*, which means the same as *pactum*. A notable survival of this remains in the formula for the surrender of Collatia. In Livy's account [1.38.1–2] it is a contract of receiving under one's power, in the form of solemn questions and answers. Hence it was with full propriety that those who had surrendered were called *recepti*, as the Roman herald said to the representatives of Collatia: *Et ego recipio*. So much for the notion that in heroic times stipulation was restricted to Roman citizens [1027]! And so much for the discernment of those who have hitherto believed that Tarquinius Priscus, in the formula for the surrender of Collatia, meant to teach the nations how surrenders were to be conducted!

1031   In this way the law of the heroic *gentes* of Latium remained fixed in the famous article of the Law of the Twelve Tables [6.1a] which reads: *Si quis nexum faciet mancipiumque, uti lingua nuncupassit, ita ius esto* ("If anyone shall make bond or conveyance, as he has declared with his tongue, so shall it be binding") [433, 570]. This article is the great fount of all ancient Roman law, and those who compare Roman with Attic law concede that this article did not come from Athens to Rome.

1032   Usucapion [at first] extended [only] as far as physical possession [1028]. Later this was feigned and the intent to possess sufficed. In the same way vindications were symbolized by a feigned force [961], and heroic reprisals were transformed into personal actions preserving the solemnity of denunciation of debtors [960]. The childhood of the world could have followed no other path; for children have a powerful faculty for imitating the truth in matters within their capacity, and it is in this that poetry consists, which is nothing but imitation [215f].

1033   Thus there appeared in the market place as many masks as there were persons (for *persona* properly means simply a mask) or as there were names. The names, which in the times of mute speech took the form of real words [435, 929], must have been the family coats of arms [433], by which families were found to be distinguished among the American Indians. And under the person or mask of the father of a family were concealed all his children and servants, and under the real name or emblem of a house were concealed all its agnates and gentiles. Thus we saw Ajax the tower of the Greeks, and Horatius alone on the bridge withstanding the whole of Tuscany, and in the returned barbarian times we encountered forty Norman heroes driving an entire army of Saracens from Salerno. Hence the reputation for amazing strength of the paladins of France (who were sovereign princes and whose name survived in [the counts palatine of] Germany), and above all of Count Roland, later called Orlando [559]. The reason for this springs from the principles of poetry discovered above [376ff]. The founders of Roman law, at a time when they could not understand intelligible universals, fashioned imaginative universals. And just as the poets later by art brought personages and masks onto the stage [910], so these men by nature had previously brought the aforesaid names and persons into the forum.

1034 The word *persōna* must not have been derived from *persōnare*, to resound everywhere, for in the quite small theaters of the first cities (when, as Horace says [A.P. 206], the spectators were so few as to be easily counted) it was not yet necessary to use masks for such resonance as would enable the voice to fill a large theater. And besides, the fact that the [second] syllable is long does not admit of this derivation, for if it came from *sŏno* it would have to be short. It must rather have come from *persōnari*, a verb which we conjecture meant to wear the skins of wild beasts, which was permitted only to heroes. The companion verb *obsōnari* has come down to us. It must at first have meant to feed on the meat of hunted game, which must have been the first rich fare on which Vergil describes his heroes as feasting [A. 3.223f]. Hence the first rich spoils must have been these skins of slain beasts brought back by the heroes from their first wars, which were waged against the beasts in defense of themselves and their families [958]. The poets clothe their heroes in these pelts, and above all Hercules, who wears that of the lion. To such an origin of the verb *persōnari*, in the primary meaning which we have restored to it, is to be traced, we conjecture, the Italian application of the term *personaggi*, personages, to men of high station and great representations.

1035 On these same principles, because they did not understand abstract forms, they imagined corporeal forms, and they imagined them, after their own nature, as animate [401]. *Hereditas*, or Inheritance, they imagined as mistress of hereditary property, and they recognized her as entire in every particular item of inherited goods, just as when they presented to the judge a lump or clod from a farm, they called it *hunc fundum* in the formula of *rei vindicatio* [961]. Thus, if they did not understand, they at least sensed in a rough way that rights were indivisible [1038].

1036 In conformity with such natures, ancient jurisprudence was throughout poetic. By its fictions what had happened was taken as not having happened, and what had not happened as having happened; those not yet born as already born; the living as dead; and the dead as still living in their estates pending acceptance. It introduced so many empty masks without subjects, *iura imaginaria*, rights invented by imagination. It rested its entire reputation on inventing such fables as might preserve the gravity of the laws and do justice to the facts. Thus all the fictions of ancient jurisprudence were truths under masks, and the formulae in which the laws were expressed, because of their strict measures of such and so many words—admitting neither addition, subtraction, nor alteration—were called *carmina*, or songs, as above we found Livy terming the formula dictating the punishment of Horatius [500]. This is confirmed by a golden passage in Plautus's *Comedy of Asses* [746ff] where Diabolus says that the parasite is a great poet, for he knows better than anybody how to invent verbal safeguards or formulae, which we have just seen were called *carmina*.

1037 Thus all ancient Roman law was a serious poem, represented by the Romans in the forum, and ancient jurisprudence was a severe poetry. Very conveniently to our argument, Justinian in the proemium of the *Institutes* speaks of the fables of the ancient law—*antiqui iuris fabulas*. He uses the phrase in derision but he must have taken it from some ancient jurisconsult who had understood the matters we have been discussing. From these ancient fables, as we here prove, Roman jurisprudence drew its principles. And from the masks called *personae* which were used in these dramatic fables, so true and severe, derive the first origins of the doctrine *de iure personarum*, of the law of persons.

1038 With the coming of the human times of the popular commonwealths, the intellect was brought into play in the great assemblies, and universal legal concepts abstracted by the intellect were thenceforward said to have their being in the understanding of the law—*consistere in intellectu iuris*. This understanding is concerned with the intention which the lawmaker has expressed in his law (this intention being called *ius* [398]), an intention which was that of the citizens brought into agreement upon an idea of a common rational utility. This they must have understood as spiritual in nature, because all those rights which did not attach to corporeal things over which they could be exercised (and which were called *nuda iura,* rights not corporeally vested) were said *in intellectu iuris consistere.* Since rights are thus modes of spiritual substance, they are therefore indivisible, and hence also eternal, for corruption is nothing else than division of parts [698].

1039 The interpreters of Roman law have rested the entire reputation of legal metaphysics on the consideration of the indivisibility of rights in their treatment of the famous subject of divisibles and indivisibles—*De dividuis et individuis.* But they have not considered the other and no less important attribute of eternity. Yet they should have noted it in the following two rules of law. The first establishes that, when the end of the law ceases, the law ceases: *cessante fine legis, cessat lex.* It does not read *cessante ratione,* for the *finis,* or end, of the law is the equal utility of causes, which may fail of realization; but the *ratio,* or reason, of the law is a conformity of the law to the fact, clothed in such and such circumstances, and whenever the fact is so clothed the reason of the law lives and governs it. The other rule establishes that time is not a mode by which a right is created or destroyed: *tempus non est modus constituendi vel dissolvendi iuris.* For time cannot give a beginning or put an end to the eternal, and in usucapion and prescription time neither produces nor terminates the rights, but is proof that he who held them intended to relinquish them. From the fact that the usufruct, for example, is said to terminate, it does not follow that the right terminates, but only that it is detached from the servitude and becomes as free as before. Herefrom spring two very important corollaries. First, that as rights are eternal in the understanding of them or in their idea, whereas men have their being in time, the rights can come to men only from God. And second, that all the countless various rights that have been, now are, or ever will be in the world, are diverse modifications of the power of the first man, who was the prince of the human race, and of the ownership which he held over the whole earth.

1040 Now, because laws certainly came first and philosophies later [1043], it must have been from observing that the enactment of laws by Athenian citizens involved their coming to agreement in an idea of an equal utility common to all of them severally, that Socrates began to adumbrate intelligible genera or abstract universals by induction; that is, by collecting uniform particulars which go to make up a genus of that in respect of which the particulars are uniform among themselves [D7, 499].

1041 Plato, reflecting that in such public assemblies the minds of particular men, each passionately bent on his private utility, are brought together in a dispassionate idea of common utility (according to the saying that men individually are swayed by their private interests but collectively they seek justice), raised himself to the meditation of the highest intelligible ideas of created minds, ideas which are distinct from these created minds and can reside only in God, and thus he reached the height of conceiving the philosophical hero who commands his passions at will.

1042 The way was thus prepared for the divine definition which Aristotle [P. 1287a 32] later gave us of a good law as a will free of passion, which is to say the will of a hero. He understood justice as queen of the virtues, seated in the spirit of the hero and commanding all the others [E. 1129b 12ff]. For he had observed legal justice seated in the spirit of the sovereign civil power and dictating prudence in the senate, fortitude in the armies, and temperance at festivals, as well as the two forms of particular justice: distributive justice in the public treasuries and commutative justice for the most part in the forum; the latter employing arithmetical proportion and the former geometrical [E. 1131b 12,29]. He must have observed distributive justice in the census which is the basic institution of the popular commonwealths [619ff] and which distributes honors and burdens in geometrical proportion according to the patrimonies of the citizens. For previously only arithmetical proportion had been understood; wherefore Astraea, heroic justice, was depicted for us with the scales [713], and in the Law of the Twelve Tables all the punishments—which philosophers, moral theologians, and professors writing on public law now say must be dispensed by distributive justice in geometrical proportion—all the punishments, we read, reduce either to the double (*duplio*) if pecuniary [6.2; 8.9,16,19,20; 12.3,4] and to the like (*talio*) if corporal [8.2]. And since the law of retaliation was invented by Rhadamanthus, he was made judge in the lower world, in which punishments are certainly distributed. In Aristotle's *Ethics* [1132b 21ff] retaliation was called Pythagorean justice, invented by the Pythagoras who founded a nation in Magna Graecia, whose nobles were called Pythagoreans [427]. This invention would be a disgrace to the Pythagoras who later became a sublime philosopher and mathematician.

1043 From all the above we conclude that these principles of metaphysics, logic, and morals issued from the market place of Athens. From Solon's advice to the Athenians, "Know thyself," came forth the popular commonwealths; from the popular commonwealths the laws; and from the laws emerged philosophy; and Solon, who had been wise in vulgar wisdom, came to be held wise in esoteric wisdom [414ff]. This may serve as a specimen of the history of philosophy told philosophically [I·8], and a last reproof, of the many brought forth in this work, against Polybius, who said that if there were philosophers in the world there would be no need of religions [179]. For [the fact is that] if there had not been religions and hence commonwealths, there would have been no philosophers in the world, and if human institutions had not been thus conducted by divine providence, there would have been no idea of either science or virtue.

1044 Now, to return to our subject and conclude the argument under discussion, in these human times in which the popular commonwealths and afterward the monarchies appeared [927], it was understood that the causes [of legal obligation], which had at first been formulae safeguarded by precise and proper words (for *cavere* is the origin of *cavissae*, of which *caussae* is the shortened form [569]), were the affairs or transactions themselves in the case of [consensual] contracts (which affairs or transactions are now solemnized by pacts, which in the act of contract are agreed upon so that they will produce the actions). In the case of those contracts which are valid titles for the conveyance of property, they solemnized the natural delivery in order to effect the transfer. And only in the contracts which are said to be completed by word of mouth (that is to say, in stipulations) did the verbal safeguards remain causes in the strict ancient sense. What we have said here illustrates further the principles above set forth for the obligations arising from contracts and pacts [570–578].

1045 To sum up, a man is properly only mind, body, and speech, and speech stands as it were midway between mind and body. Hence with regard to what is just, the certain began in mute times with the body. Then when the so-called articulate languages were invented, it advanced to ideas made certain by spoken formulae. And finally, when our human reason was fully developed, it reached its end in the true in the ideas themselves with regard to what is just, as determined by reason from the detailed circumstances of the facts. This truth is a formula devoid of any particular form, called by the learned Varro the formula of nature, *formula naturae* [C.G. 4.31], which, like light, of itself informs in all the minutest details of their surface the opaque bodies of the facts over which it is diffused [321–325].

BOOK FIVE

THE RECOURSE OF HUMAN INSTITUTIONS WHICH THE NATIONS TAKE WHEN THEY RISE AGAIN [L1–3, M1]

[INTRODUCTION]

1046 In countless passages scattered throughout this work and dealing with countless matters, we have observed the marvelous correspondence between the first and the returned barbarian times. From these passages we can easily understand the recourse of human institutions which the nations take when they rise again [1108]. For greater confirmation, however, we wish in this last Book to give a special place to this argument. Thus we shall bring more light to bear on the period of the second barbarism, which has remained darker than that of the first, though Varro, most learned student of the earliest antiquities, in his chronological division called this the dark time [52]. And we shall also show how the Best and Greatest God has caused the counsels of his providence, by which he has conducted the human institutions of all nations, to serve the ineffable decrees of his grace.

[Chapter I]   The Latest Barbaric History Explained as the Recourse of the First Barbaric History [L2]

1047 When, working in superhuman ways, God had revealed and confirmed the truth of the Christian religion by opposing the virtue of the martyrs to the power of Rome, and the teaching of the Fathers, together with the miracles, to the vain wisdom of Greece, and when armed nations were about to arise on every hand destined to combat the true divinity of its Founder, he permitted a new order of humanity to be born among the nations in order that [the true religion] might be firmly established according to the natural course of human institutions themselves.

1048 Following this eternal counsel, he brought back the truly divine times [925, 976], in which Catholic kings everywhere, in order to defend the Christian religion, of which they are protectors, donned the dalmatics of deacons and consecrated their royal persons (whence they preserve the

title Sacred Royal Majesty). They assumed ecclesiastical dignities, as Hugh
Capet, according to Symphorien Champier in his genealogy of the kings of
France (*Regum Francorum genealogia*), took the title of Count and Abbot
of Paris, and Paradin in his *Annales de Bourgogne* refers to ancient documents in which the princes of France were commonly entitled Duke and
Abbot or Count and Abbot. Thus the first Christian kings founded military
religious orders by which they re-established in their realms the Catholic
Christian religion against the Arians (by whom St. Jerome says almost the
whole Christian world was befouled), and against the Saracens and numerous other infidels.

1049   Thus there was a return in truth of what were called the pure
and pious wars—*pura et pia bella*—of the heroic peoples [958], and hence
all Christian powers still bear on the globe surmounting their crowns the
cross which they had earlier displayed on their banners when they waged
the wars called crusades [602].

1050   Amazing indeed is the recourse of these human civil institutions
in the returned barbarian times. The ancient heralds, for example, called
out the gods—*evocabant deos*—from the cities on which they were declaring war, using the elegant and splendid formula preserved for us by
Macrobius [in his *Saturnalia* 3.9.7f]; for they believed that thereby the
vanquished gentes would be left without gods [958] and hence without
auspices, which are the first principle of everything that we have discussed
in this work. For, by the heroic law of victory, the conquered were left
without any civil institutions, public or private, all of which, as we have
already fully proved principally from Roman history, were dependent in
heroic times on the divine auspices [110]. All this was comprised in the
heroic formula of surrender, applied by Tarquinius Priscus to Collatia
[1030], whereby the vanquished forfeited all their institutions, religious
and secular—*debebant divina et humana omnia*—to the conquering peoples. In the same way, the latest barbarians in taking a city made it their
principal concern to seek out and carry off famous remains or relics of
saints. So the peoples of those times were very careful to bury or hide them,
and such repositories are everywhere found in the innermost and deepest
parts of churches. That is the reason why almost all the removals of the
bodies of the saints took place in those times. A trace of this custom
survives in the rule by which conquered peoples must ransom from the
victorious commanders all the bells of the cities they have taken.

1051   Moreover, from the fifth century onward, when so many barbarous nations began to inundate Europe and Asia and Africa as well, and
the conquering peoples could not make themselves understood by the

conquered, it came about from the barbarism of the enemies of the Catholic religion that in those iron times we can find no contemporary documents in the vulgar tongues, whether Italian, French, Spanish, or even German. (As for the Germans, they did not begin to write documents in their language until the times of Frederick of Swabia, according to Johann [Tourmayer] Aventinus in his annals of Bavaria [*Annales Boiorum*], or even until those of the Emperor Rudolf of Hapsburg according to others [435].) Among all the aforesaid nations we find documents only in barbarous Latin, understood only by a very few nobles, who were also ecclesiastics. Hence we may assume that in all those unhappy centuries the nations had reverted to communicating with each other in a mute language. Because of this paucity of vulgar letters, there must everywhere have been a return to the hieroglyphic writing of family coats of arms, which, in order to give certainty to ownership, signified seignorial rights usually over houses, tombs, fields, and flocks [484–488].

1052   There was a return of certain kinds of divine judgments [955] called "canonical purgations." One kind of these judgments was the duels of the first barbarian times [959ff], though these were not recognized by the sacred canons.

1053   There was a return of heroic raids. As the heroes had counted it an honor to be called robbers, so now it was a title of nobility to be a corsair [636].

1054   There was a return of heroic reprisals, which lasted down to the times of Bartolus [960].

1055   And since the wars of the latest barbarian times, like those of the first, were all wars of religion [1049], there was a return of heroic slavery [676], which lasted a long time among Christian nations themselves. For because of the practice of duels in those times, the conquerors believed that the conquered had no god [958], and hence held them no better than beasts. This national feeling is still preserved between Christians and Turks. To a Christian the name Turk means a dog (whence Christians when they desire or are obliged to treat civilly with Turks call them Moslems, which means true believers); the Turks, on the other hand, call the Christians swine. Hence in their wars both sides practice heroic slavery, though the Christians do so with more mildness.

1056   But marvelous above all is the recourse taken by human institutions in this respect, that in these new divine times there began again the first asylums of the ancient world, within which, as we learned from Livy, all the first cities were founded [561]. For everywhere violence, rapine, and murder were rampant, because of the extreme ferocity and savagery of these most barbarous centuries. Nor was there any efficacious way of restraining men who had shaken off all human laws save by the divine laws dictated by religion [177]. Naturally, therefore, men in fear of being oppressed or destroyed betook themselves to the bishops and abbots of those violent centuries, as being comparatively humane in the midst of such barbarism, and put themselves, their families, and their patrimonies under their protection, and were received by them. Such submission and such protection are the principal constitutive elements of fiefs. Hence in Germany, which must have been the wildest and most savage of all the nations of Europe, there remained almost more ecclesiastical sovereigns (bishops or abbots) than secular; and, as we have said, in France all sovereign princes assumed the title of Count and Abbot or Duke and Abbot [1048]. Thus it came about that such an immense number of cities, towns, and castles in Europe were named after saints; for in high or hidden places [525], in order to hear Mass and perform the other offices of piety commanded by our religion, little churches were opened, which may be defined as the natural asylums of Christians in those times. Close by they built their dwellings. Hence everywhere the oldest remains we see of this second barbarism are little churches in such places as we have described, for the most part in ruins. A famous example of all this is our own Abbey of San Lorenzo of Aversa, with which was incorporated the Abbey of San Lorenzo of Capua. This abbey governed, either directly or through abbots or monks dependent upon it, a hundred and ten churches in Campania, Samnium, Apulia, and old Calabria, from the river Volturno to the Gulf of Taranto; and the abbots of San Lorenzo were barons of almost all the aforesaid places.

[Chapter II]   The Recourse the Nations Take over the Eternal Nature of Fiefs, and the Recourse Thence of Ancient Roman Law in Feudal Law [L2]

1057   These divine times were followed by certain heroic times, in consequence of the return of a certain distinction between almost opposite natures, the heroic and the human [567]. This is the reason why in feudal terminology the rustic vassals, to Hotman's surprise, are called *homines*, men [437, 600, 606]. This word must be the origin of the two feudal terms *hominium* and *homagium*, which have the same meaning. *Hominium* stands for *hominis dominium*, the baron's ownership of his man or vassal.

Helmodius, according to Cujas, considers this term more elegant than the second, *homagium*, which stands for *hominis agium*, the baron's right to lead his vassal where he pleases. Learned writers on feudal law translate this latter barbarous term into classical Latin as *obsequium*, which is an exact equivalent, since it originally meant the readiness of the man to follow the hero wherever he led in order to till the latter's fields. The word *obsequium* emphasizes the fealty owed by the vassal to the baron, so that the *obsequium* of the Latins signifies at once the homage and the fealty which must be sworn at the investiture of fiefs; and among the ancient Romans the *obsequium* was inseparable from what they called *opera militaris* and our writers on feudal law call *militare servitium*, the service which the Roman plebeians over a long period rendered to the nobles in war at their own expense [107]. *Liberti,* or freedmen, continued to owe to their patrons this *obsequium* and the services it entailed. In Roman history, this duty goes back to the time when Romulus founded Rome on the clienteles, the form of protection extended to laboring peasants received by him into his asylum [106]. These clienteles of ancient history cannot more properly be explained than as fiefs [263], and indeed the learned feudists translate the barbarous *feudum* by the elegant Latin *clientela*.

1058 These principles of institutions are clearly confirmed by the origins of the words *opera* and *servitium*. *Opera* in its original sense is the day's labor of a peasant, whom the Latins therefore called *operarius*, for which the Italian equivalent is *giornaliere*. It is as such a day laborer, without any privilege of citizenship, that Achilles complains of having been treated by Agamemnon when the latter wrongfully took from him his Briseis [597]. The Latins applied to these laborers the term "herd"—*greges operarum*, or even *greges servorum*—because both they and the later slaves were regarded as beasts, which are said to feed in herds—*pasci gregatim*. [Herds of men must have come first, and herds of beasts later;] and, correspondingly, there must first have been the shepherds of such men (whence the Homeric fixed epithet for the heroes: "shepherds of the people"), and only later the shepherds of flocks and herds [557]. This is confirmed by the Greek word *nomos*, which means both law and pasturage [607]; for by the first agrarian law the rebellious *famuli* were accorded sustenance on lands assigned to them by the heroes, and this sustenance was called *nomos*, or pasturage, as being appropriate to such beasts, even as food is proper to men [917].

1059 The property of pasturing these first herds of the world must have appertained to Apollo, the god of civil light, that is, of the nobility [533]; for fabulous history tells of him as a shepherd at the river Amphrysus, just as Paris, who was certainly of the royal house of Troy, was also a shepherd. So also is the family father (whom Homer calls a king) who with his scepter orders the roasted ox to be divided among the harvesters, as portrayed on the shield of Achilles, on which the history of the world was represented, with the epoch of the families fixed in this scene [686]. Now it is not the business of our shepherds to feed the flocks but to guide and watch over them, but pasturing [in this later sense], because of the prevalence of raiding in heroic times [636f], could have been introduced only after the confines of the first cities had been made somewhat secure. This must be why bucolic, or pastoral, poetry appeared only in the most civilized times, among the Greeks with Theocritus, the Latins with Vergil, and the Italians with Sannazaro.

1060   The word *servitium*, or service, shows that these same things returned in the latest barbarian times; and in the converse of this relationship the baron was called *senior* in the sense of lord. Thus the ancient Franks [or freedmen of the scond barbarism [1062]] who so surprised Bodin [1017] were servants born in the household, and corresponded in general to those whom [in the first barbarism] the ancient Romans called *vernae*, who gave the name *vernaculae* to the vulgar tongues introduced by the vulgar of the peoples [443], that is, by the plebs of the heroic cities [597], just as the poetic language had been introduced by the heroes or nobles of the first commonwealths [437].

1061   Once the power of the barons had been dispersed and dissipated among the peoples in the civil wars in which the powerful must depend on the people, and had hence been easily concentrated again in the persons of the monarchical kings, the *obsequium* of the freedmen passed over into what is called *obsequium principis*, in which, according to Tacitus [A.1.43], consists the entire duty of subjects to their monarchies. On the other hand, because of the supposed difference of the two natures, heroic and human [1057], the lords of the fiefs were called barons in the same sense in which, as we found above, they were called heroes by the Greek poets and men (*viri*) by the ancient Latins [684, 999]. A trace of this survives in the Spanish *varon* for a man; the vassals, because of their weakness, being regarded as women in the heroic sense above explained [989].

1062   In addition to what we have just set forth, the term *signori* for the barons can only come from the Latin *seniores*, for of such elders the first public parliaments of the new realms of Europe must have been composed, just as Romulus had applied the term *senatus* to the public council, which he must naturally have composed of the older members of the nobility. And as, from these who thus were and were called *patres*, those who give slaves their liberty came to be called *patroni*, so, from these, in Italian, the term *padroni* must have come to mean protectors. This term *padroni* retains the full elegance and propriety of its Latin original. Conversely, with equal Latin elegance and propriety the word *clientes* is used in the sense of the rustic vassals to whom Servius Tullius, in decreeing the census, conceded such fiefs by taking the shortest possible step from the clienteles of Romulus [106f]. These *clientes* are precisely the freedmen who later gave the nation of the Franks its name, as we said in reply to Bodin [1017].

1063   In this fashion the fiefs came back, springing from the eternal source assigned to them in the axioms [26off], where we indicated the benefits which may be hoped for in civil nature, whence with full Latin elegance and propriety the fiefs are called *beneficia* by the learned feudists. Hotman indeed observes, but without making use of the point, that the victors kept for themselves the cultivated fields in conquered lands and left to the unhappy vanquished the untilled fields for their sustenance. Thus the fiefs of the first world, as described in Book Two, returned, taking their new beginning, however (as by their nature we showed they must [1057]), from the personal rustic fiefs which we found the clienteles of Romulus at first to have been, and of which we remarked in the axioms that they were scattered all over the ancient world of peoples [263]. These heroic clienteles, in the splendor of Roman popular liberty, passed over into the custom by which the plebeians in their togas betook themselves in the morning to pay court to the great lords, saluted them with the title of the ancient heroes, *Ave rex*—"Hail, king!"—accompanied them into the forum, returned home with them in the evening, and were there given their evening meal by the lords, in conformity with the practice which gave the ancient heroes the title of shepherds of the people [1058].

1064   Such personal vassals must have been the first *vades*, or "sureties," among the ancient Romans [559]. This term was preserved for the defendants who were obliged to appear with the plaintiffs in court, the obligation being called *vadimonium*. The name of these *vades*, according to our "Origins of the Latin Language" [Op. 3.369], must have been derived from the nominative *vas*, the *bas* of the Greeks and the *was* of the barbarians, whence *wassus* and eventually *vassalus*. Vassals of this kind are even now to be found everywhere in the kingdoms of the colder north, which still retain a great deal of barbarism, particularly in Poland, where they are called *kmet* and are a kind of slaves, whole families of whom are gambled away by their lords and obliged to pass into the service of other masters. In these vassals we must recognize those who were chained by their ears and whom the Gallic Hercules leads whither he will by the chains of poetic gold (that is, grain) which issue from his mouth [560].

1065 Then came real rustic fiefs, reached by way of the first agrarian law of the nations, which among the Romans was the law by which Servius Tullius decreed the first census, by which he conceded to the plebeians the bonitary ownership of the fields assigned to them by the nobles under certain burdens not only personal as before but also real [107]. These plebeians must have been the first *mancipes*, a term which later designated those under real-estate bond to the public treasury [433, 559]. Of the same sort must have been the vanquished to whom the victors gave the unculti-vated fields to till for sustenance, as we found Hotman saying a short way back [1063]. Thus returned the Antaeuses bound to the soil by the Greek Hercules [618], and the *nexi*, or bondmen, of the god Fidius [602], the Roman Hercules, who were finally freed by the Petelian Law [115].

1066 These *nexi* freed by the Petelian Law [658] correspond exactly to the vassals, who must at first have been called liege men as being bound (*legati*) by this knot. Liege men are now defined by the writers on feudal law as those who must recognize as friends or enemies all the friends or enemies of their lord. This is precisely the oath Tacitus says was sworn by the ancient German vassals when they pledged themselves to serve the glory of their princes [559]. Later when these fiefs developed into the full splendor of sovereign civil fiefs, the liege vassals were the conquered kings, to whom the Roman people, in the words of the solemn formula recounted in Roman history [by Sallust in his *War with Jugurtha* 5.4], gave their kingdoms in gift—*regna dono dabat*—which is as much as to say in fief—*beneficio dabat*. They became allies of the Roman people under the kind of alliance which the Latins called unequal league—*foedus inae-quale*—and they were called royal friends of the Roman people in the sense in which the emperors spoke of their noble courtiers as friends. Such an unequal alliance was nothing but the investiture of a sovereign fief, which was conceived under the formula set forth by Livy [38.11.2] that the allied king was to uphold the majesty of the Roman people—*servaret maiestatem populi romani*—just as the jurisconsult Paulus [i.e., Proculus in D.49.15.7.1] says that the praetor renders justice *servata maiestate populi romani*; that is, he renders justice to those to whom the law grants it and withholds it from those to whom the law denies it. These allied kings were lords of sovereign fiefs subject to a greater sovereignty. There returned thus to Europe a common sense by which the title of Majesty was mostly reserved for great kings who are lords of great kingdoms and numerous provinces.

1067   Along with these rustic fiefs, from which these institutions took their beginnings, there returned the emphyteusis [575] under which the great ancient forest of the earth had been cultivated; whence the *laudimia* came to signify both the payment made by the vassal to his lord and that made by the emphyteuticary to his immediate landlord [489].

1068   There was a return of the ancient Roman clienteles called commendations, so that the vassals, with Latin elegance and propriety, are called *clientes* by the learned feudists and the fiefs themselves are called *clientelae* [1057].

1069   There was a return of the kind of census decreed by Servius Tullius, by which the Roman plebeians were for a long time obliged to serve the nobles in war at their own expense [107]. The vassals now called *angarii* and *perangarii* were the equivalent of the ancient Roman *assidui*, or tribute payers, who fought at their own expense, *suis assibus militabant*; the nobles having, moreover, the right of private imprisonment over their plebeian debtors down to the time of the Petelian Law, which freed the Roman plebs from the feudal law of *nexum* [115].

1070   There was a return of the *precaria*, which must originally have been lands granted by the lords in response to the entreaties of the poor, so that they might find their sustenance by cultivating them; for precisely such are the possessions which the Law of the Twelve Tables never recognized [638, 983].

1071   And since barbarism with its violence destroys the confidence necessary to commerce and leaves the people with no other concern than the bare necessities of natural life, and since all rents had to be in the form of so-called natural fruits, there appeared at the same time also the *libelli* as transfers of real estate. Their utility must have been apparent from the fact that one man had an abundance of fields yielding a kind of fruit which another man lacked, and vice versa, and hence they made exchanges one with another [571].

1072   There was a return of mancipations, the vassal placing his hands between the hands of his lord to signify fealty and subjection. The rustic vassals under the census of Servius Tullius were thus the first *mancipes* of the Romans [1065]. Along with mancipation there returned the division of things into *res mancipi* and *res nec mancipi*; for feudal estates are *res nec mancipi* for the vassal, who cannot alienate them, but *res mancipi* for the lord, just as the lands of the Roman provinces were *res nec mancipi* for the provincials but *res mancipi* for the Romans. In the act of mancipation there was a return of stipulations in the form of infestucations or investitures, which we showed above to be identical [569]. Along with stipulations there was a return of what in ancient Roman jurisprudence were at first properly called *cavissae*, later shortened to *caussae*, which in the second barbarian times were called *cautelae* from the same Latin origin [939, 1044]. The solemnizing of pacts and contracts by means of such *cautelae* was called *homologare*, after the *homines*, or men [i.e., vassals], to whom we traced *hominium* and *homagium* [1057]; for all the contracts of those times must have been feudal. Thus, with the *cautelae*, there was a return of pacts safeguarded [by precautionary phrases] in the act of mancipation, *pacta stipulata* as they were called by the Roman jurisconsults, from the *stipula*, or blade, which sheathes the grain; and thus in the same sense in which the barbarous doctors derived the expression *pacta vestita* from the investitures which were also called infestucations. Pacts not thus safeguarded were called by both [ancient and medieval lawyers], using the same phrase in the same sense, *pacta nuda* [569].

1073   There was a return of the two kinds of ownership, direct and useful—*dominium directum* and *dominium utile*—which correspond exactly to the quiritary and bonitary ownership of the ancient Romans [582, 600f]. Direct ownership arose first just as quiritary ownership did among the Romans. The latter was originally ownership by the nobles of the lands which they [later] granted to the plebeians [109]. If the plebeians lost possession of them, they had to resort to *rei vindicatio*, employing the formula *Aio hunc fundum meum esse ex iure quiritium* ("I declare this field to be mine by the law of the Quirites") [562, 961]. Such a revindication was nothing less than a citation of the whole order of nobles (who made up the city in the Roman aristocracy [597]) as the *auctores* from whom the plebeians derived the title of civil ownership in virtue of which they could vindicate the fields in question [603, 984]. Such ownership was always called *auctoritas* in the Law of the Twelve Tables, from the authority of ownership enjoyed by the reigning senate over the Roman territory at large, over which later the people, with the coming of popular liberty, held the sovereign *imperium* [386, 944ff].

1074   Upon this "authority," as upon numberless other institutions of the second barbarism, we throw light in this work from the antiquities of the first barbarism; so much more obscure have we found the times of the second than those of the first! The "authority" of the second has, however, left three quite clear traces in three feudal terms. First the adjective *directus*, which confirms that the action [of *rei vindicatio*] was originally authorized by the direct or immediate overlord. Next, the noun *laudimia* for the payment [made by the vassal] on taking possession of the fief to which he had laid claim by the aforesaid citation [*laudatio*] [of his lord] as *auctor*. Lastly the noun *lodo*, which must originally have signified the judicial decision in this sort of case, and which later came to mean an arbitrated decision; for these cases [concerning fiefs] seem to have been concluded on friendly terms, in contrast with cases litigated concerning alods (which Budé believes were so called from *alaudia*, just as *laus* becomes *lode* in Italian), over which the lords originally had to meet in duels [961]. This custom has lasted down to my time in our Kingdom of Naples, where the barons used to avenge not by civil suits but by duels the invasions of their feudal territories by other barons. And like the quiritary ownership of the ancient Romans, the direct ownership of the early barbarians came finally to mean ownership which gives rise to a real civil action.

1075 And here is a very clear occasion for observing, in the recourse the nations take, the recourse also which the lot of the later Roman jurisconsults took in that of the later barbarian doctors. For just as the former in their times had already lost sight of early Roman law (as we have shown above by a thousand proofs [984, 993]), so the latter in their most recent times lost sight of early feudal law. For the erudite [humanist] interpreters of Roman law resolutely deny that these two barbarian types of ownership [direct and useful] were recognized by Roman law, being misled by the difference in names and failing to understand the identity of the institutions themselves.

1076 There was a return of goods *ex iure optimo* in the alodial goods which the learned feudists define as goods free of every encumbrance public or private, comparing them with the few houses held *ex iure optimo* which Cicero says still remained at Rome in his time [601]. However, just as all notion of this sort of goods was lost in the latest Roman legislation, so in our times not a single example of these alods can be found. And like the estates *ex iure optimo* of the Romans, the alods finally became real estate free of every real private encumbrance but subject to real public encumbrances. For there was a recurrence of the transition from the census instituted by Servius Tullius to the census which was the basis of the Roman public treasury [619ff]. Alods and fiefs, then, which are the two great classes of property in feudal law, were originally distinguished by the fact that feudal goods were protected by citation of the lord and alodial goods were not. Here, for lack of these principles, all the learned feudists cannot help being at a loss as to how the alods, which they latinize with Cicero as *bona ex iure optimo*, came to be called "goods of the distaff." In their proper meaning, these were goods held under a very strong title, not weakened even by any public encumbrance. Such were the goods of the fathers in the family state and continuing for a long time into the state of the first cities, which goods they had acquired by the labors of Hercules. The difficulty is easily solved if, following our principles, we observe that this same Hercules, when he became a slave of Iole and Omphale, took to the spinning wheel. That is, the heroes became effeminate and yielded their heroic institutions to the plebeians, whom they had regarded as women (holding and calling themselves in contrast *viri*, or men [1061]), and allowed their goods to become subject to the public treasury through the census, which was first the basic institution of the popular commonwealths and later lent itself to the establishment of the monarchies.

1077 Thus through this early feudal law which was lost sight of in later times, there was a return of estates *ex iure quiritium*, by the law of the Quirites, which we explained as "the law of the Romans in public assembly, armed with lances" [603], which they called *quires* [562]. From these Quirites was conceived the formula of *rei vindicato*: *Aio hunc fundum meum esse ex iure quiritium*, which was a citation of the entire heroic city of Rome as *auctor* [1073]. Now in the second barbarism fiefs were certainly called "goods of the lance," which required the citation of the lords as *auctores*, in contrast with the later alods called "goods of the distaff" (that with which Hercules, dispirited and enslaved to women, does his spinning). This is the heroic origin of the motto of the royal arms of France, *Lilia non nent* ("The lilies do not spin"), for in that kingdom women may not inherit. For there was a return of the gentilitial successions of the Law of the Twelve Tables, which we found to be *ius gentium romanorum*, the law of the Roman gentes, just as Baldus called the Salic Law *ius gentium gallorum*, the law of the Gallic gentes. The latter was certainly observed throughout Germany, and thus must have been observed throughout all the other first barbarous nations of Europe, but was later confined to France and Savoy [988].

1078 Lastly, there was a return of armed courts such as we found above that the heroic assemblies were which were held under arms, and which were called by the Greeks assemblies of Curetes and by the Romans assemblies of Quirites [594f]. The first parliaments of the realms of Europe must have consisted of barons, as that of France certainly was of peers. French history tells us clearly that kings were heads of its parliament in the beginning and created the peers of the courts to adjudicate cases in the capacity of commissioners; whence they continued to be called the dukes and peers of France. Just as the first trial in which, according to Cicero

[*Defense of Milo* 3.7], the life of a Roman citizen was at stake, was that in which the king Tullus Hostilius created the duumvirs to act as commissioners and, in the formula preserved for us by Livy, to charge Horatius with treason—*in Horatium perduellionem dicerent*—for having slain his sister [500].

1079   This was because in the severity of those heroic times every killing of a citizen (when the cities were composed of heroes only [597]) was considered an act of hostility against the fatherland, which is precisely the meaning of *perduellio*; and every such killing was called a *parricidium*, for the victim was a father, that is, a noble, as in those days Rome was divided into fathers and plebs. The reason why from the time of Romulus down to that of Tullus Hostilius there was no trial for the slaying of a noble, must have been that the nobles took care not to commit such offenses, having among themselves the practice of dueling [1074]. But since in the case of Horatius there was no one who could privately avenge by a duel the slaying of Horatia, a trial was then for the first time ordered by Tullus Hostilius. Killings of plebeians, on the other hand, were either committed by their own lords, against whom no accusation could be brought, or by others who could indemnify the man's own lord for the loss as if he had been a slave, as is still the custom in Poland, Lithuania, Sweden, Denmark, and Norway. But the learned interpreters of Roman law did not see this difficulty because they relied on the vain opinion of the innocence of the golden age [518], just as the political theorists for the same reason relied on Aristotle's statement that in the ancient commonwealths there were no laws concerning private wrongs and offenses [269]; whence Tacitus [A.3.26], Sallust [*War with Catiline* 2.1], and other writers who are otherwise most discerning, when they speak of the origin of commonwealths and laws, relate that in the primitive state preceding the cities men led lives like so many Adams in the state of innocence. But once the cities had admitted those *homines*, or men, who so surprised Hotman [437] and from whom comes the natural law of the gentes called *humanae* by Ulpian [569], from then on the killing of any man was called *homicidium*.

1080   In these parliaments were discussed feudal causes concerning rights or successions or devolutions of fiefs by reason of felony or default of heirs. Such causes, when they had been confirmed many times by such adjudications, formed the customs of feudalism which are the most ancient of all the customs of Europe and which prove to us that the natural law of the gentes was born of these human customs of the fiefs [599ff].

1081   Finally, just as King Tullus granted Horatius an appeal to the people (which then consisted of nobles only [662ff, 666ff]) from the verdict by which he had been condemned, since against a reigning senate there was no remedy for the condemned save appeal to the senate itself [500]; even so and in no other way the nobles of the returned barbarian times must have made appeals to the kings in their parliaments, for instance to the kings of France, who at first were heads of parliament.

1082   There is a notable vestige of these heroic parliaments in the Sacred Council of Naples, for its president is given the title of Sacred Royal Majesty, the councilors are called *milites* and serve in the capacity of commissioners (for in the second barbarian times the nobles alone were soldiers and the plebeians served them in war, as we found from Homer and from ancient Roman history to have been the case in the first barbarian times [425, 558f]), and its decisions admit of no appeal to any other tribunal, but only a request for revision by the council itself.

1083   In view of all the institutions here enumerated, we must conclude that the realms were everywhere aristocratic; we do not say in constitution but in administration, as in the cold north that of Poland still is (and as those of Sweden and Denmark were until a century and a half ago). In time, if extraordinary causes do not impede its natural course, Poland will arrive at perfect [that is, at absolute but enlightened] monarchy.

1084   So true is this that Bodin himself goes so far as to say of his kingdom of France that it was aristocratic, not merely in administration as we assert but in constitution, during the Merovingian and Carlovingian dynasties.* But here we may ask Bodin how the kingdom of France became the perfect monarchy it now is. Perhaps by some royal law by which the paladins of France divested themselves of their power and conferred it upon the kings of the Capetian dynasty?—If he has recourse to the fable of the royal law invented by Tribonian [1007f], by which the Roman people supposedly divested itself of its free sovereignty and conferred it on Augustus, to prove it a fable it suffices to read the first pages of the *Annals* of Tacitus, in which he narrates the last acts of Augustus, legitimizing the beginning of the Roman monarchy in his own person, as indeed all nations perceived that it began with Augustus.—Perhaps because France was conquered through force of arms by one of the Capetian kings?—But all the histories keep it at a safe distance from such an un-

---

* Jean Bodin, *Les Six Livres de la République* (Paris, 1577), pp. 745ff, cf. 235ff; English translation by Richard Knolles, *The Six Bookes of a Commonweale* (London, 1606), pp. 729ff, 236ff. Bodin makes the distinction between constitution and administration, *estat* and *gouvernement*, on pp. 199f (Eng. tr., 199f). Vico's terms here and in 286, 663, 1004ff, and 1018 are *stato* and *governo*. Elsewhere he often uses one without the other, and without making a point of the distinction; and in most such cases they are rendered literally, but less accurately, "state" and "government."

happy fate. Bodin therefore, and with him all the other political and legal authorities who have written on public law, must recognize this eternal natural royal law by which the free power of a state, just because it is free, must be actualized. Namely, that in proportion as the optimates lose their grip the strength of the people increases until they become free; and in proportion as the free peoples relax their hold the kings gain in strength until they become monarchs [1008]. Wherefore, just as the natural law of the philosophers (or moral theologians) is that of reason [E8], so this natural law of the gentes is that of utility and of force, which, as the jurisconsults say [J.1.2.2], is observed by the nations *usu exigente humanisque necessitatibus expostulantibus*, "as occasion requires and human needs demand" [G3].

1085 From all these beautiful and elegant expressions of ancient Roman jurisprudence, with which the learned feudists do in fact mitigate and might even further mitigate the barbarousness of feudal doctrine (since the ideas of the latter fit the expressions of the former in their full propriety [1057ff]), let Oldendorp (and all the others with him) consider whether feudal law was born from the sparks of the fire set by the barbarians to Roman law. On the contrary, Roman law was born from the sparks of the fiefs practiced in the first barbarism of Latium, such fiefs as were the origin of all the commonwealths in the world. As we demonstrated this above in one of our chapters on the poetic politics of the first commonwealths [599ff], so here in Book Five, in a demonstration promised in the Idea of the Work [25], we have seen that the kingdoms of modern Europe have their origins within the eternal nature of fiefs.

1086 But finally, with the opening of schools in the universities of Italy and the teaching of the Roman laws contained in the books of Justinian, laws therein based on the natural law of human gentes [994ff, 1002], minds now more developed and grown more intelligent were dedicated to the cultivation of the jurisprudence of natural equity, which makes the common people and the nobles equal in civil rights, just as they are equal in human nature. And just as from the time when Tiberius Coruncanius [the first plebeian chief pontiff] began to teach the laws publicly in Rome their secrecy began to slip from the hands of the nobles [999], and the power of the nobles gradually declined, so it happened in the case of the nobles of the kingdoms of Europe, which had been ruled by aristocratic governments before passing into free commonwealths and thence into perfect monarchies.

1087 These last two forms of state, since both involve human governments, readily admit of change from either to the other, but a return from either to an aristocratic state is almost impossible in civil nature. So much so that Dion of Syracuse, although he was a member of the royal family and had driven into exile a monster of princes, Dionysius the tyrant, and although he was so well favored with civil virtues as to be worthy of the friendship of the divine Plato, was nevertheless barbarously slain when he attempted to restore the aristocratic state. And the Pythagoreans (that is, the nobles of Magna Graecia), for the same attempt, were all cut in pieces save for the few who had taken refuge in strongholds and were burned alive by the multitude. For the plebeians, once they know themselves to be of equal nature with the nobles, naturally will not submit to remaining their inferiors in civil rights; and they achieve equality either in free common-wealths or under monarchies. Wherefore, in the present humanity of the nations, the few remaining aristocratic commonwealths [1094] must take infinite pains and shrewd and prudent measures to keep the multitude at the same time dutiful and content.

[Chapter III]   Survey of the Ancient and the Modern World of Nations in the Light of the Principles of this Science [I·13]

1088   Carthage, Capua, and Numantia, the three cities which caused Rome to fear for her empire of the world, failed to accomplish this course of human civil institutions. The Carthaginians were prevented by their native African shrewdness, which was further sharpened by their maritime trade [971]; the Capuans by the mild climate and the fertility of this happy Campania [769]; and the Numantians, finally, in the first flower of their heroism were suppressed by the power of Rome under a Scipio Africanus, the conqueror of Carthage, assisted by the forces of the world [971]. But the Romans, having none of these obstacles, proceeded with even steps, being ruled by providence through the medium of vulgar wisdom. Through all three forms of civil states, in the natural order which has been demonstrated by so many proofs in this work, they persisted in each until it was naturally succeeded by the next. They retained the aristocracy down to the Publilian and Petelian laws [104–115]; they pre-served popular liberty down to the times of Augustus [1008]; and they clung to the monarchy as long as they could humanly withstand the internal and external causes which destroy that form of state.

1089   Today a complete humanity seems to be spread abroad through all nations, for a few great monarchs rule over this world of peoples. If there are still some barbarous peoples surviving, it is because their monarchies have persisted in the vulgar wisdom of imaginative and cruel religions, in some cases with the less balanced nature of their subject nations as an added factor.

1090   Beginning with the cold north, the Czar of Muscovy, although Christian, rules over men of sluggish minds. The Khan of Tartary dominates an effeminate people, like to the ancient Seres, who formed the larger part of his great empire, a part which is now united with that of China. The Negus of Ethiopia and the powerful kings of Fez and Morocco reign over peoples too weak and sparse.

1091   In the mid-temperate zone, however, where the nature of men is better balanced, to begin with the Far East, the Emperor of Japan practices a humanity similar to that of the Romans at the time of the Carthaginian wars. He imitates their ferocity in arms, and, as learned travelers observe, his language has a Latin ring about it. Yet, through a religion of fierce and terrible imagination with dreadful gods all armed with deadly weapons, he retains much of the heroic nature. For the missionary fathers who have been there report that the greatest difficulty they have encountered in converting the people to Christianity is that the nobles cannot be persuaded that the plebeians have the same human nature as themselves. The Emperor of the Chinese, who reigns under a mild religion and cultivates letters, is most humane. The Emperor of the Indies is rather humane than otherwise, and practices in the main the arts of peace. The Persian and the Turk have mingled the rude doctrine of their religion with the softness of Asia, which they rule; and thus both, and particularly the Turks, temper their arrogance with magnificence, pomp, liberality, and gratitude.

1092   But in Europe, where the Christian religion is everywhere professed, inculcating an infinitely pure and perfect idea of God and commanding charity to all mankind, there are great monarchies most humane in their customs. It is true that those situated in the cold north, such as Sweden and Denmark until a hundred and fifty years ago, and Poland and even England still today, although they are monarchic in constitution yet seem to be administered aristocratically; but if the natural course of human civil institutions is not impeded in their case by extraordinary causes, they will arrive at perfect monarchies [1083]. In this part of the world alone, because it cultivates the sciences, there are furthermore a great number of popular commonwealths, which are not found at all in the other three parts. Indeed, by the recourse of the same public utilities and necessities, there has been a revival of the form of the Aetolian and Achaean leagues.

Just as the latter were conceived by the Greeks because of the necessity of protecting themselves against the overwhelming power of the Romans, so the Swiss cantons and the united provinces or states of Holland have organized a number of free popular cities into two aristocracies, in which they stand united in a perpetual league of peace and war. And the body of the German empire is a system of many free cities and sovereign princes. Its head is the emperor, and in affairs concerning the imperial constitution it is administered aristocratically.

1093   We must observe here that sovereign powers uniting in leagues, whether perpetual or temporary, come of themselves to form aristocratic states into which enter the anxious suspicions characteristic of aristocracies [273, 1025]. Hence, as this [confederation] is the last form of civil states (for we cannot conceive in civil nature a state superior to such aristocracies), this same form must have been the first, which, as we have shown by so many proofs in this work, was that of the aristocracies of the fathers, sovereign family kings, united in reigning orders in the first cities [584]. For this is the nature of principles, that things begin and end in them.

1094   Now to come back to our subject, in Europe today there are only five aristocracies: namely, Venice, Genoa, and Lucca in Italy, Ragusa in Dalmatia, and Nuremberg in Germany. Almost all of them have small territories. But Christian Europe is everywhere radiant with such humanity that it abounds in all the good things that make for the happiness of human life, ministering to the comforts of the body as well as to the pleasures of mind and spirit. And all this in virtue of the Christian religion, which teaches truths so sublime that it receives into its service the most learned philosophies of the gentiles and cultivates three languages as its own: Hebrew, the most ancient in the world; Greek, the most delicate; and Latin, the grandest. Thus, even for human ends, the Christian religion is the best in the world, because it unites a wisdom of [revealed] authority with that of reason, basing the latter on the choicest doctrine of the philosophers and the most cultivated erudition of the philologists.

1095   Lastly, crossing the ocean, in the new world the American Indians would now be following this course of human institutions if they had not been discovered by the Europeans [I·13].

1096   Now, in the light of the recourse of human civil institutions to which we have given particular attention in Book Five, let us reflect on the comparisons we have made throughout this work in a great many respects between the first and last times [—that is, between those] of the ancient and modern nations. There will then be fully unfolded before us, not the particular history in time of the laws and deeds of the Romans or the

Greeks, but (by virtue of the identity of the intelligible *substance* in the diversity of their *modes* of development) the ideal history [349, 393] of the eternal laws which are instanced by the deeds of all nations [I·12] in their rise, progress, maturity, decadence, and dissolution [and which would be so instanced] even if (as is certainly not the case) there were infinite worlds being born from time to time throughout eternity [348]. Hence we could not refrain from giving this work the invidious title of a *New Science,* for it was too much to defraud it unjustly of the rightful claim it had over an argument so universal as that concerning the common nature of nations, in virtue of that property which belongs to every science that is perfect in its idea, and which Seneca has set forth for us in his vast expression: *Pusilla res hic mundus est, nisi id, quod quaerit, omnis mundus habeat*—"This world is a paltry thing unless all the world may find [therein] what it seeks." *

---

* *Natural Questions* 7.31.2: *Pusilla res mundus est, nisi in illo quod quaerat omnis mundus habeat*—"The world is a paltry thing unless it offers matter for the researches of all the world," i.e., of all ages to come [I·11–12].

CONCLUSION OF
THE WORK

ON AN ETERNAL NATURAL COMMONWEALTH,

IN EACH KIND BEST, ORDAINED

BY DIVINE PROVIDENCE [342, 629ff]

1097 Let us now conclude this work with Plato, who conceives a fourth kind of commonwealth, in which good honest men would be supreme lords. This would be the true natural aristocracy. This commonwealth conceived by Plato was brought into being by providence from the first beginnings of the nations. For it ordained that men of gigantic stature, stronger than the rest, who were to wander on the mountain heights as do the beasts of stronger natures [369–373], should, at the first thunderclaps after the universal flood, take refuge in the caves of the mountains, subject themselves to a higher power which they imagined as Jove, and, all amazement as they were all pride and cruelty, humble themselves before a divinity [377–379]. For in this order of human institutions we cannot conceive how divine providence could have employed any other counsel to halt them in their bestial wandering through the great forest of the earth, to the end of introducing among them the order of human civil institutions.

1098 Here was formed a state so to speak of monastic commonwealths or of solitary sovereigns under the government of a Greatest and Best [379] whom they themselves created for their faith out of the flash of the thunderbolts, in which this true light of God shone forth for them: that he governs mankind. Hence they came to imagine that all the human benefits supplied to them and all the aids provided for their human needs were so many gods, and feared and revered them as such. Then, between the powerful restraints of frightful superstition and the goading stimuli of bestial lust (which must both have been extremely violent in such men), as they felt the aspect of the heavens to be terrible to them and hence to thwart their use of venery, they had to hold in conatus the impetus of the bodily motion of lust [340, 504]. Thus they began to use human liberty, which consists in holding in check the motions of concupiscence and giving them another direction; for since this liberty does not come from the body, whence comes the concupiscence, it must come from the mind and is therefore properly human. The new direction took the form of forcibly seizing their women, who were naturally shy and unruly, dragging them into their caves, and, in order to have intercourse with them, keeping them there as perpetual lifelong companions. Thus, with the first human, which is to say chaste and religious, couplings, they gave a beginning to matrimony [C2]. Thereby they became certain fathers of certain children by certain women [D1]. Thus they founded the families and governed them with a cyclopean family sovereignty over their children and their wives, such as was proper to such proud and savage natures, so that later as cities arose men might be found disposed to stand in awe of the civil sovereignty [502–552]. Thus providence ordained certain household commonwealths of monarchic form under fathers (in that state princes) best in sex, age, and virtue. These fathers, in the state we must call that of nature (which was identical with the state of the families), must have formed the first natural orders, as being those who were pious, chaste, and strong. Since they were settled on their lands and could no longer escape by flight (as they had previously done in their bestial wanderings), in order to defend themselves and their families they had to kill the wild beasts that attacked them. And in order to provide sustenance for themselves and their families, as they had ceased foraging, they had to tame the earth and sow grain. All this for the salvation of the nascent human race.

1099 Meanwhile, scattered through the plains and valleys and preserving the infamous promiscuity of things and of women, there remained a great number of the impious, the unchaste, and the nefarious—impious in having no fear of gods, unchaste in their use of shameless bestial venery, and nefarious in their frequent intercourse with their own mothers and daughters. After a long time, driven by the ills occasioned by their bestial society, weak, astray, and solitary, relentlessly pursued by the robust and violent because of quarrels engendered by their infamous promiscuity, they came at last to seek refuge in the asylums of the fathers. The latter, taking them under their protection, proceeded to extend their family kingdoms to include these *famuli* through the clienteles. Thus they developed commonwealths on the basis of orders naturally superior by reason of virtues certainly heroic. First, piety, for they adored divinity, though because of their little light they multiplied and divided it into many gods formed according to their various apprehensions. (This is worked out and confirmed by Diodorus Siculus [4.2ff; 6.1ff], and more clearly by Eusebius in his *Preparation for the Gospel* [2.2], and by St. Cyril of Alexandria *Against the*

Emperor Julian [7.235ff].) And in virtue of their piety they were also endowed with prudence, taking counsel from the auspices of the gods; with
temperance, each coupling chastely with the one woman whom he had
taken under the divine auspices as perpetual companion for life; with
strength for slaying beasts and taming the earth; and with magnanimity in
giving succor to the weak and aid to those in danger [516]. Such was the
nature of the Herculean commonwealths, in which the pious, wise, chaste,
strong, and magnanimous cast down the proud and defended the weak,
which is the mark of excellence in civil governments [553].

1100 But finally the family fathers, having become great by the
religion and virtue of their ancestors and through the labors of their clients,
began to abuse the laws of protection and to govern the clients harshly.
When they had thus departed from the natural order, which is that of
justice, their clients rose in mutiny against them. But since without order
(which is to say without God) human society cannot stand for a moment,
providence led the family fathers naturally to unite themselves with their
kindred in orders against their clients. To pacify the latter, they conceded
to them, in the world's first agrarian law, the bonitary ownership of the
fields, retaining for themselves the optimal or sovereign family ownership.
Thus the first cities arose upon reigning orders of nobles [582–598]. And as
the natural order declined which had been based, in accordance with the
then state of nature, on [superiority of] kind, sex, age, and virtue, providence called the civil order into being along with the cities. And first of all
[civil orders], that which approximated most closely to nature: that in
virtue of nobility of humankind (for in that state of affairs nobility could
be based only on generating in human fashion with wives taken under
divine auspices) and thus in virtue of a heroism, the nobles should rule
over the plebeians (who did not contract marriage with such solemnities),
and now that divine rules had ceased (under which the families had been
governed by divine auspices) and the heroes had to rule in virtue of the
form of the heroic governments themselves, that the basic institution of
these commonwealths should be religion safeguarded within the heroic
orders, and that through this religion all civil laws and institutions should
belong to the heroes alone. But since nobility had now become a gift of
fortune, providence caused to arise among the nobles the order of the
family fathers themselves, as being naturally more worthy because of age.
And among the fathers it caused the most spirited and robust to arise as
kings whose duty it should be to lead the others and gird them in orders to
resist and overawe the clients who rebelled against them.

1101 But with the passage of the years and the far greater development of human minds, the plebs of the peoples finally became suspicious of the pretensions of such heroism and understood themselves to be of equal human nature with the nobles, and therefore insisted that they too should enter into the civil institutions of the cities. Since in due time the peoples were to become sovereign, providence permitted a long antecedent struggle of plebs with nobility over piety and religion in the heroic contests for the extension of the auspices by the nobles to the plebeians, with a view to securing thereby the extension of all public and private civil institutions regarded as dependent on the auspices. Thus the very care for piety and attachment to religion brought the people to civil sovereignty. In this respect the Roman people went beyond all others in the world, and for that reason it became the master people of the world. In this way, as the natural order merged more and more with the civil orders, the popular commonwealths were born. In these everything had to be reduced to lot or balance, and providence therefore, in order that neither chance nor fate should rule, ordained that the census should be the measure of fitness for office. Thereby the industrious and not the lazy, the frugal and not the prodigal, the provident and not the idle, the magnanimous and not the fainthearted—in a word, the rich with some virtue or semblance thereof, and not the poor with their many shameless vices—were considered the best for governing. In such commonwealths the entire peoples, who have in common the desire for justice, command laws that are just because they are good for all [1038]. Such a law Aristotle divinely defines as will without passions, which would be the will of a hero who has command of his passions [1042]. These commonwealths gave birth to philosophy [1043]. By their very form they inspired it to form the hero, and for that purpose to interest itself in truth [1041]. All this was ordained by providence to the end that, since virtuous actions were no longer prompted by religious sentiments as formerly, philosophy should make the virtues understood in their idea, and by dint of reflection thereon, if men were without virtue they should at least be ashamed of their vices. Only so can peoples prone to ill-doing be held to their duty. And from the philosophies providence permitted eloquence to arise and, from the very form of these popular commonwealths in which good laws are commanded, to become impassioned for justice, and from these ideas of virtue to inflame the peoples to command good laws. Such eloquence, we resolutely affirm, flourished in Rome in the time of Scipio Africanus, when civil wisdom and military valor, which happily united in establishing at Rome on the ruins of Carthage the empire of the world, must necessarily have brought in their train a robust and most prudent eloquence.

1102 But as the popular states became corrupt, so also did the philosophies. They descended to skepticism. Learned fools fell to calumniating the truth. Thence arose a false eloquence, ready to uphold either of the opposed sides of a case indifferently. Thus it came about that, by abuse of eloquence like that of the tribunes of the plebs at Rome, when the citizens were no longer content with making wealth the basis of rank, they strove to make it an instrument of power. And as furious south winds whip up the sea, so these citizens provoked civil wars in their commonwealths and drove them to total disorder. Thus they caused the commonwealths to fall from a perfect liberty into the perfect tyranny of anarchy or the unchecked liberty of the free peoples, which is the worst of all tyrannies.

1103 To this great disease of cities providence applies one of these three great remedies in the following order of human civil institutions.

1104 It first ordains that there be found among these peoples a man like Augustus to arise and establish himself as a monarch and, by force of arms, take in hand all the institutions and all the laws, which, though sprung from liberty, no longer avail to regulate and hold it within bounds. On the other hand providence ordains that the very form of the monarchic state shall confine the will of the monarchs, in spite of their unlimited sovereignty, within the natural order of keeping the peoples content and satisfied with both their religion and their natural liberty [1007f]. For without this universal satisfaction and content of the peoples, monarchic states are neither lasting nor secure.

1105 Then, if providence does not find such a remedy within, it seeks it outside. And since peoples so far corrupted have already become naturally slaves of their unrestrained passions—of luxury, effeminacy, avarice, envy, pride, and vanity—and in pursuit of the pleasures of their dissolute life are falling back into all the vices characteristic of the most abject slaves (having become liars, tricksters, calumniators, thieves, cowards, and pretenders), providence decrees that they become slaves by the natural law of the gentes which springs from this nature of nations, and that they become subject to better nations, which, having conquered them by arms, preserve them as subject provinces. Herein two great lights of natural order shine forth. First, that he who cannot govern himself must let himself be governed by another who can. Second, that the world is always governed by those who are naturally fittest.

1106 But if the peoples are rotting in that ultimate civil disease and cannot agree on a monarch from within, and are not conquered and preserved by better nations from without, then providence for their extreme ill has its extreme remedy at hand. For such peoples, like so many beasts, have fallen into the custom of each man thinking only of his own private interests and have reached the extreme of delicacy, or better of pride, in which like wild animals they bristle and lash out at the slightest displeasure. Thus no matter how great the throng and press of their bodies, they live like wild beasts in a deep solitude of spirit and will, scarcely any two being able to agree since each follows his own pleasure or caprice. By reason of all this, providence decrees that, through obstinate factions and desperate civil wars, they shall turn their cities into forests and the forests into dens and lairs of men. In this way, through long centuries of barbarism, rust will consume the misbegotten subtleties of malicious wits that have turned them into beasts made more inhuman by the barbarism of reflection than the first men had been made by the barbarism of sense [L3]. For the latter displayed a generous savagery, against which one could defend oneself or take flight or be on one's guard; but the former, with a base savagery, under soft words and embraces, plots against the life and fortune of friends and intimates. Hence peoples who have reached this point of premeditated malice, when they receive this last remedy of providence and are thereby stunned and brutalized, are sensible no longer of comforts, delicacies, pleasures, and pomp, but only of the sheer necessities of life. And the few survivors in the midst of an abundance of the things necessary for life naturally become sociable and, returning to the primitive simplicity of the first world of peoples, are again religious, truthful, and faithful. Thus providence brings back among them the piety, faith, and truth which are the natural foundations of justice as well as the graces and beauties of the eternal order of God.

1107   The clear and simple observation we have made on the institutions of the entire human race, if we had been told nothing more by the philosophers, historians, grammarians, and jurisconsults, would lead us to say certainly that this is the great city of the nations that was founded and is governed by God [B9]. Lycurgus, Solon, the decemvirs, and the like have been eternally praised to the skies as wise legislators, because it has hitherto been believed that by their good institutions and good laws they had founded Sparta, Athens, and Rome, the three cities that outshone all others in the fairest and greatest civil virtues. Yet they were all of short duration and even of small extent as compared with the universe of peoples, which was ordered by such institutions and secured by such laws that even in its decay it assumes those forms of states by which alone it may everywhere be preserved and perpetually endure. And must we not then say that this is a counsel of a superhuman wisdom? For without the force of laws (whose force, according to Dio [308], is like that of a tyrant), but making use of the very customs of men (in the practice of which they are as free of all force as in the expression of their own nature, whence the same Dio said that customs were like kings in commanding by pleasure), it divinely rules and conducts [the aforesaid city].

1108 It is true that men have themselves made this world of nations (and we took this as the first incontestable principle of our Science, since we despaired of finding it from the philosophers and philologists [330f]), but this world without doubt has issued from a mind often diverse, at times quite contrary, and always superior to the particular ends that men had proposed to themselves; which narrow ends, made means to serve wider ends, it has always employed to preserve the human race upon this earth [M9, 342, 344]. Men mean to gratify their bestial lust and abandon their offspring, and they inaugurate the chastity of marriage from which the families arise [505, 520ff]. The fathers mean to exercise without restraint their paternal power over their clients, and they subject them to the civil powers from which the cities arise [584]. The reigning orders of nobles mean to abuse their lordly freedom over the plebeians, and they are obliged to submit to the laws which establish popular liberty [598]. The free peoples mean to shake off the yoke of their laws, and they become subject to monarchs [1007f, 1104]. The monarchs mean to strengthen their own positions by debasing their subjects with all the vices of dissoluteness, and they dispose them to endure slavery at the hands of stronger nations [1105]! The nations mean to dissolve themselves, and their remnants flee for safety to the wilderness, whence, like the phoenix, they rise again [1106]. That which did all this was mind, for men did it with intelligence; it was not fate, for they did it by choice; not chance, for the results of their always so acting are perpetually the same [F6].

1109 Hence Epicurus, who believes in chance, is refuted by the facts, along with his followers Hobbes and Machiavelli; and so are Zeno and Spinoza, who believe in fate. The evidence clearly confirms the contrary position of the political philosophers, whose prince is the divine Plato, who shows that providence directs human institutions [129ff, 179]. Cicero was therefore right in refusing to discuss laws with Atticus unless the latter would give up his Epicureanism and first concede that providence governed human institutions [335]. Pufendorf implicitly denied this by his hypothesis, Selden took it for granted, and Grotius left it out of account [394]; but the Roman jurisconsults established it as the first principle of the natural law of the gentes [310, 335, 342, 584, 979]. For in this work it has been fully demonstrated that through providence the first governments of the world had as their entire form religion, on which alone the family state

was based; and passing thence to the heroic or aristocratic civil governments, religion must have been their principal firm basis. Advancing then
to the popular governments, it was again religion that served the peoples as
means for attaining them. And coming to rest at last in monarchic governments, this same religion must be the shield of princes. Hence, if religion is
lost among the peoples, they have nothing left to enable them to live in
society: no shield of defense, nor means of counsel, nor basis of support,
nor even a form by which they may exist in the world at all.

1110   Let Bayle consider then whether in fact there can be nations in
the world without any knowledge of God [334]! And let Polybius weigh
the truth of his statement that if there were philosophers in the world
there would be no need in the world of religions [179]! For religions alone
can bring the peoples to do virtuous works by appeal to their feelings,
which alone move men to perform them; and the reasoned maxims of the
philosophers concerning virtue are of use only when employed by a good
eloquence for kindling the feelings to do the duties of virtue. There is,
however, an essential difference between our Christian religion, which is
true, and all the others, which are false. In our religion, divine grace causes
virtuous action for the sake of an eternal and infinite good [136, 310]. This
good cannot fall under the senses, and it is consequently the mind that, for
its sake, moves the senses to virtuous actions. The false religions, on the
contrary, have proposed to themselves finite and transitory goods, in this
life as in the other (where they expect a beatitude of sensual pleasures),
and hence the senses must drive the mind to do virtuous works.

1111   But providence, through the order of civil institutions discussed
in this work, makes itself palpable for us in these three feelings: the first,
the marvel, the second, the veneration, hitherto felt by all the learned for
the matchless wisdom of the ancients, and the third, the ardent desire with
which they burned to seek and attain it. These are in fact three lights of
the divine providence that aroused in them the aforesaid three beautiful
and just sentiments; but these sentiments were later perverted by the
conceit of scholars and by the conceit of nations [125, 127]—conceits we
have sought throughout this work to discredit. The uncorrupted feelings
are that all the learned should admire, venerate, and desire to unite
themselves to the infinite wisdom of God.

1112   To sum up, from all that we have set forth in this work, it is to
be finally concluded that this Science carries inseparably with it the study
of piety, and that he who is not pious cannot be truly wise.

INDEX OF NAMES

(Numbers 1–1112 refer to paragraphs of the translation; A1–M10 to paragraphs of the Introduction; v–viii to pages of the Preface. "Greece," "Greek," "Rome," "Roman," "Latin" are omitted.)

Abaris   100, 745; *see also* Anacharsis
Aborigines   370, 531
Abyla Mt.   726, 750
Abyssinians   658
Abraham   526, 557
Academy of Athens   46
Achaea, Achaeans   530, 643, 748, 1017
Achaean league   1092
Acheron   719
Achilles   27, 243, 403, 432, 585, 597, 611, 617, 654, 667, 673, 681, 683, 693, 708, 712, 724, 726, 742, 750, 781, 782, 783, 786, 793, 794, 797, 801, 809, 868, 879, 908, 920, 923, 934, 966, 977, 1058, 1059
Achivi, *see* Achaea
Acosta, José de (1539?–1600)   337
Actaeon   528
Adam   13, 51, 310, 371, 381, 401, 430, 1079
Aebutius, Sextus   1001
Aeëtes   760
Aegaeon   437
Aegean Sea   635
Aelian (Claudius Aelianus)   79, 469, 854
Aeneas   86, 307, 432, 512, 546, 558, 611, 660, 716, 721, 742, 761, 764, 770–773
Aeolia   724, 753
Aeschylus   906, 910, 911
Aesculapius   98, 749
Aesop   91, 424, 425, 426, 499, 559
Aetolian league   1092
Africa   44, 93, 369, 435, 543, 636, 644, 658, 748, 750, 778, 1051
——, South   334
Agamemnon   191, 425, 517, 585, 597, 611, 667, 680, 683, 708, 782, 783, 786, 801, 968, 1058
Agathocles, tyrant of Syracuse   517

Agis III, king of Sparta   592, 668, 985, 1021
Agricola, Cneius Julius   644
Ailly, Pierre d', Cardinal (1350–1420)   169, 740
Ajax, son of Telamon   559, 1033
Alba Longa, Albans   75, 76, 532, 595, 641, 645, 770, 771, 963, 1021
Alcinous   786, 789, 795, 870, 879
Alcmena   508
Alexander the Great   46, 103, 243, 297, 441, 1023
Alexandria   46–47, 89
Alfonso X, king of Castile (1221–84), Tables of   169
Allacci, Leone, librarian of Vatican (1586–1669)   788, 989
Alphonsine Tables, *see* Alfonso
Alps   117
America, American Indians   I·13; 89, 170, 375, 437, 470, 486, 517, 538, 542, 546, 562, 658, 841, 1033, 1095
Amphion   81, 338, 523, 615, 647, 661, 734, 901
—— of Methymna, *see* Arion
Amphipolitans   612
Amphitryon   858
Amphrysus river   1059
Amulius   76, 641, 645
Anacharsis   100, 128, 745; *see also* Abaris
Anchises   512
Ancus Marcius   736, 769, 770, 771
Andromeda   635
Andronicus, Livius   438, 471
Androtion, Athenian historian   79
Angles   657
Antaeus   614, 618, 653, 721, 1065
Antenor   86, 660, 761
Antilles   334
Antinous [i.e. Eurylochus]   558

427

Date Due

DEMCO NO. 25-370

	CANISIUS		
MAY	CANISIUS		
JUN 1 9 '69	CANISIUS		
OCT 31 '75	CANISIUS		
FEB 12 '76	CANISIUS	OCT 2 7 2004	
OCT 23 '85			
DEC 1 6 1994			